NEGOTIATIONS

NEGOTIATIONS

SOCIAL-PSYCHOLOGICAL PERSPECTIVES

Edited by

DANIEL DRUCKMAN

SAGE PUBLICATIONS   Beverly Hills   London

For information address

SAGE PUBLICATIONS, INC.
275 South Beverly Drive
Beverly Hills, California 90212

SAGE PUBLICATIONS, INC.
28 Banner Street
London EC1Y 8QE

Printed in the United States of America

Library of Congress Cataloging in Publication Data

Main entry under title:

Negotiations, social-psychological perspectives.

Includes index.
1. Negotiations. I. Druckman, Daniel.
BF637.N4N43   158   76-58353
ISBN 0-8039-0829-6

FIRST PRINTING

CONTENTS

FOREWORD

Daniel Druckman's invitation to all of us interested in negotiation to help make things "add up" is welcomed. His authors clearly demonstrate the great headway we've made in the empirical grounding of our ideas about negotiation since Sawyer and I attempted to put together the foundations more than a decade ago (Sawyer and Guetzkow, 1965). But perhaps the greatest gain has obtained in terms of the reconstruction of the overriding frameworks, so elegantly summarized in Druckman's "Introduction and Overview" to the essays of this volume. At least fifteen perspectives have been utilized, as Druckman's coding of the essays in Table 1 reveals. When they are contrasted with the pretheoretical ideas presented by Iklé in his pioneering work on negotiation (Iklé, 1964), their breadth and profundity are most encouraging.

To be sure, there is much work yet ahead, as Druckman argues at the end of his conclusions. It is necessary to do a comprehensive, systematic job in making the consolidations, in the style of Rubin and Brown (1975). The contributors to this volume inspire us, as they indicate the fruitfulness of their approaches. I am especially awed by the willingness of the researchers to tackle the problem of negotiations as a longitudinal process, in their drive to capture the ongoing nature of the complex interactions. It is fascinating to realize that it is necessary to integrate both the mini-processes and the macro-processes—and that a willingness to work at a single level of explanation seems narrow-gauged, if not indolent. There's an excitement generated in these essays, as the authors seek to push toward the creation of new and alternative processes. Not content only to tie the "artificial" phenomena of the laboratory to the field, a number of the researchers are creating new phenomena in their experiments and simulations. These social "inventions" portend policy applications to negotiation processes that are of significance to those practitioners working within a myriad of sites, from labor-management relations to international affairs.

Although as yet we have developed no science about our social science to give us guidance, it just may be that the complexity we find in our work on negotiations to date is a reflection of our failure to have discovered cuts which yield greater parsimony. Therefore, in addition to attempting to consolidate our cumulative findings in more programmatic ways, would it be wise that some of us—perhaps only a few of our most creative colleagues—be given the opportunity to attempt end-runs? Let us insist on a division of our labors. Many of us will build consolidations, making iterations of them every five to ten years. Others of us will create "soft technologies," permitting the application of knowledge by the thousands whose task it is to conduct negotiations. And a few will remain aloof, probing for paradigms of greater simplicity, so that the complexity of our understanding does not overwhelm us.

For sure, those of us who are concerned with negotiations and work in the "think-tanks" and the universities need to accelerate our researches, making them more cumulative and framing them within more adequate consolidations of extant knowledge. The gatekeepers in both private and public funding agencies can gain guidance from these essays, so that they ensure a more rapid and fruitful expansion of ongoing programs of research and application. We have moved beyond the case study approach, even though some are still content with inadequate methodologies and theories derived from speculation (Campbell, 1976).

Let us use these essays to spur ourselves on—as users, as managers of research, and as investigators. Let us build solidly by working together—systematically, rigorously, and imaginatively.

Harold Guetzkow
Fulcher Professor of
Decision-Making
Northwestern University

REFERENCES

CAMPBELL, J. C. [ed.] (1976) *Successful Negotiation: TRIESTE 1954.* Princeton, N.J.: Princeton University Press.

IKLE, F. C. (1964) *How Nations Negotiate.* New York: Harper.

RUBIN, J. Z. and B. R. BROWN (1975) *The Social Psychology of Bargaining and Negotiation.* New York: Academic Press, Inc.

SAWYER, J. and H. GUETZKOW (1965) "Bargaining and negotiation in international relations," pp. 464-520 in H. C. Kelman (ed.) *International Behavior: A Social-Psychological Analysis.* New York: Holt, Rinehart, and Winston.

PREFACE

Negotiations is a presentation of perspectives that draw on a common body of work loosely referred to as a social-psychological approach. The chapters are original statements of investigators who for some time have made significant contributions to the literature. These statements represent, for the most part, attempts by the investigators to integrate or organize their most recent findings. While their work is embedded within the social-psychological tradition, the contributors do not dwell on this background. Each effort is creative and forward-looking. Each investigator is a craftsman-specialist who envisions the real possibility of a science of negotiating behavior.

This volume emphasizes basic research. It presents concepts and methodologies that are intended to advance our understanding of negotiation processes and influences on negotiating behavior. Our primary purpose is to provoke, stimulate, and encourage further investigations along the lines defined by the contributors. But advances in the development of a science are not without implications for practitioners. The contributors develop systematically the concepts that precede (and form the basis for) advice and application. These concepts can be refined and tailored for application, which should render the craft of negotiating more effective.

Attempts to translate scientific findings and concepts on negotiating into useful advice are facilitated by a meaningful integration of that knowledge. However, integration is difficult, since knowledge does not come in neat packages, and negotiation is not a unitary phenomenon. The differing emphases, presuppositions, and perspectives *on* negotiation pose the same problems for integrators as do the different components, aspects, and contexts *of* negotiation. By joining the varying themes or approaches to the topic with the diverse aspects of the phenomenon, this volume takes a first step on the way to a unified body of knowledge about negotiation. The next steps consist of two kinds of linking efforts: (1) linking the part-processes identified and probed in this volume, and (2) developing linkages between the theory and practice. Some progress in achieving the first type of linkage is indicated in the introductory essay. The second type of linkage depends on parallel efforts in developing taxonomies of concepts and situations.

Another impetus for this project was a desire to present in one volume the major work on negotiations being done in the social-psychological tradition. Most of the work in this field has been reported in a variety of professional journals, and in chapters of volumes intended for other purposes. The task was facilitated by earlier literature reviews done by the Editor and by the formation some years ago of the Conflict Research Group (CRG). The CRG is an interdisciplinary group of social psychologists, sociologists, political scientists, and management scientists whose purpose has been to develop, critique, and disseminate research on conflict processes. These efforts have taken the form of newsletters, exchanging of draft manuscripts, panels at professional conferences, and special conferences—convened in various locations—on negotiation and conflict. This volume is a major product of these activities, and the contributors have been active participants in, and reflect the interdisciplinary composition of, the CRG as a whole.

On a more personal note, this volume reflects my desire to present in one place the concepts and perspectives that have influenced my research over the past decade. The chapters represent the themes that have guided my investigations of negotiation and related processes as these occur in a variety of settings and at several levels of analysis. These are the themes that provide the ingredients for the larger task of consolidation in keeping with the goals of knowledge organization and utilization that have been stated so eloquently by Harold Guetzkow. These goals have guided my work from the outset.

These various purposes and motives for preparing this volume have resulted, it is hoped, in a work that will be a unique addition to the literature. Our diversified approach to the study of negotiation, which emphasizes objectives and incentives, strategies, influences, and settings, contrasts with the more narrowly focused treatments of Fouraker and Siegel (*Bargainings Behavior* [1963]), Bartos (*Process and Outcome of Negotiations* [1974]), or Coddington (*Theories of the Bargaining Process* [1968]). Our reliance on experimental data is in contrast with approaches that rely primarily on events or documented quotes (e.g., Iklé's *How Nations Negotiate* [1964]), personal experience (e.g., Lall's *Modern International Negotiation* [1966]), or case study material (e.g., Walton and McKersie's *A Behavioral Theory of Labor Negotiation* [1965] and Zartman's *The 50% Solution* [1976]). Our theoretical emphasis differs from the prescriptive approach taken by Karrass in *Give and Take* (1974) and other books on "gamesmanship," or the descriptive case studies of Newhouse in *Cold Dawn* (1973) and of Young in *Negotiating with the Chinese Communists* (1968). And our social-psychological orientation complements the economic and political treatments of most previous works but is similar to that of such publications as Deutsch, *The Resolution of Conflict* (1973), and Rubin and Brown, *The Social Psychology of Bargaining and Negotiation* (1975). In scope and emphasis, this volume is perhaps closest to Rubin and Brown's integration of literature, the main differences being in choice of, and depth of treatment of, certain themes. It might be regarded as a companion to the Rubin and Brown effort. In fact, the differences notwithstanding, we offer this volume as a companion to all of the earlier works. Together, these various volumes present an exciting body of research on negotiations; continued effort along these lines should move us closer to a more fully integrated theory of negotiation.

As Editor, I consider myself fortunate to have such a talented and cooperative group of contributors. Most of them produced a draft manuscript in keeping with the general plan for the volume, and all cooperated in responding to my suggestions for revisions. In no case was there a problem in "negotiating" the final version, which was produced in a reasonable period of time. For these efforts I am deeply grateful. Yet in spite of this cooperation, the editorial process was more involved and took longer than I had anticipated. Through it all Sage's Senior Editor, Rhoda Blecker, remained patient, understanding, and helpful. For this too I am deeply grateful.

Special gratitude is extended to Virginia Haaga, whose skillful editing improved the style of presentation considerably and whose work on index preparation resulted in thorough indexes for this volume. She edited the entire manuscript for style, often working long hours to meet deadlines. I consider her help to have been invaluable.

I would also like to acknowledge the typing services provided by Emma Davis and Alma Hall. They too responded often "beyond the call of duty." And the institutional resources provided by Mathematica aided this project considerably. Perhaps the most essential resource provided was the atmosphere created by my colleagues.

As always, however, my greatest debt of gratitude is owed to my wife, Marjorie. Her help, understanding, and warm encouragement during this project, and through the years, have been invaluable.

Daniel Druckman
Bethesda, Maryland

INTRODUCTION AND OVERVIEW

SOCIAL-PSYCHOLOGICAL APPROACHES TO
THE STUDY OF NEGOTIATION

DANIEL DRUCKMAN

Mathematica, Inc.

Over the past decade or so, considerable attention has been paid to the systematic analysis of the social-psychological aspects of negotiation. There has been a steady growth of theory and empirical research on problems of negotiation behavior in general, and this research has included the use of social-psychological concepts and methods. This development has consisted of attempts to define aspects of negotiation as researchable problems to which the tools of behavioral science can be applied. What has emerged is a subdiscipline, a new area of specialization, which, while cutting across several disciplines, can be defined as the "social psychology of negotiation." The scope of this area of specialization is presented in this volume.

In this introductory essay, an attempt is made to provide an overview of the volume and of the issues and themes that define the field. Our intention is to assist the reader in developing a broad perspective on the work that has been done, including an understanding of the boundaries of the field. After an overview is presented, each of four themes that have guided the research is discussed, and the essay concludes with a brief section on considerations toward an integrated theory of negotiation.

OVERVIEW OF THE VOLUME

This volume continues the tradition of blending hard evidence with broad interpretation in order to achieve a more encompassing framework for analyzing negotiations (as in Druckman, 1973, 1976). Hard evidence takes the form of data or observations made under specified conditions and subjected to a series of analyses designed to isolate the critical factors that tend to facilitate or impede efforts to reach agreement. Each contribution explores systematically the effects on negotiating behavior of a particular aspect of negotiation. The aspects treated are divided into four categories that serve as sections. Through broad interpretation an attempt is made to place the analysis into a mosaic of influences on negotiating behavior. The findings obtained can be placed in a more general framework which organizes the dimensions and processes of negotiation into a temporal and spatial sequence that depicts the interplay among preconditions, background factors, conditions, processes and outcomes, and settings (see Sawyer and Guetzkow, 1965; Druckman, 1973, for examples). The integration that results reflects a juxtaposition of this framework and the blending of styles represented in each essay.

Systematic exploration and integration are pitted against diversity of approach as the volume attempts to represent a variety of methodological strategies and settings within which negotiation occurs. In their search for empirical regularities, the contributors use different approaches. Three dimensions of difference in particular distinguish among the various approaches: the extent to which conceptual framework, context, or negotiating is emphasized. The contributors who emphasize the general conceptualization see negotiations as one type of activity within the purview of that formulation (e.g., McClintock; Brehmer and Hammond; Tedeschi and Bonoma). The frameworks represented are both robust and relevant: Each extends to diverse situations, and each presents concepts that are essential for the analysis of negotiation. The contributions that emphasize context construe negotiation as a form embedded within that setting (e.g., Stern et al.; Winham; Hopmann and Walcott). The contexts represented are those in which negotiating is a prevalent, if not a ubiquitous, activity. The chapters that focus on negotiation per se adapt concepts and frameworks to a construal of the negotiating process (e.g., Hamner and Yukl; Pruitt and Lewis; Walcott et al.; Midgaard and Underdal). The processes represented and the dimensions discussed—bargaining, debating, problem-solving, conference size, coalitions—are essential aspects of *any* negotiation.

Other chapters are more difficult to categorize in terms of these dimensions. Some present a more balanced emphasis on context, conceptualization, and negotiating; for example, Druckman et al. create a general conceptualization that describes a negotiation process as it takes place in certain types of political decision-making committees. Others can be located at the boundary between two of the dimensions, as when Brown focuses on face-saving in negotiations but recognizes the relevance of the conceptualization for other types of social behavior, or when Hopmann and Walcott move between international negotiating and the broader arena of international relations. And the Hermann and Kogan chapter uses a gaming representation of negotiation in order to explore the effects of several personality/attitudinal variables. Neither context nor broad theory is emphasized as personality effects are woven in a particular conception of negotiating.

The diversity presented in this volume provides the material for integrators who attempt to bridge the gap between conceptualization and relevance on the way to a context-relevant theory of negotiation. The integration envisioned is one that will take account of the various processes, settings, and conceptual approaches represented here. Each treatment can be regarded as an "island of theory"—an explication of a process of negotiation or an influence on negotiating behavior. Taken together, these are the dimensions of negotiation. A next step entails the development of linking hypotheses, a prerequisite to the positing of relationships between the dimensions. From these efforts, a framework will emerge, although the construction will be continually revised as new "islands of theory" are created and new contexts for negotiating are discovered.

Counterpoised against the diversity of approaches are similarities among the contributors. The similarities result from the types of chapters that were solicited according to the plan for the volume. This volume is in the tradition of a cumulative, experimental social science. Each contributor has an impressive history of work in this tradition. Each chapter reviews, summarizes, or integrates the most recent of those contributions. The form that most of these treatments take consists of:

(a) a conceptual framework with supporting evidence, although some are more like integrative literature reviews (Tedeschi and Bonoma; Hamner and Yukl; Walcott et al.);

(b) a characterization of the conference in abstract terms rather than a depiction of a specific negotiation or even a particular type of negotiation (exceptions are the case-study portions of the Winham, and the Hopmann and Walcott chapters); and

(c) a presentation of empirical evidence based on laboratory experiments or simulations (only Midgaard and Underdal do not rely primarily on this methodology).

In all chapters, the approach taken is systematic, with an eye on moving closer to the goal of theory-building. An additional step in this direction was taken by contributors who extended their base of observation to field settings (viz., Brehmer and Hammond; Druckman et al.; Hopmann and Walcott; Winham). Recognizing the limitations of the laboratory as a source of generalizable insights, these investigators sought either parallel data sets from nonlaboratory settings for comparison, or additional data to buttress conclusions derived from the experiments. Moreover, the heuristic value of the field setting was demonstrated in these chapters: The field setting would often suggest new insights that were not provided by the laboratory work. These advantages should encourage those who have limited their work to laboratory demonstrations. Indeed, a number of the investigators who did not present field data in their chapters *advocated* a strategy of moving between the laboratory and the field (note especially Pruitt and Lewis; Hermann and Kogan; Brown).

FIGURE 1

Schematic Representation of the Influences and Processes of Negotiation Treated in This Volume*

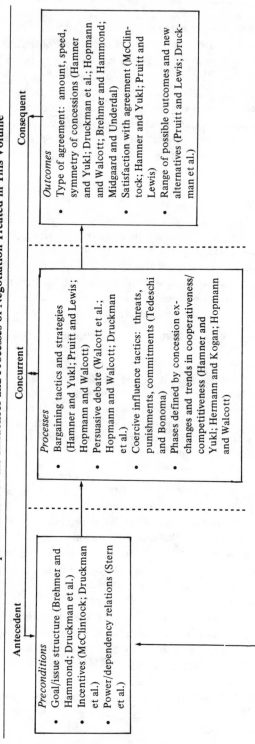

Antecedent   Concurrent   Consequent

Preconditions
- Goal/issue structure (Brehmer and Hammond; Druckman et al.)
- Incentives (McClintock; Druckman et al.)
- Power/dependency relations (Stern et al.)

Processes
- Bargaining tactics and strategies (Hamner and Yukl; Pruitt and Lewis; Hopmann and Walcott)
- Persuasive debate (Walcott et al.; Hopmann and Walcott; Druckman et al.)
- Coercive influence tactics: threats, punishments, commitments (Tedeschi and Bonoma)
- Phases defined by concession exchanges and trends in cooperativeness/competitiveness (Hamner and Yukl; Hermann and Kogan; Hopmann and Walcott)

Outcomes
- Type of agreement: amount, speed, symmetry of concessions (Hamner and Yukl; Druckman et al.; Hopmann and Walcott; Brehmer and Hammond; Midgaard and Underdal)
- Satisfaction with agreement (McClintock; Hamner and Yukl; Pruitt and Lewis)
- Range of possible outcomes and new alternatives (Pruitt and Lewis; Druckman et al.)

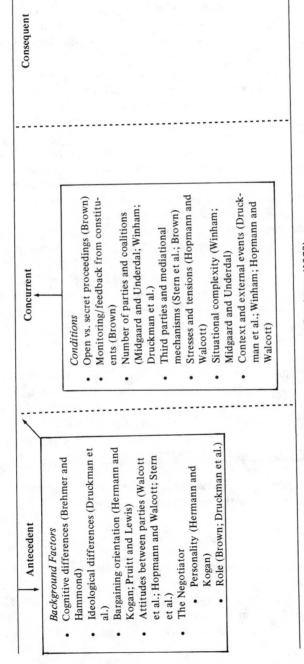

Antecedent | **Concurrent** | **Consequent**

Background Factors
- Cognitive differences (Brehmer and Hammond)
- Ideological differences (Druckman et al.)
- Bargaining orientation (Hermann and Kogan; Pruitt and Lewis)
- Attitudes between parties (Walcott et al.; Hopmann and Walcott; Stern et al.)
- The Negotiator
  - Personality (Hermann and Kogan)
  - Role (Brown; Druckman et al.)

Conditions
- Open vs. secret proceedings (Brown)
- Monitoring/feedback from constituents (Brown)
- Number of parties and coalitions (Midgaard and Underdal; Winham; Druckman et al.)
- Third parties and mediational mechanisms (Stern et al.; Brown)
- Stresses and tensions (Hopmann and Walcott)
- Situational complexity (Winham; Midgaard and Underdal)
- Context and external events (Druckman et al.; Winham; Hopmann and Walcott)

*Adapted with modification from Sawyer and Guetzkow (1965) and Druckman (1973).

[19]

The cumulation of efforts demonstrated in each of these papers is the result of applying a strategy that consists of systematic and controlled variation and the assessment of effects produced by such (experimental or statistical) manipulation. Yet this is not a narrow-gauged experimental approach: All of the chapters make explicit the broader implications of the work. Some draw out implications in terms of a well-developed framework that is used also to generate experiments on other topics (e.g., McClintock; Brehmer and Hammond; Tedeschi and Bonoma; Stern et al.); others discuss implications in terms of the negotiation process per se (e.g., Hamner and Yukl; Winham; Pruitt and Lewis; Hopmann and Walcott). The former may be construed as *discipline-oriented* approaches, while the latter are *phenomenon-oriented*. Together, the two approaches reflect the dual objective of this volume: to advance theory-development in social psychology and to con-tribute to an understanding of negotiation. These goals, it is felt, can best be achieved by the attempt made in each chapter to juxtapose experimental work with an explicit conceptual framework. It is this form that defines the essential contribution of the volume to the literature on negotiation.

The dual theme of the volume makes it difficult to assess its principal contribution. For some, the contributions to social psychology may be more evident; for others, advances in understanding negotiation processes might be emphasized. Preferences for one theme or the other notwithstanding, it is possible to suggest a list of topics from social psychology and a list of variables relevant to negotiation to which this volume contributes. Topics in social psychology include utility theory (McClintock), social judgment theory (Brehmer and Hammond), influence theory (Tedeschi and Bonoma), social facilitation theory (Brown), coalition theory (Druckman et al.; Midgaard and Underdal), and relative effects of person and situation (Hermann and Kogan). Negotiation variables include objectives (McClintock), incentives (Druckman et al.), strategies (Hamner and Yukl; Pruitt and Lewis), tactics (Hamner and Yukl; Tedeschi and Bonoma), role reversal (Walcott et al.; Stern et al.), size of conference (Midgaard and Underdal), issue complexity (Winham), accounta-bility to constituencies (Brown), and stresses and tensions (Hopmann and Walcott) (see Figure 1). The heuristic contribution of this volume derives from both emphases: The negotiation arena provides another setting for applying the paradigms, and the paradigms serve to highlight processes of, and influences on, negotiating as this occurs in situ.

ORGANIZATION OF THE VOLUME

The order of presentation of the chapters in this volume is intended to facilitate comparisons among them. The chapters are arranged into four parts according to the perspective adopted and the issues addressed. The parts are: Objectives, Incentives, and Conflict; Processes, Strategies, and Outcomes; Influences: Conditions and Background Factors; and Complex Processes and

Settings. Each of the first three parts contains chapters that take different perspectives on a broad issue concerned with a particular aspect of negotiation. The fourth consists of chapters that converge on a common theme: Each emphasizes the complexity of negotiation as it occurs in situ. The issues and themes serve as common foci for organizing and dividing the papers. Viewed separately, the sections provide alternative analytic cuts on negotiation. Taken together, the sections suggest the various components that must be woven into a mosaic on the way to developing an integrated theory of negotiation. One type of mosaic is the framework presented in Figure 1. This schematic representation, adapted from Sawyer and Guetzkow (1965) and Druckman (1973), is used to depict and organize the various components treated by the contributors.

The three chapters in the first part concern the relative importance of motivational (McClintock) and cognitive (Brehmer and Hammond) factors in negotiation, culminating in a chapter that attempts to arbitrate the issue (Druckman et al.). The second part consists of four chapters that treat the various processes that occur in negotiation, including bargaining (Hamner and Yukl), debating (Walcott et al.), influencing (Tedeschi and Bonoma), and integrative bargaining—a process that consists of both bargaining and debate (Pruitt and Lewis). The relative importance of these processes is likely to vary both with the stages of a negotiation and with the type of negotiation. The chapters in the third part deal with influences. The coverage suggests the issue of whether the negotiator (Hermann and Kogan), his role obligations (Brown), or the negotiating situation (Brown; Hopmann and Walcott) is a more important determinant of negotiating behavior. And the contributions in the final section attempt to make comprehensible the complexity of negotiation. Each offers a framework for conceptualizing certain types of conference settings, including those that are multilateral (Midgaard and Underdal), those in which multiple issues are contended (Winham) and those where mediational mechanisms operate to facilitate negotiation among organizations (Stern et al.). In what follows, these themes are discussed by interspersing salient insights with issues and conclusions drawn from each of the sections.

MOTIVATIONAL VERSUS COGNITIVE EXPLANATIONS

The literature on the psychology of negotiation has been written largely from the standpoint of a clash of motives, where motives are construed as preferences for outcomes, utilities, or incentives. This view holds that negotiation is a contest between two rivals, both of whom are intent on winning. Construing negotiation in this way has had advantages. It has permitted students to borrow from progress that has been made elsewhere in psychology and economics. Most relevant has been the work in such areas as scaling of preferences, game theory, and other formal models of social interaction, including arms races. These developments have provided a lexicon and a paradigm for the analysis of negotiation behavior.

The widespread acceptance of, and excitement generated by, this paradigm has resulted in a large amount of literature on both experimental studies and prescriptive analyses. These two literatures, however, have been largely parallel developments. The empirical and normative traditions have for the most part remained separate developments. One consequence of this has been that prescriptions for maximizing joint gain (or own gain) have not been tempered by empirical evidence. The empirical literature makes evident the difficulties of motivational analysis. Efforts to derive outcomes from an analysis of preferences, and to offer calculation aids for achieving these outcomes (see Midgaard and Underdal), are confounded by such problems as the interpersonal comparison of utilities, the multidimensional scaling of preferences, and the attribution of motives to actors whose situations cannot be fully appreciated by an outside observer. In addition, McClintock reminds us of the difficulties in inferring motives from behavior, in distinguishing between strategies and underlying motives, and in detecting the predominant motive in particular situations. But these problems may not be severe. Their solution awaits further progress in the development of new methodologies and technologies (the McClintock chapter shows what can be done). More problematic for motivational analysis is the contention that motives are not the *primary* source for behavior in negotiation. Certain aspects of negotiation may be rooted in other psychological processes.

Less likely to benefit from a motivational analysis are the aspects of negotiation that are conceptual and the functions performed by negotiators that consist of steering or directing the course of the deliberations. These aspects are rooted primarily in cognitive processes. They are problems to be solved or directions to be charted, rather than contests to be won. Conceptual problems often prevent the parties from defining issues in a way that would render them negotiable. This was clearly the case in a number of international negotiations, including the Vietnam Peace Talks, the Strategic Arms Limitation Talks (SALT), and the Mutual and Balanced Force Reduction talks (MBFR): in the Vietnam talks, the parties had to agree on an acceptable formula before the details could be a subject of bargaining; in SALT, a discussion of the details of disarmament depended on a shift in the parties' conception of nuclear parity from one permitting deterrence to one foreclosing coercion; and MBFR is an example of a negotiation that has not gotten beyond the conceptual stage as the parties continue to struggle with a definition of offensive force strength. Before the parties can bargain over an exchange of money for facilities or an equivalence ratio of backfire bombers to cruise missiles, they must agree that this is in fact the purpose of the negotiation. And as the examples presented here illustrate, such matters of definition may be the primary activity of negotiators.

While working out acceptable definitions of purpose, as well as haggling over the details, negotiators on both (all) sides engage in a process of steering the deliberations toward desired objectives. Steering involves both monitoring and strategizing. Monitoring consists of assessing the interest of various parties in the negotiation and seeking instructions and guidance from "superiors." Strategizing involves using the tactics necessary to move the negotiations along. These are actions that are taken to influence the course of the negotiations, such as tabling issues, decomposing and aggregating relevant information, and proceeding point by point to reconcile the different positions of the parties. These essential activities, which are performed in any negotiation, are rooted primarily in cognitive processes.

The importance of conceptual processes in negotiation was recognized by a group of cognitive psychologists who have attempted to extend their paradigm to the study of conflict resolution as this occurs in negotiation settings. This group has contributed an alternative lexicon and a paradigm that competes with the game-theoretic approach in the analysis of negotiation behavior. The results of experimental work generated by this paradigm have largely supported the premises of the approach (see Hammond, 1965), including:

(a) that cognitive factors are sufficient to cause interpersonal conflict;

(b) that cognitive factors are sufficient to explain why negotiations are made difficult;

(c) that the level of conflict is determined by the structure of the situation that confronts negotiators; and

(d) that aids can be designed to facilitate the resolution of cognitive conflict.

The Brehmer and Hammond chapter recounts the achievements of this research as it has moved from laboratory to field studies. These achievements consist both of evidence relevant to predictions derived from the framework and of prescriptions in the form of techniques for resolving cognitive conflicts.

Yet in spite of these achievements the work has not been appropriately translated for use by negotiators. It will be necessary to attempt systematically to bridge the gap between the experimental problems designed for research and the conceptual problems that confront negotiators in theatres where the major decisions of the day are being hammered out (see examples above).

Without denigrating the scope of the contributions made by each approach, it can be claimed that both suffer from a lack of balance; i.e., the one does not acknowledge the relevance of the central process explored by the other. In any particular negotiation, both motivational and cognitive processes operate. Or, put another way, negotiating behavior is *driven* by preferences and *directed* by a plan. While the relative importance of these processes is likely to vary (a) with the stage of the negotiation, as when conceptual problems must be resolved before bargaining can occur (see above), or (b) with types of negotiation (cf. trade negotiations with arms control deliberations), the relevance of both must be acknowledged. Indeed, the importance of both processes is acknowledged in the research program presented in the chapter by Druckman et al. In that research, motives (defined as interests in the outcome) and cognitive factors (defined as ideological orientations) are conceived as either interacting or independent influences on decisions made in negotiations. Even more complex is the notion that the two sources for behavior are inextricably intertwined, with preferences deriving from conceptualizations, and vice versa. Moreover, new conceptualizations may alter preferences and thus pave the way toward an acceptable resolution. (An elaboration of some of these interactions is presented in the Druckman et al. chapter.) It is just this sort of process that must be taken into account if our models are to approach the complexity and depict the reality of negotiation as it occurs in situ.

BARGAINING, DEBATING, AND INFLUENCING

Just as Anatol Rapoport (1960) offered fights, games, and debates as three modes of conflict, one can view bargaining, debating, and influencing as three cuts on negotiation. Rapoport developed his modes as alternative frameworks for analyzing conflict, although any particular conflict might contain all three processes. Each mode has developed from a particular set of assumptions, has served as an organizing concept for an extensive interdisciplinary literature, and has stimulated the development of sophisticated models that have proven useful for understanding the dynamics of arms races, the range of strategic options available in certain situations, the contagion of psychological epidemics, and the difficulties involved in attempts to resolve conflicts caused by ideological or attitudinal differences. Similarly, each of the three cuts on negotiation has developed on the basis of certain assumptions, has stimulated model development and experimentation, and has proved to be a compelling characterization of the negotiation process. Each process is a paradigm for the analysis of negotiation. However, the fact that all three processes operate in any *particular* negotiation renders incomplete an analysis that does not document the interplay among them. In what follows, these points are elaborated further.

Bargaining is a cut on negotiation not unlike the type of conflict that is characterized by Rapoport as the "game." According to Rapoport,

> Games of strategy . . . offer a good model of rational behavior in situations where (1) there are conflicts of interest; (2) a number of alternatives are open at each phase of the situation; (3) people are in a position to estimate consequences of their choices, taking into consideration the very important circumstance that outcomes are determined

not only by one's own choices but also by the choices of others, over whom one has no control [1960: 108].

Bargaining then is a kind of game that can be defined (following Hamner and Yukl) as an interaction process "that occurs when two or more persons attempt to agree on a mutually acceptable outcome in a situation where their orders of preferences for possible outcomes are negatively correlated" (see Chapter 4, p. 138). The bargaining process consists of converging decisions that are construed as concession exchanges.

Three approaches to the bargaining problem can be distinguished: (a) concern solely with the bargaining outcome or settlement point; (b) concern with the process of concession-making and the relation between the process and the observed outcome; or (c) a focus on attempts by the bargainers to change some of the basic parameters of the situation. A theory of bargaining should encompass all of these concerns. As Coddington (1968: 24) suggests, a theory of bargaining should provide answers to such questions as: (a) What agreement is likely to result from the bargaining? (b) What factors play an important part in influencing the outcome of the process? (c) Given the initial conditions, what will be the course of developments leading to either an agreement or a breakdown of the bargaining? (d) What distinguishes the conditions under which an agreement of some form is likely to occur from those under which a breakdown is likely? and so on. Some of the progress toward providing answers to these questions is reviewed by Hamner and Yukl.

Since the publication of Siegel and Fouraker's (1960) work, students of bargaining behavior have devoted considerable attention to the effects of alternative strategies for eliciting concessions from an opponent. The Hamner and Yukl review makes evident the amount of work that has been completed to date on this problem. Much of the experimentation has been designed to arbitrate among competing prescriptions. However, the results of these studies have not produced a "most effective strategy." Rather they have alerted us to the complexity of the problem. Two conclusions in particular emphasize the need to consider new frameworks for exploring the bargaining process.

One conclusion concerns the dynamics of the bargaining process. It has been suggested, for example, that, contrary to an assumption of the game-theoretic paradigm, a bargainer *may not* respond directly to the other's strategy. A response may be determined by *expectations* of the other's concession-making pattern. Moreover, these expectations are in flux, constantly undergoing revision to take account of changes in the other's behavior. Recognizing the role of expectations in bargaining, some investigators (e.g., Druckman and Bonoma, 1976) are considering an alternative framework based on what Coddington (1968) described as a decision/expectation/ adjustment approach. This framework should enable investigators to take into account variables that have previously been neglected.

A second conclusion concerns elaboration and context. Hamner and Yukl note the need to design more elaborate studies in order "to map and extend the network of relationships among the various independent and dependent variables" (Chapter 4, p. 157). Furthermore, they note the need to create better representations of actual bargaining situations or more studies conducted in field settings. Such studies would direct the elaboration toward a consideration of contextual influences. The effects on bargaining of such factors as market conditions in the economic system or budget allocations to committees in the legislative system have remained outside the purview of most studies completed to date. Together the two conclusions noted here should lead to the development of approaches that advance our understanding of bargaining by enhancing both the internal and external validity of the obtained results.

Models of bargaining cast the process in terms of *incremental convergence:* initial bargaining positions are opposed—as at opposite ends of a continuum— and bargainers move gradually toward one another. To claim, however, that this is also a model of negotiation would be misleading. Bargaining is only one of several activities that occur during the course of a negotiation. Negotiation is also a rhetorical contest characterized by discussion, explication, posturing, and persuasive appeals. Together these activities can be referred to as the *debating* aspect of negotiation. Debate is more difficult to construe in terms of models based on a process of incremental convergence. The debating process requires a different conceptualization.

Although debate in negotiation is becoming an increasingly popular subject for investigation, this aspect has not benefited as much from research and theory as has the bargaining process. The work to date has not been guided by a unified conception or paradigm. The development of a paradigm is considered a goal by investigators who have devoted their attention primarily to problems of definition and measurement. Progress along these lines is reflected in the chapter by Walcott and his colleagues. Two developments in particular are worth noting: an explication of the functions of debate and the development of content-analysis systems.

The dialogue of negotiation reveals its mixed-motive quality. On the one hand, negotiators use rhetoric to cajole, persuade, and wheedle their opposite numbers. Each attempts to steer the talks in a direction that will lead to a favorable outcome for himself. On the other hand, negotiators use rhetoric to solve problems caused by revealed differences in conception or purpose. These differences impede progress; until they are resolved, the talks cannot move forward. Persuasion and problem-solving can be regarded as the two functions of debate in negotiation. Both functions are evident in the literature reviewed by Walcott et al. They parallel the distinctions drawn by Walcott et al. between competition and conflict resolution and by Pruitt and Lewis between distributive and integrative strategies.

These themes are prevalent in the negotiation literature. Tactics for winning are emphasized in the various guides for effective negotiating (e.g., Karrass, 1974), while strategies for resolving differences are suggested in the more therapeutic-oriented treatments (e.g., Rapoport, 1964). The former approach is based on the assumption that both (all) players cannot win since their goals are in opposition. The latter approach assumes that both (all) players can win by promoting shared goals through mutual understanding. One relies on techniques that are designed to maximize the difference between the negotiators; the other relies on techniques designed to minimize the differences. In both cases, the techniques suggested are essentially rhetorical devices. An assessment of the effects produced by using, for example, the "ploy" or the "region of validity," depends on the development of a content-analysis system designed to code the substance of discussion in negotiation.

The several attempts to construct a content-analysis system are reviewed in the chapter by Walcott et al. These efforts reflect both the persuasive and the problem-solving function of debate in negotiation. The persuasive function is emphasized in the Bargaining Process Analysis system, where the substance of discussion is divided into hard (threats, commitments, and retractions) and soft (initiations, accommodations, and promises) bargaining strategies. The problem-solving function is emphasized in such indices as the ratio of task-oriented to affect-oriented behavior, in the distinctions made between cognitive and value statements, and in the derived measures of sequences that reveal cognitive differences, cognitive similarities, value differences, and value similarities (see the Walcott et al. chapter for details). These categorical distinctions can be used in assessing the effects produced by tactics that are designed for "winning" or by strategies designed for "resolving differences." If effective, the "tactics" should produce an increase in the opponent's soft (as compared to hard) behaviors. Effective "strategies" should *decrease* the number of sequences that reveal cognitive or value differences while *increasing* the number of sequences that reveal similarities in cognitive or value statements. The few studies that were designed to make such assessments are encouraging. The results obtained suggest directions for further work. One outstanding effort is the programmatic research presented in the chapter by Pruitt and Lewis.

These investigators use process analysis to suggest strategies conducive to achieving integrative solutions. Their prescriptions derive directly from observations of negotiating behavior that are made under controlled conditions. Their research addresses two issues: Which strategies are most likely to lead to integrative outcomes? And, under what circumstances will these strategies be used? The notion of *flexible rigidity* combines elements of persuasion (rigidity with respect to goals) and problem-solving (flexibility with respect to means). Strategies that contain a "proper" mix of these elements are most conducive to integrative outcomes. Thus circumstances that promote such strategies should be nurtured. Pruitt and Lewis in their research have identified *both* the strategies and the circumstances and so have contributed to the resolution of the mixed-motive dilemma that is inherent in *both* bargaining and debate: the value of integrative solutions is that they satisfy everybody's ultimate limits or aspirations. The work also bridges the distinction between bargaining and debate. The negotiation process examined consists of both of those activities, and the recommendations that are made apply to both.

Bargaining and debate are the predominant *activities* in negotiation. However, they are not the only *processes* of negotiation. Negotiators occasionally use less subtle forms of influence tactics, comparable in some respects to the mode of conflict referred to by Rapoport as the "fight." These tactics include warnings, threats, ultimatums, shows of force, commitments, and other forms of coercive behavior. That these behaviors are relatively infrequent (see Hopmann, 1974) is not surprising. When they do occur, a crisis may be imminent. The negotiator who uses these tactics runs the risk of jeopardizing the deliberations. He can either succeed in persuading the other to "see it his way" or cause him to retaliate with counter-threats that lead to a breakdown in the talks. It would seem imperative to estimate the likely consequences of attempts to coerce the other. In their chapter, Tedeschi and Bonoma suggest some of the circumstances under which such tactics may succeed.

Coercion may succeed when the course of events makes it appear to be an appropriate response or when gestures are made to diffuse the other's retaliation or counter-aggressive responses. Some of the justifying events include periods of intense conflict, threats to face (see also the Brown chapter), and the experience of inequity through relative deprivation. Under these conditions, one's coercive attempts should be seen by the other as being supported by the norms of the situation, as being defensively motivated, and as being nonselfish. Rationalizing gestures include the expression of guilt, self-criticism, and the suggestion that negative consequences were unintended. Above all, the other must not consider his acquiescence to be the result of having been exploited. The success of one's coercive acts depends on the other's willingness to concede. And willingness depends in turn on the extent to which he can justify the coercion as having been supported by the norms of the situation or by other circumstances. These mitigating circumstances notwithstanding, however, coercion and aggression in negotiation should be considered "measures of last resort."

THE PERSON, ROLE, AND SITUATION

Of all the issues raised by social psychologists, none is more central to the discipline than the relative importance of the person, role, and situation as determinants of behavior. It is considered by some to be the defining issue of the discipline, placing social psychology at the interdisciplinary juncture where personality psychology, sociology, and experimental psychology meet.

This issue has stimulated considerable empirical activity; yet despite these efforts, it has not been arbitrated. Rather than clarifying the issue, the literature has shown its complexity. What emerges is an interactive model summarized by the general observation that "under certain conditions, particular 'person' variables influence behavior when these are not moderated by role demands." Progress at the theoretical level lags far behind. What is lacking is a paradigm to organize the findings and to guide further developments.

Of all the settings in which this issue has been explored, none is more relevant than negotiation. Negotiators are individuals, they are usually in the role of representative, and their behavior is influenced by the negotiating situation. The negotiation literature has addressed the issue. Here too complexity is revealed by empirical investigation. The few experiments completed to date support the "interaction model." What remains to be determined is: What are the conditions? Which "person" variables affect behavior? And when do role demands moderate (or enhance) the impact of person or situational variables? Some of the progress that has been made is presented in the chapters by Hermann and Kogan, Brown, and Hopmann and Walcott. These chapters summarize portions of this literature and/or present new data. They hint at the possibility of an integration which will foster the development of a conceptual structure that can guide research in much the way this is done in the parallel effort by Druckman (1976).

The conceptual structure must take account of the complexity made evident by the empirical literature. The interaction model suggested by the findings is also a differentiated model. Different personality variables affect different aspects of the negotiating process. Representational role obligations can be considered in terms of components that determine the impact of "representation" on negotiation behavior. And different aspects of the situation may either moderate or enhance the effects obtained for selected person and role variables. Moreover, the interactive effects of these variables are likely to differ from one stage of the negotiation to another. This sort of complexity impedes the development of an overarching conceptual structure, which may be a goal that can be approached only piecemeal. If this is the case, then the most plausible strategy is one that moves gradually toward this goal by resolving one issue at a time. Indeed, the literature seems to have progressed in this manner. In what follows, the progression is highlighted.

The Hermann and Kogan chapter calls attention to the complex relationship between personality and negotiating behavior. The literature that is summarized and the results that were obtained by these investigators suggest that personality variables may affect negotiations in a subtle way. For example, different negotiators seem to respond differently to a previous sequence of "moves" and to demonstrate different trends in cooperativeness/competitiveness over long periods of time. The direction of these effects may depend on the particular mix of characteristics of the opponents engaged in negotiating. Other effects include reactions to the other's shift in strategy, interpretation of the other's concessions, and initial orientations toward the negotiating situation. Moreover, personality is most likely to affect negotiating behavior very early in the deliberations (before the structural aspects of the interaction become the major determinant) and during the middle phase of the conference. Most of these findings were obtained in isolated experimental settings. The extent to which they increase our understanding of the way in which personality variables operate in other negotiating theatres remains to be determined.

Efforts to extrapolate to the field the findings obtained in the laboratory are impeded by several dimensions of difference between the settings. Laboratory negotiators are not professionals. They are screened for participation on dimensions unlikely to be used in recruiting professional negotiators, the definition of their roles is more ambiguous, and they operate in an environment that is less complex (in terms of strategic options) and less tense than the noncontrived settings in which negotiations take place. Under these conditions, the impact of personality characteristics is likely to be enhanced. Personality differences among professionals are minimized by similar selective recruiting procedures, the development of a "negotiator subculture," and the constraining effects of role obligations (see Bartos, 1967). They are likely to differ more on such dimensions as ideology or national culture. For these reasons, among others, personality effects may be stronger in the laboratory.

These observations have several implications. First, it may be more fruitful to focus on *interactions* among personality, role, and situation variables. Second, more concentration on the components of role obligations and on aspects of the negotiating situations is warranted. And third, systematic research on the effects of ideological and cultural differences should be encouraged (see, e.g., Druckman et al., 1976). The first two recommendations are developed by the chapters in this section. The third may be found in the research reported in the earlier chapters by Brehmer and Hammond, and Druckman et al.

The negotiator as representative fills a role that prescribes his options and makes him responsible for the consequences of his performance. As an agent, the negotiator's posture may range all the way from that of an emissary commissioned to "deliver the position," to a free agent with considerable latitude in his attempts to achieve an agreement. This range of responsiveness, referred to as "decision latitude," covaries with the extent to which individual characteristics are likely to influence the negotiation process—i.e., the more the latitude, the stronger the effects of "person" variables. The Brown chapter summarizes the results of experiments that documented the behavioral consequences of being responsive to one's role obligations (a more extensive review is presented in Druckman, 1976).

One way of characterizing these effects is that such responsiveness legitimizes a pattern of behavior that prevents a negotiator from responding spontaneously to his opposite number. These effects are most pronounced

under certain conditions, such as (1) when a negotiator has little latitude in determining either his positions or his posture, (2) when he is held accountable for his performance, (3) when he has sole responsibility for the outcome, (4) when he is obligated to a constituency that is present during the negotiations, and (5) when he is appointed rather than elected. Under these conditions, a negotiator's behavior is constrained by his obligations. The more latitude a negotiator has in formulating his positions, the more dispersed the responsibility for the outcome, the more abstract the constituency (e.g., cultures, ideologies), the less is the impact of his role obligations on negotiating behavior. The "uncommitted" representative is relatively free from constituent or administrative demands; instead, he is free to respond to the demands of his opposite number.

The research completed to date has made us aware of the importance of role obligations in negotiation. The way in which a negotiator responds to these obligations influences the negotiation process. Most interesting perhaps is the conflict experienced by the negotiator, who, as a representative, occupies a boundary role between the demands of his own and the other side. As a negotiator, the representative is expected to make concessions toward achieving an agreement. As a representative, the negotiator must be cautious in offering concessions and must demand reciprocation for concessions made. As a tactician, the negotiator-representative does not want to convey the impression that because he made a concession, further concessions are forthcoming or that he has conceded to the "superior" position of his opposite number. The more effective a negotiator is in conveying the impression that his performance coincides with his own party's expectations, and at the same time conveying the impression to his opposite number that he cannot concede beyond a clearly defined point, the easier the negotiations are. His effectiveness depends on the skillful execution of impression-management tactics.

Impression-management tactics are devices that help a negotiator avoid loss of face (e.g., humiliation, intimidation). In his boundary role, the representative is confronted with a potential loss of face in the eyes of two or more parties who are making conflicting demands on him. Concessions offered could be interpreted by his constituents as a "sellout" and by his opponents as a "sign of weakness." Both interpretations are a threat to face. How he responds to these threats could either strengthen or weaken his negotiating position. At stake is his bargaining reputation. To be effective, a negotiator must be firm without appearing too rigid, and at the same time he must be willing to yield without appearing too conciliatory. Brown follows Stevens (1963) in referring to this as the "inherent paradox" of negotiation. He views this paradox as the reason for "building pressures toward face-maintenance into the structure of negotiation" (Chapter 9, p. 278).

Brown presents a compelling argument for the importance of face-maintenance motives in negotiation. It may be regarded as a pivotal concept—a primary motive that impels negotiators to resolve their boundary-role dilemma. It is a motive that is regulated by aspects of the negotiating situation. As such, it may provide the link between investigations of representational role obligations and explorations of the effects of (a) the opposing party's actions, (b) various kinds of audiences, (c) third-party interventions, and (d) salient features of the negotiation situation.

These factors affect the negotiator's attempts to achieve a balance between firmness and accommodation. A negotiator reacts to his opponent's actions and to his own perception of his constituent's expectations. An effective negotiator is one who can influence his opponent's actions and structure his constituent's expectations in a direction that makes agreement inevitable. He can be aided by structurally prominent solutions or by third parties. He is hindered by actions and expectations that evoke face-maintenance motives. The former contribute to mutual accommodation by permitting a negotiator to "save face." The latter contribute to mutual firmness by calling forth efforts designed to assert or reassert one's strength. The results of several studies suggest how prominent solutions and/or intermediaries can relieve negotiators of the feeling of personal inadequacy that may result from actions taken or received during the deliberations.

Brown cites the definition of prominence found in the bargaining literature: It refers to features of the negotiation situation that draw attention to themselves by virtue of physical configuration, uniqueness, or precedent. These features can take the form of procedures for face-saving or face-restoration actions, or bargaining solutions that are salient because they are equitable. The former can be used to assert strength in the face of threatened intimidation. Their availability enables a negotiator to prevent a loss of face that would result from acquiescing to the opponent's demands. The latter solutions prevent either party from claiming victory or feeling defeated. These solutions are attained through equal compromises made by all parties. They facilitate concession-making. In fact, experiments have shown that it is safer to offer concessions through an intermediary; direct offers raise an opponent's expectations of further concessions significantly higher than when the same offers are initiated by a third party. He can also "help a negotiator making a concession to avoid a loss of face through such devices as creating the impression that the player is conceding to the pressures of public opinion rather than to the superior position of the other players" (Young, 1972: 58). If they are used effectively, these mechanisms should relieve negotiators of the feeling of personal inadequacy that results from making concessions to an opponent.

The discussion of face-saving points to the importance of performance evaluation in negotiation. As Hermann and Kogan suggest, "In a sense, negotiators act in a fishbowl: everyone is interested in their performance" (Chapter 8, p. 270). The evaluation anxiety experienced by negotiators enhances the stresses and tensions involved in the negotiating task. Stress is a condition of negotiation. How negotiators cope with it could affect the process and determine the outcome, as Hopmann and Walcott demonstrate in their chapter.

The evidence presented by Hopmann and Walcott indicates that high levels of stresses and tensions are dysfunctional for negotiation. Among the effects obtained were greater hostility among negotiators, harder bargaining strategies, and less successful outcomes. These observed effects may occur because of the way in which stress affects individual perceptual and cognitive structure, as well as group structure. Numerous studies, some of which are reviewed in the Hopmann and Walcott chapter, suggest that increases in tension beyond a certain point may decrease the amount of integration in the group and may result in a simplified cognitive structure on the part of members, making them less capable of evaluating information and making the fine discriminations that are necessary in order to achieve a mutually satisfactory agreement. While these psychological effects may be general, affecting negotiators who have a wide variety of backgrounds and role obligations, they can be magnified or reduced by the way in which an individual reacts to a stressful environment.[1]

The Hopmann and Walcott study documents the effects on negotiating behavior of stress in the external system. Their results support the proposition (stated by Druckman, 1973) on the linkage between the international environment and negotiations and illustrate the reciprocal effects of "systemic tension" and "conference tension." But systemic tension is only one cause of the level of stress experienced by negotiators. Other factors include time pressures, the consequences of nonagreement (or an unfavorable agreement), performance evaluation pressures (see above), and unexpected actions taken by opponents. The effects of these variables have been explored in a number of experimental studies. Some of the studies are reviewed in other chapters (e.g., Hamner and Yukl on time pressures). However, these and other relevant situational variables do not form the basis for chapters in this volume.[2]

The discussion in this section makes evident the abundant amount of research stimulated by questions of the manner in which person, role, and situational variables influence negotiation behavior. Most of this research has concentrated on one or the other factor. Relatively few studies have examined interrelationships. Plausible interactions are suggested in the chapter by Hermann and Kogan, and the chapter by Brown. These investigators also cited studies designed explicitly to address issues of interrelationships in both laboratory (e.g., Druckman, 1967) and field settings (e.g., Douglas, 1957). But this work merely suggests the outlines of a conceptual structure that can guide efforts designed to arbitrate such issues as how different negotiators under varying degrees of responsiveness to their role obligations (or accountability for the outcome) and under varied conditions (e.g., secrecy versus openness) attempt to resolve their boundary role dilemmas. Other examples of two- and three-way interactions (see Druckman, 1976) are worthy of further exploration in an attempt to ascertain the relative impact of these sources of variation on negotiation behavior.

COMPLEX SETTINGS AND PROCESSES

The contributors to this volume make evident the complexity of negotiations, which is revealed in process and in context. Negotiators must deal with this complexity. They do this by decomposing and aggregating relevant information, by monitoring their opposite numbers to determine "where they are at," by tactically moving a negotiation along a desired course, and by attempting to control the impact of factors that may disturb an orderly progression toward the attainment of a balanced agreement. These activities are designed to keep the deliberations "on the track." The skillful negotiator is a competent manager of information, a sensitive analyst of the others' revealed intentions, a canny tactician, and a person who can prevent unpredictable events or sudden changes in policy from disrupting the momentum of a negotiation. The success of a negotiation depends largely on the negotiator's ability to perform these functions. And these activities can be aided by analyses designed to identify the relevant internal and external factors that "drive" a complex negotiation. The three chapters in the final part of this volume contribute to the development of such analyses.

Complexity poses problems for the analyst of negotiation. Extant paradigms are limited in scope and provide a structure only for the analysis of selected problems—those that arise in the context of brief negotiations among a small number of parties. These problems may be fundamentally different from those that occur in large conferences that are conducted over long periods of time. Indeed, Midgaard and Underdal make a case for fundamentally different processes, claiming that complexity obscures the operation of processes observed in the bilateral case. Their contention is supported by the Stern et al. analysis of the difficulties involved in attempting to implement mechanisms that are designed to facilitate negotiation. New paradigms may be needed to guide the study of complex negotiations. One example is provided by Winham's perspective for conceptualizing complexity in international negotiations. Along with the other contributors to this section, he suggests a new direction for research on negotiation. Moreover, each of these investigators promotes a methodology based on systematic observation of negotiations as these occur in situ.

The chapters by Midgaard and Underdal, Winham, and Stern et al. call attention to the considerations that must be entertained by those intent on investigating complex processes. The chapters present considerations from the standpoint of the negotiation process (Midgaard and Underdal), negotiators' adaptations (Winham), and third-party attempts to engineer or mediate the conflict situation (Stern et al.). Some of these considerations concern the variable of *conference size;* others relate to *conference structure.* Large variegated conferences are difficult to analyze. Their increased complexity militates against analytic solutions. The structures and processes that must be analyzed require either a shift in perspective (see Winham) or an extension of analyses designed for problems that arise in less complex settings (see Midgaard and Underdal).

The broadened perspective entails a shift in the level of analysis from that of dyadic bargaining, or small-group interaction, to the large-scale conference. The bargaining dynamic of smaller conferences is replaced by mechanisms that are designed to manage complexity. The mechanisms consist of structures and processes that have received scant attention in the social-psychological literature. The structures are those of interorganizational relations. The processes are those of collective decision-making. These are the factors over which individual negotiators have little control. The dynamics of large conferences reflect the combined operation of these structures and processes. Decisions emerge from the interplay of bureaucratic politics and interorganizational relations. The chapters in the last part are first attempts to use these types of factors in an analysis of negotiation. The analyses are suggestive. The propositions generated are useful. The insights achieved suggest that more sustained efforts are warranted.

A prototype for large negotiation conferences is the plenary of international negotiations. Plenaries are the official sessions. All delegates attend to hear the formal statements of their principals. The work of smaller committees is represented in the "record" of the plenary. This conference form is characterized by identifiable structures and processes. The structures are those of formalized rules, differentiation of role and functions, specialized working committees, coalitions of similar interests, and mechanisms for facilitating decision-making. Processes include networks of informal communication channels, a repetitive review of arguments for or against a few alternatives or principles, discussion that is less exploratory or adventurous, reluctance to initiate concessions (offers are vague and tentative), and a more impersonal and anonymous form of interaction (see Midgaard and Underdal). These are the structures and processes that the analyst of large-scale conferences must include in his framework.

Increased conference size also affects the negotiator. Midgaard and Underdal note the increased strain and frustration caused by complexity. Winham emphasizes the effects of complexity on cognitive structuring. These effects are not independent. One affects the other in a cycle of reciprocal relations: The increased strain limits the amount of information processed by the negotiator (see also the Hopmann and Walcott chapter); the negotiator's need to manage the complex situation confronting him increases his level of tension. The result is that prospects for rational choice and value maximization are diminished. While these effects might actually facilitate agreements, as Winham notes, the agreement is likely to be partial and suboptimal—e.g., covering only some agenda items, signed by only some parties, and ambiguous (see Midgaard and Underdal).

The two variables that begin to differentiate simple from complex negotiating situations are size and uncertainty. From the negotiator's standpoint, size presents a problem of information-processing; uncertainty poses problems of availability and reliability of information. To operate effectively, negotiators must manage these problems. Winham uses data obtained from field and laboratory investigations to illustrate some strategies. These include the following:

(a) Concentrate more on aspects that are relatively certain (stated positions) than on aspects that are less understandable (value of alternative proposals).

(b) Monitor concessions as a trend, noting in that trend a willingness of the other party to negotiate.

(c) Concentrate on keeping abreast of where the other parties stand on issues rather than on the size of the concessions offered.

(d) Make simple measurements in order to negotiate over complex data. These can be used to create a structure for communication and decision-making.

These strategies emphasize the monitoring problems (i.e., adducing "where I am at" and "where he is at") for negotiators in multilateral situations. These problems are construed in terms of an information-processing framework. Winham draws from developments in organizational decision-making and cybernetics for his perspective. The perspective can be used for organizing observations of multilateral conferences. More practically, it can be used to develop calculation aids for helping a negotiator structure his situation (see examples in Winham and in Midgaard and Underdal).

Another effect of complexity is that it obfuscates the negotiating situation. It makes it difficult to develop a coherent framework for organizing the issues, parties, and networks of communication that define a negotiation. Different parties are likely to develop different conceptions of the situation, disagree on the objectives of the negotiation, and prefer a different structure for framing the issues for discussion (see the Brehmer and Hammond chapter). Impasses result from an inability to resolve these differences. The resolution of such impasses may require altered perceptions or definitions of purpose by some or all parties. This can be accomplished by the skillful use of mediational mechanisms.

The chapter by Stern et al. presents several mediational devices designed to restructure a complex negotiating situation. These are exchange of persons, superordinate goals, and diplomacy. The effectiveness of each depends on the nature of the relationship among the parties and the extent to which each party is willing to attend to the processes involved in executing the procedures implied by the mechanism(s). According to Stern et al., the interrelationships must be typified by mutual dependence, symmetric power, and relative intensity. Moreover, the energy level of the parties must be sufficiently high to permit them to maintain the enthusiasm needed for sustained participation in the program or procedure. These are the underlying social-psychological processes that promote or inhibit the operation of the mediational mechanisms. If they are to be implemented effectively, a subtle balance must be achieved among them. How to achieve such a balance is problematic: Stern et al. highlight some of the difficulties of implementation.

Perhaps the most interesting implication of the mediational mechanisms discussed in the final chapter is that they can be used prior to a negotiation to set the stage for meaningful deliberations. They can foster the climate needed for effective negotiating. The increased trust and mutual understanding achieved by such techniques as role reversal and diplomacy should enable the parties to discuss openly their differences on sensitive issues. Such "negotiating in good faith" can promote mutually beneficial agreements. However, the techniques are less likely to be useful as intrusions during the course of a negotiation. While they can prevent crises from emerging, they are less likely to help negotiators extricate themselves from a crisis. Other forms of mediation may be called for at these junctures.[3]

Finally, the chapters in this part suggest several implications for the analyst of complex negotiations. First, he must broaden his perspective on the processes and contexts of negotiation. Second, he must consider structures and processes that have been neglected in the literature on negotiation. Third, he must tailor his analyses to this "reality." Fourth, he must develop a sensitivity to the ways in which negotiators can manage complexity and suggest possible "structuring" devices. And, fifth, he should recognize the relevance of various mediational mechanisms as processes that can effectively restructure a complex situation for negotiators: Such recognition entails distinguishing between appropriate and inappropriate procedures. These implications suggest directions for systematic programs of research on complex negotiations. More conjectural, however, is the question as to what extent these directions portend the shape of future developments.

TOWARD AN INTEGRATED THEORY

The overview presented in Table 1 highlights the diversity of the contributions. The various emphases, settings, concepts, and methods define the state of the art. This volume is a bench mark for the ongoing programs of research: Progress to date is recorded, and new directions are charted. And it explicates the considerations that must be entertained by the serious student of negotiation structure and process. These considerations are a first step toward the juxtaposition needed for an overall framework that encompasses the various "components" listed in Table 1 and depicted in Figure 1. They are precursors to model development. They suggest the broad outlines for a general theory.

TABLE 1
An Overview of the Contributions

Chapters	Aspects Examined	Types of Effects	Settings	Conceptual Approaches	Methodological Approaches	Stylistic Approaches
McClintock	Motivational orientation; strategy; expectations for other's behavior and outcome preferences	Level of conflict; predictive accuracy of other's choices; satisfaction with outcome	Negotiation situations as individualistic, cooperative, competitive, altruistic	Value maximization/utility theory	Gaming experiments	Theoretical propositions with illustrative experiments
Brehmer and Hammond	Cognitive structure of conflict; nature of task; positions on issues	Level (and structure) of conflict; position convergence/divergence); deadlock/resolutions	Simulated political decision-making; city councils; union-management negotiations	Social judgment theory; Brunswik's "probabilistic functionalism"	Laboratory and field experiments	Review of experimental results derived from a conceptual framework or model
Druckman et al	Incentives and outcome preferences; ideologies and positions on issues; context for negotiation	Level of conflict; direction of resolution of issues; probable alliances on issues in multilateral negotiations	Simulated political decision-making	Utility theory; coalition theory; sociology of conflict	Experimental simulation; process-outcome relationships	Review of experiments derived from a conceptual framework or model
Hamner and Yukl	Bargaining tactics; bargaining strategies; type of bargainer and bargaining situation	Frequency and size of concessions; rate of concession-making; speed to agreement; type of (and satisfaction with) agreement	Buyer-seller games; reward allocation games; bargaining simulations	Alternative theoretical approaches to the "most effective strategy"	Experimental design: studies use real or confederate opponents	Organized review of literature for deriving conclusions on the "most effective strategy"
Pruitt and Lewis	Bargaining strategies: distributive; information exchange; heuristic trial and error. Bargaining orientation: problem-solving or win-lose	Choice of strategy; coordination of strategies; effects of one's strategy on the other; level of satisfaction with outcome	Simulated buyer-seller interactions	Joint value-maximization; information-processing	Process analyses of data from experimental simulations; process-outcome relationships	Review of experimental results on effectiveness of alternative bargaining strategies

TABLE 1
An Overview of the Contributions [a]

Chapters	Aspects Examined	Types of Effects	Settings	Conceptual Approaches	Methodological Approaches	Stylistic Approaches
Walcott et al.	Debating; meaning of rhetorical aspects; role reversal; phases of negotiation	Attitudinal change/resistance; timing for bilateral focus, misunderstandings	Laboratory simulations; international negotiations	Small group interaction processes; assumptions underlying bilateral focus/region of validity	Alternative process or content analysis systems for analyzing the rhetorical aspects of negotiation; process-outcome relationships	Review of techniques and studies
Tedeschi and Bonoma	Forms of coercion: contingent/non-contingent threats; offensive/defensive threats; types of punishments. Commitment tactics	Compliance; retaliation; retribution; costly escalation	Laboratory experiments	"Coercion theory;" extensions of reinforcement/learning theory	(Chapter emphasizes concepts rather than methods)	Conceptual framework and review of related research
Hermann and Kogan	Eight personality variables; type of negotiating dyad; orientations, strategies, and behaviors	Level of cooperative/competitive orientation and behavior; trends in cooperation/competition through time; reaction to previous contingent responses or shifts in strategy	Prisoner's Dilemma game	Findings from previous studies suggest hypotheses of personality/behavior relationships	Laboratory experiment	Hypotheses derived from literature review and tested by an experiment
Brown	Situational regulators of face-saving, including monitoring/feedback from constituents and other audiences, role-obligations, and third-parties; open vs. secret negotiations	Assertions of strength, costly retaliation; tacit bargaining; rate and amount of concession making	Laboratory experiments/simulations	Framework for indentifying the arousal and effects of face-saving motives	(Chapter emphasizes concepts rather than methods)	Conceptual framework and review of related research

[39]

TABLE 1
An Overview of the Contributions

Chapters	Aspects Examined	Types of Effects	Settings	Conceptual Approaches	Methodological Approaches	Stylistic Approaches
Hopmann and Walcott	Stresses and tensions	Over- and under- reactions to other's provocations; soft/ hard bargaining strategies; ratio of agreements to disagreements, and negative to positive affect; hostile attitudes and perceptions	Laboratory simulation of test-ban treaty; transcripts of the actual negotiation (1962-1963)	Mediated stimulus – response model; four approaches to the relation between tensions and disarmament negotiations	Comparisons between methods drawn from parallel analyses of simulation and referent materials	Hypothesis testing in two settings: laboratory and *in situ*
Midgaard and Underdal	Number of parties, from bilateral to multilateral conferences	Partial, suboptimal agreements; types of coalitions; increased situational complexity obfuscates strategic calculations	Multilateral international conferences such as UNCTAD, Law of the Seas, EEC used as examples for arguments	Game theory; small group theory; coalition theory	Models and empirical results suggest normative or prescriptive implications	Propositions and sources from which they are derived
Winham	Complexity: size of situation and uncertainty of information	Effects of complexity including simplified cognitive structures, facilitating agreements in the form of packages, and concessions seen as breakthroughs	Kennedy Round of trade negotiations and simulation of this negotiation	Adaptations of "decision theory" to account for decision-making in complex (multilateral or organizational) settings	Comparison of observations made *in situ* and in a simulation	Framework for organizing and describing effects of complexity in multilateral settings
Stern et al.	Alternative mediational mechanisms	If effective, mechanisms can foster favorable atmosphere, increase understanding, and increase chances of accommodation and compromise among boundary-role members	Inter-organizational relations; laboratory and field studies of intergroup relations	Explication of underlying social-psychological processes for effective operation of the mechanisms	(Chapter emphasizes concepts rather than methods)	Selected literature review for conceptual insights and generalizations

An adequate general theory of negotiation must encompass the following observations, gleaned from the contributions, about objectives, processes, behaviors, and influences.

(1) Negotiation is a method of social decision-making. It differs from forms of decision-making that involve choices against the environment; it consists of choices against another person or party and is accomplished by persuasion and haggling (Winham; Tedeschi and Bonoma).

(2) Negotiators sometimes face situations where they must arbitrate between clear-cut alternatives and easily ordered priorities (McClintock; Druckman et al.; Hamner and Yukl; Hermann and Kogan). More often perhaps they must balance incommensurates on the way to an agreement (Brehmer and Hammond; Hopmann and Walcott; Midgaard and Underdal; Winham).

(3) Negotiating situations differ in the extent to which the negotiators' attention is focused on the negotiating situation. Contesting negotiators may or may not be able (or be willing) to: (a) define the issues in the same manner, (b) enter a process consisting of gradual convergence toward a compromise solution, (c) make utility and cost calculations in terms both of positions on issues and of bargaining time, and (d) agree on relative bargaining power (compare McClintock; Hamner and Yukl; Pruitt and Lewis; Hermann and Kogan; and Midgaard and Underdal with Brehmer and Hammond; Druckman et al.; Walcott et al.; Winham; and Stern et al.).

(4) Most negotiating situations contain elements of both bargaining and debate (Druckman et al.). Negotiations consist of making concessions to achieve an agreement (Hamner and Yukl; Brown) and using rhetoric to clarify issues and to persuade (Walcott et al.; Pruitt and Lewis; Tedeschi and Bonoma).

(5) Negotiators operate within two limits: They act to increase common interests and expand cooperation; they also act to maximize their own interests and to prevail in terms of ensuring that an agreement is valuable for themselves (McClintock; Pruitt and Lewis; Hermann and Kogan).

(6) It is difficult to find an overarching criterion by which to judge negotiations, negotiators, or negotiated outcomes. Opposing parties rarely agree that one outcome derives from mutually agreed procedures for deducing that outcome (compare Brehmer and Hammond; Druckman et al.; and Winham with Pruitt and Lewis).

(7) Bargaining reputation is an important variable. Face-saving is a powerful motive in negotiation (Brown). Negotiators are reluctant to yield or concede, and even after having made a concession are often unwilling to acknowledge it. For this reason, concessions may appear only in the context of an apparent quid pro quo or for an obvious strategic advantage (Winham).

(8) Negotiating behavior is conditioned by the *context* for negotiation. Issues, complexity, team structure, and style are determined in part

by the larger setting for negotiation (Druckman et al.; Hopmann and Walcott; Winham; Stern et al.).

More generally, these observations suggest that an analysis of negotiation be made in terms of actors and interactions, power, and interests, and that explanations of outcomes are found in parties and process, structure, and communication (see also Zartman, 1976). Such an analysis entails moving between levels of conceptualization and weaving together diverse data sources into a mosaic of influences (see Figure 1) that contribute to an understanding of the phenomenon. Acquiring the insights then is a first step toward the development of a conceptual framework that makes comprehensible the way in which various aspects are related. This step takes the form of identifying these aspects and clarifying, to some extent, their effects on the negotiation process. These tasks are accomplished by the efforts reported in this volume (see Table 1).

But have we also developed a purview of the field that permits us to move beyond the heuristic implications of identification and clarification of effects? What are the prospects for developing a general theory? The progress to date merely suggests directions and provides a glimpse at the broad outlines. For some, this level of achievement is adequate—the search is more rewarding than the product. For others, it is disappointing: While promoting the possibilities for application and predictability, they are reluctant to offer a "warranty for their services." The *situation* or *dilemma* is captured well by Zartman, who appraises the state of the art as follows:

> Theory about negotiation is still not well developed, either in abstract terms or *a fortiori* in terms that can be used to explain real outcomes. Concepts that can be operationalized, relationships of observed regularity, hypotheses about causal influences—all need more work. . . .To be sure, the idea of theoretical unpredictability can be cited to discourage further work in explanatory theory of negotiation. But the notion of theoretical inadequacy leads one to suspect that current theory is not sufficiently developed to leave us with theoretical unpredictability as the last word! [Zartman, 1976: 483-484]

The issue is not resolved in this volume. Rather, the chapters to follow are offered as "further work [toward an] explanatory theory of negotiation."

NOTES

1. Some suggestions for coping are made in a recent work by Alex George (1976). He offers advice to international decision makers, who are often confronted with the potentially incapacitating effects of post-decision malaise that is experienced after making a critical decision. These prescriptions may also help the international negotiator who must deal with high levels of stress that accompany crises or impending crises.

2. The interested reader is referred to Druckman (1976) and Druckman and Mahoney (1976) for a review of literature on the effects of such relevant factors as prenegotiation experience, procedural conferences, rules of conduct, agendas, and the size, content, and ranking of issues.

3. One form is traditional mediation. Like the Stern et al. mechanisms, effective mediation depends on certain perceptual and situational factors. These include the nature of the conflict, whether his decisions are binding, the amount of background information he has, and the extent to which he is perceived as unbiased (see Druckman, 1973, for a review). Further research might examine the relative effectiveness of various forms of mediation, including when each is likely to be most useful.

REFERENCES

BARTOS, O. J. (1967) "How predictable are negotiations?" J. of Conflict Resolution 11: 481-496.

CODDINGTON, A. (1968) *Theories of the Bargaining Process.* Chicago: Aldine.

DOUGLAS, A. (1957) "The peaceful settlement of industrial and intergroup disputes." J. of Conflict Resolution 1: 69-81.

DRUCKMAN, D. (1976) "The person, role, and situation in international negotiations," in M. G. Hermann and T. W. Milburn (eds.) *A Psychological Examination of Political Leaders.* New York: Free Press.

――― (1973) "Human Factors in International Negotiations: Social-Psychological Aspects of International Conflict." Sage Professional Paper in International Studies 02-020. Beverly Hills: Sage Publications.

――― (1967) "Dogmatism, prenegotiation experience, and simulated group representation as determinants of dyadic behavior in a bargaining situation." J. of Personality and Social Psychology 6: 279-290.

――― and T. V. BONOMA (1976) "Determinants of bargaining behavior in a bilateral monopoly situation II: Opponent's concession rate and similarity." Behavioral Science 21: 252-262.

DRUCKMAN, D. and R. MAHONEY (1976) "Processes and consequences of international negotiations," in T. W. Milburn and T. V. Bonoma (eds.) Social Conflict: Another Look. (Special Issue of the Journal of Social Issues)

DRUCKMAN, D., A. A. BENTON, F. ALI, and J. S. BAGUR (1976). "Cultural differences in bargaining behavior: India, Argentina, and the United States." J. of Conflict Resolution 20: 413-452.

GEORGE, A. (1976) "Minimizing Irrationalities." Report to the Commission on the Organization of the Government for the Conduct of Foreign Policy. Washington, D.C.

HAMMOND, K. R. (1965) "New directions in research on conflict resolution." J. of Social Issues 11: 44-66.

HOPMANN, P. T. (1974) "Bargaining in arms control negotiations: The Seabeds Denuclearization Treaty." International Organization 28: 313-348.

KARRASS, C. L. (1974) *Give & Take: The Complete Guide to Negotiating Strategies and Tactics.* New York: Thomas Y. Crowell.

RAPOPORT, A. (1964) *Strategy and Conscience.* New York: Harper & Row.

――― (1960) *Fights, Games, and Debates.* Ann Arbor: University of Michigan Press.

SAWYER, J. and H. GUETZKOW (1965) "Bargaining and negotiation in international relations," in H. C. Kelman (ed.) *International Behavior: A Social-Psychological Analysis.* New York: Holt, Rinehart & Winston.

SIEGEL, S. and L. E. FOURAKER (1960) *Bargaining and Group Decision Making: Experiments in Bilateral Monopoly.* New York: McGraw-Hill.
STEVENS, C. M. (1963) *Strategy and Collective Bargaining Negotiation.* New York: McGraw-Hill.
YOUNG, O. R. (1972) "Intermediaries: Additional thoughts on third parties." J. of Conflict Resolution 16: 51-66.
ZARTMAN, I. W. (1976) *The 50% Solution.* Garden City, N.Y.: Doubleday Anchor.

PART I

OBJECTIVES, INCENTIVES, AND CONFLICT

EDITOR'S INTRODUCTION

From one standpoint, negotiating behavior can be viewed as a set of strategies in the service of social motives. *From another standpoint, cognitive factors are, in themselves, sufficient to explain why conflict is not resolved and why negotiation is made difficult. The issue is confronted in this section. The chapters by McClintock and by Brehmer and Hammond present contrasting views on the role of motives and cognition in interpersonal conflict and negotiations. According to McClintock, the problem for the observer of (or participant in) negotiation is to detect the intentions of the actors with regard to their preferred distribution of outcomes. According to Brehmer and Hammond, the remedy for negotiating difficulties is to assist negotiators in clarifying the "real causes" of their disagreement and in changing their policies systematically, while maintaining consistency. Each makes a good case for his perspective. The ingenuity shown by the investigators in both camps makes difficult an appraisal of the issue. Are we to conclude from the separate arguments and evidence that motivational and cognitive factors are equally important? Or can the issue be arbitrated more directly? The third chapter of this section provides a paradigm that can be used to assess relative importance.*

The balancing approach of Druckman et al. makes possible an evaluation of the extent to which interests or cognitive factors affect negotiating behavior. The results of the experiments conducted by these investigators suggest that relative importance varies with the situation and context in which negotiations take place: Negotiators in the multilateral experiments weighed the factors equally, while those in the bilateral experiments were influenced more by one type of factor or the other. Further specification of relationships is made possible by a research strategy that consists of conducting similar experiments in varied settings. This approach also shows promise in uniting the two traditions of research on sources of conflict in negotiations. And, as Druckman et al. make evident, the integration of perspectives may take the form either of a weighting process, where interests and cognitive factors are independent, or of an interaction process, where the sources of conflict influence one another in a reciprocal manner.

Each of the chapters in this section represents a bench mark in an ongoing research program. The programs have been developed along similar lines.

Experimental work has been related closely to a well-defined conceptual emphasis, and this emphasis has guided the design of paradigms that have served, in turn, to organize and structure the experimentation. However, more recently, the programs have moved in different directions. McClintock's work has become more theoretical, focusing on broader implications. The Brehmer and Hammond effort has turned toward practical implications as they attempt to design tools or aids for conflict managers. And Druckman and his collaborators have become more concerned with developing new methodological approaches for exploring complex processes and concepts. These new directions present new challenges, and the progress to date suggests the possibility of important breakthroughs. We look forward to the future developments projected in each chapter.

Chapter 1

SOCIAL MOTIVATIONS IN
SETTINGS OF OUTCOME INTERDEPENDENCE

CHARLES G. McCLINTOCK

University of California, Santa Barbara

The study of negotiations is necessarily a broad area of inquiry. There are obviously many psychological, interpersonal, or collective processes that may contribute to the occurrence of conflict between two or more actors and determine the nature of their subsequent negotiation process. The present chapter considers a restricted set of variables that may contribute to an understanding of the behavior of actors whose outcomes are interdependent and between whom conflict and negotiation may occur. First, we will be concerned with defining certain motivational orientations that occur in settings of interdependence; second, we will show how variations in such motivational orientations toward own and others' outcomes may affect the strategies actors use in relating with others.

Before a formal definitional structure of social motives is set forth, several more general observations need to be made. First, James Coleman (1973), in his recent book, *The Mathematics of Collective Action,* observes that there are two major models for describing social action—causal and purposive. Causal models view human behavior generally in mechanistic and drive-reduction terms as the result of prior, more or less proximal, environmental

AUTHOR'S NOTE: It should be acknowledged that many of the ideas in this chapter derive from collaborative conceptual and empirical work with Professor David M. Messick. The author would like to thank Professor D. Michael Kuhlman and Alfred Marshello for permission to describe in detail their study entitled "Individual Differences in Game Motivation as Moderators of Preprogrammed Strategy Effects in Prisoner's Dilemma" (1975). Finally, the author would like to thank Daniel Druckman and Judy Maki for their helpful editorial comments.

and organismic events. Purposive models, on the other hand, employ a somewhat more dynamic and descriptive paradigm in which the organism is seen as monitoring its environment, including future states, and selecting actions that in some manner produce preferred outcomes. This latter orientation underlies much of the work in contemporary decision and game theory. Although neither of these orientations tends to exist in a pure form, this chapter's theoretical approach derives more from the purposive than the causal model, and it attempts to extend the notion of preferred outcomes for self to settings of social interdependence where actions affect not only own but other's outcomes.

In addition to the distinction between causal and purposive models of action, there is another dichotomy which is somewhat related. One approach to human behavior focuses on the individual as the unit of analysis, with other actors or environmental events as independent or contextual variables. The second considers any actor as part of a system of relationship that includes other actors where there is the occurrence of mutual control of actions and outcomes. The present paradigm is more closely related in orientation to the second than to the first of these approaches.

SOCIAL MOTIVATION—A SET OF PROPOSITIONS

The propositions and corollaries that follow establish a basic assumptive structure for defining social motives in purposive and systemic terms. It should be noted again that motives represent only one of a large number of classes of variables that help determine patterns of conflict and negotiation behavior. Other chapters in this book will address other sets of variables that must be taken into account for the development of adequate models for describing and understanding conflict, negotiation, and other related forms of social behavior.

> Proposition 1. Human behavior is governed to a significant degree by the values attached to various behavioral alternatives. Given a choice among a set of available alternatives, we may normally assume that an individual selects the alternative for which the perceived value of the accompanying outcome is as high as or higher than the values attached to any other alternatives available at the time of the choice.

This initial proposition invokes the principle of hedonism, which in one form or another underlies almost all models of human behavior. Individuals are assumed to select the outcomes that afford them the greatest reinforcement, those that they find the most attractive. Unlike causal models, the above proposition is not concerned primarily with what or how prior events (e.g., rewards and punishments) determine the value of the various alternative outcomes. Rather it emphasizes that, given a range of possible outcomes, an actor will respond purposively so as to achieve that which he finds most attractive.

Proposition 2. Values can be assumed to be made up of two components: a subjective utility component that reflects the "reward-ingness" of the outcome associated with a particular alternative, and an expectation component that reflects the choice maker's evaluation of the likelihood that the outcome will follow from his choice of the alternative.

This proposition reflects a basic tenet underlying most purposive models of behavior—namely, that behavior reflects some combination of the utility (goodness) of available outcomes, and an expectancy of obtaining each more or less available outcome (its subjective probability). The reader will recognize that this proposition incorporates the fundamental assumptions that underlie contemporary decision theory where the value of outcomes is seen to be a function of their subjective utility multiplied by the subjective probability of their occurrence. Extensive reviews have been made of this area by Becker and McClintock (1967), and Rapoport and Wallsten (1972).

Given that one can assume that the organism is active, then one is confronted with explaining the direction and intensity of activity. The matter of direction raises two questions: (1) What determines the direction of activity? (2) Why do certain types of activities rather than others occur at a particular time and in a particular context? The first asks the historical or causal question of what prior experiences or inborn characteristics determine the behaviors that the organism displays in a given setting; the second asks the more purposive question of what utilities and expectancies, operating at a particular time, account for the organism's preference for X rather than Y or Z? The construct of value is relevant to both questions. Question 1 asks how individuals acquire those utilities and expected likelihoods that define the values of various activities. Question 2 concerns how an organism's utilities and expectancies combine to define its behavior in a particular setting. Intensity of motivational orientation in causal models of motivation is defined in terms of the effects that prior environmental and organismic events have in producing higher levels of arousal or drive in the organism. In purposive models, intensity is determined by the magnitude of the values associated with various outcomes.

Insofar as the question of motivation is one of defining the origin, determinants, and intensity of directed activity on the part of the human organism, then the process of value maximization or satisfaction is central to the description and understanding of human motives, and their impact upon behavior. And if values are thus central to defining human behavior, then it becomes critical to determine what indeed are the central values in human existence, how they are formed, what environmental contingencies affect their absolute and relative strengths, and what behavioral strategies can and are employed to achieve outcomes that are reflections of preferred values.

Proposition 3. A significant portion of human behavior occurs in social matrices where an individual's outcomes are determined not only by his behavior but by that of one or more other persons in the matrix and vice versa—i.e., where there is outcome interdependence.

The implications of the above proposition for the development of a theory of human motivation are profound, and yet it is only in recent years that its importance has been acknowledged. To be sure, most behavioral scientists have recognized that people are social animals and that our behavior and our values are conditioned by our social and cultural environment. Our parents' attitudes have shaped our own; culture plays a significant role in defining the range of behavior and values of its inhabitants. But given the highly individualistic orientation of most behavioral theories, the human organism has generally been viewed as an entity with a preprogrammed set of behavior potentials activated and modified by a myriad of external physical and social stimuli.

Such an individualistic approach is not without utility. It is indeed important to know about behavior potentials, and about how the physical and social environments have shaped these potentials. But it is also essential that one recognize that people frequently operate within a social matrix of which they are individually only one part or component and that it is necessary to understand the relationships and the interdependencies between the parts before one can predict or understand the behavior of one or more components. Thus, for an understanding of social motivation and the behavior of individuals who are interdependent in terms of achieving a great variety of valued outcomes, an individualistic model is not sufficient.

Corollary 1. In a situation of social interdependence, an individual is unable to optimize his own outcomes independent of the choices of others who are part of his social matrix since outcomes obtained are necessarily a function of the choices of both.

Corollary 2. The values an individual attaches to the behaviors associated with various outcomes, given interdependence, may be a function not only of the behavior he would engage in, but also of the behavior the other would engage in at the same time.

It should be emphasized that neither Proposition 3 nor its two corollaries should be viewed as contradicting Propositions 1 and 2. People are still assumed to seek their most valued outcomes, but when behavior occurs within a social matrix, these choices must reflect the limitations or constraints that the mutual determination of outcomes imposes on any actor, as well as the fact that the values associated with a given behavioral alternative for one actor (e.g., watching TV) may vary as a function of the state the other actor(s) will be in—e.g., also watching TV, going to a movie, or eating out.

In summary, then, Propositions 1 and 2 assume that a person operates upon his environment in a manner consistent with the assumptions underlying a purposive model of human behavior. Proposition 3 asserts that social action frequently occurs in a context of outcome interdependence between participating actors. Furthermore, it asserts that not only is achieving valued outcomes dependent upon the actions of others, but that the very value of a behavior for Actor A may vary as a function of the behavior of Actor B. These are essential characteristics of human interdependence, and they are central to an understanding of the etiology of human conflict and the nature of interpersonal negotiation and accommodation.

> Proposition 4. In any choice situation where actors are interdependent in terms of the attainment of outcomes, a preference may reflect either an actor's most valued outcome (a social goal or motive where value is defined both in terms of likelihood and utility of available alternatives) and/or a strategic response designed to affect the other's subsequent choices so as to increase the likelihood that an actor can subsequently achieve a highly valued outcome.

The above proposition obtains in situations where (1) an individual has the possibility of stating at least one preference or engaging in one act prior to making a terminal choice, or (2) the individual is part of a relationship in which interactions will occur through time. If an individual can make one and only one choice, and if there is to be no future interaction with another with whom he is interdependent in terms of outcomes, then the individual's choice can have no meaningful effect upon the other's future choice behavior. Hence, there can be no strategic rationale for a single choice other than that it maximizes the expected value of that act.

In effect, Proposition 4 distinguishes between choices that are means versus those that are ends. An example may help to clarify the difference. Let us imagine that you and a friend want to go and see a movie and that you are forced to make a decision between two alternative pictures, A and B. Further, let us assume that some type of joint accord must ultimately be reached because you are determined to go to a movie together. Suppose that you have a distinct preference for picture A over picture B. Now, suppose that I, as an observer who is unaware of your internal preferences, hear you tell your friend that you want to see picture B. If I assume that your stated preference reflects your value structure, then I would incorrectly infer that you prefer B to A. However, if I recognize that strategy may also affect choice, then I cannot be certain; for it may be that you recognize that your friend is of the species that has a tendency to prefer the alternative that you least prefer. If so, proposing B may become a highly effective strategy or means for obtaining A. Such strategies of disguising preferred outcomes are not uncommon in bargaining and negotiation.

Proposition 4 has a number of implications for utilizing preferences as a procedure for measuring motives or values in a social setting. Choices may reflect either goals, strategies, or some combination of the two for achieving preferred outcomes. Beating his head against a wall may not imply that the child highly values the pain that ensues. It is more likely to mean that he has discovered that this pattern of behavior produces responses in an observer that enable him to achieve some other more highly desired outcomes, such as parental attention. From both a conceptual and a measurement standpoint, it is important to recognize that in social settings where there is interdependence of outcomes between actors, an observer must have more information than mere overt choices to make a distinction between strategies and goals and that behaviors that often seem to an observer to be irrational as ends may in reality be more or less effective means for achieving a particular desired outcome.

Proposition 5. In situations of social interdependence, one's access to one's own valued outcomes is dependent upon the values assigned by others to their possible outcomes (and vice versa). Furthermore, the attractiveness of outcomes for one actor may be influenced not only by the outcomes he receives but also by the outcomes he judges the other(s) will receive.

The reader will recall that Propositions 1 and 2 assert that individual actors seek to attain those outcomes with the highest value as defined by the joint consideration of utility and likelihood. Proposition 3 states that the access to valued outcomes in situations of social interdependence is determined mutually by the behaviors of two or more actors and that the value that a given actor attaches to his outcome may reflect both the behavior he would engage in and that which others would engage in—e.g., the value of watching TV may be enhanced if the other also watches. Proposition 4 indicates that a given choice on the part of an actor may reflect his preferred outcome, or it may be a strategic response made to affect another's behavior to permit the actor eventually to achieve some preferred outcome. The above proposition, Proposition 5, asserts that an actor may evaluate the attractiveness of various outcomes not only in terms of the rewards and the costs to himself, but also in terms of the rewards and costs to others with whom he is interdependent.

Since the present proposition is central to our subsequent discussion of major social motives, let us consider one formal example of how an individual actor judges the attractiveness or value of a given outcome—not only in terms of his own payoffs but of those obtained by others. A fundamental assumption of current game research is that an individual will (or at least should) make choices that maximize that which he values most. The assumption that is contained in Proposition 1 states simply that given some valued commodity or group of commodities—e.g., money, love, prestige, or peanuts—an individual will select the alternative that affords him the outcome with the highest expected value. But now let us examine what is the typical behavior of subjects when they are confronted with a choice situation where there are points attached to alternatives, and where the outcomes for both self and other are mutually determined.

The choice situation is one that was originally defined as a maximizing-difference game (McClintock and McNeel, 1966). It is, in effect, a two-person, two-choice decision situation in which the outcomes are jointly determined. As is illustrated in Figure 1.1, Person 1 has the option of selecting between alternatives A and B; Person 2 can select X or Y. The outcomes afforded to each person are represented in the cells of the matrix, with that below the diagonal in each cell being Person 1's outcome and that above being Person 2's.

An examination of the point payoff structure of the game in Figure 1.1 immediately reveals that if the players are intent on maximizing the number of points they can receive individually, they should select alternatives A and X. However, most studies using the above game have found that even when subjects are told to obtain as many points as possible for themselves, they select a majority of B and Y alternatives. If indeed the numbers in the matrix represent the potential values attained by the subjects, this is clearly irrational behavior and severely violates Proposition 1 of the present system. However, it also has been repeatedly observed that subjects define the value to themselves of the outcomes, not in terms of the absolute number of points each receives—even when points can be translated into meaningful sums of money (McClintock and McNeel, 1966, 1967)—but in terms of how many points or dollars more or less than the other player they attain. And indeed if one values having more points or money than the other, then the appropriate strategy in the above game is to select a B or a Y since the other player can never receive more than oneself and one has the opportunity to receive more than the other. In effect, one cannot lose, but one can win.

We have cited the above example to point out that, in order to understand behavior occurring within a social matrix, not only must one take into account the utilities an individual has learned to attach to his own alternative outcomes (as well as the strategies that he anticipates may affect other's choices), but one must also consider the standards or rules of interpersonal comparison he uses to determine the attractiveness of outcomes as they determine both his own and others' rewards and punishments.

Corollary 1. Values, to the extent that they define consistent preferences for distributions of outcomes to self and other, can be represented as motivational vectors in a two-dimensional space.

Griesinger and Livingston (1973) describe a spatial model of social motives in which the magnitude or quality of one actor's outcomes is defined on the

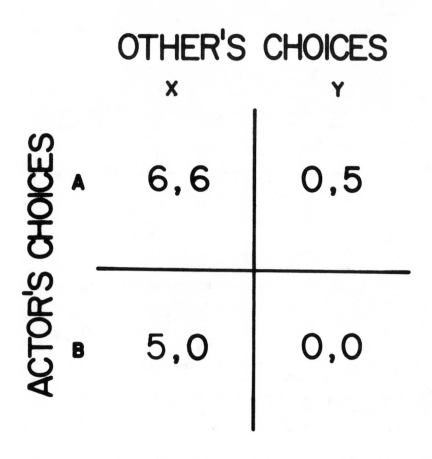

Figure 1.1. Maximizing Difference Game.

horizontal axis, and those of another on the vertical axis. Combinations of own and other's outcomes are represented as points in the two-dimensional space formed by these axes. Values are defined as vectors consistent with commonly observed preferences for distributions of outcomes to self and other. Figure 1.2 illustrates a set of motivational vectors that are frequently observed in settings where there are two interdependent actors:

(1) altruism, maximizing other's outcomes;
(2) cooperation, maximizing joint outcomes;
(3) individualism, maximizing own outcomes;
(4) competition, maximizing relative advantage of own over other's out-comes or minimizing other's relative advantage; and
(5) aggression, minimizing other's outcomes.

The model assumes that an actor will prefer that combination of own and other's outcomes that has the greatest projection on the motivational vector he values most highly. Thus, for example, if an actor is confronted with a choice between an outcome that affords him 5 of some valued commodity and other 5 and an outcome that affords him 3 and other 2, then his choice should be consistent with his preferred vector. If he is altruistic, cooperative, or individualistic in orientation, he should prefer 5,5; if he is competitive or aggressive, he should prefer 3,2. To separate altruism, cooperation, and individualism as preferred goals, one would have to provide the actor with choices that permitted this discrimination. The same would obtain for discriminating between a competitive and an aggressive goal.

Corollary 2. The number of vectors that are possible in a two-dimensional space is infinite (Wyer, 1971). However, a limited set of outcome vectors dominates human action.

It would be unreasonable to think that humans use an infinite or very large set of outcome vectors to define their goals in settings of interpersonal dependence. Indeed, when one reviews the philosophical and scientific attempts to explain man's social values or motives, they include a limited set of outcome vectors. These dominant vectors afford nonnegative or positive payoffs to an actor (see Figure 1.2), and include the previously defined predispositions of altruism, individualism, competition, and aggression. Mead (1934), for example, was able to rank thirteen primitive societies according to whether they were organized socially on the basis of the three more dominant orientations: competition, cooperation, or individualism.

Describing competition, cooperation, and individualism as more dominant does not imply that under certain conditions the motives of altruism and aggression may not obtain. There are indeed instances where someone may jump into a raging river to save a drowning person, without regard for his own outcome, and there are instances where an individual may act to inflict negative outcomes on another without considering their own payoff, as may

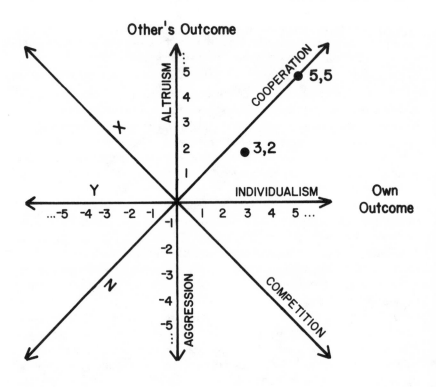

Figure 1.2. Motivational Vectors in a Two-Dimensional Space with Two Hypothetical Self-Other Outcome Combinations: 5,2 and 3,2.

be the case in Milgram's (1963) research on obedience. These are indeed interesting and significant forms of social behavior. At the same time, it does not seem likely that a great amount of human social behavior can be understood in terms of motives where an individual will forego individualistic, cooperative, or competitive outcomes for altruistic or aggressive ones. It seems likely that altruistic and aggressive acts are more often strategic responses.

These outcome vectors labelled X, Y, and Z in Figure 1.2 represent goals which imply preferences for outcomes that include negative outcomes to self. They are designated by letter because, rather interestingly, there are no self-evident descriptive labels to attach to these vectors. The Z vector implies preferences for outcomes that afford negative outcomes to self and other. The phrase, "Better dead than Red," may imply such a preference structure in certain environmental states, since dying implies a negative payoff to self. It also implies a negative payoff to those who might utilize one as a resource if one were not dead.

The Y vector might be labelled "masochistic." Beating one's head against the wall might represent such a goal if the behavior, as was noted earlier, is not merely a strategy to influence others in order to obtain more positive own outcomes. The X vector is sometimes described as altruism insofar as it is a popular notion that the most altruistic act is one that involves self-sacrifice; e.g., Christ suffered on the cross to save mankind. Although behavior consistent with the X vector may make it easier for an observer to attribute altruistic motives to an actor, it seems likely that a person concerned with other's outcomes, if he had the choice, would prefer to increase other's outcomes without inflicting negative outcomes upon self. What makes the attribution of altruism more compelling under conditions of self-sacrifice, of course, is that an actor would not afford a positive outcome for others, given a negative outcome to self, unless he was deeply concerned about the other's welfare.

In many instances, behaviors consistent with a preference for negative outcomes to self seem to represent strategic acts rather than indications of actors' goals. For example, Herman Kahn's (1960) proposed "doomsday machine," which would trigger a nuclear holocaust throughout the world if someone attacked the United States with nuclear weapons, was not a statement of preferred outcome for destroying both self and other (at least one would hope not), but a strategy intended to influence others, to deter them from using nuclear weapons against the United States. And, indeed, the threat of inflicting negative outcomes upon self, though not often reflecting a preferred outcome, is frequently used as an interpersonal strategy in settings where there is conflict and subsequent bargaining and negotiation (Schelling, 1960).

Corollary 3. Orderings of preference for own and other's outcomes exist that can be characterized as social motives but cannot be expressed as a single vector in a two-dimensional outcome space.

One orientation that cannot be characterized as a single vector is a preference for equal outcomes. In terms of an own-and-other's-outcome space, equality can be represented as a set of parallel lines, each equally distant from the cooperation vector. An individual in an equality state would prefer any outcome within the parallel lines to any outside. In effect, an actor so motivated would rather minimize the difference between his own and another's outcomes—his most preferred state being equality.

Although equality of outcome may be a social goal, it seems likely in many instances to reflect a strategy. It may be a way in which two individualistic or competitive actors resolve a conflict over outcomes so as to ensure the maintenance of a relationship. Hence, we have such strategic rules as "one divides, the other chooses," "split it down the middle," and "take turns" that serve to reduce potential conflict between actors. Benton and Druckman (1973) have indeed observed that the presence of an equality point in a bargaining setting facilitates reaching agreements when opposing actors are representing different constituencies.

Recently Van Avermaet (1975) has demonstrated that equity can also be formally defined as a distinct motive, but cannot be represented as a single vector. Expressing a preference for an equitable distribution of outcomes may in many instances also serve as a strategic act to maintain a relationship or to serve other motivational orientations. Van Avermaet, for example, found that, in a private setting, actors who deserved less by an equity rule preferred equality and those who deserved more preferred equity. In both instances, equality and equity permitted actors to maximize both their own and relative outcomes while making a normative response. And, in fact, historically it is the "have nots" who demand equality, whereas the "haves" describe the present allocation of resources as equitable according to some convenient criteria. Hence, it seems likely that both equality and equity often serve as strategic rules in the service of other, more fundamental goals. However, equity and equality may also serve as goals that can be distinctly represented in an own-other outcome space but cannot be uniquely defined by single vectors.

Corollary 4. Given a particular motivational orientation, an actor may use different criteria for defining preferred outcomes depending upon the region of the payoff space in which alternatives are represented.

MacCrimmon and Messick (1976) have recently set forth examples of what may form secondary motives that condition preferences for outcomes, depending on the specific outcomes in the own-other payoff space. For example, actors may prefer ratios of payoffs. Proportionate competition implies that an actor is willing to forego an absolute level of competitive advantage in favor of a proportionate one. Hence, confronted with the choice of receiving a payoff of $300 for self and $200 for other, as against $100 for self and $10 for other, an actor attempting to maximize his relative position proportionate to the other would prefer the outcome that afforded him a 10 to 1 advantage rather than the one that afforded him only a 3 to 2 advantage. MacCrimmon and Messick observe that there are indeed instances in which "business firms may focus on market share rather than on profit differentials, and nations may bargain in terms of ratios of missile strength or kill capability rather than in terms of absolute numbers," (1976: 90).

Proportionate cooperation is defined as a joint gain associated with a secondary motive of increasing the product of own and other's payoff. Such a preference implies that one not only is concerned with maximizing the total of own and other's outcomes but also is interested in the distribution of these payoffs. In effect, proportionate cooperation would imply that one would accept a smaller total payoff in certain cases for outcome distributions that were more equal. Hence, given a choice between a distribution of $17 for self and $3 for other or $10 for self and $9 for other, the actor preferring to maximize proportionate joint gain would choose the latter (10 x 9 = 90 > 17 x 3 = 51) even though it yielded less absolute joint gain.

A third example of a secondary motive comes from a number of relatively recent empirical investigations (Messick and Thorngate, 1967; McClintock, et al., 1973; MacCrimmon, 1973), which indicate that when an actor is confronted with one or more outcomes that afford him fewer points than the other actor, he is more likely to prefer outcomes that maximize competitive gain rather than individualistic or cooperative gain. In effect, an actor is more likely to behave in a manner consistent with individualistic or cooperative motives when the alternatives available are located in that part of the payoff space where he obtains more than the other actor.

A final example of a secondary motive can be seen in competitive sports, where actors can pursue winning by maximizing their own score or minimizing other's score through offensive or defensive acts. Track is mainly a sport that demands maximization of own outcomes in order to win since the ways of minimizing other's outcomes are limited. In basketball, on the other hand, a team may play principally either to maximize their own score or to minimize the other team's score. Winning by maximizing own points is generally viewed with more favor than winning by minimizing other's points. Most basketball teams would prefer to win by a score of 100 to 98 than 20 to 18.

In summary, we see that what appeared initially to be a relatively simple method of characterizing social motivation in terms of own and others' outcomes becomes increasingly complex as one attempts to describe the variety of preferences that humans may express in situations of outcome interdependence. At the same time, developing ways to represent potential patterns of own-other outcome preferences in simple terms provides a beginning point for meaningful elaborations of more complex forms of social behavior, including those of conflict and negotiation.

> Proposition 6. The environment may operate to define the availability of outcomes to self and other in such a way as to increase or decrease the likelihood that a given motivational predisposition will be dominant.

The kinds of choice situations available to the individual can vary markedly in terms of what orientations can be satisfied independently or in combination with other orientations. We wish now to examine instances where the environment helps to define the availability of outcomes and may operate to predispose the individual toward one or more motivational orientations. For purposes of this discussion, we will consider settings that may more or less predispose the individual toward individualistic, cooperative, competitive, or altruistic orientations.

Individualistic Settings

If an individual is not in a situation of social interdependence, then his choice behavior can reflect only a predisposition toward own-gain maximization. Such was the case with Robinson Crusoe on his island prior to the arrival of Friday. Further, to the extent that an individual is unaware that he is in an interdependent relationship, he will assume an own-gain orientation though his behavior may have implications for both his own and others' outcomes. For instance, in research by Sidowski (1957) and Kelley et al. (1962), where subjects were unaware that they were in a situation of social interdependence and in which their rewards and punishments were completely determined by the other, it was observed that subjects were able to learn a coordinated pattern of responding, with each maximizing the other's payoffs. In this instance, although the subjects' choices resulted in the maximization of joint and other's outcomes, the informational constraints were such that the subjects were pursuing maximization of own gain.

Similarly, there are instances in which individuals may unknowingly be interdependent in settings where maximization of own gain also minimizes the other's outcomes. Thus, in situations of scarce resources, maximizing own gain may also maximize the difference between own and other's gains. This situation relates to the classic definition of competition as it is used in population biology and economics. However, even though in terms of outcomes a given choice or action leads to a maximization of difference, the actors, because of a restriction in information, are pursuing own-gain maximization. Interpersonal conflict and negotiation are not likely to occur in settings where there is no awareness of outcome interdependence.

Cooperative Settings

There also exist cooperative settings in which the orientation to maximize joint gain is more or less a requisite for successful performance. Such situations tend to be those in which the individual is aware of his own and others' outcomes and in which success is defined in terms of the total outcome achieved by members of a collectivity who share an interdependent relationship. The most classic example of a setting that requires a joint gain orientation is that of team members who are cooperating in order to outdo another team. In such instances, own, relative, and other gain orientations become secondary within a team to considerations of maximizing joint gain.

A cooperative setting does not necessarily give rise to joint-gain orientations in actors. It does imply interdependence of outcomes, however. For example, I may wish to move an object that requires the help of someone else. To obtain such assistance, I may agree to help the other with some comparable activity. Although the task requires a coordination of effort, neither I nor the other may be concerned with maximizing joint outcomes. In fact, both might prefer not to help the other if a way could be found to perform the task ourselves. Any division-of-labor task represents a setting in which actors are interdependent in terms of outcomes, but in which the motivation for cooperative activity may be restricted to maximizing own outcomes. In general, actors who are in interdependent cooperative settings in which joint or own-gain motives are dominant are not likely to experience conflict, and to negotiate. They are limited principally to finding the most effective ways to coordinate activities to maximize own and/or joint outcomes. Schelling (1960) describes such settings as coordinative tasks. (See also Brehmer and Hammond in this volume.)

Competitive Settings

There exist, of course, settings that lead to a maximizing relative gain orientation. In many competitive sport situations, the name of the game is maximizing difference between one's own score and that of another. In classroom settings, the same demand characteristics may exist in regard to certain activities. In European schools, for example, the practice may be found of providing not only letter grades at the end of a grading period, but also public information to the members of the class regarding their rank within that class. Hence, it is not surprising to observe children evaluating the goodness of their outcomes in terms of how much better or worse they have done than their fellow classmates. Such forms of evaluation are likely to lead a student to evaluate his learning performance not in terms of how much knowledge he has acquired, but how much more or less he knows than do his peers.

A competitive setting may also give rise to individualistic orientations in actors. For example, I may wish to obtain as much money as possible for myself at a poker game and may be indifferent about others' wins and losses. However, the structure of the game is such that the amount of money I win is directly related to the amount others lose. In effect, I am interdependent with others in terms of my outcomes, and furthermore I am aware of this interdependence. In general, actors in a competitive setting are in a state of interpersonal conflict. They cannot simultaneously maximize their preferred outcomes whether these are defined in own or in relative-gain terms. It is in this social setting that bargaining and negotiation generally occur. And it should be noted that negotiated solutions to interpersonal conflict in competitive settings are likely to vary in terms of difficulty of achieving and, in kind, depending on whether actors are own- or relative-gain-oriented toward outcomes.

Altruistic Settings

It should be acknowledged that the author has had some difficulty in finding a group of attributes to characterize settings that are likely to give rise to an altruistic orientation rather than to one of the other three. Altruism as a predisposition does seem to occur more frequently in settings where actors are strongly identified with a common group and where the outcomes that one perceives another will receive far exceed the rewards that he foregoes. Thus, a parent may forego winning a game with a child because he recognizes that the rewards the child receives in winning far exceed those the parent would attain by winning. Or a motorist may stop to give aid to an unknown disabled motorist because he recognizes that the rewards the other will receive will far exceed his own costs in time and energy. Or, as we have observed occasionally in game studies, a player may begin to select alternatives that meet our definition of altruism—maximizing the other's outcomes—when he has built up an enormous lead over another player.

What seems to characterize all three of these situations is a difference in an individual's estimate of the cost of an act to self in terms of his available resources or power, and the positive outcomes afforded another, and an assumption concerning responsibility toward or dependency of the other. An altruistic setting is not likely to give rise to conflict and negotiation since the intent of one actor's behavior is to increase another's outcomes. There are, of course, gift-giving rituals in some societies where actors compete fiercely to provide to the other higher outcomes than they receive.

> Proposition 7. Individuals vary in terms of their likelihood of adopting one of the four motivational orientations across settings in which there is outcome interdependence.

This proposition asserts that if one controls on situational factors as well as on outcomes afforded self and other, differences will emerge between individuals in terms of how likely it is that they will assume a maximum own, joint, relative, or other's gain orientation. We have, for example, found that the relative strength of these orientations changes as a function of age and cultural background. For example, children in Japan, Belgium, Greece, and the United States become increasingly competitive in motivation as they progress from first to sixth grade (McClintock and Nuttin, 1969; McClintock, 1972).

There have been a number of other studies using the Prisoner's Dilemma Game (PDG) that have shown that individuals who vary in terms of certain values are more or less likely to make choices that reflect differing orientations, although, as was noted earlier, social motives are confounded in the PDG. Deutsch (1960), for instance, observed that subjects high in authoritarianism, as measured by the California F-Scale, were less likely on the first trial of a PDG to select that alternative that maximizes joint outcomes than those who scored low on authoritarianism. Lutzker (1960) investigated the relationship between persons who scored high and low on a measure of internationalism and found fewer relative gain choices on the part of subjects who held more internationalistic values. McClintock et al. (1963) obtained similar findings. Terhune (1968) provides a summary of a number of PDG studies in which individual differences are related to game behavior and goes on to demonstrate empirically that achievement, affiliation, and power motives predispose individuals to behave in different ways when playing various Prisoner's Dilemma games. McNeel (1969) found that, in the same setting, some individuals were more predisposed to maximize own gain, whereas others more consistently maximized relative gain.

Proposition 7 is, of course, a statement concerning individual differences in motivational predisposition. It seems indeed likely that some individuals are more predisposed than others to be individualistic, or cooperative, or competitive, or altruistic. The major task, of course, is to find methods for identifying these differences in orientation, to understand their etiology, and to examine the impact of differing orientations on the formation and maintenance of social relationships and the resolution of social conflict.

Conclusion

In the present section we have outlined a propositional statement defining social motives as they occur in settings of social interdependence. Basically what is provided is a taxonomy of social motives derived from a limited set of assumptions regarding human action. These assumptions define human behavior as purposive or goal-oriented where goals take into consideration both own and other's outcomes.

The subsequent section has two major purposes: First, by reviewing in detail a recent study of social decision-making, we hope to illustrate the relevance of each of the previous propositions. Second, we will use the findings of this specific study to document the final proposition of our social motivational paradigm:

Proposition 8. In settings of outcome interdependence, actors in attempting to maximize their most preferred outcomes will
adapt their behavior to take into account the acts of
others.

It is, of course, the purposive *and* mutually adaptive actions that human
actors pursue in settings of outcome interdependence that require one to
define human social behavior in systemic or interactive terms.

SOCIAL MOTIVES AND OTHERS' STRATEGY:
AN EMPIRICAL EXAMPLE

To illustrate empirically some of the implications of the foregoing propositions, we will first examine in detail the procedures and findings of a recent
study conducted by Kuhlman and Marshello (1975). This study considers the
interaction of an actor's motivational orientation and the strategy of another
in determining the actor's behavior in a setting of outcome interdependence.

The Assessment of Social Motives

Kuhlman and Marshello first assessed the motivational orientations of
actors by measuring their preferences for alternative outcomes to self and
other, across a series of triple-choice decomposed games. In constructing the
games and evaluating subject choices, the investigators considered the three
orientations most commonly observed in experimental game studies: cooperation, competition, and individualism. Examples of the four classes of decomposed games that are used in the present study are presented in Table 1.1.
The Triple Dominance game is a choice situation where each of the possible
alternatives maximizes one of the three preceding motivational orientations.
In the Prisoner's Dilemma game (in decomposed rather than matrix form),
one alternative maximizes own and relative outcomes; a second, joint; and a
third, none of the three motivational orientations. In the decomposed form
of the Maximizing Difference game, one of the alternatives maximizes own
and joint gain, a second, relative, and a third, none of the three motivational
orientations. Finally, in the Single Dominance game, one of the alternatives
maximizes all three of the motivational orientations, and the other two
choices are nondominant.

Pairs of subjects of the same sex were asked to state their outcome
preferences in six games in each of the four game classes. Subjects were seated
at separate tables, facing a common projection screen but visually isolated
from one another. They were informed that their total score would be a
function of both the points they afforded self and those that the other person
afforded them, and that they would receive $.10 for each 1,000 points they
accumulated throughout the experimental session.

In this initial measurement phase, choices were made in a setting of limited
outcome interdependence insofar as, for any given choice, each actor deter-

mined both his own and the other's outcomes. Furthermore, information concerning what choices the other was making was not provided to subjects, and they did not know how many points either they or the other was accumulating. Thus, a person's choice could not reflect an attempt to change the choice behavior of the other since he did not have information concerning other's choices. The mere fact, however, that final outcomes for both members of the dyad were determined both by own and other's choices defines the setting as one of outcome interdependence, as was elaborated in Proposition 3. The restriction in information concerning other's choices ensured that actor's choices reflected goals rather than strategies, a possible source of confounding outlined in Proposition 4.

Proposition 6 asserts that in settings of social interdependence, there is an infinite number of possible motivational preference vectors, but three motivational orientations are particularly likely to obtain: cooperation, individualism, and competition. As illustrated in Table 1.1, the game classes employed in the present study provide a means for estimating actors' preferred outcomes in terms of these orientations. Kuhlman and Marshello, invoking a criterion of consistency of motive associated with choice across the 24 games, observed that the 167 male and female participants in the study could be classified as follows: 26 percent were individualistic in orientation, 28 percent were cooperative, 21 percent were competitive, and 25 percent were unclassifiable because they did not meet the consistency criterion. Hence, 75 percent of the participants demonstrated a consistent preference for outcomes reflecting one of the three motivational orientations.

As noted in Proposition 6, the nature of the social setting, including the alternatives available to an actor, plays a role in defining what social motives can and will be expressed. In the present instance, the demand characteristics of the setting, in terms of which motivational orientation might be more appropriate, was purposely kept ambiguous. And this was indeed reflected in the different motivational orientations that were observed. The ambiguity of the setting, the consistency of choices within 75 percent of the subjects, and

TABLE 1.1
Examples of Four Classes of Decomposed Games

	GAME CLASS										
	Triple Decomposed Alternatives			Prisoner's Dilemma Alternatives			Maximizing Difference Alternatives			Single Dominance Alternatives		
	A	*B*	*C*	*A*	*B*	*C*	*A*	*B*	*C*	*A*	*B*	*C*
Own Points	50	40	40	50	40	20	70	60	40	90	70	60
Other's Points	20	0	40	10	30	0	60	40	30	10	20	20

the variability of choices in terms of the three measured motivational orientations is consonant with Proposition 7.

Thus the initial phase of the present study was structured and obtained
results that are consistent with the preceding propositional statement. But the
study goes further, and in a direction that is consonant with Proposition
8. In effect, it asks how persons with differing motivations respond to
differing behaviors of others with whom they are in relation of outcome
interdependence.

Motives and Other's Strategy

The goals or motives of an actor represent but one of a number of classes
of variables and relationships that determine behavior in settings of social
interdependence. Figure 1.3 depicts, in very generalized form, other factors
that affect decision-making in social settings. As indicated, the alternatives
available to an actor, as well as his motivational orientation, can influence his
strategies, behaviors, and eventual outcomes. Alternatives are in part dictated
by the physical or nonreactive social environment, but they are also defined
by an actor's information and expectations concerning the alternatives, motives, strategies, and likely behaviors of others. These expectations affect, of
course, which strategy an actor should select in order to obtain the mutually
determined outcome that is most consistent with his own motivational
orientation. The same, of course, obtains for the other actor or actors who
share in a relationship of outcome interdependence.

The second part of the Kuhlman-Marshello study can be translated into
this more general paradigm. The first part assessed the probable goals of
individual actors. The second part had actors play a matrix form of the
Prisoner's Dilemma game with a simulated other. An actor playing a PDG
knows that he has two choices, that the other has two choices, and that both
his and the other's payoffs will depend upon the intersection of both choices.
Hence, both actors have and know that the other has complete information
concerning what outcome states are *potentially* available. However, neither
knows before beginning to play what the other's motives, strategies, or
choices will be, and hence they cannot predict on an a priori basis which
outcome cells in the matrix they can enter.

Kuhlman and Marshello were interested in determining how subjects
would behave in a PDG (see Figure 1.4) as a function of their own motivational states and systematic variations in the choices of the other. In order to
vary the behavior of the other systematically, participants were informed
they were playing with another person when, in fact, the experimenter
actually made the choices in a preprogrammed fashion of the simulated other.
In making these choices, the experimenter followed one of three strategies:
Other made 100 percent competitive (Y) choices or 100 percent cooperative
(X) choices, or played tit-for-tat (TFT). The investigators proceed to examine

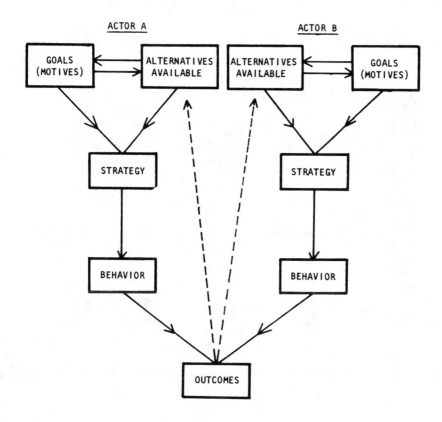

Figure 1.3.   Variable Affecting Decision Making in Settings of Outcome Interdependence.

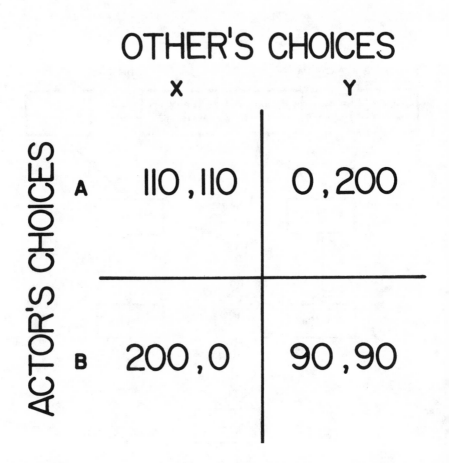

Figure 1.4. Prisoner's Dilemma Game Employed in Kuhlman and Marshello Study.

what are the strategic and behavioral implications of each strategy of other for actors with varying motivational orientations.[1]

Let us consider the payoff matrix in the PDG from the standpoint of actors with differing motivational orientations. For the individualistically oriented actor who wants to maximize his own gain, the most preferred outcome cell would be BX. For the competitively oriented actor, the most preferred outcome would be BX also. For the cooperatively oriented actor, AX would be most preferred. However, access to any of the four outcome cells in the matrix is mutually determined, and given differing strategies on the part of other, differing actor choices become optimal in approximating their goal.

In the case of the individualistically oriented actor, a 100 percent cooperative strategy by other enables him to achieve his most preferred outcome cell, BX. Hence, one would expect that, confronted with consistent X choices by another, the individualistic actor would select the B row. Confronted with another making 100 percent competitive (Y) choices, an individualistic actor would again prefer the B choice since the BY cell affords him greater individual gain than the AY cell.

The appropriate choice for an individualistic actor, given that other follows a tit-for-tat strategy, is a bit more complex. However, it can be demonstrated that the B choice is no longer optimal for an individualistic actor. The B choice limits the actor's outcomes to the BX or BY cells.[2] It turns out that, in order to maximize own gain, give a tit-for-tat (TFT) strategy by other, the most effective own-gain strategy is to continue selecting the cooperative choice, A. In this manner, an individualistically oriented subject assures himself, given the present game matrix, 110 points on each trial. Should he consistently select the competitive B choice, he would receive only 90 points per trial, and should he alternate, his average outcome would be 100 points per trial. McNeel (1973) found that individualistically oriented actors do indeed learn to make cooperative choices consistently when confronted by a tit-for-tat strategy by other.

What about a competitively oriented actor? His choices are clear. Given a 100 percent cooperative other, he can maximize both own and relative gain on each trial by selecting a competitive (B) choice. A 100 percent competitive strategy by other also poses no problem, although it offers little in the way of reward in terms of achieving a competitive advantage. But obviously the actor cannot make a cooperative choice since that would afford other the opportunity to achieve a competitive advantage over him. Given a TFT strategy by other, there is again no way in which the actor can achieve a competitive advantage unless other selects cooperatively on the first trial while actor competes. Hence, one would expect a competitively oriented actor to select competitive choices (B) regardless of other's pattern of responding.

Finally, what would be optimal behavior for a cooperatively oriented subject, given the three variations in other's strategy? Obviously, if other cooperates by selecting X 100 percent of the time, then the subject by selecting A achieves his most preferred outcome cell, AX. Similarly, if other is playing a TFT strategy, selecting A on each trial assures that other will match with X on the subsequent trial, and consistent AX outcomes are again assured. One might predict that even if other competes by selecting Y 100 percent of the time, a cooperative actor would persevere in making A choices on each trial since the total outcome to self and other in the AY cell is greater (200) than in the BY cell (180). However, prior research suggests that even cooperative subjects are not willing to live in a world where on each trial they would receive 0 and other 200. Kelley and Stahelski (1970) indeed report that subjects who had cooperative intentions demonstrated competitive choice behavior when paired with another who consistently competed. Hence, though one might expect somewhat less competition over trials for a cooperative actor, given a 100 percent competitive strategy by other, it is too much to expect that they will not generally forego cooperative choices for competitive ones to avoid being continually exploited.

Procedures and Results

The previously discussed expectations regarding the relationship between the three motivational states and the three strategies of other served as the major hypotheses of the study. These hypothesized relationships were tested, using a 3 motive x 3 other's strategy factorial design, with a minimum of five female and five male Ss in each of the nine resulting conditions. All Ss played thirty trials of the PDG described in Figure 1.4. Ss were again informed that they would receive $.10 for every 1,000 points they accumulated by the end of the experimental session. During the course of play, Ss were, of course, aware of their own and other's choices on each trial and their respective payoffs. However, information concerning total points being accumulated was not provided while Ss played the PDG.

The results of the first phase of the study, in which Ss were classified in terms of motivational orientation, have already been noted. The dependent variable in the PDG phase of the study was the proportion of cooperative choices (A) made by Ss across the thirty trials. Figure 1.5 plots the proportion of cooperative choices by actor's motivational orientation and other's strategy. It is readily apparent that there is a highly significant interaction between these two variables. In fact, all of Kuhlman's hypothesized relationships between motives and strategies were strongly supported: Competitive actors did not cooperate (they competed) regardless of other's strategy; cooperative actors cooperated in response to cooperative or TFT strategies by other, but competed when confronted with strictly competitive choices by others; and individualistic Ss tended to compete given a cooperative or

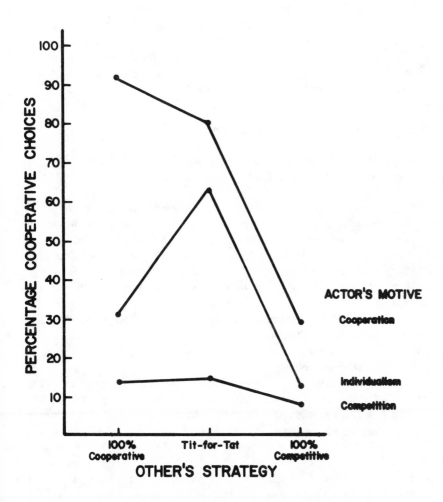

Figure 1.5. Percentage Cooperative Choices in PDG by Actor's Motive and Other's Strategy.

competitive other's strategy, but cooperated given a tit-for-tat strategy on the part of other.

Thus, Kuhlman and Marshello's study of social decision-making clearly demonstrates that it is possible to define and measure the social motivational dispositions of actors in situations where their choices can affect both own and other's outcomes. It demonstrates further that actors do take into consideration other's strategies in making choices where there is outcome interdependence and that their choices are modified to obtain those outcomes that are most consonant with their dominant motivational orientation. Finally, the fact that the data so closely parallel the patterns of predicted interaction between actor's motives and other's strategy provides empirical support for the propositions set forth in this chapter.

CONCLUSIONS

In concluding, several general ways in which an understanding of social motives can contribute to a more precise understanding of the negotiation process will be noted.

(1) Interpersonal conflict and negotiation are more or less likely to occur, given a particular motivational orientation of one actor or a combination of orientations across two or more interdependent actors. A knowledge of social motives can thus contribute to the prediction of the likelihood of conflict and negotiation. Furthermore, it seems likely that both the character of conflict and the types of negotiation pursued will vary according to the motivational orientations of the participants.

(2) Differences in outcome settings can affect the likelihood of occurrence of particular motivational orientations within and across actors. The effects of setting upon orientation and subsequent conflict and negotiation were noted earlier in this chapter.

(3) For an observer to understand the meaning of a given behavior on the part of an actor, whether the observer be external to or a participant in a relationship, it is necessary that he be able to infer the intent of an actor as regards the latter's preferred distribution of own and other's outcomes. Thorngate (1973) has clearly demonstrated that if subjects observe outcome choices being made by another that correspond to a given motivational vector, as defined in Figure 1.2, they can learn to infer other's subsequent choices in a manner consistent with that vector. Although this obtained for all the motivational vectors in Figure 1.2, Thorngate found that the rate it took subjects to reach asymptote, as well as their level of accuracy in predicting choices consistent with a given vector, was greater when the observed choices reflected an individualistic or competitive vector than when they reflected a cooperative or altruistic vector. Thus, it appears that we are more sensitive in detecting behaviors that are own- or relative-gain-oriented

than those that are joint- or other-gain-oriented. It is, of course, own- and relative-gain motives that are most likely to produce conflict and negotiation.

(4) Detecting an actor's orientation is considerably more difficult in a naturalistic than in a laboratory setting, such as that employed by Thorngate, since motives and strategies are often confounded. In fact, in negotiations, actors often deliberately employ strategies to disguise their preferred outcomes. Furthermore, as was noted earlier in this chapter, there are settings in which a given behavior or behaviors may simultaneously satisfy more than one motivational orientation. Thus, in a zero-sum game, where winning maximizes both own and relative gain, it is difficult to ascertain the specific intent of an actor. Yet it remains important for understanding the negotiation process to know the intent of an actor and how co-actors perceive that intent.

(5) The behavior of an actor in a setting of outcome interdependence is a function of actor's motivational orientation, strategy, and expectations regarding the behavior of others. Thus, to understand negotiation behavior, one must not only be cognizant of an actor's motives and strategies, but also know how the actor perceives the preferred outcomes and strategies of others with whom he shares dependence. In effect, as was diagrammed earlier (Figure 1.3) and as is demonstrated in the Kuhlman and Marshello study, behaviors that occur in settings of outcome interdependence, including those that are defined as negotiations, must be understood in systemic or interactive terms.

(6) Finally, we would assert that negotiation behavior represents primarily a set of strategies in the service of social motives. Such strategies may include more or less normative outcome distribution rules—e.g., equity and equality—or behaviors directed at influencing the behaviors and expected outcomes of others—e.g., promises, threats, and ingratiation. An understanding of the negotiation process requires a definition and classification not only of social motives, but also of negotiation strategies. The other chapters in this volume will undoubtedly contribute toward such a classification.

NOTES

1. Reviewing Figure 1.4, it is important to remember that the payoffs on the lefthand side of the comma in each cell of the matrix are those for the row player—in this case, the actor. Those to the right are payoffs for the simulated other. The subject, of course, can select row A or B; other can select row X or Y; and the payoff cell itself is jointly determined by the intersection of these two choices.

2. The implications of choice for the individualistic actor can be illustrated. If the actor selects the competitive B choice on trial n, then other competes (Y) on trial n + 1. If on this trial the actor cooperates, (A), the AY cell is entered, which provides an individualistic actor with his lowest outcome. If the actor selects B, then he enters cell BY, which affords him his second lowest outcome. If the subject cooperates, (A), on trial n, then other cooperates, (A), he receives the second highest own payoff by entering cell AX. If subject competes, (B), then BX cell is entered and he receives his highest own

payoff. But there is a problem. If the BX cell is entered, actor has competed, and on the next trial the other will reciprocate with a competetitive, (Y), choice, and to return to the preferred BX cell actor must cooperate. But if he cooperates, the AY cell is entered, and subject receives 0 points for that trial.

REFERENCES

BECKER, G. and C. McCLINTOCK (1967) "Value: Behavioral decision theory." Annual Rev. of Psychology 18: 239-286.

BENTON, A. and D. DRUCKMAN (1973) "Salient solutions and bargaining behavior of representatives and non-representatives." International J. of Group Tensions 3: 28-39.

COLEMAN, J. (1973) The Mathematics of Collective Action. Chicago: Aldine.

DEUTSCH, M. (1960) "Trust, trustworthiness and the F-Scale." J. of Abnormal and Social Psychology 61: 138-140.

GRIESINGER, D. and D. LIVINGSTON (1973) "Towards a model of interpersonal motivation in experimental games." Behavioral Science 18: 173-188.

KAHN, H. (1960) On Thermonuclear War. Princeton, N.J.: Princeton University Press.

KELLEY, H. and A. STAHELSKI (1970) "The social interaction basis of cooperators' and competitors' beliefs about others." J. of Personality and Social Psychology 16: 66-91.

KELLEY, H., J. THIBAUT, R. RADLOFF, and D. MUNDY (1962) "The development of cooperation in the 'minimal social situation.' " Psychological Monographs 76:19, Whole No. 538.

KUHLMAN, D. M. and A. MARSHELLO (1975) "Individual differences in game motivation as moderators of preprogrammed strategy effects in Prisoner's Dilemma." J. of Personality and Social Psychology 32: 922-931.

LUTZKER, D. (1960) "Internationalism as a predictor of cooperative behavior." J. of Conflict Resolution 4: 426-435.

McCLINTOCK, C. "Game behavior and social motivation in interpersonal settings," pp. 271-297 in C. McClintock (ed.) Experimental Social Psychology. New York: Holt, Rinehart & Winston.

——— (1972) "Social Motives: A set of propositons." Behavioral Sci. 17: 438-454.

——— and S. McNEEL (1966) "Societal membership, score status, and game behavior: A phenomenological analysis." International J. of Psychology 1:263-279.

——— (1967) "Prior dyadic experience and monetary reward as determinants of cooperative behavior." J. of Personality and Social Psychology 5: 282-294.

McCLINTOCK, C. and J. NUTTIN (1969) "Development of competitive behavior in children across two cultures." J. of Experimental Social Psychology 5: 203-218.

McCLINTOCK,C., A. HARRISON, S. STRAND, and P. GALLO (1963) "Internationalism, isolationism, strategy of other player and two-person game behavior." J. of Conflict Resolution 4: 426-435.

McCLINTOCK, C., D. MESSICK, D. KUHLMAN, and R. CAMPOS (1973) "Assessing social motives in a triple decomposed game." J. of Experimental Social Psychology 9: 572-590.

MacCRIMMON, K. (1973) "The effect of social orientation and relative resources on social motives." Vancouver: Faculty of Commerce and Business Administration, University of British Columbia: Working Paper 183.

—————and D. MESSICK (1976) "A Framework for social motives." Behavioral Science 21: 86-100.

McNEEL, S. (1969) "Choice rules and dimensions of interpersonal rewards in mixed motive games." Unpublished doctoral dissertation. University of California, Santa Barbara.

MEAD, M. (1934) *Cooperation and Competition Among Primitive Peoples.* New York: McGraw-Hill.

MESSICK, D., and W. THORNGATE (1967) "Relative gain maximization in experimental games." J. of Experimental Social Psychology 3: 85-101.

MILGRAM, S. (1963) "Behavioral study of obedience." J. of Abnormal and Social Psychology 67: 371-378.

RAPOPORT, A. and T. WALLSTEN (1972) "Individual decision behavior." Annual Rev. of Psychology 23: 131-176.

SCHELLING, T. (1960) *The Strategy of Conflict.* Cambridge: Harvard University.

SIDOWSKI, J. (1957) "Reward and punishment in a minimal social situation." J. of Experimental Psychology 54: 318-326.

TERHUNE, K. (1968) "Motives, situations and interpersonal conflict." J. of Personality and Social Psychology, Monograph Supplement 8: 1-24.

THORNGATE, W. (1973) "Person perception and the prediction of behaviour in decomposed games." Social Psychology Labs, Department of Psychology, University of Alberta, Edmonton, Canada TSG 2E9: 1-56.

VAN AVERMAET, E. (1975) "Equity: A theoretical and experimental analysis." Unpublished doctoral dissertation. University of California, Santa Barbara.

WYER, R. (1971) "Effects of outcome matrix and partner's behavior in two-person games." J. of Experimental Social Psychology 1: 190-210.

Chapter 2

COGNITIVE FACTORS IN INTERPERSONAL CONFLICT

BERNDT BREHMER

University of Umeå, Umeå, Sweden

KENNETH R. HAMMOND

Institute of Behavioral Science, University of Colorado

Ever since Freud, explanations of interpersonal conflict have concerned only motivation. The basic assumption is that persons quarrel because they want to satisfy drives that lead to material and/or psychological gain. And even when they fail to achieve goals that apparently are mutually important to them (peace, for example), it will be said that their efforts failed because their self-serving motives interfered. In short, the common explanation of humanity's failure is that motives flaw the rational cognitive process that would otherwise lead to mutual achievement; our constant despair is that we are the victims of our motives. Negotiations are frustrated by self-interest that will not be denied.

This thumbnail sketch of the present world view of interpersonal conflict may be oversimplified, but it is precisely the view that caused Freud to be pessimistic about prospects for international peace. That pessimism has had far-reaching effects, from the time Einstein asked Freud to participate in a public debate on "the causes and cure of wars" (Nathan and Norden, 1965)

AUTHORS' NOTE: Support for Brehmer's participation in this article came from the Swedish Council on Social Science Research. Support for Hammond's participation was provided by NIMH Grant MH16437. Both authors wish to thank K. Will and B. Ramsay for their assistance.

until the present. Freud's gloomy reply to Einstein dwelt on man's aggressive instincts and drives, and although it made his views of the causes of war clear enough, it offered no hope for their elimination. There is only one reference to human capacity for thought in Freud's letter to Einstein, and that reference is a disparaging one. Nothing came of the exchange of letters between the two great intellectual leaders, both of whom were deeply interested in peace, and the people of the world lost another opportunity; fundamental views about the roles of motivation and cognition in conflict make a difference.

The role of motivation in interpersonal conflict has been so overemphasized (see the McClintock chapter), and extrapolated so far beyond its empirical base, that even today one would be led to believe that human beings have no capacity to think. As a result, that unique human capacity has not been examined with regard to its contribution to the generation and reduction of conflict. Strangely enough, never in the history of the study of interpersonal conflict has there been a significant systematic effort to investigate the role of cognitive factors in conflict, except for the one described below. Even the most prominent *cognitive* psychologist of the first half of the twentieth century, Edward Tolman, analyzed conflict in terms of "*drives toward war*" (1942; italics added).

Without denying that motivational factors can contribute to conflict, we will argue that the cognitive aspects of interpersonal conflict should be given as much consideration as the motivational, if not more. Indeed, we will show that cognitive processes in themselves can cause conflict and that it is not always necessary to use motivational factors to explain it. Because the contribution of purely cognitive factors to conflict has been totally neglected, we shall consider only these in this chapter. (For a discussion linking the role of both motivation and cognition in conflict, see Druckman and Zechmeister, 1973; Druckman, 1973; and the Druckman et al. chapter in this volume.) We shall be explicit about our theory, indicate the basis of our research methods, provide a set of laboratory findings, and offer a technique for conflict management and negotiation that can be, and has been, tested outside the laboratory. In short, we offer a testable, modifiable, and cumulative approach that explicitly acknowledges the role of human cognition in human conflict. The work to be described has grown out of social judgment theory (for an overview see Hammond, Stewart, Brehmer, and Steinmann, 1975), which in turn has developed from Tolman's and Brunswik's approaches to cognition (see Brunswik, 1956; Tolman, 1932; and Tolman and Brunswik, 1935; see also Hammond, 1966).

HUMAN JUDGMENT AND INTERPERSONAL CONFLICT

Social and political problems that require negotiation are highly complex and uncertain. They can seldom, if ever, be solved by scientific means since the effects of different causes cannot be isolated. Therefore it becomes necessary to rely on human judgment—a cognitive activity of last resort. In addition to the intrinsic complexity of these tasks, the covert nature of the judgment process makes it difficult for others to understand the basis for the decisions that are made. Negotiation is not made easier by covertness.

Disagreements are hard to resolve, and successful negotiation is hard to achieve, not only because the judgment tasks are complex but because judgments are produced by a poorly understood process; they are not the product of an explicit, fully analytical procedure that is easily retraceable. Human judgment instead is best characterized as a *quasi-rational* process—a mixture of analysis, intuition, and experience. Quasi-rational thinking is only partly rule-based and only partly recoverable, and it processes only part of the available information. Most important, the process is uncertain; it may (unpredictably) rely on different information at different times. As a result, judgments cannot be fully accounted for in terms of the available information. As will be shown below, these conditions can induce and prolong disagreement and frustrate negotiation.

We begin with a brief discussion of the formal analysis of human judgment and its role in cognitive conflict, and then present the social judgment theory (SJT) research paradigm, as well as the reasons for its adoption. The next section reviews the results of a series of laboratory experiments suggested by the theory and conducted within the SJT research paradigm. Based on the results of these experiments and the general principles of SJT, cognitive aids were developed to help reduce cognitive conflict. These aids are described in the fourth section. The fifth and final section of the paper describes the findings of four applications of the results of theory and research to instances of conflict and negotiation outside the laboratory.

THE ANALYSIS OF JUDGMENT

A general finding of studies of human judgment is that the subjects studied are seldom able to describe consistently, accurately, and completely how they arrive at their judgments (e.g., Summers et al., 1969; Balke et al., 1973; Brehmer and Qvarnström, 1973; Brehmer et al., 1973; Cook and Stewart, 1975). Therefore, judgment analysts know that they cannot rely on the introspective descriptions of judgment policies provided by their subjects. Indeed, the inability to describe judgment policies accurately and completely is one of the major reasons why cognitive conflict between persons is so hard to resolve and successful negotiation is so elusive. For while the student of human judgment will realize that the descriptions of judgment policies produced by introspection are likely to be inaccurate and incomplete because of human *inability* to be otherwise, the lay person will attribute inconsistencies, inaccuracies, and incompleteness to an *intention to be devious;* current folklore insists that it is naive to do otherwise. Failure to acknowledge the limitations of human judgment results in the attribution of evil intent to the other person.

Methods of judgment analysis have been developed, however, that make it less necessary to guess at the judgment processes of the other person. These methods are based on the premise that it is possible to develop a reasonably accurate quantitative description of the judgment policy used by a person. This is accomplished by fitting a mathematical model to the judgments and to the information on which the judgments are based. The mathematical model describes how judgments are related to information, and the judgment policy is thus specified and described in terms of equations. The equations then provide a means for predicting the judgments from the information on which they are based. Of course, the utility of this procedure must be tested by empirical research in the real world as well as in the laboratory.

Linear statistical models have been tested in this way and have proved to be useful tools. They make it possible to analyze a judgment policy on two major bases: (a) the systematic aspects of the policy, and (b) the unsystematic aspects. The systematic aspects can be analyzed in terms of three major sources of variance: the *relative weights* of the various sources of information, the *forms of the functions* relating judgments to information, and the *organizing principle* according to which information from different sources is combined. The unsystematic aspect of judgment is its *inconsistency*. Thus it is possible to analyze judgment in terms of the four parameters of judgment, namely, (a) cue weights—i.e., the relative importance of different sources of information; (b) function forms—i.e., whether cues are used in a linear or a nonlinear fashion; (c) organizing principles—i.e., how information from different cues is integrated; and (d) consistency—i.e., the extent to which a given judgment policy is executed in the same manner under the same conditions.

The Role of Human Judgment in Conflict and Negotiation

The lens model equation (LME), originally developed by Hursch et al. (1964), and later modified by Tucker (1964) and Stewart (1976), makes analysis of the cognitive aspect of conflict and negotiation possible. The LME provides an index of the extent to which two persons agree in their judgments and divides for analysis their agreement into two components: the degree to which the systematic aspects of their judgment policies are similar, and the degree to which they are consistent in applying their policies. For analyzing agreement and its components, the form of the LME suggested by Tucker (1964) and adapted to the study of conflict by Brehmer (1971) has proved to be useful; namely,

$$r_A = G\, R_{S1} R_{S2}, \qquad\qquad [1]$$

where r_A is the correlation between the judgments made by person S1 and those made by S2; G is the correlation between the judgments predicted from a regression equation fitted to the judgments made by S1 and those predicted from a regression equation fitted to the judgments made by S_2; R_{S1} is the multiple correlation between the cues and the judgments made by S1; and R_{S2} is the multiple correlation between cues and judgments made by S2.

In equation 1, r_A is an index of the level of agreement between S1 and S2. G shows the extent to which the systematic aspects of the policies of S1 and S2 are similar. Specifically, G shows the extent to which the relative weights given to the cues by S1 are similar to the relative weights given to the cues by S2. And, finally, R_{S1} and R_{S2} show the extent to which S1 and S2 tend to use the same weights from trial to trial. Thus, these multiple correlations can be interpreted as indices of the consistency of the policies.[1]

As can be seen from equation 1, disagreement—i.e., $r_A < 1.00$ (which, of course, implies that the judgments of the persons differ), can occur for two reasons: First, two persons may fail to agree because their *policies* differ systematically—i.e., $G < 1.00$, implying that the two persons differ with respect to the weights they give to the cues. Second, disagreement may occur because one or both of the persons are *inconsistent* in applying their policies— i.e., R_{S1} and/or $R_{S2} < 1.00$. Disagreement, therefore, does not necessarily imply that there are fundamental differences between the policy of S1 and that of S2; it is sufficient that they are inconsistent. That is, due to inconsistency, we may have disagreement in fact, despite agreement in principle. From time to time, inconsistency will also cause the persons who have different policies to make similar judgments, and thus inconsistency may also cause agreement in fact, despite disagreement in principle. Inconsistency, then, will tend to hide the real causes of their disagreement from the decision makers, as well as from the conflict analyst who is unable to disentangle these components.

In short, in order to see the true nature of conflict it is necessary to go beyond the observable judgmental differences and analyze the unobservable structure of conflict. This can be done by using the LME, which gives us a means for breaking down cognitive conflict into its components. Thus, one of the preconditions for studying conflict is fulfilled. The other precondition is a suitable research paradigm.

THE SJT RESEARCH PARADIGM

SJT provides the investigator with a frame of reference for choosing the situation—the experimental paradigm—for investigating cognitive conflict, as well as a rationale for deciding which variables should be considered. According to SJT, the basic cognitive conflict situation involves three systems, one being the task system and the other two the cognitive systems of the persons in conflict. The task system is described in terms of the relations between a set of cues (the information available for the judgments), and a criterion variable (the variable about which judgments are made); and the cognitive systems are described in terms of the relations between the cues and judg-ments of each person. Furthermore, SJT requires that tasks should contain multiple cues and that the relations between cues and criterion should be probabilistic; i.e., the task should contain uncertainty (see Figure 2.1). These requirements follow directly from the general theory of inductive tasks in SJT (see Hammond, Stewart, Brehmer, and Steinmann, 1975).

In addition to specifying the nature of cognitive tasks that evoke conflict, SJT also specifies the parameters of the cognitive systems of the two persons. That is, SJT indicates that their cognitive systems may differ with respect to the different cue dependencies or different *relative weights* given to the cues, the *form of the functions* relating judgments to cues, the *organizing principle* for combining information from the cues, and the *consistency* of the system. SJT also requires that the cognitive systems be quasi-rational in character and specifies a general procedure for creating quasi-rational policies in the cog-nitive systems of the subjects. Thus SJT identifies the major sources of conflict in terms of (a) the general characteristics of a cognitive conflict situation and (b) the characteristics of the cognitive systems. Therefore SJT gives clear direction to the study of cognitive conflict.

Creating Cognitive Conflict Between Persons

Experiments on conflict and negotiation that are carried out within the social judgment theory research paradigm simulate a situation where two persons must exercise their judgment with regard to a set of problems that require them to make their judgments from cues that provide uncertain

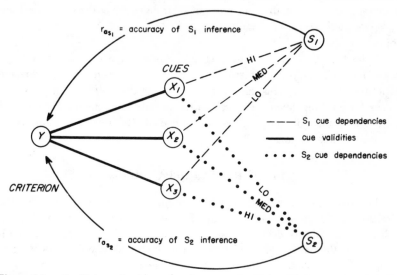

Figure 2.1. Conflict results from the different sets of cue dependencies or relative weights (high, medium, or low) that each subject (S1, S2) brings to the task in an effort to make accurate inferences (r_a) about a criterion variable (Y) on the basis of multiple cues ($X_{1,2,3}$) of less than perfect validity.

information. They disagree in their judgments, however, because each person uses the cues differently. That is, one may *weight* cues differently or use different *function forms* than another. Judgmental differences may be induced in the laboratory situation by *training* the persons to have different judgment policies. It is also possible to determine and quantify the differences in judgment policies that stem from differences in pre-experimental experiences. The results so far indicate that it makes little difference whether the judgment policies are acquired in or outside the laboratory; essentially the same results are obtained in both cases (Hammond and Brehmer, 1973).

An experiment in the SJT paradigm is conducted in two stages. The first may involve training or selection. Its purpose is to create a conflict based on reasons that are perfectly understood by the experimenter. That is, the experimenter creates a situation in which pairs of subjects will have judgment policies that differ in ways specified by, and known to, the experimenter. If training is involved, the subjects will learn specific judgment policies (determined a priori by the experimenter) according to a multiple-cue probability learning paradigm. The subjects will learn to use the cues in the required manner by observing cue values that are probabilistically related to criterion values. This procedure leads to judgment policies that have all the characteristics of quasi-rational thought in that such policies will have both regularities and irregularities and in that the subjects cannot fully describe their judgment policies (see, e.g., Brehmer et al., 1973). If, on the other hand, the first stage is a *selection* stage, standard policy-capturing procedures are used to obtain the subjects' policies (see, e.g., Hammond, Stewart, Brehmer, and Steinmann, 1975).

Once the experimenter is confident that the subjects function cognitively, as is required by the purposes of the experiment, they enter the conflict stage. In this stage, the subjects are given a series of problems and are required to negotiate in order to find a common judgment they can agree on. On each trial, they (a) study the cues, (b) make individual judgments about the criterion variable, which they (c) communicate to each other; and if these judgments differ, they (d) discuss the problem until (e) they reach a joint judgment agreeable to both of them, and they are then (f) given feedback in the form of the correct answer for the problem. After having had an opportunity to discuss this answer, they then continue with the next trial.

Depending on the purposes of the experiment, various modifications of this standard procedure are possible. In some experiments, task feedback is omitted; in others the subjects are not required to negotiate a joint judgment; and in still others the subjects may be required to make additional individual judgments that are not communicated after the joint judgment.

As is clear from the above description, the SJT paradigm simulates a form of conflict that is wholly cognitive in origin. All aspects of conflict that have to do with differential gain have been removed. The paradigm thus allows the investigator to study (a) the interaction of the cognitive systems of two persons and a cognitive task and (b) the effects of the parameters of cognitive systems described above. We turn now to the results of studies carried out within this framework.

LABORATORY STUDIES OF CONFLICT AND NEGOTIATION

Four major problems have been studied so far: The first concerns the structure of cognitive conflict; the second, the importance of the task relative to that of the other subject; the third, the effects of the specific characteristics of the task on conflict and negotiation; and the fourth, the manner in which specific characteristics of the subjects' judgment policies affect conflict and changes in judgment policies. The results pertaining to these four problems are reviewed below.

The Structure of Conflict

A striking finding in the first studies of cognitive conflict with the SJT paradigm was that there was little or no conflict reduction (Hammond et al., 1966; Hammond et al., 1968; Rappoport, 1965; Summers, 1968; Todd, Hammond, and Wilkins, 1966). That is, despite the fact that there were no motivational differences and despite the fact that simple judgment tasks were employed, the subjects failed to resolve their differences.

These surprising results led Brehmer (1969a) to analyze conflict by means of the LME. The results of this study were similar to those of the earlier studies in that there was very little reduction of conflict over a twenty-trial sequence. However, when the results were analyzed by means of the LME in order to obtain separate measures of the contribution of consistency and systematic differences in policy to agreement, the subjects were found to have reduced their systematic differences in policy very rapidly. At the same time, however, the consistency of their policies decreased. Thus, although there was very little reduction in the *amount* of conflict, the *structure* of conflict changed. That is, in the beginning of the conflict stage, most of the conflict was caused by systematic differences in policy, but at the end, most was caused by inconsistency.

These results were subsequently replicated over a wide variety of conditions, including (a) subject conditions, such as sex (Hammond and Brehmer, 1973) and nationality (Brehmer et al., 1970), (b) task conditions with respect both to the content of the task (Hammond and Brehmer, 1973) and to its formal characteristics (Brehmer, 1973a, 1974a, 1975a; Brehmer and Hammond, 1973; Brehmer and Kostron, 1973), and (c) situational conditions, such as communication (Brehmer, 1971). Brehmer (1975b) gives a detailed review of these results.

Further analysis showed that the change in the structure of conflict was due to the manner in which subjects *changed their policies*. It is important to note that in order to maintain consistency while changing their judgment policies, the subjects must decrease their dependency on the cues that they depended on heavily at the start, while they must *at the same rate* increase their dependency on cues that they did not previously depend on (that is, the cues used by the other person). However, the subjects do not change their cue dependencies at the same rate. Rather, they give up their dependency on the cues that were used heavily at the start more rapidly than they increase their dependency on cues that they at first gave little weight to. As a result, their consistency decreases.

Thus, contrary to the popular belief that conflict persists because people refuse to change, conflict persists because they give up their judgment policies too rapidly. If this empirical result (which is verified in many studies—see Brehmer, 1975b; and Hammond, Stewart, Brehmer, and Steinmann, 1975) taxes the reader's credulity, he or she should remember that in actual disputes, the change in underlying policies is not observable. Therefore this result could not be discovered under the ordinary conditions of argument; it could be discovered only by the methods used in these studies. In short, the results are unexpected only because the means for detecting them have not heretofore been available.

These results make it possible to derive an interesting prediction for circumstances in which two persons have the *same* judgment policy and the task requires them to change. Since changes in judgment policies lead to inconsistency, disagreement would be expected to develop, even if the persons maintained high policy similarity (see equation 1). This prediction has been confirmed for both (a) the case where the subjects have had to change because the nature of the task has changed and (b) the case where there is no feedback from the task and change takes place only on the basis of discussion (Brehmer, 1972).

The results reviewed so far point to the central importance of the concept of inconsistency. However, in these analyses, inconsistency is defined only in terms of the model used for data analysis; i.e., it is a statistical concept. This leads to the question of whether or not this concept is merely a mathematical fiction without behavioral implications.

Brehmer (1974b) investigated this question by recording the number of questions the subjects asked each other during the conflict and negotiation phase. Only direct questions of the type "What are you doing?" were recorded. The results showed that more questions about the other person's judgment policy were asked when consistency was low than when it was high, despite the fact that there were essentially no systematic differences in judgment policies in either condition. Inconsistency therefore apparently prevented the subjects from finding out what the features of the other person's policy were as well as from detecting the fact that the systematic differences between their judgment policies had disappeared. The findings from the above study were subsequently replicated in two new experiments under somewhat different conditions (Brehmer, 1975a).

The results of these studies are important because they show that the concept of inconsistency has behavioral implications. In addition, the studies show that this concept is important for understanding not only what people may say to each other in a conflict situation, but why their questions may have little effect on the behavior of the other person.

Further evidence of the general usefulness of the concept of inconsistency comes from experiments that show that it is related to various independent variables in a systematic way. That is, consistency varies with task characteristics, such as the predictability of the task (Brehmer, 1973a), the function forms in the task (Brehmer and Kostron, 1973), and the number of cues (Brehmer, 1974b), as well as with situation factors, such as feedback (Brehmer and Kostron, 1973). Moreover, it can be modified systematically by certain psychoactive drugs (Gillis, 1975; for a series of studies involving psychoactive drugs and SJT, see Hammond and Joyce, 1975).

The Importance of the Task

As was indicated, conflict is not significantly reduced under the circumstances described above. Nevertheless, the subjects do change their policies as they interact with each other and with the task. There are at least two possible explanations for this change in policies: The subjects may change in an attempt to reduce the conflict between them, or they may change to reduce the inaccuracy of their judgments with respect to the task.

Brehmer carried out a series of experiments to discover which of these explanations is more plausible. Specifically, the experiments were designed so that one of the subjects in each pair started with a judgment policy that was optimal for the task, while the other started with a judgment policy that was the opposite of what was required. If policy change is motivated by a desire to reduce conflict, both subjects should change their policies. If, on the other hand, policy change is an attempt to reduce the inaccuracy of the policies, only the subject with the inaccurate policy should change. The results (see Brehmer, 1973b, 1973c, 1975a; Brehmer and Kostron, 1973) clearly support the second alternative, since only the subjects with the inaccurate policy show any appreciable change in policy. Moreover, the process of policy change varies with the nature of the task (Brehmer, 1975a). When the task contains a high level of uncertainty, subjects who start out with an optimal policy tend to change their policy at the beginning of the conflict stage, apparently because they are uncertain whether their policies are correct or not. However, they quickly change back toward the initial policy after further trials. These results are important because they show that policy change should not always be interpreted as evidence that a person is willing to compromise. Instead, the change in policy may simply express misguided attempts to reduce judgmental inaccuracy.

Further support for this interpretation comes from an experiment by Brehmer and Garpebring (1974). In this experiment, subjects in an experimental group were paired with a pre-instructed confederate who did not change his policy in the conflict stage even though it was inaccurate. Subjects in a control group were paired with subjects who did change their inaccurate policies. The results showed that the subjects in *both* groups changed their policies in the direction of the optimal policy for the task. That is, the unchanging confederate could not induce the subjects in the experimental group to give up accuracy for agreement (cf. Asch, 1958).

These results illustrate the need to analyze cognitive conflict in terms of three systems, rather than in terms of only two systems, as is done in analyses of conflicts of interest. In the latter kind of conflict, there are no restrictions on the ways in which a conflict may be resolved and in which agreement can be negotiated. If the persons in conflict agree, any kind of policy change will do. In cognitive conflict, this is not the case. The course of action agreed upon has to be a good solution to the problems posed by the task. If this is not achieved, no one will derive any benefits from the negotiations, and it is unlikely that agreement will persist. Thus, the only way in which a stable agreement can be negotiated in cognitive conflict is with a good judgment policy for the task. As can be seen from the results reviewed above, this is what the subjects are trying to do, and only by analyzing the situation in terms of three systems could we have discovered this.

Conflict as a Function of the Characteristics of the Task

Tasks that require judgment may vary both with respect to their *sub-stantive* characteristics—i.e., their content—and their *formal* characteristics—i.e., their quantitative properties. Present results show that whereas substantive task characteristics do not affect conflict, formal characteristics do (Hammond and Brehmer, 1973). Therefore, the effect on conflict of variations in the formal characteristics of tasks will be dealt with in this section.

The formal characteristics of policy tasks have seven formal dimensions. The first three dimensions are called surface characteristics of the task, since they pertain to the cues—i.e., to those characteristics of the task that are perceived directly by the subjects. These characteristics are:

(a) the metric characteristics of the cues (the cues may be quantitative or nominal in character);
(b) the number of cues; and
(c) the intercorrelations among the cues

The remaining four dimensions pertain to the relations between the cues and the variable to be predicted—the criterion. These characteristics are called system characteristics, and they include:

(d) the relative validities of the cues (the cues may have the same or different validity);
(e) the forms of the functions relating the cues to the criterion (the form may be linear or nonlinear);

(f) the organizing principle according to which the cues should be combined (which may be additive or configural); and

(g) the total predictability of the task, given the optimal organizational principle.

Studies of the formal characteristics of the tasks have focused on the effects of three of the system characteristics: cue validities, function forms, and task predictability; and on one of the surface characteristics: cue intercorrelations. The results (see Brehmer, 1975b, for a review) show that all have strong effects on both the *level* and the *structure* of conflict. Specifically, (a) when the task requires the use of multiple cues, (b) when the relations between cues and the criterion are nonlinear, and (c) when the task has a high degree of uncertainty, the level of conflict is higher than when the task requires the use of few cues, when the cue-criterion relations are linear, and when the task has a low degree of uncertainty.[2] The formal characteristics of the task affect the structure of conflict because they decrease the consistency of the subjects' policies. Consequently they lead to lower agreement despite the fact that they do not affect the subjects' ability to reduce the systematic differences between their policies.

A further example of the importance of task characteristics brought out by studies of cognitive conflict concerns cue intercorrelations. This characteristic of judgment tasks differs from the other dimensions in that not only does it affect the structure of the subjects' policies, it also affects agreement, policy similarity, and judgmental accuracy. When the cues in the task are intercorrelated, the subjects may find negotiation easy because they reach a high level of *false* agreement, despite substantial differences in judgment policy. That is, when cues are intercorrelated, persons may agree, but for the wrong reasons. Consequently it would be expected that people would reach a lower level of policy similarity and negotiation would be more difficult when the cues are orthogonal. These predictions are supported by the data (see Brehmer, 1975a; Mumpower and Hammond, 1974).

The results with respect to the effects of task characteristics on conflict further underline the need to analyze conflict, not only in terms of the persons involved but also in terms of the task. Specifically, these results show the need to consider the formal characteristics of the task, something traditional studies of conflict never do. Indeed, the formal characteristics of the task prove to be the most important determinants of the level and structure of cognitive conflict.

Subject Characteristics and Conflict

The above results illustrate the importance of the task and lead to the unconventional hypothesis that subject characteristics will be important only insofar as they affect the subjects' ability to adapt to the task. Specifically, we would expect, for example, that the nationality and sex of the subjects would not affect conflict, but that the formal characteristics of their cognitive systems would. The results support these hypotheses. Cross-cultural comparisons involving subjects from Czechoslovakia, Japan, Greece, Sweden, and the United States have yielded no significant differences in conflict reduction, or in the structure of conflict (Brehmer et al., 1970). Indeed studies of conflict involving subjects in a dozen different countries yield essentially the same results (Hammond and Brehmer, 1973). Similar results were obtained in a study comparing males and females (Hammond and Brehmer, 1973). In this respect, the results obtained with the SJT paradigm differ from those achieved in Prisoner's Dilemma experiments (Rapoport and Chammah, 1965).

The formal characteristics of the subjects' cognitive systems, on the other hand, do affect conflict. It is important to remember that these effects cannot be discussed apart from the effects of the formal characteristics of the task, since it is these which affect the formal characteristics of the cognitive systems (Brehmer, 1969b, 1976). In fact, these two sets of characteristics interact; focusing only on the characteristics of the subjects' cognitive systems that would lead to incorrect conclusions, as the following studies show.

Many experiments in the SJT paradigm have used two-cue policy tasks, with one linear and one nonlinear cue, in which one subject in each pair is trained to rely on the linear cue while the other subject is trained to rely on the nonlinear cue. Thus the subjects' policies differ with respect to both function form and the relative weights given to the cues. Because both cues have equal validity in the conflict stage, the linearly trained subject has to reduce his dependence on the linear cue and increase his dependence on the nonlinear cue. The nonlinearly trained subject, on the other hand, has to decrease his dependence on the nonlinear cue and increase his dependence on the linear cue.

Under these conditions the nonlinearly trained subjects change faster than do the linearly trained. Not only do the nonlinear subjects give up the use of their trained cue faster, they also learn to use their opponents' cue faster and to a greater extent (Brehmer, 1972).

In sum, the above results reflect general cognitive processes rather than processes specific to conflict (see Hammond, 1955; Brehmer, 1975b). The results, therefore, support our contention that cognitive conflict and negotiation are to be understood in terms of the cognitive processes involved in coping with uncertain tasks, rather than in terms of social processes evoked by interpersonal conflict. (The reader should note that the present results lead to interpretations of conflict that are sharply different from those offered by students of Prisoner's Dilemma games and bargaining situations; see Chapters 1, 4, and 9.)

Cognitive factors also indicate why the nonlinearly trained subjects learn more about the cue of their opponents than do the linearly trained subjects. The results show that a linear cue is easier to learn about, regardless of the cognitive system of the learner. Thus, both linearly and nonlinearly trained subjects learn more about the cue of their opponents if there is a linear cue than if it is a nonlinear cue. Thus, both linearly and nonlinearly trained subjects learn more about the cue of their opponents if there is a linear cue than if it is a nonlinear cue. (Brehmer and Hammond, 1973: for replications with patients treated with psychoactive drugs, see Gillis and others in Hammond and Joyce, 1975). Indeed, linearly trained subjects are affected by communication to a greater extent than are nonlinearly trained subjects. Thus, nonlinearly trained subjects learn to use a linear cue regardless of whether or not they have a linearly trained partner, but linearly trained subjects need communication from a nonlinearly trained partner to learn to use a nonlinear cue (Earle, 1973). This clearly suggests that communication serves less to *persuade* than simply to *give information* that is difficult for subjects to extract from the task. In short, in order to understand how subjects change, both the nature of the subjects' cognitive system and the nature of the task are the more significant matters to consider.

Summary and Implications

The results described above suggest the following general conclusions:

(1) Cognitive factors are, in themselves, sufficient to *cause* conflict; motivational explanations of interpersonal conflict are not mandatory, contrary to what Freud, folklore, and a contemporary, motive-oriented social psychology would lead us to believe.

(2) Cognitive factors are, in themselves, sufficient to explain why conflict is *not resolved* and why negotiation is made difficult. Although persons are able to reduce the systematic differences between their policies, these reductions are not apparent to them because inconsistency develops in the process of change; such inconsistency masks the convergence of judgment policies and frustrates negotiation.

(3) Cognitive factors account for *inconsistency;* inconsistency develops because people give up judgment policies faster than they acquire a new policy from an opponent. Differential rates of abandonment and acquisition of policies depend on cognitive factors.

(4) The nature of the task determines the *level and structure* of conflict. Task characteristics can create false agreement as well as false disagreement.

(5) Once the formal characteristics of the task, such as uncertainty and cue intercorrelations, are understood, conflict reduction *can be facilitated.* Contrary to conventional views, conflict reduction is more likely to come about as a consequence of clarification of the nature of the task than through direct attempts to change the persons involved in conflict.

A COGNITIVE AID FOR CONFLICT REDUCTION AND NEGOTIATION

The above conclusions suggest a remedy for conflict: Cognitive processes should be supplemented with cognitive aids in order to help people overcome those cognitive limitations that prevent them from reaching agreement. Specifically, cognitive aids should help people do two things: (a) clarify judgment processes so that the true nature of disagreement can be ascertained and (b) assist people to change their policies in a visible, controlled way, while maintaining consistency.

Such an aid has now been developed by social-judgment theorists in the form of an interactive computer program that analyzes human judgment policies, as well as the relations between the policies of two subjects, and displays the results immediately on a computer terminal (Hammond, 1971; Hammond and Brehmer, 1973; Stewart and Carter, 1973; Hammond, Stewart, Brehmer, and Steinmann, 1975). Specifically, the program displays a representative series of cases to the subjects, accepts their judgments, which are entered directly into the console, analyzes those judgments by means of the lens model equation described above, and displays the results in pictorial form to the subjects, thus providing clear information about the policy of each subject as well as about the nature of their disagreement. This information is displayed in terms of the relative weights given to the cues, the forms of the functions relating the judgments to the cues, and the consistency of the policy, as well as of the nature of the subjects' agreement. That is, the system externalizes, by nonverbal means, the judgment policies and the differences between them, thus permitting the subjects to see what was formerly obscured by language. As a result, they can see what the real causes of their disagreement are and can direct their efforts toward solving their real problems. Figures 2.2 and 2.3 provide an illustration of the information provided at the interactive computer terminal.

Externalization of the characteristics of a person's judgment policy facilitates communication, but this is not enough. People also need help in *changing* their policies if negotiation is to succeed (as is illustrated in the above experiments). Therefore, the procedure allows the persons to modify their policies by enabling them to indicate the changes they want to make in weights or function forms. The computer program then changes the policy according to the person's directions and executes the new policy with perfect consistency.

The procedure thus makes it possible for people to explore the consequences of new policies—a critical aspect of any situation requiring negotiation. Persons can now investigate the consequences of the new policies for agreement with another person and the extent to which the new policy requires judgments that are different from those made under the old policy. Furthermore, it allows one to investigate the characteristics of the policy under conditions where the policy is executed with perfect consistency. Thus the consequences of the policy will not be obscured by inconsistency, and persons can now observe the consequences of the policy they have chosen.

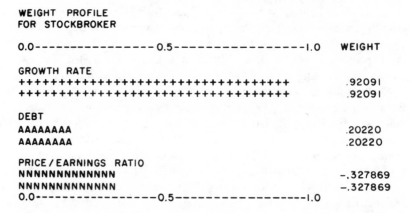

Figure 2.2. An example of a computer-generated display of relative weights for one person's judgments in response to three cues. In a two-person situation weights are displayed side-by-side for easy comparison.

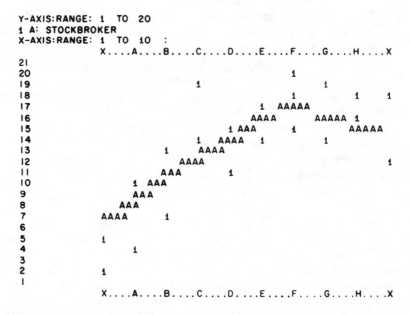

Figure 2.3. An example of a computer-generated display of a function form (the relation between a cue [e.g., growth rate] on the X-axis and a person's judgments [e.g., desirability of ownership] on the Y-axis). The numerals (1) on the graph indicate data points; the letters (A) indicate the (least squares) best-fit line. In a two-person situation, such graphs are presented side-by-side for easy comparison.

The question, however, is not whether such cognitive aids can be invented; they have been. The question is whether cognitive aids have any value in conflict situations outside the laboratory, a matter to which we now turn.

APPLICATIONS

The conclusions set forth above regarding the cognitive sources of conflict and the use of cognitive aids in negotiation were derived from the conjunction of cognitive theory and the results of laboratory research. What remains to be seen is whether these conclusions can be brought to bear on conflict situations in the real world outside the laboratory. Four attempts that have been made to test the utility of the present approach are described below. Each illustrates one of the four problems studied in the laboratory.

Structure of Conflict

Adelman et al. (1975) studied conflict among the managers of an educational research corporation, who were attempting to decide whether to extend their work to a new form of research. The results of a judgment analysis showed that the structure of conflict between persons contained the same systematic and nonsystematic components observed in the laboratory. And, as in the laboratory, the nonsystematic components obscured the nature of the systematic policy differences. Therefore understanding of the issues was poor, as in the laboratory, despite a year-long effort at negotiation. Externalization of judgment policies resulted in progress toward a solution. Other parallels with laboratory research were also observed (see Adelman et al., 1975, for details).

Importance of the Task

Steinmann, Smith, Jurdem, and Hammond (1975) attempted to help the members of a municipal board achieve a policy for making decisions about which parcels of land the city should buy for "open space" in the city. The five members of the board were appointed on the assumption that they represented different vested interests in the city (e.g., environmentalists and real estate developers). The assistance offered by the judgment analysts was to provide a mechanism whereby the board members focused on the task, rather than on one another's motives. Asked to evaluate the desirability of a series of parcels of land, as well as to predict how other board members would evaluate these parcels, the board members discovered that they were incorrect in their predictions of one another's judgment policies. In fact, use of the interactive computer system (described above as a cognitive aid) for externalizing judgment policies showed that there were in fact few differences in the actual choices of land parcels; thus, a compromise policy was readily achieved.

The point to be observed here is that if (a) initial policies are not widely separated and (b) nonsystematic components of judgments are removed, then (c) the decisions made by a compromise policy will be very similar to the decisions desired by each of the various parties—a fact not easily realizable by decisions desired by each of the various parties—a fact not easily realizable by decision makers who must work without cognitive aids. The computer system makers, thus enabling them to see that they may be giving up less than they had anticipated in adopting the compromise policy. This strategy was successful in the present study, and the compromise policy was adopted by the board as its official policy. It is clear, however, that this strategy will be useful only under certain circumstances—that is, when moderate differences among the initial policies are obscured by incorrect assumptions (which, of course, are common). To determine the range of conditions under which this strategy will be useful is an important problem for future studies.

Task Characteristics

As was indicated earlier, intercorrelation among cues is one of the more important task characteristics leading to incorrect inferences about other persons' judgments, particularly because persons may implicitly assume either the presence or absence of such intercorrelations incorrectly, and therefore false disagreement (or false agreement) may ensue. A study carried out by Hammond, Stewart, Adelman, and Wascoe (1975) illustrates a situation where a severe community-disrupting conflict occurred because a perfect correlation between task variables was incorrectly assumed to exist. Judgment analysis subsequently showed that the intercorrelation between the variables was less than perfect, and, as a consequence, room for compromise was found, and the conflict was resolved.

The problem involved a conflict over the type of handgun ammunition the police department of a large city would be allowed to use. Finding a bullet that was acceptable to all segments of the community, including the police department, turned out to be a highly emotional matter that divided the community. The difficulty was that persons believed that two aspects of a bullet—(a) its power to stop a suspect from firing back at the officer (or anyone else) after being hit, and (b) the amount of injury caused by the bullet—were perfectly correlated. This led persons who wanted to maximize stopping power to prefer a bullet totally different from that preferred by those who wanted to minimize the amount of injury caused by the bullet. Task analysis showed, however, that even though these two aspects of bullets were indeed correlated to some degree, the correlation was not perfect. It was therefore possible to find a bullet that had more stopping power than the bullet currently used (thus satisfying one segment of the community) but that did not increase injury (thus satisfying the other segment of the community). Once this was made clear, a satisfactory bullet could be found, and the conflict was resolved. In these two studies, then, task clarification achieved what discussion could not achieve—a result consistent with our analysis of cognitive conflict.

Specific Characteristics of Judgment Policies and Their Effect on Negotiation

Earlier we explained that in our laboratory research both linear and nonlinear function forms were induced into the cognitive systems of the persons studied as well as differential weighting of cues. Was this tactic appropriate? Do such function forms appear in the cognitive systems of people outside the laboratory who may be involved in conflict and negotiation? A study involving a reenactment of a labor-management negotiation carried out by Balke et al. (1973) illustrates not only (a) that inaccurate estimates of differential weighting occur and (b) that curvilinear function forms are used, but (c) that misunderstanding resulting from inconsistency can occur. Moreover, such misunderstanding can occur not only *between* negotiators, but *within* teams of negotiators, thus complicating and frustrating agreement.

Despite their participation in negotiations that had lasted at least seven months, both union and management negotiators were found to be inaccurate in their predictions of the differential weights the other side placed on various negotiating issues (see Figure 2.4), a result that underscores the inadequacy of verbal communication. Both sides used curvilinear function forms (see Figure 2.5); but, as can be seen from Figure 2.6, the three members of the

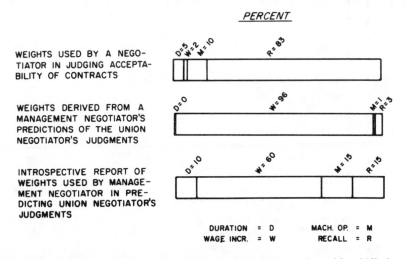

Figure 2.4. Illustration of misunderstanding: Comparison of top bar with middle bar shows that the management negotiator incorrectly assumes that the union negotiator attaches nearly all importance to wages (96 percent), whereas the union negotiator attaches nearly all importance to the question of how many strikers are to be recalled to work. Comparison of the lower bar with the middle bar shows that the management negotiator misunderstood his own weights in predicting the union negotiator's judgments.

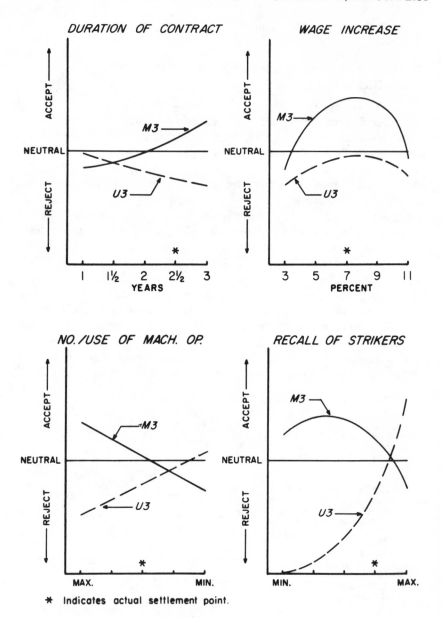

* Indicates actual settlement point.

Figure 2.5. Illustration of computer-generated display of functional relations (function forms) between judgments of contracts and four contract issues. The display provides a comparison between the function forms of a management negotiator (M3) and a union negotiator (U3).

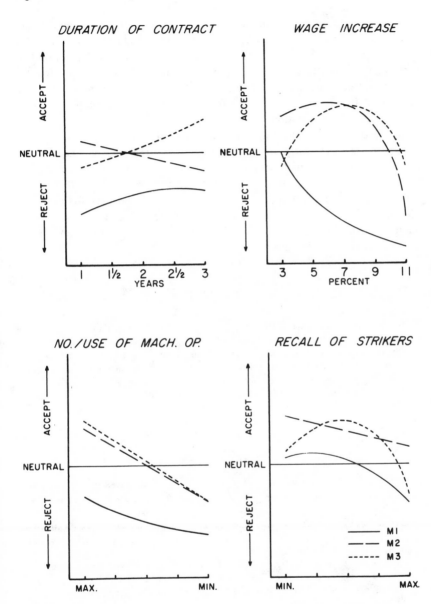

Figure 2.6. Illustration of the disparity in function forms in the judgment policies of the managment negotiators.

management negotiating team did not use them in the same way, again indicating the inadequacy of verbal communication. This differential use of function forms means, of course, that management did not have a unified negotiating policy. Under these circumstances, it was virtually impossible for the union negotiators to predict accurately the management negotiators' judgments. Finding agreement, therefore, would be more a matter of chance than of reasoned negotiation.

In short, these results indicate that both theory and the findings of laboratory research carry meaning for conflict situations outside the laboratory and that the application of the principles derived from the laboratory studies leads to a better understanding of actual instances of conflict. These studies merely mark a beginning, however, and much more theoretical development, as well as systematic laboratory and field research, must be conducted so that a more secure grasp of the nature of interpersonal conflict and negotiation can be achieved.

NOTES

1. These interpretations of R_{S1}, R_{S2}, and G hold only when the relations between the judgments and the cues are linear. When there are nonlinear relations, they are usually transformed to linear relations before the analysis (see Brehmer and Kostron, 1973, for an example). However, it is also possible to add nonlinear components to the IME (see Hammond, Stewart, Brehmer, and Steinmann, 1975).

2. There is some evidence to suggest that these conditions are the ones in which a subject is least likely to be able to report accurately on the characteristics of his judgment policy (Hammond, Stewart, Brehmer, and Steinmann, 1975).

REFERENCES

ADELMAN, L., T. R. STEWART, and K. R. HAMMOND (1975) "A case history of the application of Social Judgment Theory to policy formulation." Policy Sciences 6: 137-159.

ASCH, S. E. (1958) "Effects of group pressures upon modification and distortion of judgments," in E. E. Maccoby et al. (eds.) Readings in Social Psychology. New York: Holt, Rinehart & Winston.

BALKE, W. M., K. R. HAMMOND, and G. D. MEYER (1973) "An alternative approach to labor-management relations." Administrative Sci. Q. 18: 311-327.

BREHMER, B. (1976) "Note on clinical judgment and the formal characteristics of clinical tasks." Psych. Bull.

———(1975a) "Policy conflict and policy change as a function of the characteristics of the task: IV. The effect of cue intercorrelations." Scandinavian J. of Psychology 16: 85-96.

——— (1975b) "Social judgment theory and the analysis of interpersonal conflict." Umea Psychological Reports No. 87. Umea, Sweden: University of Umeå.

———(1974a) "Policy conflict and policy change as a function of task characteristics: III. The effect of the distribution of the validities of cues in the conflict task." Scandinavian J. of Psychology 15: 135-138.

——(1974b) "Policy conflict, policy consistency, and interpersonal understanding." Scandinavian J. of Psychology 15: 273-276.

——— (1973a) "Policy conflict and policy change as a function of task characteristics: II. The effects of task predictability." Scandinavian J. of Psychology 14: 220-227.

——— (1973b) "Effects of cue validity on interpersonal learning of inference tasks with linear and nonlinear cues." American J. of Psychology 86: 29-48.

——— (1973c) "Effects of task predictability and cue validity on interpersonal learning of inference tasks involving both linear and nonlinear cues." Organizational Behavior and Human Performance 10: 24-46.

——— (1972) "Policy conflict as a function of policy differences and policy complexity." Scandinavian J. of Psychology 13: 208-221.

——— (1971) "Effects of communication and feedback on cognitive conflict." Scandinavian J. of Psychology 12: 205-216.

——— (1969a) "The roles of policy differences and inconsistency in policy conflict." Umeå Psychological Reports No. 18. Umea, Sweden: University of Umeå.

——— (1969b) "Cognitive dependence on additive and configural cues." American J. of Psychology 82: 490-503.

——— and S. GARPEBRING (1974) "Social pressure and policy change in the lens model interpersonal conflict paradigm." Scandinavian J. of Psychology 15: 191-196.

BREHMER, B. and K. R. HAMMOND (1973) "Cognitive sources of interpersonal conflict: Analysis of interactions between linear and nonlinear cognitive systems." Organizational Behavior and Human Performance 10: 290-313.

BREHMER, B. and L. KOSTRON (1973) "Policy conflict and policy change as a function of task characteristics: I. The effects of cue validity and function form." Scandinavian J. of Psychology 14: 44-55.

BREHMER, B. and G. QVANRSTROM (1973) "Feedforward, feedback, and subjective weights in multiple-cue judgments." Umeå Psychological Reports No. 76. Umeå, Sweden: University of Umeå.

BREHMER, B., H. AZUMA, K. R. HAMMOND, L. KOSTRON, and D. D. VARONOS (1970) "A cross-national comparison of cognitive conflict." J. of Cross-Cultural Psychology 1: 5-20.

BREHMER, B., J. KUYLENSTIERNA, and J. LILJERGREN (1973) "Effects of function form and cue validity on the subjects' hypotheses in probabilistic inference tasks." Organizational Behavior and Human Performance 11: 338-354.

BRUNSWIK, E. (1956) Perception and the Representative Design of Psychological Experiments. Berkeley and Los Angeles: Univ. of California Press.

COOK, R. L. and T. R. STEWART (1975) "A comparison of seven methods for obtaining subjective descriptions of judgment policy." Organizational Behavior and Human Performance 13: 31-45.

DRUCKMAN, D. (1973) "Human factors in international negotiations: Social-psychological aspects of international conflict," in V. Davis and M. A. East (eds.) Sage Professional Papers in International Studies, Volume 2. Beverly Hills and London: Sage Publications.

——— and K. ZECHMEISTER (1973) "Conflict of interest and value dissensus: Propositions in the sociology of conflict." Human Relations 26, 449-466.

EARLE, T. C. (1973) "Interpersonal learning," in L. Rappoport and D. Summers (eds.) Human Judgment and Social Interaction. New York: Holt, Rinehart & Winston.

GILLIS, J. (1975) "Effects of Chlorpromazine and Thiothixene on acute schizophrenic patients," in K. R. Hammond and C. R. B. Joyce (eds.) Psychoactive Drugs and Social Judgment: Theory and Research. New York: John Wiley.

HAMMOND, K. R. (1974) "Human judgment and social policy." Program of Research on Human Judgment and Social Interaction Report No. 170. Boulder: University of Colorado, Institute of Behavioral Science.

——— (1971) "Computer graphics as an aid to learning." Science 172: 903-908.
——— [ed.] (1966) The Psychology of Egon Brunswik. New York: Holt, Rinehart & Winston.
——— (1965) "New directions in research on conflict resolution." J. of Social Issues 21: 44-66.
——— (1955) "Probabilistic functioning and the clinical method." Psych. Rev. 62: 255-262.
——— and B. BREHMER (1973) "Quasi-rationality and distrust: Implications for international conflict," in L. Rappoport and D. Summers (eds.) Human Judgment and Social Interaction. New York: Holt, Rinehart & Winston.
HAMMOND, K. R. and C. R. B. JOYCE [eds.] (1975) Psychoactive Drugs and Social Judgment: Theory and Research. New York: John Wiley.
HAMMOND, K. R., T. R. STEWART, L. ADELMAN, and N. WASCOE (1975) "Report to the Denver City Council and Mayor regarding the choice of handgun ammunition for the Denver Police Department." Program of Research on Human Judgment and Social Interaction Report No. 179. Boulder: University of Colorado, Institute of Behavioral Science.
HAMMOND, K. R., T. R. STEWART, B. BREHMER, and D. O. STEINMANN (1975) "Social judgment theory," in M. Kaplan and S. Schwartz (eds.) Human Judgment and Decision Processes: Formal and Mathematical Approaches. New York: Academic Press.
HAMMOND, K. R., F. J. TODD, M. WILKINS, and T. O. MITCHELL (1966) "Cognitive conflict between persons: Application of the 'lens model' paradigm." J. of Experimental Social Psychology 2: 343-360.
HAMMOND, K. R., G. B. BONAIUTO, C. FAUCHEUX, S. MOSCOVICI, W. D. FROHLICH, C. R. B. JOYCE, and G. DiMAJO (1968) "A comparison of cognitive conflict between persons in Western Europe and the United States." International J. of Psychology 3: 1-12.
HURSCH, C. J., K. R. HAMMOND, and J. L. HURSCH (1964) "Some methodological considerations in multiple-cue probability studies." Psych. Rev. 71: 42-60.
MUMPOWER, J. L. and K. R. HAMMOND (1974) "Entangled task dimensions: An impediment to interpersonal learning." Organizational Behavior and Human Performance 11: 387-399.
NATHAN, O. and H. NORDEN (1965) Einstein on Peace. New York: Schocken.
RAPOPORT, A. and A. M. CHAMMAH (1965) Prisoner's Dilemma: A Study in Conflict and Cooperation. Ann Arbor: Univ. of Michigan Press.
RAPPOPORT, L. (1965) "Interpersonal conflict in non-competitive and uncertain situations." J. of Experimental Social Psychology 1: 323-333.
STEINMANN, D. O., T. H. SMITH, L. G. JURDEM, and K. R. HAMMOND (1975) "Application and evaluation of Social Judgment Theory in policy formulation: An example." Program of Research on Human Judgment and Social Interaction Report No. 174. Boulder: University of Colorado, Institute of Behavioral Science.
STEWART, T. R. (1976) "Components of correlations and extension of the lens model equation." Psychometrika.
——— and J. E. CARTER (1973) "POLICY: An interactive computer program for externalizing, executing, and refining judgmental policy." Program of Research on Human Judgment and Social Interaction Report No. 159. Boulder: University of Colorado, Institute of Behavioral Science.
SUMMERS, D. A. (1968) "Conflict, compromise, and belief change in a decision making task." J. of Conflict Resolution 12: 215-221.
———, J. D. FLETCHER, and D. J. TALIAFERRO (1969) "Subjective vs. objective description of judgment policy." Psychonomic Sci. 18: 249-250.

TODD, F. J., K. R. HAMMOND, and M. WILKINS (1966) "Differential effects of ambiguous and exact feedback on two-person conflict and compromise." J. of Conflict Resolution 10: 88-97.

TOLMAN, E. C. (1942) Drives Toward War. New York: Appleton-Century.

——— (1932) Purposive Behavior in Animals and Men. New York: Appleton-Century.

——— and E. BRUNSWIK (1935) "The organism and the causal texture of the environment." Psych. Rev. 42: 43-77.

TUCKER, L. R. (1964) "A suggested alternative formulation in the developments by Hursch, Hammond, and Hursch, and by Hammond, Hursch, and Todd." Psych. Rev. 71: 528-530.

Chapter 3

CONFLICT OF INTEREST AND
VALUE DISSENSUS: TWO PERSPECTIVES

DANIEL DRUCKMAN

Mathematica, Inc., Bethesda, Maryland

RICHARD ROZELLE

University of Houston, Houston

and

KATHLEEN ZECHMEISTER

Conflict of interest between two parties is defined as a discrepancy between their preferences for the distribution of a scarce resource. The conflict is caused by differing utilities for the range of possible outcomes, different expected payoffs for the same outcome, or different vested interests of nonoverlapping constituencies in the various possible outcomes. The parties become contestants when both are strongly motivated to achieve their most

AUTHORS' NOTE: Among the participants in this research program who have made notable contributions are Roger M. Krause, Rhonda Love, Robert Mahoney and Maurice Mittelmark. We are indebted to these collaborators, whose labors and insights are well represented in this chapter. An earlier version of this chapter was presented at the annual meeting of the American Psychological Association in New Orleans, 1974. Partial support for some of the work reported here came from the National Institutes of Health General Support Grant FR-05666-02, from the National Institute of Dental Research Grant 5T IDE00138-09, and from a grant-in-aid awarded by the Society for the Psychological Study of Social Issues.

desired outcome under conditions that permit only one to be realized. This situation is familiar to experimental social psychologists who have developed extensive research programs designed to separate the components of variance in efforts to resolve conflicts of interests. (See, for example, the McClintock chapter in this volume.) It is the prototype for experimental studies of coordination using matrix games or bargaining simulations.

An alternative conceptualization of interparty conflict, which is less well known among bargaining and gaming specialists, is that proposed by Hammond and his associates. (See the chapter by Brehmer and Hammond in this volume.) These investigators have conducted a number of experiments designed to explore the determinants of the resolution of *cognitive conflicts* or conflicts caused by different ideas, values, ideologies, policies, and so on. This type of conflict is defined operationally by differences in the probabilistic relationship between cues or predictors and a criterion that represents the solution to a shared problem. The parties disagree over the best way to achieve a particular outcome rather than over what that particular outcome should be. The conflict is noncompetitive insofar as there are no payoffs or other vested interests contingent on the outcome; that is, the criterion of achievement is "correctness" rather than "return." This conflict is likely to be most intense when (a) there are several possible strategies leading to the same outcome and (b) the criterion is somewhat ambiguous. It has been found that, under these conditions, cognitive conflicts are rather difficult to resolve without mediational devices provided by the experimenter.

A third paradigm designed to explore interparty conflict resolution is based on the *interplay* between interests and cognitive factors or values. These are conflicts caused both by different utilities for the range of possible outcomes *and* by different values or policy preferences. This type of conflict is defined by the interaction between differing interests and differing values; the two types of differences influence one another reciprocally (see Druckman and Zechmeister, 1973). A series of experiments has been designed to explore the effects of this interplay on the resolution, through negotiations, of conflicts between two or more parties. Some of the studies are presented in this chapter after a discussion of the conceptualization and examples of the phenomenon as it occurs in various settings.

Three features in particular distinguish this paradigm from both the conflict-of-interest and the cognitive-conflict paradigms: (a) The focus is on the *interplay* between values and interests, rather than on one or the other; (b) the effects of this "interplay" are assessed by examining a negotiation process that consists of both debate and bargaining, rather than one or the other; and (c) variables and processes are embedded within context-relevant simulations of policy-making conferences, rather than explored in the abstract-experimental mode. The simulations are considered to represent the processes as they occur in situ. In many policy-making settings, values and interests interact in the process of intensifying conflicts over the distribution of resources that are worked out in a format consisting of both debate and bargaining. In fact, it has been suggested by several sociologists (e.g., Van Doorn, 1966; Coser, 1956) that the pattern of conflict is related systematically to the institutional context within which decision-making on policy occurs. This is explored further below.

The paradigm focuses on the "mixed" cases, where conflicts of interest derive from value or ideological differences (or where contrasting ideologies develop out of a conflict of interest; see Druckman and Zechmeister, 1973), or where one component must be balanced against the other in decision-making (see Druckman et al., 1974). It is difficult to imagine a "pure" conflict of ideas in which a vested interest, such as saving face or winning new advocates for an ideological position, is not at stake. That is, a confrontation for the purpose of persuading another to accept one's beliefs and attitudes, or presumed facts, is likely to involve a potential "payoff" to the advocate in the form of a new adherent and his enthusiastic admiration. Moreover, vested interests might be made explicit by the presence of an aligned constituency or by invoking representational role obligations. When these pressures are made explicit, the intensity of the conflict between contrasting ideological proponents is likely to be exacerbated (see, e.g., Druckman et al., 1972).

Similarly, "pure" conflicts of interest seem to occur rarely. For example, contesting parties might offer alternative rationales for the use of scarce resources and justify their needs in different terms. In his analysis of Ghanaian elites, Nayak (1973) claimed that Nkrumah, who was believed to be an ideologue, used ideology to serve his own interests. In Nayak's words,

> His ideology was a mere montage to disguise, rationalize, and legitimize the contest for power. Political decisions were based not on advertised ideological foundations of the political kingdom but on the realities of power equations. Ideology was no more than a "political formula" to wheedle the masses, to raise their sense of importance, and to justify Nkrumah's "actual exercise of power by resting it on some universal moral principle" [1973: 60].

Thus, while Nayak makes a case for the importance of interests, it is clear that these interests were justified in terms of a broader ideological posture, which through time may have emerged as a source of conflict in addition to the contesting interests.

This chapter is organized into five sections. The first section describes each of the two perspectives. The second discusses briefly the simulation methodology used for the experiments. The third presents the procedures and results of the multilateral and bilateral negotiation experiments that were conducted to assess the relative importance of interests and values. Then the negotiation experiments, which were designed to explore the process by which values and interests *interact,* are presented, followed by a discussion of refinements in the conceptual framework. And finally the work that has been completed to date is summarized, and suggestions are made for further developments.

THE "INTERPLAY": TWO PERSPECTIVES

In this section, each of the two perspectives is described. The examples used are intended as illustrative settings in which the processes occur. Other examples could also be cited. Indeed, other examples were used in developing scenarios for the simulation experiments that are reported in later sections.

Balancing Values Against Interests

A number of examples of the interplay between values and interests as it occurs in various contexts can be cited. Some of these examples give rise to the notion that actors balance ideological considerations against interests in the decision-making process. Especially prominent is Axelrod's (1970) study of coalition formation in Italian legislative politics. He demonstrated that if *both* ideological similarity and utilities are taken into account, predictions of coalition formation and duration of coalitions improve significantly over predictions made on the basis of theories that consider only utilities. Leiserson (1970) represented this process in terms of weights assigned to each component by actors who are conflicted by acting in a direction suggested either by their beliefs or by their interests. In legislative politics, ideology does play a prominent role in decision-making. However, the relative weight attached to these factors is likely to vary with the decision-making context.

In international relations, a nation's interests are likely to predominate. Lall (1966), in his classic treatment of international negotiations, presents a number of examples which show that even the most ideological countries pay more attention to their vital interests than to their ideologies when these two factors conflict. In his words, "a country which is imbued with a strong ideological belief does not let these beliefs dominate its representatives in negotiations with other countries" (1966: 288). He goes on to illustrate that at the negotiating table, or in informal exchanges, the ideological beliefs of a country tend to have less influence on its demands and attitudes regarding matters of substance. The nation's assessment of its own best advantage in terms of military power, and the protection and promotion of its other vital interests, will predominantly determine its conduct. This kind of behavior is typical of the *Realpolitik* approach, which implies that ideological factors are less important than material ones in shaping policy. It also implies that if, for example, the material environment offers incentives to freeze the arms race, a negotiated agreement will be struck regardless of the parties' divergent world views. This approach may be characteristic of the Soviet Union, where, as Clemens (1973: 9) notes, "Ideology has over time been adapted to reflect the imperatives of the military and economic conditions faced by the Soviet state." Such observations suggest that "Moscow's proposals to control the arms race have generally been more consonant with its military-strategic interests than with ideological or cultural imperatives" (Clemens, 1973; 9). Even the most ideological nation—Red China—attempts to reduce negotiations to matters concerned with its interests. This observation led Young (1968: 372) to comment that "the need to identify and analyze Peking's pattern of being in favor of negotiations but against haggling over principle requires a proper assessment of the relative weight attached at any one time to adherence to ideology and principled policies on the one hand, and tactical flexibility on the other." An assessment of this weighting process is central to the research reported below.

The balancing process can be conceived of in terms of a continuum ranging from "pure" conflict of interest at one end through varying degrees of "mix" to "pure" cognitive conflict at the other. The various positions along the continuum may reflect either situation- or person-variance. That is, the relative importance of the two components can be defined by the structure of the situation or by weights assigned by persons operating under the same conditions. These alternative perspectives—situation or person—suggest two empirical questions: Which type of conflict situation defined by its position on the continuum, is most difficult to resolve? And what factors affect the relative weights assigned to the components by actors who must balance them in decision-making? These questions have formed the bases for two related programs of research. The former has guided investigations into the effects of varying conflict situations on the negotiation behavior of representatives who must attempt to reach a joint decision on the allocation of resources to alternative programs sponsored by a council to which they both belong. The latter has guided investigations of coalition formation where decision makers had to decide whether to support or oppose various council programs by entering into funding or blocking coalitions; the decision required an assessment of the relative importance of their values or beliefs and interests. The results of these studies are presented below.

The Interaction Between Values and Interests

Other examples of the interplay between values and interests give rise to the notion that the two sources of conflict are interdependent and that one derives from or causes the other. The cleavages are overlapping and interacting, one intensifying or polarizing the other in a pattern of reciprocal relations (see Druckman and Zechmeister, 1973). This conceptualization is in contrast to the "balancing" notion, which posits that the components can be untangled, separated, and made orthogonal. Moreover, it develops out of the literature on the sociology of conflict rather than the utility theory framework, which has guided the operationalization of the "balancing" process. Ideologies and vested interests are intertwined as sources of preferences for programs and policies. This was clearly the case in a recent interdepartmental dispute, documented by Druckman and Bonoma (1976), over policy in a health service-delivery bureaucracy.

The problem concerned the assignment of predoctoral trainees to service teams that were responsible for delivering psychological services to the community. The parties were administrators who were responsible for training and those who were responsible for administering the community service-delivery unit of a service/training/research institute. While external pressures compelled the parties to ensure that trainees spent a portion of their time on the community teams, they could not agree on a policy for assignments. The training directors were reluctant to commit themselves to the community team experience as a training device, while the service directors were reluctant to require their team leaders to supervise trainees. The emergence of a policy to guide assignments depended on a mutual commitment to the service teams as an essential training device. Differences both in preference for a training model and in interests prevented such a commitment. Those responsible for training were oriented toward a clinic model of service-delivery and exposed their trainees to this mode of delivering services; those responsible for service were oriented toward a community model, and they viewed trainees as a resource in the sense of being members of the service-delivery teams. The conflict of interest was caused by an organizational structure that separated training from service: The trainers did not have responsibility for trainees on the teams, and the service team leaders were not responsible for training team members who were predoctoral trainees. The trainers were especially reluctant to relinquish control of a portion of their training program. Taken together, the interests and the differences in conceptual preference militated against a negotiated agreement on policy. A solution to the structural problem that is responsible for the conflict of interest should reduce the amount of polarization on conceptual preferences; or, to put it the other way, a depolarization in conceptual differences should reduce the intensity of the conflict of interest caused by structural factors. Such solutions were proposed in a workshop designed to encourage a negotiated settlement of the dispute. Steps were also taken toward implementing the proposals (see Druckman and Bonoma, 1976, for details).

The interplay between conceptual preferences and interests can be illustrated by other examples drawn from the literature on the sociology of conflict and debate. Several of these are presented in Druckman and Zechmeister (1973), including Snow's (1959) characterization of a dissensus in the academic-intellectual community, Rapoport's (1964) discussion of foreign-policy formulation, interpersonal relations within the family, disputes over funding priorities in a grants allocation office, and so on. In all these cases, conflicts of interest over resource distribution derived explicitly from a value dissensus. This type of link formed the basis for a paradigm designed to test propositions that were derived from the conceptualization of interacting sources of interparty conflict. A summary of the results obtained to date is presented below, together with an elucidation of the processes, following a review of the work completed on the "balancing" perspective. First, however, the simulation methodology used to investigate the processes is discussed.

SIMULATION

The simulation methodology used represents an attempt to bring an experimental approach to interparty conflict and negotiations closer to the nonlaboratory settings in which such conflict occurs. Context-relevance is not forfeited in the interest of analytical rigor. Experiments are conducted by manipulating variables that are defined in terms of the backgrounds in which they are ensconced. This strategy is suggested by a conceptualization which posits that the pattern of conflict is embedded·within a broader context (see Van Doorn, 1966; Druckman, 1971). The interplay between values and interests cannot be considered apart from the context within which it operates: Values and ideologies refer to substantive issues, and interests concern decisions that are made with respect to the distribution of very specific resources. For this reason, among others, it is necessary to reproduce certain aspects of that context. The expanded perspective gained in the process contributes to an understanding of the phenomenon (see Druckman, 1971). Moreover, the effects of context can be assessed by comparing the results obtained in two or more simulations or by comparing the results obtained from a simulation with the real-world referent (see Druckman et al., 1974, for an example of such a comparison).

Two strategies were used for representing context: (a) Context was *incorporated* in design by reproducing relationships between variables as they existed in situ; and (b) context was *represented* in the scenarios that served as background for manipulating variables that were made orthogonal. The former strategy was used in the coalition experiments, while the latter was used in designing the negotiation experiments. The incorporation strategy often involves reproducing relationships among variables that are nonorthogonal. Such nonorthogonality can be taken into account in analysis, although it is especially problematic when it occurs among a system of several variables. The representation strategy deals with complexity at another stage: The relationship between values and interests is built into the materials presented to those who are participating in the simulation. The nature of the "link" as it is presumed to occur in the context being simulated must be made explicit in the background scenarios. Complexity is represented in the details of scenario construction rather than in statistical analysis procedures (for further discussion of these strategies, see Mahoney and Druckman, 1975).

These strategies are part of the more general methodology that has guided the experiments designed to explore propositions derived from the two perspectives on the interplay between the components of interparty conflict. The experiments were embedded within various simulation-models, including an interdenominational council, a prison services committee of an interdenominational council, a population-control policy-making committee, and a city council responsible for allocating resources to a number of urban programs. These models can be regarded as prototypes for the many settings within which the "interplay" between values and interests occurs, including those cited above as examples. We not turn to a summary of the procedures and results of these investigations.

THE BALANCING PROCESS: VALUES VERSUS INTERESTS

The simulated situation was a meeting of an interdenominational council that was modeled in some respects on the Houston Metropolitan Ministries—a nonprofit organization formed to sponsor a number of programs, including prison services, community centers, interfaith television and services, child nutrition, foster grandparents, economic development, and so on. Representatives of the participating denominations were responsible for setting priorities and distributing resources among these projects. Responsibility for decision-making rested with a committee of the whole, which set priorities, and a subcommittee structure, which dealt with the details of particular programs. The smaller committees were responsible to the council, which had final authority on policy. Decisions were generated by two types of activities: coalition formation and bilateral negotiations. These activities corresponded loosely to the decision-making format, with coalition formation occurring in the committee of the whole and two-party negotiations occurring in the subcommittees. Each of these processes was simulated: The first type took the form of a multiparty conference among four denominational representatives, while the latter took the form of two-party negotiations between representatives on the prison services committee. These are discussed in turn.

Coalition Formation in Multilateral Negotiations

The decision-making conference consisted of representatives from four denominations who were responsible for deciding whether to sponsor each of three projects—a community hospital, an advertising campaign, and an interfaith chapel. Their preferences for each of these projects were determined by denominational beliefs[1] related to each project and the prospective consequences of the decision for their membership. The beliefs and interests were represented by values on 11-point scales, ranging from -5 to $+5$, which were assigned on the basis of estimates made for four "real" denominations: Unitarians, Methodists, Lutherans, and Baptists. Each role player represented one of these groups. Each group had a particular set of values on the "belief" and "interest" scales for each of the proposed projects. For each project, one representative had positive values on both scales (e.g., $+4$, $+2$), while another had negative values (e.g., -2, -4) on the two scales. The other two representatives were mixed, with a positive value on one scale and a negative value on the other (e.g., $+4$, -2; or -4, $+2$). The representatives were rotated through the four combinations of positions in such a way that each would be in a different position on each of the three projects. (A third scale represented the amount that each representative had to invest in each project, with some denominations having more than others on some projects and less than others on other projects. For any one denominational representative, the investment amount was less than the minimum necessary to fund the project, thus making a coalition of two or more representatives necessary in order to ensure that a project would be funded.)

Following role-induction procedures, the four representatives began deliberations—consisting of note-passing—in order to reach a decision to fund or to block a particular project. Representatives exchanged offers and replies through several decision periods until a coalition formed. The winning coalition consisted of representatives who agreed to contribute their funds to the construction of a project (a funding coalition) or who agreed to withhold their funds (a blocking coalition). A successful funding coalition contained members whose contributions exceeded the "minimum amount necessary to fund"; a viable blocking coalition contained members whose pooled resources were used to prevent the attainment of a funding coalition. The coalitions that formed on each project provided most of the information necessary for computing regression analyses and for estimating model parameters. For details on design, scenario construction, and simulation procedures, see Druckman et al. (1974). For our purposes in this chapter, only the final equation (which was evaluated by multiple regression procedures) and a brief description of its component parameters are presented. The full derivation of the model and various extensions are worked out in Krause et al. (1975).

This procedure was used to generate data that would provide estimates for parameters and test a simple model of the balancing process. The model is expressed as follows:

$$U_d = \text{theta} \cdot w_I + (1 - \text{theta}) \cdot w_M + \text{process} + \text{error},$$

where U_d is the utility for denomination d; theta is a subjective term that reflects the extent to which the representative finds ideology to be more important than interests; w_I is the "objective" worth of the ideological term as reflected in the number of scale units assigned a representative for that term; $1 - \text{theta}$ is the one-complement of the subjective evaluation term theta; w_M is the "objective" worth of the interest (materialism) term as reflected in the number of scale units assigned a representative for that term; "process" reflects the amount of variance accounted for by communications sent and received on the way to a final decision; and "error" is residual variance.

Values for w_I and w_M were provided by the design, while theta was estimated through questionnaire and behavioral procedures. (A process-analysis coding system was devised to analyze the communications sent and received during the conference.) Following the conference, representatives were asked to indicate on a seven-step scale "the extent to which your ideology or membership gain was a more important consideration in your decisions to form an alliance on each issue." The behavioral measure was more complex and involved a procedure that was based on combinatorial logic, using coalition outcomes in conjunction with a contrived ratio of the values of the parameters w_I and w_M (see Krause et al.,1975, for a step-by-step description of this index). The questionnaire estimates of theta were used in a series of regression analyses to assess the relative importance of the various model components in predicting a coalition outcome index, which ranged from being in a successful blocking coalition (1) to being in a successful funding coalition (4). The two intermediate values were: being out of a successful funding coalition (2) and being out of a successful blocking coalition (3). The behavioral estimates of theta were used in a model-fitting analysis that was designed to determine the distribution of this parameter for the sample used in the simulation.

The salient empirical issues, from the standpoint of the "balancing" perspective discussed above, are: Which are weighted more, interests or ideologies, in the decision-making process? And how important is the balancing process, which consists of weighing one component against the other, in predicting coalition outcomes? Both of these issues involve the subjective parameter that is designated in the model as theta. These questions were evaluated by the use of data collected from twenty-five replications of the simulated interdenominational policy-making conference. In these runs, students were assigned to roles of denominational representatives. An additional set of eight runs was conducted, with ministers playing the appropriate role in the conference. The minister-runs served, inter alia, as a source for validation of the results obtained in the student replications. Components of variance for the parameters of the model were compared for the two data sets.

The values of theta ranged from 0 to 1. A representative who weighed the two components equally had a theta value of .5. A theta above .5 indicated that he was motivated more in the direction of his ideology, with 1 signifying an "ideologue." A theta below .5 indicated that he was motivated more by material concerns, and a value of 0 signified a "pure materialist." The first analysis compared the obtained distribution of values with various theoretical distributions for "goodness of fit." The theoretical distributions included a null distribution, which assumed that choices were made randomly; a "pure ideologue" distribution, which assumed that all parties disregarded their material stakes; a "pure materialist" distribution, which assumed that all parties disregarded their ideological stakes; and four types of "mixed" distributions—all of which assumed that parties weighed both components but differed as to the shape of the resulting distribution, with some positing a near-normal distribution and others positing distributions that were closer to rectangular.

One of the mixed distributions provided the best fit as determined by the square root of the sum of the squared deviations between each theoretical distribution and the obtained distribution. This was a distribution in which

theta was more or less normally distributed, with a mean of .5 and some
distribution in the tails: 10 percent of the sample had thetas greater than .67,
and 10 percent had thetas less than .33. (The mean deviation score was
.216—better than a distribution in which all parties had a theta of .5 [X̄ =
.277] and considerably better than the null distribution [X̄ = .362].) Thus,
the best estimate for most representatives in the sample was approximately
.5, indicating that they were weighing the two components about equally.
(See Druckman et al., 1974: 231-233, for the results of goodness-of-
fit tests that compare the obtained distribution with seven alternative theoretical distributions.) The next step will be to compare the distributions obtained for various populations and contexts. A comparison of special interest
is that between the simulated interreligious setting and an international-
negotiation setting where several writers claim that vested interests predominate (see citations above), or a legislative setting where a rectangular distribution might exist.[2]

The second analysis was designed to determine the relative importance of
the balancing process. In other words, it was designed to determine how
much variance in coalition outcomes is explained by theta, over and above
that explained by the other components of the prediction equation. This
analysis consisted of an assessment of the increment in variance explained by
the entire utility equation, over and above that explained by the "objective"
parameters alone. The increment can be evaluated by an F test, which makes
allowances for statistical dependencies among the correlated predictor variables (see Cohen, 1968: 435). The results of the analysis, computed for each
project, are shown in Table 3.1. It can be seen that in each case the result is a
highly significant *increment* in variance explained (R^2). These findings attest
to the importance of the subjective balancing process, represented by theta,
in predicting coalition outcomes.

A third analysis was designed to examine the effects of the negotiation
process on coalition outcomes. The process was coded into some ten categories, including the type of offer; implied tactics, such as threats, promises,
and commitments; the context referred to by the message; the inner or outer

TABLE 3.1
Multiple Correlations and Variance Accounted for in
Outcome Index by Joint Sum and U_d

	Interfaith Chapel		Advertising Campaign		Community Hospital	
	Mult. R	R^2	*Mult. R*	R^2	*Mult. R*	R^2
$w_I + w_m$ (Joint Sum)	.49	.24	.58	.34	.51	.26
Joint Sum + U_d	.61	.37	.67	.45	.57	.32
Increment		.13		.11		.06
$F_{1/93}$		19.5**		18.6**		8.1*

*p $<$.01
**p $<$.001

direction of the message (i.e., self or other); and so on. To date only the community hospital project has been analyzed. The extent to which each of these variables served to increment the variance explained in the outcome index, over and above that explained by the other components of the utility equation, was assessed for this project/issue. None of these variables added significantly to the variance explained (R_2) by the other parameters of the utility equation. For this project/issue, process factors were negligible influences on the outcomes.

The minister data present a different picture. The results of the analyses of this data-set indicated that the process categories accounted for significantly more variance ($R^2 = .33$) in the outcome index than the "objective" parameters ($R^2 = .25$), the theta estimate ($R^2 = .19$), and the utility equation (excluding process) ($R^2 = .23$) when each was entered first in the regression equation. Moreover, the net increment of process over the "objective" parameters (.08), the theta estimate (.14), and the utility equation (.10) were significant as evaluated by the Cohen F test (Cohen, 1968).[3] In contrast to the student data, the utility equation (without process) did not result in a significant increment in variance explained over the "objective" parameters ($R^2 = .26$ versus $R^2 = .25$, respectively), indicating that theta was not as important a factor in predicting the coalitional outcomes.[4] Interestingly, one of the three process categories that correlated strongly with the outcome index was "context-related messages." This category consisted of those communications that referred directly to the religious institution that was simulated. Thus it appears that extra-laboratory experience made a difference. This experience, as reflected in the process categories, overwhelmed the effects of those factors (namely, experimental variations, instructions, theta estimates) which accounted for the outcomes attained by the student sample.

The different results obtained for the two populations have implications for simulating. By responding differently to the built-in aspects of the model, the ministers served to alert us to the importance of "experienced role players." Simulations that include this factor may indeed be better representations of the context being simulated. However *the extent* to which such experience increases the validity of the construction remains to be determined by corresponding analyses of parallel data-sets obtained by making probes in situ.

Bilateral Negotiations

A second decision-making conference was convened for the purpose of distributing a $40,000 budget among four programs proposed for prison services. This conference was composed of the members of one of several subcommittees of the Houston Metropolitan Ministries. Deliberations among committee members did not result in a decision: Two factions formed, each preferring to support different programs. The prolonged deadlock led committee members to consider a different format for resolving their differences.

They agreed to appoint two members, one representing each faction, to negotiate the differences and make recommendations to the entire committee that would then be communicated to the council. These two-person negotiations were simulated under varying conditions.

The factions were divided according to preferences for four alternative programs: religious services, a counselor-training program, a criminal justice action group, and reform of the prison system. One negotiator represented a faction that supported the first two programs, suggesting that $20,000 be allocated to each, while the other negotiator represented a faction that supported the latter two programs and suggested that $20,000 be allocated to each of these. Their program preferences derived from more general ideological orientations, with services and training programs reflecting a "system-maintenance" ideology and an action group and reform reflecting a "social-change" ideology (see Druckman and Zechmeister, 1970, and Zechmeister and Druckman, 1973, for summary statements). An elaborate role-induction session preceded the deliberations. Detailed statements of these opposing orientations and each of the four programs were presented to each negotiator prior to the deliberations; the link between the ideologies and corresponding programs was also made explicit. Each representative was given time to prepare position statements and a strategy before the face-to-face negotiations.

Following the role-induction preparation, the two representatives engaged in negotiations for a maximum of thirty minutes. They were under pressure to reach an agreed-upon decision, within this time period, on the distribution of the budget across the four programs: They could agree to allot none, some, or all of the $40,000 in any way among the programs. However, any money that remained unallotted would be returned to the council to be used for other kinds of programs. They were prompted to reach a decision as soon as possible since every five minutes represented a day of negotiations, and time was costly. The decisions were to be recorded on special forms consisting of four scales, one for each issue, ranging from 0 to 20 (see Figure 3.1 for examples of these scales). An agreed-upon decision would be initialed by botn negotiators. All sessions were tape-recorded, and some were videotaped for process analyses.

This procedure was used to probe the same general question that was explored in the coalition experiments: Do interests or ideology explain more of the variance in the decision-making process and outcomes? However, in contrast to the coalition situation, where role-players were assigned scores representing their interests and ideology, the components were defined in terms of the structure of the situation that confronted the negotiators. Experimental conditions ranged from a conflict that was primarily ideological (extreme difference in values; shared interests) to one that was primarily a conflict of interest (moderate difference in values; conflicting vested interests), with varying degrees of "mix" in between.

Figure 1. Examples of Contrasting Issue Scales from Decision-Making Form

Solution M_1: Religious Activities

0 2 4 6 8 10 12 14 16 18 20

(thousands of dollars)

Solution C_1: Establishing Criminal Justice Action Group

0 2 4 6 8 10 12 14 16 18 20

(thousands of dollars)

Solution M_2: Counselor-Training Program

0 2 4 6 8 10 12 14 16 18 20

(thousands of dollars)

Solution C_2: Reform of the Prison System

0 2 4 6 8 10 12 14 16 18 20

(thousands of dollars)

FIGURE 1. Examples of Contrasting Issue Scales from Decision-Making Form

The amount of ideological conflict was defined as the extent to which each faction was unanimous or split in support of the orientations from which the program preferences were derived. A condition in which all members of both factions endorsed a rather extreme statement was compared to a condition in which both factions were split on the degree to which they supported the statement, with both "moderates" and "extremists" being members of the same faction. In the former condition, role players were told that the two factions were becoming *more* disparate in their views, with members gravitating toward the more extreme statement of the orientation. In the latter condition, role players were told that the two factions were becoming *less* disparate in their views, with some members in each faction adopting a more moderate statement of the orientation. (Note that this operational definition ensured against an interpretation of results in terms of initial position distance. The split between factions was at the level of underlying ideology rather than programs; contesting negotiators in *all* conditions had the same initial positions on preferred allocations to each of the four programs.)

Size of the interest conflict was defined by the extent to which the outcome of negotiations would have consequences for the other members of each faction (i.e., "constituents") being represented. A condition in which each faction had high vested interests in the outcome was compared to a condition in which each faction had low vested interests in the outcome. Vested interests were defined in terms of source of funding of programs and source of control over the programs: In the high-interest condition, the budget was contributed by the denominations and controlled by the faction that supported the funded programs; in the low-interest condition, the budget was contributed by external granting agencies, with control over the funded programs shared by both factions.

One of the experiments completed was carried out by Love (1975). In this experiment, interests were made orthogonal to ideological differences, with high and low interests crossed against cohesive and split factions on endorsement of the "social change" or "system maintenance" ideology. A third variable, sex, made this a 2 x 2 x 2 design, with six replications in each cell. This design permitted an assessment of the components of variance accounted for by each of the factors and also by possible interactions among them. The results are clear. Significant main effects were obtained for each dependent variable: time to resolution, amount allocated, asymmetry of resolution, and frequency of resolved conflicts. The results for three of these variables are shown in Table 3.2. High-interest dyads took longer ($\bar{X} = 24.67$), allocated less funds ($\bar{X} = 25.00$), and had more asymmetrical resolutions (i.e., one negotiator conceded more than the other [$\bar{X} = .32$]) than low-interest dyads (20.17, 36.58, and .14, respectively). None of the other main effects or interactions approached significance (see Table 3.2). Moreover, there were more unresolved conflicts (9) or fewer resolved conflicts (15) among nego-

TABLE 3.2

Analyses of Variance on Negotiation Time, Amount Allocated, and Symmetry of Resolution

Source	df	Negotiation Time		Amount Allocated		Symmetry of Resolution	
		MS	F	MS	F	MS	F
Interests (A)	1	242.55	5.96*	1,610.08	6.22*	.407	11.50**
Ideology (B)	1	14.08	1.00	30.08	<1	.025	<1
Sex (C)	1	61.58	1.51	36.75	<1	.010	<1
A x B	1	0.28	1.00	850.08	3.29	.095	2.71
A x C	1	57.86	1.42	310.08	1.20	.095	2.71
B x C	1	48.13	1.18	36.75	<1	.399	1.13
A x B x C	1	78.71	1.94	310.08	1.20	.010	<1
Within groups	40	40.67	-	258.75	-	.035	-
Total	47						

*p < .05
**p < .01

tiating dyads in the high-interest condition than in the low-interest condition (2 and 22, respectively).

Other findings from this experiment indicate that perceptions of the situation corresponded to the observed negotiating behavior. Negotiators in the high-conflict-of-interest condition viewed the conflict as more of a win-lose competition ($\bar{X} = 5.16$) than did those in the low-conflict-of-interest condition ($\bar{X} = 6.12$: F [1,40] = 7.33, p < .01). They were less willing to compromise ($\bar{X} = 2.93$) than were negotiators in the low-conflict-of-interest condition ($\bar{X} = 2.37$: F [2,40] = 5.91, p < .05), and they perceived compromise as being more like defeat ($\bar{X} = 3.95$) than did those in the low-conflict condition ($\bar{X} = 4.41$: F [1,40] = 5.60, p < .05). In ratings of the negotiating session, high-conflict dyads were less satisfied with the session ($\bar{X} = 2.81$) than were low-conflict dyads ($\bar{X} = 2.00$: F [1,40] = 6.55, p < .05). When asked to rate the general atmosphere of the session, high-conflict dyads viewed it as more emotional ($\bar{X} = 4.93$) and more idealistic ($\bar{X} = 3.47$) than did low-conflict dyads, who saw it as more rational ($\bar{X} = 5.75$) and practical ($\bar{X} = 2.35$) (p < .05 and p < .01, respectively). Moreover, they saw the negotiations as being more competitive ($\bar{X} = 4.27$), more hostile ($\bar{X} = 2.29$), and more futile ($\bar{X} = 4.91$) than did the negotiators in the low-conflict-of-interest condition, who viewed it as being more cooperative ($\bar{X} = 5.66$), more friendly ($\bar{X} = 1.60$), and more productive ($\bar{X} = 5.68$) (p < .01, p < .01, p < .05, respectively).

The observed correspondences between perceptions and behavior are bolstered by correlations among these types of variables: The more funds that were allocated, the more the session was perceived as a problem-solving debate instead of a win-lose competition (r = .68); the less compromise was perceived as defeat (r = .43); and the less important it was to come out favorably in the negotiations (r = .37). As the amount funded increased, the negotiators became more satisfied with the outcome (r = .32), felt the negotiations were more production (r = .37), more rational (r = .41), more friendly (r = .37), more calm (r = .30), and perceived the opponent as fair (r = .36), more compromising (r = .38), and more cooperative (r = .45). Finally, the more time spent in negotiating, the more important it was to come out favorably in the session (r = .65).

Taken together, these results clearly demonstrate the importance of interests in this political decision-making arena. The extent of the conflict of interest between negotiating opponents influenced their perceptions of the situation and their negotiating behavior. Negotiating behavior may have resulted from perceptions of the situation induced by the experimental manipulation: High-conflict-of-interest dyads had more trouble resolving their initial position differences *and* perceived the situation as more competitive, less productive, and so on.[5] These results appear to be rather conclusive, but are they generalizable to other political decision-making contexts where similar conflicts occur? Might the relative importance of the two sources vary with contextual factors, as was suggested by the coalition experiments discussed above? Pilot data, collected in a related series of experiments, suggest that this may be the case.

A conflict of interest was compared to a conflict over policy in a simulated conference convened to allocate funds to programs in the area of population control. The issue explored was: Which source of conflict is more difficult to resolve? The effects of the two types of conflict were assessed as each "policy-making" dyad attempted to resolve first one type and then the other. The policy/ideological conflict was between the "family planners" and the "social structuralists." Among the programs defended by the former was "birth control counseling," while the latter defended such programs as "manipulation of tax incentives." The interest conflict was between those who advocated administering funds through local agencies and those who preferred that federal agencies be responsible for their distribution. Vested interest in type of agency was created by having one negotiator represent a local agency while his opposite number represented a federal agency. The order of problem was made orthogonal to type of conflict: One group attempted to resolve the policy/ideology conflict first and then the funding problem; another group negotiated these problems in the reverse order.

In an analysis of time to resolution, the conflict type was highly significant (F [1,14] = 12.12, p < .001), with the conflict of interest being resolved more quickly than the conflict over policy/ideology. A significant conflict type x order of conflict interaction (F [1,14] = 4.93, p < .05) indicated that the conflict of interest was settled more quickly when it was negotiated as the first topic, while there was no difference in time to resolution for the policy conflict as a function of order. Moreover, when the policy conflict was negotiated first, less time was spent overall in negotiating both types of conflict. Supporting the behavioral results were the obtained differences in perceptions of the two types of conflict situations: The policy conflict was viewed as more competitive, more difficult to resolve, and as a more important source of conflict than the conflict of interest over funding. Even though the settings and tasks are not directly comparable, it is appropriate to speculate on reasons for the contrasting findings.

The differences obtained may be related to differences between the two contexts in the extent to which policy has been institutionalized. In the population area, policy issues are still in dispute, and successful programs have yet to be institutionalized. The public attention that has focused on these issues has made the diversity of opinion on the issues salient. Under these conditions it is likely that policy differences are a more important source of conflict than are vested interests. Interests have not yet crystallized, and are better defined in areas where policies have been established. One such area is that of prison services programs. Counseling and rehabilitation programs have been carried out by public-service and religious organizations for years. Thus, as is suggested by the data, conflicts are affected more by interests than they are by policy differences. Vested interests crystallize in an area where positions on policies are clear. Moreover, when policy differences are large, the resolution is more likely to be in favor of the more established policies. This is suggested by differences in the type of resolution achieved under the various conditions in the "prison services" simulation: Allocations were significantly more asymmetrical in favor of the counseling and rehabilitation policies in the high-policy-difference, low-interest condition than in the other three conditions.

While this interpretation is speculative, it does point us in the direction of an ecological model of conflict resolution (see also Krause and Druckman, 1973). Such a model would suggest that the relative importance of interests and policy or ideological differences varies with the policy-making arena under consideration. This is also the direction in which we are moving with the coalition experiments, where it was suggested that the distribution of weighting of ideology and interests varies with context. However, at this point we are merely proposing the framework and projecting the structure of a research program in which experiments are embedded within policy contexts. The substantive breakthroughs can be realized only as a result of linking systematic variation of contextual dimensions to observed attempts at resolving conflicts over resource allocation.

THE INTERACTION PROCESS: VALUES *AND* INTERESTS

The way in which values and interests interact in affecting the intensity of a conflict depends upon three factors: the salience of the link between the two sources of conflict, their relative intensity, and the relative importance, in terms of future significance, of each source. The experimentation completed to date has consisted of investigations of the first factor—the salience of the link between values and interests. The results of these experiments are summarized in this section, followed by an elucidation of refinements in the model based on this perspective.

Bilateral Negotiation Experiments

The situation that was simulated was a meeting of a city government-appointed committee that was commissioned to decide on the allocation of funds to programs that were designed to solve certain urban problems. The city had given the committee a budget of $8 million to spend on solving the problems. Subjects role-played the two committee co-chairmen, each representing a different faction of interest. One decision-maker represented a faction that preferred to divide the budget equally across four of the eight programs (e.g., a guaranteed annual income program), while his opposite number preferred to split the budget across the other four proposed solutions (e.g., a program of increased enforcement of fair-employment legislation). The initial conflict of interest was depicted as position differences on each of eight allocation scales ranging from $0 to $2 million.[6] The decision-makers were appointed to resolve this conflict. The simulation consisted of ten phases, including a session of orientation in the decision-making roles, pre-conference planning and caucusing, a decision-making conference with an announced deadline, and a postnegotiation session, during which questionnaires were completed (see Zechmeister and Druckman, 1973, for the details).

The first series of experiments was designed to explore the effects of making explicit the ideological differences underlying the conflicting positions defended by the co-chairmen/decision makers. In one condition, the contrasting set of programs derived directly from ideologies representing opposing views about the presumed source of social problems, as well as from assumptions concerning the impact and feasibility of social change. The decision makers were to represent the solutions that followed from statements of these ideologies. In the other condition, the contrasting sets of programs were derived from the same five-page statement of "neutral" background information. In this condition, decision makers did not represent explicit ideological orientations, and an attempt was made to take the focus off ideological differences as the source for the contrasting programs considered as alternative solutions to the problems identified by the city council.

It was hypothesized that the conflict would be more difficult to resolve through negotiation when the contrasting positions on resource allocation were linked explicitly to a value dissensus than when the relationship between interests and values remained implicit. The experiments confirmed the relationship and revealed the conditions under which it was especially likely to occur. In the first experiment, significant differences between the conditions were found in number of dyads reaching agreement, proportion of the dyads distributing the total budget, asymmetry of resolution, and perception of similarity in beliefs between self and opponent. Negotiating dyads in the "ideological link" condition displayed fewer resolutions, had fewer successes in distributing the entire budget, had more asymmetrical resolutions (i.e., deviations from a compromise solution), and perceived a larger discrepancy in beliefs between the opposing negotiators than did dyads in the "background information" condition (see Druckman and Zechmeister, 1970). Further experiments indicated the effects of some population and situational variables on responsiveness by negotiators to the manipulation.

The next experiment consisted of instituting real payoffs in addition to the simulated allocations that resulted from the agreed-upon decisions. Several types of real-payoff conditions were run, using both the "ideological-link" and the "background-information" scenarios. These included payoffs to ideological and nonideological organizations and payoffs to the decision-making participants themselves. Instituting payoffs had the effect of "washing out" the differences between conditions obtained when payoffs were simulated. Negotiators were "cooperative" in all conditions; those in the "ideological link" condition were as "cooperative" (i.e., resolved their differences as quickly) as those in the "background information" condition.

The two conditions were then replicated without real payoffs and with a larger sample of both males and females. The differences between the conditions obtained in the initial experiment were replicated for males but not for females. (That is, there was a condition x sex interaction.) Postnegotiation questions indicated greater involvement of the male negotiators in the simulation and suggested that, as a result of their involvement, they may have been more sensitive to the role requirements of an ideological representative than were the females (see Zechmeister and Druckman, 1973). However, additional experiments showed that female negotiators who took a more extreme position on the issues considered in the simulation responded to the manipulation in the same manner as the male negotiating dyads. In other words, the differences between the conditions were significant for those females who identified strongly with the ideological orientations from which the positions were derived—e.g., $\bar{X} = 6.07$ versus $\bar{X} = 7.67$: $t = 1.81$, $p < .05$, on amount allocated (see Druckman, 1971). Perhaps these females were more responsive to the role requirements of an ideological representative.

In summary, over all the experiments, it appears that real payoffs and sex affected a person's responsiveness to the condition variation. When payoffs were simulated, males responded in a way predicted by the hypotheses. (That is, the conflict was more difficult to resolve in the "ideological link" condition.) For females, the effect occurred only among those dyads who took a more extreme position with respect to the types of issues represented in the simulation. When payoffs were real, neither sex responded to the condition variation; instead, they appeared to be responding in the same way to the payoffs that were provided. Thus, as in the conclusion reached in the previous section, it can be stated that, by isolating the conditions (situations, contexts) under which a hypothesized relationship is confirmed, we move closer to an ecological model of conflict resolution. However, the particular type of relationship investigated in these experiments (i.e., the effect of a link between ideologies and interests on resolution attempts) is only one aspect of the *interaction perspective.* We turn now to an elaboration of other aspects of the framework.

Further Developments

The central proposition of this perspective is that the intensity of a conflict between parties is affected by the reciprocal relationship between the two components of the conflict—values (or ideologies) and interests. This is not simply a function of the salience of the link between these components. Other factors come into play. These include the relative intensity of the two components, their relative importance in terms of future significance, and changes in each of them through time and repeated interaction between the parties. Relative intensity determines the type of effect one component has upon the other; relative importance determines the direction of influence; and the salience of the link affects the strength of the relationship between the components of conflict. The way in which these factors operate in influencing the intensity of a conflict will now be described.

Direction and type of influence depend for their effects on the strength of the link between the components. The stronger the link, as when conflicting positions on resource allocation derive explicitly from a value dissensus (see above experiments), the more will relative importance and relative intensity influence the total intensity of the conflict. With respect to direction, when the two components are unequal in importance (e.g., future significance), the more important component (ideology or interests) has a greater impact. When the components are of equal significance, the "flow of influence" is the same (i.e., equally strong) in both directions. With respect to type, an initially high-intensity component (e.g., high conflict of interest, as defined in Love, 1975) will raise the level of intensity of the second component (e.g., moderate distance in ideologies, as in Love, 1975); an initially low-intensity component will lower the level of intensity of the second component. When both components are high (low) in intensity, the "bidirectional flow of influence" will increase (or further reduce) the intensity of both components and thus the total level of conflict intensity. (This is a comparison of the high-interest, high-ideology and low-interest, low-ideology cells in the Love [1975] experiment discussed in the previous section.) Zechmeister (1976) draws upon examples from a variety of social contexts to illustrate the operation of this process as it occurs in situ.

The effects on conflict of relative importance and relative intensity of components are reduced when the link between the components is weak (e.g., as in the "background information" condition of the experiments reviewed above). The weaker the link, the closer the model comes to resembling a balancing process where components are orthogonal. When the components are orthogonal, such reciprocal influences as direction and type are precluded. Under these conditions, a simple averaging of component intensity will yield an estimate of the intensity of the total conflict. Such estimates will differ from those based on an interaction model. This is illustrated in Figure 3.2. It can be seen that the averaging model predicts a higher-intensity conflict under "low/low" and "low/high" conditions, while the interaction model predicts a higher-intensity conflict under "high/low" and "high/high" conditions. There are actually only three points for the averaging model—low, medium, and high. Orthogonal components render the "low/high" and "high/low" conditions irrelevant. Interacting components, on the other hand, make this distinction important. When one component is of greater significance than the other, the level of intensity of that component will serve either to moderate ("low/high") or to enhance ("high/low") the intensity of the total conflict. The result is a difference in predicted intensity of total conflict, as is

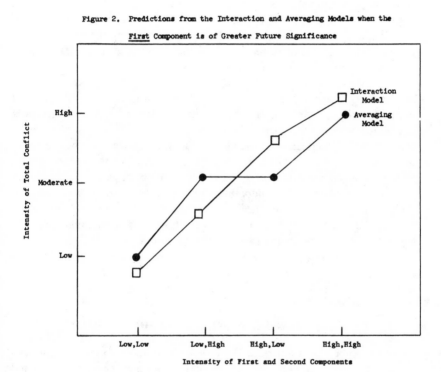

Figure 2. Predictions from the Interaction and Averaging Models when the First Component is of Greater Future Significance

Figure 3.2. Predictions from the Interaction and Averaging Models when the First Component is of Greater Future Significance

illustrated in Figure 3.2. Empirical tests of these competing predictions, derived from the alternative models, have yet to be made.

The preceding discussion has highlighted the relationship between the reciprocal effects of two components (or sources) of conflict and the intensity of the conflict at one point in time. As depicted, the model is *static:* The experiments were cross-sectional condition comparisons of an "explicit link" versus "no link," and the criterion variable in Figure 3.2 is the *initial* intensity of the conflict. However, the presentation was intended to be illustrative rather than definitive. It is a first step in unraveling the components of a complex process that may impede attempts to resolve a conflict through negotiations. A further development will entail extending the description to an elucidation of the *dynamics* of the process. Some progress has already been made toward such specification.

The interrelated set of propositions presented by Druckman and Zechmeister (1973) are a "first cut" on the dynamics of the interplay between sources of conflict. In that treatment, changes, through time and repeated interaction between the parties, in the intensity of a conflict were related to changes in the polarization of the ideological differences and to the operation of mediational mechanisms built into the situation. The mediational mechanisms served to moderate the spiral of increasing polarization as the parties repeatedly contested their competing interests. Such a process was viewed in terms of countervailing influences on the intensity of a conflict. However, as is suggested in this section, this process effects changes in the intensity of the conflict by (a) strengthening (weakening) the *link* between the components, (b) changing the relative *importance* of the components, and (c) changing the relative *intensity* of the components. Further specification of the way in which this occurs awaits development of the dynamic aspects of the model.

SUMMARY AND CONCLUSION

This chapter has summarized the progress to date of a series of investigations designed to explore the effects of the interplay between values and interests on decision-making and conflict resolution. Two perspectives on this interplay have given rise to alternative experimental paradigms. One paradigm is based on the notion that actors, in the process of decision-making, balance their interests against their values. The empirical question of concern is: Which are assigned greater weight, interests or values? This issue was explored in two types of simulated political decision-making situations: multilateral negotiations, involving coalition formation, and bilateral negotiations. In both of these settings, actors were to decide on an allocation of resources to alternative programs. The second paradigm is based on the notion that the two sources of conflict interact, the one deriving from and influencing the other in a reciprocal manner. The empirical question of interest is: How does the reciprocal relationship between interests and values affect the intensity of a conflict? The reciprocal relationship includes three factors: the salience of the link between the two sources of conflict, the relative intensity of the two sources, and their relative importance. To date, only the effects of the salience of the link between the sources of conflict have been investigated. The setting was a simulated bilateral negotiation between members of a city government-appointed committee.

The work on the balancing perspective has produced several compelling results. Of particular interest are the findings that suggest that the relative importance of interests and values varies with context. That most actors assign these factors an equal weight may be a finding that applies only to the interdenominational setting simulated for the coalition experiments reported above. It was speculated in this chapter and elsewhere (e.g., Krause et al., 1975) that a distribution in which interests are more important than values may obtain in a legislative setting, while a distribution that is even more skewed in the direction of interests, reflecting a disregard for ideological positions, would obtain in an international context. These hypotheses have yet to be explored. Less speculative, however, are the relative effects of the two sources of conflict on attempts to reach decisions in bilateral negotiations. The results of the experiments summarized above indicated clearly that interests were more important than ideology in the prison services negotiations, while the reverse occurred in the population policy negotiations. Further experimentation along these lines is planned as we move toward a clarification of the contextual determinants of decision-making behavior.

The work on the interaction perspective has concentrated primarily on an elaboration of the process. The effort expended on this task was necessitated by the complexity of the formulation. The nature of this formulation requires more work on the descriptive phase of theory development than that required by the less-complex balancing perspective. But this effort has been intertwined with the development of an appropriate experimental paradigm. The paradigm has been used to test hypotheses (which are derived from the perspective) on the effects of making salient the link between the sources of conflict. Now that additional factors have been identified, the experimental work can proceed to test systematically the effects of variations in these aspects. Moreover, the competing predictions of the averaging and interaction models can be arbitrated. The outcome of such a test will inform us of the extent to which the added complexity of the interaction model increases (or decreases) predictability.

NOTES

1. In all of the experiments reported in this chapter, participants were assigned roles on the basis of attitudes expressed on a questionnaire administered prior to the time when the experiment was conducted. Assigned roles were coincident with expressed attitudes. Session times were arranged with the selected respondents by phone.

2. There has been progress toward making such a comparison. A recently designed experiment compared a simulated interdenominational and a simulated legislative condition. Selected dimensions of difference between the two contexts (e.g., money versus votes) were varied, and coalitional outcomes were observed. In the first experiment that has been completed, the two conditions were compared on investment behavior. As expected, there were more votes invested in legislative coalitions than money invested in interdenominational coalitions ($\bar{X}$ = 8.16 versus $\bar{X}$ = 3.43: p < .001, using standardized metrics in order to compare votes and money). Moreover, individual investments relative to the total amount invested were higher in the legislative condition than in the interdenominational condition ($\bar{X}$ = 2.86 versus $\bar{X}$ = 2.51: p < .025, using a standardized ratio). These results confirmed the hypothesis relating the manipulated dimensions of differences between the conditions to investment behavior. Other dimensions of difference between the contexts must be considered if we are to construct more elaborate models. Such elaboration is essential for a comparison of the distribution of theta between the two systems.

3. The *net* increment is the difference between the increments in variance explained (R^2) when a variable (e.g. "process") is entered first and when it is entered second, following the other variable it is being compared with (e.g., "objective" parameters) in a stepwise regression analysis.

4. The distribution of theta was not determined for the minister sample. This was due to a relatively small number of runs and the nonsignificant increment in variance accounted for by this variable.

5. The results of an even more recent experiment suggest that the effects obtained for the conflict-of-interest variable may depend on the *extent* of representational pressures on the decision-maker. In that study, the conflict-of-interest variable was significant when representational pressures were high (as was also the case in the Love experiment discussed above): High conflict-of-interest dyads had more trouble resolving their differences than low conflict dyads. The differences between the conditions under low representational pressures were nonsignificant. Interestingly, however, the ideological conflict variable was significant when representational pressures were low: High conflict-of-ideology dyads had more trouble resolving their differences than did low conflict dyads. Put another way, opposing decision-makers were more responsive to their differences in ideology when they were not accountable directly to a group or constituency. One implication of these findings is that representational pressures mediate the effects obtained for "type of conflict." The extent to which these effects vary with other situational and contextual factors is currently being explored.

6. This procedure was used in most of the experiments reported in this section. However, the number of issues and length of issue scales varied somewhat from one series of experiments to another depending upon the purpose of the experiment. For example, in the Zechmeister and Druckman (1973) study, four issue scales, ranging from $0 to $4 million (in intervals of one-half million), were used. In the Love (1975) experiment, reported above, four issue scales ranging from $0 to $20 thousand (see Figure 3.1) were used.

REFERENCES

AXELROD, R. (1970) Conflict of Interest: A Theory of Divergent Goals with Applications to Politics. Chicago: Markham.

CLEMENS, W. C. (1973) The Superpowers and Arms Control. Lexington, Mass.: D. C. Heath.

COHEN, J. (1968) "Multiple regression as a general data-analytic system." Psych. Bull. 70: 426-443.

COSER, L. (1956) The Functions of Social Conflict. New York: Free Press.

DRUCKMAN, D. (1971) "Understanding the operation of complex social systems: Some uses of simulation design." Simulation and Games 2: 173-195.

——— and T. V. BONOMA (1976) "A conflict resolution workshop for health service-delivery professionals: Design and appraisal." International J. of Group Tensions.

DRUCKMAN, D. and K. ZECHMEISTER (1973) "Conflict of interest and value dissensus: Propositions in the sociology of conflict." Human Relations 26: 449-466.

——— (1970) "Conflict of interest and value dissensus." Human Relations 23: 431-438.

DRUCKMAN, D., D. SOLOMON, and K. ZECHMEISTER (1972) "Effects of representational role obligations on the process of children's distribution of resources." Sociometry 35: 387-410.

DRUCKMAN, D., R. ROZELLE, R. KRAUSE, and R. MAHONEY (1974) "Power and utilities in a simulated interreligious council: A situational approach to interparty decision-making," in J. Tedeschi (ed.) Perspectives on Social Power. Chicago: Aldine.

KRAUSE, R. M. and D. DRUCKMAN (1973) "Toward an ecological generality model of conflict." Presented at the meetings of the Peace Science Society, Lake Cumberland, Kentucky, April 18-21.

KRAUSE, R. M., D. DRUCKMAN, R. ROZZELLE, and R. MAHONEY (1975) "Components of value and representation in coalition formation." J. of Peace Science 1: 141-158.

LALL, A. (1966) Modern International Negotiation: Principles and Practice. New York: Columbia Univ. Press.

LEISERSON, M. A. (1970) "Power and ideology in coalition behavior: An experimental study," in S. Groennings et al. (eds.) The Study of Coalition Behavior. New York: Holt.

LOVE, R. (1975) "Resolving conflicts of interest and ideologies: A simulation of political decision-making in an interreligious council." Unpublished doctoral dissertation, University of Houston.

MAHONEY, R. and D. DRUCKMAN (1975) "Simulation, experimentation, and context: Dimensions of design and inference." Simulation and Games 6: 235-270.

NAYAK, S. (1973) "An analytical model of hegemonical tension among Ghanaian elites," in D. Sidjanski (ed.) Political Decision-Making Processes: Studies in National, Comparative and International Politics. San Francisco: Jossey-Bass.

RAPOPORT, A. (1964) Strategy and Conscience. New York: Harper & Row.

SNOW, C. P. (1959) The Two Cultures and the Scientific Revolution. Cambridge: Cambridge University Press.

VAN DOORN, J. A. A. (1966) "Conflict in formal organizations," in CIBA Foundation, A. de Reuck and J. Knight (eds.) Conflict in Society. London: Churchill.

YOUNG, K. T. (1968) Negotiating with the Chinese Communists: The United States Experience, 1953-1967. New York: McGraw-Hill.

ZECHMEISTER, K. (1976) "Conflict of interest and value dissensus: Further developments toward a theory." Unpublished.

——— and D. DRUCKMAN (1973) "Determinants of resolving a conflict of interest: A simulation of political decision-making." J. of Conflict Resolution 17: 63-88.

PART II

PROCESSES, STRATEGIES, AND OUTCOMES

EDITOR'S INTRODUCTION

How should the negotiation process be construed? What type of model captures the reality of most negotiations? There is disagreement on the answers to these questions. For some, negotiation consists primarily of offer-counteroffer bargaining. For others, it is primarily a persuasive debate. And still others conceive the process as a problem-solving forum where parties engage in a joint search for solutions. These conceptions were referred to earlier as alternative "cuts" on negotiation. The different cuts imply different types of models. Each model is a structure within which a particular process—bargaining, debating, or problem-solving—unfolds. These alternative structures and processes are represented by the chapters in this section.

Whether considered as an aspect *of negotiation or as the* essence *of negotiation, one's preferred "cut" determines his strategy for investigation. Hamner and Yukl survey the large literature on bargaining to ascertain which of various concession-making strategies is likely to be most effective in eliciting concessions from an opponent. While their search did not produce a "most effective strategy," it did highlight important variables and new approaches to the bargaining problem. The Pruitt and Lewis chapter broadens the traditional conceptualization of bargaining by considering a process that combines elements of persuasion and problem-solving. The authors demonstrate how a "proper mix" of these elements can lead to mutually desirable outcomes. Their notion of flexible rigidity is a prescription for negotiators who aspire to integrative solutions to the bargaining problem.*

The Walcott et al. chapter focuses exclusively on the rhetorical aspects of negotiation. To these investigators, the negotiation process is primarily one of debate. Like Pruitt and Lewis, they view debate as an activity that combines the processes of persuasion and problem-solving: Their content-analysis categories reflect both of these processes. However, unlike that of Pruitt and Lewis, their analysis does not include a concession-making (or bargaining) dynamic. Finally, Tedeschi and Bonoma offer a framework for conceptualizing a relatively neglected aspect of negotiation. Their treatment of the effects of coercive tactics is suggestive. Their conclusions could alert negotiators to the circumstances under which such tactics may be effective. The risk inherent in the use of these tactics renders useful a taxonomy that could distinguish between appropriate and inappropriate conditions.

A prevalent emphasis in this section is the mixed-motive dilemma of negotiation. This dilemma makes difficult an attempt to separate cooperative from competitive goals or behaviors. The two forms of activity are intertwined in the process of negotiating. Tough bargaining postures must be tempered by concessions if an agreement is to be attained. Problem-solving and persuasive debate are implied in the rhetoric of negotiators, just as problem-solving and win-lose orientations are coterminous goals. And negotiations are a blend of cautious diplomacy and aggressive acts: The success of a deliberation may depend on the balance achieved between these postures. The search for integrative solutions is one approach to resolving the dilemma. The Pruitt and Lewis research program has identified strategies that could lead to such outcomes.

Chapter 4

THE EFFECTIVENESS OF DIFFERENT
OFFER STRATEGIES IN BARGAINING

W. CLAY HAMNER

Graduate School of Management
Boston University

GARY A. YUKL

Baruch College, City University of New York

> *"A Belgian banker's private size-up of U.S. Treasury Secretary John B. Connally as a bargainer on international monetary problems: 'He does not seem to realize that to succeed in these matters you must be extremely frank and that there must be concessions from both sides. Negotiation needs a spirit of compromise. I haven't seen much sign of that.' "*
>
> U.S. News & World Report *(Dec. 6, 1971, p. 3)*

> *"Diplomats use a standard jargon to describe high level discussions between heads of state. As a guide to better understanding of diplomatic terms, we offer these definitions:*
> *'Useful'—No progress, but we learned where the other side stands, and that could prove fruitful.*
> *'Fruitful'—This round was deadlocked, but the next could be productive.*
> *'Productive'—Still no agreement, but we are proceeding in an atmosphere that is frank and open.*
> *'Frank and open'—Complete and total disagreement, but something meaningful may come of it.*
> *'Meaningful'—Everybody enjoyed the tour of the museum."*
>
> Copley News Service, Readers Digest,
> *(October, 1975, p. 82)*

INTRODUCTION

What is bargaining? The occurrence of international strife, labor-management conflict, and fights for social and sexual equality have led in recent years to increased study of conflict resolution processes. Social scientists are interested in studying these processes as they relate to the behavior of people, since the timely management of conflict has important consequences for organizational effectiveness and individual success. While there are many approaches to handling conflict (e.g., assigning the conflict to a panel of judges, forming a coalition, taking conflict to court, withdrawing from the situation, etc.), settlements of disagreements between parties usually involve some sort of bargaining, whether implicit or explicit. The process of bargaining can be defined as interaction that occurs when two or more persons attempt to agree on a mutually acceptable outcome in a situation where their orders of preference for possible outcomes are negatively correlated. In this negotiation situation, a number of proposed settlements of the mixed-motive conflict can be offered so that both sides will have the possibility of improving their outcomes if an agreement can be reached. The conflict involves one or more issues, and each issue can be settled in one of two or more ways ("settlement positions").

Since interpersonal bargaining is a common method of resolving conflict, it is receiving greater emphasis in the research of behavioral scientists who are interested in conflict in various environments. The most prevalent concern in bargaining research has been to identify the factors that determine: (1) whether an agreement will be reached, (2) the amount of time required to reach an agreement, (3) the nature of the agreement, and (4) the degree of satisfaction with the agreement and the commitment to carry it out. The purpose of this chapter is to examine the research evidence presented by those behavioral scientists in an attempt to determine to what extent and under what conditions various strategies and tactics affect bargaining outcomes.

BARGAINING TACTICS AND BARGAINING STRATEGIES

A *bargaining tactic* can be defined as a position to be taken or a maneuver to be made at a specific point in the bargaining process. A *bargaining strategy*, on the other hand, consists of a series of bargaining tactics to be used throughout the bargaining process. It implies a commitment to a long-range position to be taken with the bargaining opponent from initial contact.

Bargaining Tactics

Since most of the tactics that have been researched are components of one or more of the bargaining strategies discussed below, a brief description of possible tactics for use in a negotiation session will suffice here. One frequently used tactic is to open with an extreme or hard initial offer (IO). Supposedly, this tactic indicates to the bargaining opponent that you are not going to retreat from your position easily and that therefore he or she should not expect or aspire to get the better of you in the exchange. By shifting his or her aspiration level to a personally less favorable position, the bargaining opponent is thus more likely to concede more than he or she had originally expected. For example, assume that you are trying to buy a used car from a friend. He knows he can sell the car to a used car dealer for $1,000, and you know you can buy the same car from the dealer for $2,000. Your friends tell you he will sell the car to you for $1,800. The bargaining range has shifted by $200 from $1,000-to-$2,000 to $1,000-to-$1,800. It is now up to you to make a counteroffer. You decide to be tough and offer him $1,000, thus giving a $0 concession in response to his $200 concession and causing the midpoint or even split position to shift from $1,500 to $1,400, a $100 advantage to you. Since there seems to be a norm of "meeting in the middle" in most "equal-power" or peer bargaining situations, your tactic has violated this norm, and thus the seller is forced to shift his goal from $1,500 to $1,400.

Following from this same reasoning, a second tactic that should give you an advantage over your opponent is to make *relatively small subsequent concessions.* Many would argue that a bargainer has two overriding goals: first to reach an agreement and second to obtain equal or better outcomes than the bargaining opponent. It is obvious that if one is to meet the first objective, he or she should make concessions when offered a concession. The norm of reciprocity in exchange explains this principal. However, if one is to meet the second objective, the bargainer must make the size of his or her average concession equal to or less than that offered by the opponent. Nevertheless, it should be evident that the opponent has the option of refusing to reach an agreement rather than reach an inequitable agreement.

A third tactic, which is very similar to the size-of-concession tactic, deals with the *frequency and rate of concessions* made. One position for reaching an agreement is to make a few large concessions over the bargaining period. A second position would be to make many small concessions. Both these positions, dealing with the frequency and rate of concessions, will be elaborated when bargaining strategies are discussed.

A fourth tactic deals with the terminating or *last-clear-chance offer.* The last-clear-chance offer tactic was first described by Schelling (1960), who stated that at some point in bargaining a "final" offer should be made. The person who decides to, or is forced to, make this offer should have the advantage since he or she leaves the opponent with the responsibility of either accepting the last (and often less advantageous) offer or refusing to reach an agreement and making no profit on the deal. In the above example, assume that the buyer had responded to the seller's $1,400 offer (which was made after a series of other offers) by saying that he would under no circumstances pay more than $1,320 for the car and that the seller could take it or leave it. This forces the seller to decide whether he will forfeit a $320 profit and have an additional $40 loss (the midpoint between $1,400 and $1,320, which was arrived at after a series of $100 concessions by the seller and was followed by counteroffers of $80 by the buyer) or whether he will accept the offer knowing that the buyer is making a $680 profit ($1,320 from the seller versus $2,000 from the dealer). Most people, it is assumed, would not refuse to accept the $320 profit, but as we will see when we examine the research, this assumption may not always hold.

General Offer Strategies

This section of the chapter will present four major theories dealing with strategies of concession-making. The four strategies reviewed are: (1) Siegel and Fouraker's (1960) "tough" strategy, (2) Bartos (1967) and Komorita's (1972) "moderately tough" or "intermediate" strategy, (3) Osgood's (1962) "soft" strategy, and (4) Schelling's (1960) "fair" strategy. Each of these strategies can involve a series of tactics to be used against the bargaining opponent, including those discussed below.

It is important to examine strategies of bargaining since one of the key problems facing a bargainer in a conflict situation is deciding what type of concession-making strategy is most effective. For instance, is it better to concede less often or more often than your opponent? Making many concessions can be effective in the sense that it may lead to agreement sooner and may reduce tension. However, such an agreement may be disadvantageous in terms of the payoff to the party who makes more concessions. Therefore, the dilemma facing a bargainer is whether to risk not reaching an agreement at all in order to reach an advantageous agreement.

Two of the theories that deal with general offer strategies—the Siegel and Fouraker (1960) tough or "level of aspiration" model and the Osgood (1962) soft or "graduated reciprocation in tension reduction" model—make apparently contradictory predictions about what type of concession-making strategy is most effective. Osgood (1962) describes his concession-making model in terms of an arms race—a series of reciprocal initiatives in which each side alternatively contributes to international "tension" and distrust. His suggestion for a solution to this kind of situation is for an "arms race in reverse," with each side alternatively taking tension-reducing initiatives. To produce such a reversal, it is necessary for one side to adopt a policy he called *graduated reciprocation in tension reduction.*

Osgood's model suggests the following guidelines:

(1) Unilateral initiatives must not reduce the capacity to inflict retaliation on an opponent.

(2) Unilateral initiatives must be graduated in risk according to the degree of reciprocation obtained from the opponent.

(3) Unilateral initiatives should expect and invite reciprocation in some form.

(4) Unilateral initiatives must be continued over a considerable period.

Osgood implies that his soft-strategy proposal is valid when (1) the two parties have equal power, (2) the parties are stalemated or moving away from a range of acceptable solutions (high-initial-position tactic), and (3) the two parties are facing mutually applied high pressure to reach agreement. He says that in this situation one side should initiate concessions, each of which is small (many small concession tactic). Osgood's reasoning is that a bargainer will fail to make concessions because he distrusts his opponents. A person who makes unilateral concessions will thereby remove the main obstacle to his opponent's concession-making.

Siegel and Fouraker (1960), on the other hand, argue that a bargainer should make a concession only if his opponent makes no concession. If he experiences success—i.e., his opponent makes a generous offer—a bargainer should not make a concession. This reasoning is based on the changing level of aspiration of the bargainer where it is assumed that success will raise one's level of aspiration and failure will lower it. Therefore, the demands a bargainer makes reflect his level of aspiration. The implication, then, is that a bargainer who wants to maximize his own payoff should make few, if any, concessions when his opponent is conceding (the few small concessions tactic).

Siegel and Fouraker describe a typical pattern of bargaining as one where a bargainer opens negotiations at a high level, usually his highest level of expectancy (the high-initial-position tactic). The bargainer soon learns, from his rival's early bids, that it will probably be necessary for him to make concessions before agreement can be reached. According to the Siegel and Fouraker model, as negotiations progress, the successive bids seem (1) to give experience to the bargainer, enabling him to establish a realistic level of aspiration and (2) also to enable the bargainer to find means by which concessions can be made to the opponent without making offers below his aspiration level. Aspiration levels should be modified as bargaining continues, although bargainers are assumed to begin the bargaining with an a priori minimum level of expectancy. If his opponent makes no concessions, then Siegel and Fouraker suggest that a bargainer should make concessions, until his level of aspiration approaches, or coincides with, his minimum expectancy. On the other hand, if a bargainer's rival is making discernible concessions, the bargainer should modify the maximum concession he is willing to make and raise his level of aspiration to a higher, more advantageous level.

For success in bargaining, therefore, Siegel and Fouraker recommend that a bargainer should follow the "toughness" principle, which was first presented by Fellner (1949). This principle suggests that a bargainer who wants to make a relatively higher payoff than his opponent should (a) open the negotiation with a high request, (b) have a small rate of concession, (c) have a high minimum level of expectation, and (d) be unyielding.

It thus appears that both of these theories recommend that once his opponent is no longer making concessions (a stalemate), a bargainer must begin making concessions. Both theories also imply that bargainers should start high in the initial stages of bargaining in order to allow the other bargainers room to make concessions. The basic differences between the two models are in (1) the motive for concession-making (agreement versus winning), and (2) the prediction of the rival's reaction to the bargainer's concession.

For Siegel and Fouraker (1960: 2) the motive of the bargainer is to "maximize his personal total profit," i.e., to win. Siegel and Fouraker predict that concessions in general will not be reciprocated but rather will raise the level of aspiration of the opponent and increase his demands. Osgood, on the other hand, views concession-making as a method for gaining trust and inviting reciprocity so that equality can be maintained (i.e., to reach a mutually satisfactory agreement).

The Siegel and Fouraker models and the Osgood model represent extreme bargaining positions concerning concession-making strategies. Several additional strategies have also gained some prominence. Komorita (1972) and Bartos (1967) both follow the basic assumption that it pays to be tough in bargaining, but there is a limit to this principle. They suggest that a position somewhere between a tough and a soft approach may prove to be an optimal strategy in terms of the payoff it produces. A *moderately tough* strategy, they contend, will induce opponent concessions and at the same time decrease the chances of not reaching an agreement.

Schelling (1960), on the other hand, suggests that bargainers often perceive that a certain "prominent" settlement would be *fair* to both parties. In the case of symmetrical payoff tables, the fair solution is a 50-50 split, the midpoint of the payoff table. From the viewpoint of equity theory (Adams, 1965), bargainers should readily agree once the prominent or fair solution is identified. The bargainer, in following the fair strategy, should not attempt to "bluff" his opponent but instead should propose a settlement at the point where the prominent solution is reached. If communication is allowed, the bargainer should point out the fact that this is the equitable solution and stay at this point until agreement is reached.

Pruitt (1972) points out that, unfortunately, there are many different standards of fairness and equity, and wishful thinking is fully capable of determining which standard an individual chooses. Hence, bargainers often disagree about which alternatives are fair and equitable, and they may spend considerable time and energy debating the matter. In a more recent article, Pruitt (1974) noted that, when there is disagreement about the nature of a fair solution, bargainers are often tempted to use pressure tactics in order to force the other party to accept an alternative he considers unfair, and that the relationship may thus be impaired.

It appears, therefore, that there is considerable disagreement about which strategy will be most effective in reaching mutually acceptable outcomes over a long period of time. Before we examine the research evidence on offer tactics and strategies, let us examine the general approaches used by researchers for studying offer effects in bargaining.

GENERAL APPROACHES FOR STUDYING BARGAINING STRATEGIES

The conflict simulations used most often to study the effectiveness of bargaining strategies have been bargaining games and matrix games. There are several types of bargaining games, including: (1) bilateral monopoly, (2) buyer-seller games, (3) "pure-issue" bargaining games, and (4) reward allocation decisions.

Bilateral monopoly games simulate the economic relationship between a single seller and a single buyer who are trying to agree on the price and quantity of a commodity. In *buyer-seller* games, only the price must be negotiated, and the market is usually not limited to a single buyer or seller. In *pure-issue* bargaining games, there is a conflict of interest on one or more issues, but the nature of the conflict and the issue content are not usually specified, only the possible settlements and their respective payoffs. In *reward-allocation* games, there is a fixed amount of some scarce resource (usually money), and the bargainers try to agree on how to allocate this resource among the parties.

Some studies have used bargaining simulations with a programmed opponent instead of a real opponent. That is, the offers and comments of one bargainer were predetermined by the experimenters without the other bargainer's knowledge in order to manipulate some independent variable, such as the opponent's offer strategy. This approach permits better inferences regarding causal relationships than does correlational analysis of the behavior of two real negotiators. However, a number of important phenomena, such as the mutual influence of the parties over time, the probability that they will reach an agreement, and the duration of negotiations, usually cannot be investigated with programmed opponents. In some of these studies, the programmed opponent's offers have been contingent upon the subject's offers, while in other studies a noncontingent-offer strategy has been used by the programmed opponent. When a contingent-offer strategy is used, the programmed opponent makes a concession only after each subject concession, and the magnitude of the opponent's concession is a predetermined percentage of the subject's concession (e.g., 50 percent, 100 percent). In a few cases this percentage has been systematically increased or decreased during the negotiation session, but usually the percentage remains constant throughout the negotiations. In studies in which a noncontingent strategy is used by the programmed opponent, a predetermined schedule of offers is made, regardless of the subject's offers and concessions.

In studies without programmed opponents, one of three approaches is generally used to analyze the effects of different offer strategies. The first approach is to correlate the mean level of payoff demanded, or the mean offer made by each negotiator, with the negotiator's actual payoff from the settlement. A second approach is to correlate the mean demand or mean offer of one negotiator with the corresponding index for his opponent, across pairs of negotiators. The third approach is to classify the offers of one negotiator in terms of some set of strategy categories and then test for differences among categories in the opponent's final offer, concession magnitude, payoff from the settlement, etc.

Unlike negotiation games, matrix games such as the Prisoner's Dilemma game do not involve an explicit exchange of offers. Instead, each player must choose either a cooperative (C) or an uncooperative (UC) option. A player is usually provided with information about the payoffs that will result for each combination of choices by himself and the opponent (e.g., C-C, C-UC, UC-C, UC-UC), but the player will not know for certain whether the opponent will choose a cooperative or an uncooperative option. On each trial of a matrix game, the two players usually make their choices simultaneously, and the resulting outcome is then announced. The game can be repeated for as many trials as desired to study how a player's choice behavior has been influenced by the opponent's behavior during previous trials. When a programmed opponent is used, the choices made by the opponent are predetermined by the experimenter, although the subject is usually led to believe he is playing against another subject.

Summary

In this section, we have noted the difference between a bargaining tactic (i.e., a position or maneuver to be taken at a specific point in the bargaining process) and a bargaining strategy (a planned series of bargaining tactics). Four bargaining tactics were discussed, including the size of the first offer (opening bid), the size of concessions made, the frequency of concessions, and the rate at which they are made, and the final offer maneuver (last-clear-chance offer). Combinations of these four tactics are found in the basic bargaining strategies discussed. The strategies examined here include (1) Siegel and Fouraker's (1960) "tough" strategy, (2) Bartos' (1967) and Komorita's (1972) "moderately tough" strategy, (3) Osgood's (1962) "soft" strategy, and (4) Schelling's (1960) "fair" strategy. As is implied by the names, each of these strategies recommends different approaches to successful bargaining. We will now examine the research evidence generated from various bargaining paradigms (i.e., bargaining games and matrix games) in order to see under what circumstances these various strategy recommendations are successful.

RESEARCH EVIDENCE FROM STUDIES USING NEGOTIATION GAMES

The review of research using bargaining games will be divided into studies with real opponents, studies with programmed opponents using non-contingent strategies, and studies with programmed opponents using contingent offer strategies.

Studies with Real Opponents

A substantial number of studies without programmed opponents have been conducted by Bartos (1966, 1967, 1970). For most of his studies, he found a significant negative correlation between one negotiator's mean demand and the opponent's mean demand, as well as a significant positive correlation between a negotiator's mean demand and his profits. The magnitude of the correlation between own and opponent's mean demand in some of these studies was small. This may have been due to the fact that there were five parties to the negotiations, which could have diluted the effects of each negotiator's offers on those of the other negotiators. Even in the experiments with only two parties, the correlation between a negotiator's mean demand and his profits was significant only for the "abstract" experiments, in which subjects did not know the opponent's priorities and could not infer them from the nature of the simulation. When the relationship between toughness and profit for all of his studies was plotted, Bartos (1970) found it to be curvilinear, with a moderately tough offer strategy being as effective as a very tough offer strategy. Apparently, as a negotiator's toughness increased, he obtained greater concessions from the other negotiator, but fewer agreements occurred. Since deadlocks resulted in zero profit, more than a moderate degree of toughness failed to produce any increase in the mean level of profits.

In his studies, Bartos (1970: 14) obtained support for both the Osgood and the Siegel and Fouraker theories: "We are thus drawn to the conclusion that, in our negotiations, the subjects tended to respond to high offers by making high demands, while at the same time reciprocating concession by concession." However, those who made large concessions tended to obtain somewhat lower payoffs than did negotiators who made small concessions. "Concession-making helps as well as hinders obtaining high payoff; in our experiments, the hindrance was somewhat larger than the help" (1970: 19).

Bartos summarizes his research by saying that the bargainer who wishes to make a higher-than-average payoff is well advised to make fewer concessions than his opponent, but that one should avoid being extremely uncooperative because, by so doing, the bargainer drastically reduces his chances of reaching an agreement. He seems to be making an argument for a "moderately" tough strategy. He argues, as does Osgood, that the negotiator must consider the future payoffs as well as the present one. Such a position is well stated by Morgan and Sawyer (1967: 40), who suggest that "wise persons, however, do not treat every encounter like a used-car transaction where they never expect to see others again; friends, instead, also take care that the other obtains an outcome sufficiently rewarding so that he is willing to interact again."

Hinton et al. (1974) conducted a study in which the subjects bargained many times with the same opponent in order to simulate a continuing relationship between the parties, as in the case of collective bargaining between a labor union and management. The zero-order correlations indicated a significant positive relationship between a negotiator's concession rate and his profit, but profit was not related to the hardness of the negotiator's initial offer. Since initial offer and concession rate were highly confounded ($r = .97$), the authors used partial correlations in an attempt to separate the effects of the two offer parameters. The partial correlation in both cases was significant, but low ($r = .17$), and the authors interpreted their results as indicating that a negotiator should make either a soft initial offer or large concessions in a situation where there is a continuing relationship between parties.

Harnett et al. (1973) classified their subjects into four strategy categories according to the subject offers during the first half of the negotiations: "tough strategy" (hard IO and infrequent small or moderate concessions), "intermediate strategy" (moderate IO and moderate concessions), and "soft strategy" (soft IO or early concession to a fair offer with small or no concessions thereafter). Bargainers using the tough strategy earned the largest profit, and negotiators using the fair strategy earned the smallest profit. The soft and intermediate strategies were equivalent, and were intermediate in effectiveness. A zero-order correlational analysis was also made for separate offer tactics. A negotiator's profit was positively correlated with his initial offer and negatively correlated with the size of his concessions, but it was not significantly correlated with the frequency of his concessions. However, since these three offer parameters were not independent, a stepwise multiple regression was conducted to estimate their unique effects, and concession magnitude was found to account for most of the variance in the bargainers' profits. A comparison of the effects of making a few large concessions or many small concessions revealed no significant difference in the bargainer's profit. Bargainers in the fair and intermediate strategy conditions took less time to reach a settlement than did negotiators in the soft and hard strategy conditions. Surprisingly, the latter two conditions were nearly equal in duration of negotiations.

In a study by Starbuck and Grant (1971), an offer parameter called "negotiator commitment" was used. Commitment was defined as the average deviation of a negotiator's offers from the settlement finally reached. In the first experiment, the correlation between commitment and settlement price was positive and significant for the sellers (who made the first bid) but was not significant for the buyers. In the second experiment, where the seller had the advantage of being able to make a last-chance offer, as well as the first bid, commitment was not significantly correlated with the settlement price for either party.

Studies on Noncontingent Offers by a Programmed Opponent

Hardness of initial offer. Three studies have investigated the effects of the opponent's initial offer when manipulated independently of any other offer tactic. Chertkoff and Conley (1967) found that the final subject offer or settlement was more favorable to the opponent when the opponent's initial offer was hard than when it was soft, but there was no significant difference in the subject's initial offer, concession magnitude, or concession frequency. Yukl (1974b) found that subjects made a more favorable initial offer and a more favorable final offer when the programmed opponent's initial offer was hard than when it was soft, but the opponent's initial offer did not affect the amount of overall concessions by subjects. In both of these studies, subjects were not informed about the opponent's payoff from each possible settlement. In another study by Yukl (1972), in which the subjects were given partial information about the opponent's payoffs, there was no effect of opponent's initial offer on the subject's initial or final offer.

Size of concessions. Several studies reported the effects of opponent concessions when manipulated independently of other offer tactics. In four separate experiments, Yukl (1972, 1973, 1974a, 1974b) found that subjects made a more favorable final offer when the opponent's concessions were small than when they were large, but some limiting conditions were also found for the effects of opponent concessions. The subject's final offer was not affected by the opponent's concessions in the following situations:

(1) when opponent offers were so extreme that they provided only negative payoffs (i.e., losses rather than profits) for the subjects (Yukl, 1974b),
(2) when the opponent made concessions on only 33 percent of his offers, as opposed to a 100 percent concession frequency (Yukl, 1974b),
(3) when there was little time pressure and subjects knew the opponent's payoff at each possible settlement (Yukl, 1974a).

In a study by Pruitt and Drews (1969), opponent concessions did not affect the final offer of (uninformed) subjects under either high or low time pressure. The absence of a significant effect in this study was probably due to the use of opponent offers providing mostly negative payoffs for subjects, which is one of the limiting conditions just discussed.

Concession frequency and timing. Three studies investigated the independent effects of opponent-concession frequency, which was defined as the percentage of opponent offers that are concessions. In the first two studies (Chertkoff and Conley, 1967; Yukl, 1974b), concession frequency was manipulated by varying the number of concessions while holding the number of offers constant. In the other study (Pruitt and Johnson, 1970), the number of offers was varied and the number of concessions held constant. These studies did not find a significant effect of opponent concession frequency on the subjects' concessions or final offer. It made no difference if the opponent made few large concessions or many small concessions. That is, the subjects reciprocated the frequency but not the magnitude of opponent concessions.

Four articles reported research on the timing of opponent concessions or the slope of the opponent's offer curve. Yukl (1974a) attempted to determine whether it is best (1) to make larger concessions early in the negotiations and smaller concessions during the later stages of negotiations, (2) to make uniform concessions throughout the negotiations, or (3) to make smaller early concessions and larger later concessions. Three separate experiments by Yukl showed no effect of the opponent's timing of (non-contingent) concessions on the final subject offer or the settlement reached. Hatton (1967) conducted a study in which he compared the strategy of rapidly conceding a predetermined amount with the strategy of conceding the same amount more slowly over a larger number of offers. There was no effect of opponent-offer strategy on the subject's final offer. Several studies compared mixed, noncontingent offer tactics. Rubin and Dimatteo (1972) found that a consistently hard offer strategy (hard IO and small CM) by the opponent resulted in a more favorable final subject offer than a consistently soft offer strategy (soft IO and large CM). Liebert et al. (1968) compared a hard initial opponent offer, followed by large concessions, to a soft initial offer, followed by small concessions. The results indicated that when subjects were informed about opponent payoffs, there was no effect of the opponent's offer strategy on the subject's initial offer or profit from the settlement. However, when they were not informed, the subjects made a more favorable initial offer and earned less profit when the opponent used a hard IO/large concession strategy than when the opponent used a soft IO/small concession strategy. Yukl (1974b) found no significant difference between the effects of a hard IO/small concession strategy and a soft IO/large concession strategy on the final subject offer or settlement. The data from this study suggest that the Liebert et al. results were due primarily to the initial opponent offer.

Benton (1971) and Benton et al. (1972) compared the following three mixed strategies: hard IO/no concession, hard IO/moderate concession, and soft IO/no concession. The subjects, who were informed about opponent payoffs, tended to reciprocate the hardness of the initial opponent offer, but there was no effect of opponent offer strategy on the final subject offer. When the opponent was assigned zero profit for any deadlocks, so that the magnitude of earned profit depended on reaching an agreement, as well as on obtaining concessions from the subject, then opponent profits were largest in the hard IO/moderate concession condition.

Last-clear-chance-offer. Two studies have attempted to study the effect of the "last-clear-chance" offer tactic recommended by Schelling (1960). Chertkoff and Baird (1971) found that a bargainer who was tough (in terms of concession rate) is less successful in using an unrealistic last-clear-chance strategy than is a softer bargainer whose last offer is more realistic for both parties. In the second study by Hamner (1974) the programmed buyer made the last offer, and therefore it was up to the seller to accept or reject this offer. If he rejected the offer on the last trial, neither he nor his "hypothetical" opponent would receive any money for their efforts. All of the uninformed sellers who were offered an equitable last-chance offer accepted the buyer's last-clear-chance offer, whereas 48 percent of the sellers who received an inequitable last-clear-chance offer rejected it.

Studies on Contingent Offers by a Programmed Opponent

Several studies have investigated the effectiveness of contingent offer strategies. Komorita and Brenner (1968) compared four offer strategies: hard contingent concessions (50 percent reciprocation), very hard contingent concessions (10 percent reciprocation), concession-matching (100 percent reciprocation), and a final-offer-first strategy (i.e., a fair initial offer and no subsequent concessions). The final subject offer was least favorable to the opponent in the final-offer-first condition and most favorable to the opponent in the hard and very hard contingent concession conditions, which were equally effective. Komorita and Barnes (1969) compared concession matching with a hard contingent concession strategy (50 percent reciprocation) under two time-pressure conditions and found no effect of opponent offer strategy on subjects without any time cost. But for subjects with a high cost of delay, a more favorable final offer was made when the opponent used a hard contingent concession strategy than when the opponent used a matching strategy.

Cann et al. (1973) compared two offer strategies used by the programmed opponent: matching concessions, and a strategy of initial hard contingent concessions (20 percent reciprocation) which continued until a stalemate occurred, after which the opponent made a single noncontingent concession and then adopted a concession-matching strategy. There were also three levels of initial opponent offer, and since a harder initial opponent offer resulted in a larger bargaining range, the absolute size of the opponent's concessions within a given condition was larger the harder the initial offer. In view of this confounding of independent variables and the fact that subjects knew they had the advantage of making a last-chance final offer to the opponent, it is not surprising that the researchers found that the opponent's offer strategy did not affect the final subject offer.

Druckman et al. (1972) compared four offer strategies: concession-matching, noncontingent concessions of a constant magnitude, contingent concessions with the percentage reciprocation increasing over trials from 10 percent to 110 percent ("positively acelerated"), and contingent concessions with the percentage of reciprocation decreasing over trials from 110 percent to 10 percent ("negatively accelerated"). The most favorable final subject offer occured in the positively accelerated condition, and the negatively accelerated condition was second, with the matching- and constant-concession conditions least effective and equal to each other. Druckman et al. also used supplementary measures of subject offers to control for lack of comparability between conditions, and the results for these measures were generally similar to those for the final subject offer.

Michener et al. (1975) conducted a study to compare 50 percent and 150 percent reciprocation strategies in two power situations. When the opponent had more power than the subject, the subject concession rate was greater in the soft-strategy condition (150 percent reciprocation) than in the hard strategy condition. When the subject had more power than the opponent, the opponent's concession strategy did not significantly affect the subject's concession rate.

Esser and Komorita (1975) compared a concession-matching condition (100 percent reciprocation) with two conditions in which the programmed opponent conceded the same amount as the subject, but the concessions were delayed and combined into periodic "catch-up concessions." There was also a 50 percent reciprocation condition. Subjects made a more favorable final offer when the opponent made immediate matching concessions than when reciprocity was delayed. This difference was found to occur for subjects who had a competitive orientation, but not for subjects with a cooperative orientation. The final subject offer was more favorable in the 100 percent reciprocation condition than in the hard strategy condition (50 percent reciprocation), which is directly contrary to the results in the earlier study by Komorita and Brenner (1968). The difference in results is probably due to the fact that subjects in the earlier study did not have information about opponent payoffs, whereas such information was provided in the later study. Esser and Komorita concluded that immediacy, size, and frequency are all important aspects of reciprocity.

Hamner (1974) conducted a study to determine whether, after a stalemate in a negotiation session had been reached, there was a bargaining style which led to a distinctively superior outcome. The four bargaining styles replicated in a stalemated bilateral monopoly paradigm, under both high- and low-pressure-to-reach-agreement conditions, were "tough" (50 percent reciprocation), conciliatory or "soft" (100 percent reciprocation), "intermediate" or moderately tough (75 percent reciprocation), and "fair" (one even-split offer).

The results of this study indicated that: (1) a soft strategy resulted in significantly higher payoffs in both pressure conditions; (2) the subjects who faced a soft strategy opponent responded with a higher concession rate in both time pressure conditions; and (3) the probability of not reaching an agreement was significantly greater when a tougher strategy was used (as measured by the number of "last-clear-chance" offers refused).

Hamner interpreted this study as showing that, while a tough strategy is superior when agreements are reached, it is an inferior strategy overall because it results in fewer agreements. One plausible explanation suggested for these results was that bargainers believe that if they accept the tougher opponent's offer, they will be earning considerably less than their opponent.

Therefore, for many subjects, the utility of saving "face" may be greater than the utility of the money given up.

Summary

This section of the chapter examined the evidence supporting or refuting the success of the various bargaining tactics and strategies from research with bargaining games using (1) real opponents, (2) programmed opponents who used a noncontingent strategy, and (3) programmed opponents using contingent strategies. The research findings from "real opponent" studies give some evidence that: A bargainer who wishes to make a higher than average payoff is advised to make fewer concessions than his opponent, but that one should avoid being extremely uncooperative because, by doing so, the bargainer is drastically reducing his own chances of reaching agreement. From the research evidence presented, the initial offer and the size of concessions appear to be the major tactics that affected bargaining outcomes.

Studies where programmed opponents used a noncontingent strategy showed that:

(1) Subjects made a more favorable final offer when the opponent made a tough initial offer;

(2) subjects tended to make a more favorable final offer when the opponent's concessions were small rather than large;

(3) concession frequency had little, if any, effect on the subject's final offer, except when combined with a hard IO; and

(4) tough bargainers, unlike soft bargainers, found the "last-clear-chance" strategy unsuccessful.

The studies where the programmed opponent used a contingent strategy found that various strategies were successful under different situations. The situations which tended to affect the success of various bargaining strategies included timing of the concessions, relative power, pressure to reach agreement, stalemate versus no stalemate, and competitive orientation. In general, a harder strategy was less successful than a softer strategy, especially when a stalemate or high pressure was present and actual payoff was used as the dependent variable.

Other Related Research

Behavioral scientists have used matrix games with a programmed opponent to study the following tacit bargaining strategies:

(1) Unconditional cooperation (extremely soft): The programmed opponent cooperates on every trial regardless of the subject's moves.

(2) Unconditional defection (extremely tough): The programmed opponent is uncooperative on every trial.

(3) Matching strategies: Matching may be a function of the subject's present choice or previous choice (tit-for-tat). Cooperation is thus a function of his own performance.

(4) Partial cooperation strategy: The programmed opponent cooperates on a predetermined percentage of trials (e.g., 90 percent, 50 percent, 10 percent).

(5) Partial reinforcement strategy (moderately tough): The programmed opponent responds at one probability level if the choice is uncooperative and another probability level if the choice is cooperative.

If Osgood's theory applies to the type of mixed-motive situation portrayed by a matrix game, then these studies should have found the bargainer's cooperation to be highly correlated with the programmed opponent's cooperation. In total unilateral cooperation, Rapoport and Chammah (1965) found that about half the subjects exploited the programmed opponent while the other half cooperated completely. Sermat (1964) and Vanden Heuvel (1968) found that a tit-for-tat strategy produced more cooperative behavior than a strategy that deviated from reciprocity. Solomon (1960) found that a tit-for-tat strategy led to more cooperative behavior by the bargainer than an unconditional cooperative strategy. However, no significant difference in subject cooperation was found between tit-for-tat and unconditionally cooperative strategies in two studies with a much longer series of trials (Wilson, 1969).

Komorita (1972: 2) believes that "earlier (matrix game) studies (before 1972) both supporting and refuting the theories proposed by Osgood and by Siegel and Fouraker are quite equivocal." He states that in none of the cases has the research been based on a long history of uncooperative choices where both sides are deadlocked. He reports a study conducted by Komorita and Koziej (1970) designed to discover under what conditions it was likely choice was perceived to be a sign of weakness and was met with exploitation (as implied by Siegel and Fouraker), and under what conditions it was likely to be perceived as "honest" or "fair" and to be reciprocated (as implied by Osgood). Two situational variables were investigated: (a) the length of the competitive stalemate prior to conciliatory acts, and (b) the consequences or cost to the party initiating such acts. The dependent variable was the number of cooperative choices on the last block of trials.

There were three phases in this simulated PD game: (a) extinction phase, where the experimenter made ten consecutive uncooperative choices; (b) repentance phase, where the experimenter made consecutive cooperative choices matching the number of the cooperative choices made by the subjects in phase 1; and (c) reconciliation phase, where the experimenter played either a "tit-for-tat" strategy for sixty trials or a martyr strategy, so that whenever the subjects made five consecutive uncooperative choices, the experimenter made a cooperative choice and then went to a "tit-for-tat" strategy.

A second experiment that slightly changed the experimenter's behavior during the three phases was also run by Komorita (1972). Komorita found that there was no significant difference in the martyr or tit-for-tat strategy.

The conclusion was that it may pay to be tough with a tough person, but not necessarily with a cooperative person because a tough strategy against a cooperative person may subsequently evoke a tough strategy in return (see also Druckman and Bonoma, 1976). Komorita stated that he would hypothesize that the Siegel and Fouraker proposal is valid at the initial and intermediate stages of negotiation, but that Osgood's proposal is valid in the later stages when the negotiations are deadlocked for an extended period of time.

Of all the research found on the Osgood/Siegel-Fouraker debate, this study by Komorita is one of the best attempts at testing the Osgood hypothesis using a PD game. However, several aspects of this research should be noted:

(1) There was no attempt to simulate a Siegel-Fouraker strategy—i.e., in phase 3, to make small cooperative choices only when the subject is uncooperative for an extended period of time, and then to make uncooperative choices when the subject is predominantly cooperative. No comparison between the two strategies can be made directly, since neither tit-for-tat nor martyr represents a Siegel-Fouraker strategy.

(2) While tit-for-tat would represent the second phase of Osgood's theory, a martyr strategy would never be recommended by Osgood, since he proposes that one not leave himself vulnerable over an extended period of time.

(3) There is no cost for a stalemate (UC-UC condition). The payoff matrix shows that when both subjects and opponents compete, they receive a zero payoff. (Normally one would expect a negative cost for being stalemated.)

(4) The percentage of cooperation is used as the dependent variable. Again, the real test of a strategy would be the payoff one receives. No mention of which subjects received the highest payoff was given. As Harsanyi (1962: 145) observed, "In the absence of a theory yielding determinate predictions as to the *outcome,* even the mere description of many social situations in a satisfactory way becomes impossible."

Summary

In matrix game research, the findings tend to show that a matching strategy usually resulted in greater cooperation by the subject than did an unconditionally cooperative strategy (soft), an unconditionally competitive strategy (very tough), or a partially cooperative strategy.

Simulated and Field Research

In addition to studies with bargaining games and matrix games, there have been a few studies that attempted to test the Osgood hypothesis in a different kind of situation. The Osgood hypothesis was originally formulated as a proposal for facilitating mutual disarmament. Pilisuk and Skolnick (1968) simulated an arms race where the subjects had the option of converting their missiles into factories. In the matching strategy condition, the experimenter conceded three missiles on the first trial (unilateral concession), and thereafter the number of missiles the subject showed on trial n was revealed as the number shown by the opponent on trial n + 1. In the conciliatory strategy condition, the experimenter conceded three missiles on the first trial, and thereafter one missile less than the subject showed on trial n was revealed as the number shown by the opponent on trial n + 1.

Pilisuk and Skolnick found that a subject's behavior on the first trial may predict cooperation on later trials. They reported support for the Osgood proposal in that small, consistent, unilateral overtures of good intentions, combined with an honest prior announcement of moves, apparently did produce markedly more cooperation than was found in a control group. But they found a rate of increase only marginally higher than that found in a comparable matching strategy. They suggest that perhaps a combination strategy is best—one that uses conciliatory moves in the beginning and then switches to tit-for-tat.

Osgood's strategy has also been tested by Crow (1963) in an inter-nation simulation, with students representing the leaders of imaginary nations. One student was an accomplice of the experimenter and functioned in a similar capacity as a programmed opponent. When a high level of tension had been created (e.g., hostile communications, armaments race), the accomplice made a series of unilateral conciliatory actions. After some initial suspicion, the actions were reciprocated by the opposing nation, and tension was reduced. The results can be interpreted as evidence of the effectiveness of the Osgood strategy, although no other strategy was tested. Additional support comes from some case studies of actual historical events and disarmament negotiations between the United States and the USSR (Etzioni, 1967; Jensen, 1963).

Dorris (1972) contends that laboratory studies have not provided an adequate test of reciprocity because they usually restrict normal opportunities for social influence, and they include instructions that suspend reciprocity norms and encourage exploitation. He designed a field study to avoid these limitations. The sixty-five subjects were rare-coin dealers who were offered a chance to buy a small collection of rare coins from an unconditionally cooperative seller. Comments made by the coin seller before giving the coins to the dealer determined whether the subject received a "moral" or a "neutral" appeal. Since the coin seller made it quite clear that he had no idea what the coins might be worth, the dealer was led to believe that he had an opportunity to buy the coins as cheaply as he desired. (The coins were never sold to the dealer.) In the *moral* appeal, the seller explained that he needed to sell the coins to get money to help pay for some school books and that he was going to sell the coins to this dealer on the basis of the recommendation of another customer, an acquaintance of the seller. In the *neutral* appeal, the seller explained that he simply had some coins that he wanted to sell because he was not interested in becoming a collector. In both appeals, the seller's ignorance of the coins' value and his desire to sell them to this dealer were clearly evident. The results indicated that the moral appeal was found to elicit higher bids than the neutral one did. This difference was attributed by Dorris to considerable helping behavior by the moral-appeal dealers combined with some exploitative attempts by the neutral-appeals dealer.

Cialdini et al. (1975) recently conducted a field study to investigate reciprocity in another realistic social situation. College students were approached as they walked across campus and asked to do volunteer work. More students agreed to a small request (donate two hours' time) when it was preceded by a large request (which was refused by the student) than when the two requests were made at the same time and the subject was asked to accept either one, or when only the small request was made (similar to a "fair offer" strategy), or when the large request was made earlier by another person. The results were interpreted as evidence for a reciprocity process. That is, starting from a hard position and conceding to a soft one will prompt the other person to also make a concession. This is the case especially under high time pressure (see Druckman et al., 1972).

SUMMARY OF RESEARCH FINDINGS

The large variety of *bargaining simulations* that were used and the differences in choice of offer parameters and dependent variables, make comparison and integration of the results of research on offer tactics and strategies difficult. Nevertheless, some general consistency of findings was evident. Negotiators usually conceded when the opponent conceded, but the frequency of opponent concessions did not affect the size of a negotiator's concessions, his final offer, or the location of the settlement. A hard initial offer by the opponent usually resulted in a more favorable final offer by negotiators who did not have information about the opponent's payoffs. Small contingent or noncontingent concessions by the opponent usually resulted in a more favorable final offer by a negotiator, especially if he did not have information about the opponent's payoffs and was under substantial time pressure. The probability of a settlement was greater when the opponent used a soft- or intermediate-offer strategy rather than a hard-offer strategy. In situations where a deadlock would result in zero profits, a negotiator usually earned a larger profit if he used a matching-concession strategy or an intermediate-offer strategy rather than a hard-offer strategy.

In research with *matrix games*, a matching strategy usually resulted in greater subject cooperation than did an unconditionally cooperative strategy (soft), an unconditionally competitive strategy (very hard), or a partially cooperative strategy. The matching strategy can be viewed as "fair play," since a player who adopts this strategy neither exploits the opponent nor allows himself to be exploited. An unconditionally cooperative strategy permits exploitation by the opponent, but the likelihood of exploitation rather than cooperation appears to be strongly influenced by certain features of the experimental procedure. In a situation where two players have been "locked into" a long series of mutually uncooperative choices, a strategy of unconditionally cooperative choices by one player can be an effective way of eliciting cooperation from the opponent, as Osgood proposes. Once mutual cooperation is reestablished, a matching strategy can be used to discourage subsequent exploitation by the opponent although such exploitation may be unlikely.

Some research using approaches other than negotiation games or matrix games tended to support the effectiveness of the Osgood hypothesis, and the hypothesis that cooperation will be reciprocated. However, this research did not explicitly compare different bargaining strategies.

Problems of External Validity

Recent criticisms of the internal and external validity of PD games (Dorris, 1972; Nemeth, 1970, 1972; Tedeschi et al., 1973) have pointed out the difficulty of drawing conclusions from such games about relative strategy effectiveness. Subjects may not understand the matrix, or they may not perceive the opponent's choices in terms of cooperation and noncooperation, as is assumed by the experimenter. Furthermore, many aspects of the experiment itself (e.g., payoff matrices, number of trials, nature of instructions to subjects, and method of displaying payoffs) condition the effects of the strategies. The results also appear to be influenced by the use of simultaneous rather than sequential choices and the absence of direct communication between players. These conditions, which are typical of matrix game research, create a highly artificial situation that has little similarity to most real bargaining situations.

The research on bargaining games also has problems and limitations. One problem is the use of nonequivalent criteria to evaluate strategy effectiveness. Some studies have used the final subject offer or concession rate, while other studies have used the payoff resulting from a settlement or deadlock. A limitation of the final offer and concession rate as criteria is that they do not take into account the probability of an agreement. It is possible in some real bargaining situations to follow a tough bargaining strategy until the opponent has made an attractive final offer and then suddenly accept this offer. However, there are many situations where this strategy would not work (e.g., when the opponent can retract his favorable offer), and, in any case, it is not likely to be effective more than once with the same opponent. On the other hand, a payoff criterion also has limitations. The assumption of a zero payoff from a deadlock is not always valid. In some cases, a real bargainer has the alternative of dealing with another party besides the immediate opponent. Furthermore, the probability of a settlement with a programmed opponent is unrealistically low in most studies, since the opponent is not allowed to accept a subject offer unless it is a complete capitulation to the opponent's current position.

The most serious limitation of laboratory negotiation research is probably the failure to establish its external validity. Since most studies have used inexperienced negotiators and a relatively simple negotiation task, it is possible that the results from this research apply, if at all, only to comparable situations in real life. A further problem is the lack of emotional involvement by subjects in laboratory negotiations. Thus we do not know whether the findings from laboratory research can be generalized to the most important kinds of real negotiations (e.g., international, labor-management, etc.) which are typically complex in nature and emotionally charged.

CONCLUSIONS

From this review, it is obvious that various characteristics of the bargainers and of the bargaining situation play a large part in determining whether a particular bargaining strategy will be effective. No tactic or strategy was found to be superior in all situations or against all types of opponents in any given situation.

Even though, after twenty years of study of bargaining tactics and strategies, no one superior strategy emerges, our review did suggest that a soft approach to bargaining, where steady concession-making takes place, leads to more mutually satisfactory agreements in most situations. However, when the bargainer has a long time to reach agreement, is more interested in "winning" (i.e., reaching a larger outcome than his opponent) than in reaching a mutually satisfactory agreement, or is bargaining with an opponent with low aspirations, then it pays to be tough.

It appears that while we have made great progress as researchers in isolating variables and strategies that affect bargaining success, we need more research, in both laboratory and field settings, before prescriptions of behavior can be made. Unfortunately, previous research has examined only a few of the significant variables at a time and has randomized other variables or held them constant. As Patchen (1970: 389) has noted, "Such studies are often useful but it is usually hard to know how the results are affected by other important but unspecified variables, nor is it usually easy to see how the results of many studies concerning many apparently disparate variables may be fitted together."

It is obvious that more elaborate studies will be needed to map and extend the network of relationships among the various independent and dependent variables. Furthermore, if bargaining research is to become more than an empty academic exercise, we must learn to create better laboratory simulations of actual bargaining situations. Laboratory simulation research should be closely coordinated with field studies so that their relative advantages can be realized. Recent attempts to study reciprocity processes in a natural setting are promising, but much more field research will be needed to evaluate the external validity of laboratory findings about the consequences of different bargaining strategies.

Once we have designed more elaborate studies and are more confident about the external validity of our findings, our next important challenge is to train bargainers in the strategies and skills necessary for reaching the goal at hand.

REFERENCES

ADAMS, J. S. (1965) "Inequity in social exchange," in L. Berkowitz, Advances in Experimental Psychology. New York: Academic Press.

BARTOS, O. J. (1966) "Concession-making in experimental negotiations," in J. Berger et al., Sociological Theories in Action. Boston: Houghton Mifflin.

––– (1967) "How predictable are negotiations?" J. of Conflict Resolution 11: 481-496.

––– (1970) "Determinants and consequences of toughness," in P. Swingle, The Structure of Conflict. New York: Academic Press.

BENTON, A. A. (1971) "Some unexpected consequences of jeopardy." Proceedings of the 79th Annual Convention of the American Psychological Association. Washington: 223-224.

–––, H. H. KELLEY, and B. LIEBLING (1972) "Effects of extremity of offers and concession rate on the outcomes of bargaining." J. of Personality and Social Psychology 24: 73-83.

CANN, A., J. K. ESSER, and S. S. KOMORITA (1973) "Equity and concession strategies in bargaining." Presented at the Annual Meeting of the Midwestern Psychological Association, Chicago, May 12.

CHERTKOFF, J. M. and M. CONLEY (1967) "Opening offer and frequency of concession on bargaining strategies." J. of Personality and Social Psychology 7: 181-185.

CHERTKOFF, J. M. and S. L. BAIRD (1971) "The application of the big lie technique and the last clear chance doctrine to bargaining." J. of Personality and Social Psychology 20: 298-303.

CIALDINI, R. B., J. E. VINCENT, S. K. LEWIS, J. CATALAN, D. WHEELER, and B. L. DARBY (1975) "Reciprocal concessions procedure for inducing compliance: The door-in-the-face technique," J. of Personality and Social Psychology, 31: 206-215.

CROW, W. J. (1963) "A study of strategic doctrines using the internation simulation." J. of Conflict Resolution 7: 580-589.

DORRIS, J. W. (1972) "Reactions to unconditional cooperation: A field study." J. of Personality and Social Psychology 22: 387-397.

DRUCKMAN, D. and T. BONOMA (1976) "Determinants of bargaining behavior in a bilateral monopoly situation II: Opponent's concession rate and similarity." Behavioral Science 21.

DRUCKMAN, D., K. ZECHMEISTER, and D. SOLOMON (1972) "Determinants of bargaining behavior in a bilateral monopoly situation: Opponent's concession rate and relative defensibility." Behavioral Science 17: 514-531.

ESSER, J. K. and S. S. KOMORITA (1975) "Reciprocity and concession making in bargaining." J. of Personality and Social Psychology 31: 864-872.

ETZIONI, A. (1967) "The Kennedy experiment." Western Pol. Q. 20: 361-380.

FELLNER, W. (1949) Competition Among the Few. New York: Alfred A. Knopf.

FOURAKER, L. E. and S. SIEGEL (1963) Bargaining Behavior. New York: McGraw-Hill.

HAMNER, W. C. (1974) "Effects of bargaining strategy and pressure to reach agreement in a stalemated negotiation." J. of Personality and Social Psychology 30: 458-467.
HARNETT, D. L., L. L. CUMMINGS, and W. C. HAMNER (1973) "Personality bargaining style and payoff in international bargaining." Sociometry 36: 325-345.
HARSANYI, J. C. (1962) "Bargaining in ignorance of the opponent's utility function." J. of Conflict Resolution 1: 29-38.
HATTON, J. M. (1967) "Reactions of Negroes in a biracial bargaining situation." J. of Personality and Social Psychology 7: 301-306.
HINTON, B. L., W. C. HAMNER, and M. F. POHLEN (1974) "The influence of reward magnitude, opening bid and concession rate on profit earned in a managerial negotiation game." Behavioral Sci. 19: 197-203.
JENSEN, L. (1963) "Soviet-American bargaining behavior in the post-war disarmament negotiations." J. of Conflict Resolution 7: 522-541.
KOMORITA, S. S. (1972) "Tacit communication and cooperation in a two-person game," in V. H. Sauermann (ed.) Contributions to Experimental Economics. Vol. 3. Frankfurt: J. C. B. Mohr Tübingen.
——— and M. BARNES (1969) "Effects of pressures to reach agreement in bargaining." J. of Personality and Social Psychology 13: 245-252.
KOMORITA, S. S. and A. R. BRENNER (1968) "Bargaining and concession-making under bilateral monopoly." J. of Personality and Social Psychology 6: 349-353.
KOMORITA, S. S. and R. KOZIEJ (1970) "Tacit communication in a Prisoner's Dilemma game." Presented at the Midwestern Psychological Association Meetings, April.
LIEBERT, R. M., W. P. SMITH, J. H. HILL, and M. KEIFFER (1968) "The effects of information and magnitude of initial offer on interpersonal negotiation." J. of Experimental Social Psychology 4: 431-441.
MICHENER, H. A., J. J. VASKE, S. L. SCHLEIFER, J. G. PLAZEWSKI, and L. J. CHAPMAN (1975) "Factors affecting concession rate and threat usage in bilateral conflict." Sociometry 38: 62-80.
MORGAN, W. R. and J. SAWYER (1967) "Bargaining expectations, and the preference for equality over equity." J. of Personality and Social Psychology 6: 139-149.
NEMETH, C. (1970) "Bargaining and reciprocity." Psych. Bull. 74: 297-308.
——— (1972) "A critical analysis of research using the Prisoner's Dilemma paradigm for the study of bargaining," in L. Berkowitz, Advances in Experimental Social Psychology. New York: Academic Press.
OSGOOD, C. (1962) An Alternative to War or Surrender. Urbana: Univ. of Illinois Press.
——— (1959) "Suggestions for winning the real war with Communism." J. of Conflict Resolution 3: 295-325.
PATCHEN, M. (1970) "Models of cooperation and conflict: A critical review." J. of Conflict Resolution 3: 389-407.
PILISUK, M. and P. SKOLNICK (1968) "Inducing trust: A test of the Osgood proposal." J. of Personality and Social Psychology 8: 121-133.
PRUITT, D. G. (1972) "Methods for resolving differences of interest: A theoretical analysis." J. of Social Issues 28: 133-154.
——— (1974) "Power and bargaining," in B. Seidenberg and Snadowsky, A Social Psychology. New York: Free Press.
——— and J. L. DREWS (1969) "The effects of time pressure, time elapsed, and the opponents' concession rate on behavior in negotiation." J. of Experimental Social Psychology 5: 43-60.
PRUITT, D. G. and D. F. JOHNSON (1970) "Mediation as an aid to face-saving in negotiations." J. of Personality and Social Psychology 14: 239-246.
RAPOPORT, A. and A. M. CHAMMAH (1965) Prisoner's Dilemma. Ann Arbor: Univ. of Michigan Press.

RUBIN, J. and M. R. DIMATTEO (1972) "Factors affecting the magnitude of subjective utility parameters in a tacit bargaining game." J. of Experimental Social Psychology 8: 412-426.

SCHELLING, T. (1960) The Strategy of Conflict. Cambridge: Harvard Univ. Press.

SERMAT, V. (1964) "Cooperative behavior in a mixed-motive game." J. of Social Psychology 62: 217-239.

SIEGEL, S. and L. F. FOURAKER (1960) Bargaining and Group Decision Making. New York: McGraw-Hill.

SOLOMON, L. (1960) "The influence of some types of power relationships and game strategies upon the development of interpersonal trust." J. of Abnormal and Social Psychology 61: 223-230.

STARBUCK, W. and D. F. GRANT (1971) "Bargaining strategies with asymmetric initiation." J. of Applied Social Psychology 1: 344-363.

TEDESCHI, J. T., B. R. SCHLENKER, and T. BONOMA (1973) Conflict, Power, and Games: The Experimental Study of Interpersonal Relations. Chicago: Aldine.

VANDEN HEUVEL, K. (1968) "Game strategy as a function of 'partner's strategy.'" Unpublished master's thesis, University of Toronto.

WILSON, W. (1969) "Cooperation and the cooperativeness of the other player." J. of Conflict Resolution 13: 110-117.

YUKL, G. A. (1972) "The effect of opponent concessions on a bargainer's perception and concessions." Proceedings of the 80th Annual Convention of the American Psychological Association: 229-230.

——— (1973) "The effects of the opponent's initial offer and concession magnitude on bargaining outcomes." Proceedings of the 81st Annual Convention of the American Psychological Association: 143-144.

——— (1974b) "Effects of the opponent's initial offer, concession magnitude, and concession frequency on bargaining behavior." J. of Personality and Social Psychology 29: 327-330.

———(1974b) "Effects of the opponent's initial offer, concession magnitude, and concession frequency on bargaining behavior." J. of Personality and Social Psychology 29: 327-330.

Chapter 5

THE PSYCHOLOGY OF INTEGRATIVE BARGAINING

DEAN G. PRUITT

State University of New York at Buffalo

STEVEN A. LEWIS

Wayne State University

This chapter deals with the processes by which bargainers reach agreements that reconcile their separate needs and values and thus offer high joint utility. Some definitions of terms and examples of their usage are needed before we go further.

By "bargaining" is meant a process of communication between two or more parties aimed at resolving initial differences in preference. Bargaining always involves joint consideration of two or more "options" or potential agreements. Some options are more "integrative" than others in the sense of providing greater joint utility to the bargainers taken collectively. The term "integrative bargaining"[1] refers to the processes by which bargainers locate and adopt such options. One process is considered to be more "integrative" than another to the extent that it is more capable of locating the best among the options available to the bargainers.

There are several ways of defining "joint utility," each with its strong and weak points. For example, Sen (1970) has suggested that it can be defined as (a) the sum of the utilities incurred by each bargainer as an individual, (b) the product of these utilities, or (c) the utility incurred by the least successful bargainer. In addition, an ordinal definition (d) is possible, in which one

AUTHOR'S NOTE: Prepared under the sponsorship of National Science Foundation Grants S042686 and BNS7610963 and National Institutes of Health Grant 5I·22MH02624-02.

option is said to have higher joint utility than another if it is better than the other for both parties. However, at this rather primitive stage of theory development, such fine distinctions do not seem worth pursuing, and we have arbitrarily adopted the first (sum-of-utilities) definition.

By "options available to the bargainers" we refer to the set of all *possible* solutions to the bargaining problem at hand. This set can be contrasted to the usually smaller set of options that are *known* when bargaining commences. The latter set sometimes contains the most integrative options, but often does not. Hence, integrative bargaining is frequently a creative process in which new options are discovered.

A contrast can often be drawn between integrative bargaining and the process of "compromise," by which bargainers concede along some obvious dimension to a point partway between their initial preferences. We admit that compromise can sometimes lead to the best available agreement, but we argue that more integrative solutions are usually available if bargainers will only seek them. Indeed, we suspect that the search for an acceptable compromise, with all its overtones of fairness and equitability, is sometimes responsible for failure to discover more integrative options.

The contrast between compromise and integrative bargaining can be seen in the following example: A married couple is trying to decide where to spend the husband's two weeks of vacation time. The husband prefers the mountains, and his wife the seashore. A possible compromise would be to divide the available time down the middle and spend one week in the mountains and one at the seashore. But there may be other, more integrative solutions. For example, with a little discussion, they may decide that two extra weeks of vacation is worth the income that would be lost if the husband took a leave of absence from his work. With four weeks, each can have the kind of vacation he wanted. Alternatively, in discussing the needs and values underlying their preferences, they may discover that the husband's main interest is fresh-water fishing while the wife's is swimming and sunbathing. This might lead them to search for a mountain resort on a lake or a seashore near a well-stocked stream. Two weeks at either kind of location would presumably be mutually more satisfying than a simple compromise.

The concept "integrative bargaining" is closely related to the notion of "constructive conflict," which Deutsch (1973: 17) defines as conflict in which "the participants all are satisfied with their outcomes and feel that they have gained." But Deutsch does not distinguish between available and known options. People are often satisfied with an initially known option unless and until they learn of (or take seriously) a better one. Deutsch would logically label as "constructive" a process that led bargainers to choose an option that was initially available and mutually satisfying. But we would hesitate to label such a process "integrative" until we were certain that there were no hidden options that were better for both parties.

WHY STUDY INTEGRATIVE BARGAINING?

There are at least six reasons why it is important to study integrative bargaining:

(1) The satisfaction of human needs and values has intrinsic ethical interest.

(2) Where limits or aspirations are high, integrative bargaining reduces the likelihood that negotiations will fail, by making it possible to locate options that satisfy everybody's ultimate limits (absolute minimal aspirations, fall-back positions).

(3) Integrative bargaining leads to speedier settlements. It often takes a lot of time to reach a compromise, because people do not like to reduce their aspirations. If an integrative option can be found, aspirations need not be substantially reduced, and hence a settlement can be reached more rapidly.

(4) Integrative bargaining reduces the danger that one or both bargainers will repudiate an agreement after it has been reached, inasmuch as agreements that are more integrative are ordinarily more satisfactory to one or both parties (Follett, 1940).

(5) Members of groups that persistently achieve integrative agreements are likely to find their relationships with one another mutually satisfying. Hence, their groups will be cohesive and persistent (Lott and Lott, 1965). It follows that the theory of integrative bargaining is relevant to such topics as communication and conformity (Festinger, 1950) and marital stability.

(6) We can conceive of an organization as composed of many units (individuals, work groups, departments), each with its own distinct needs and values. These needs and values largely reflect the responsibilities assigned to the unit. Hence, the organization as a whole will prosper to the extent that its units are satisfied. It follows that integrative bargaining among such units will contribute to organizational effectiveness. In this interpretation, integrative bargaining is a route to greater *total power*, as this term is used by Tannenbaum (1968).

FORMS TAKEN BY INTEGRATIVE OPTIONS

There are at least three forms that integrative options can take, three ways in which new options can be constructed that have greater joint utility than the old:

(1) Broadening the pie. The conflict underlying bargaining often results from some sort of shortage. (There is only one apple and two hungry boys.) If this shortage can be alleviated, an integrative agreement can be reached in which both parties achieve the options they favor. An example would be the case of the husband and wife who thought of the idea of taking a four-week instead of the usual two-week vacation.

(2) Alternation. When there is no way to broaden the pie, it may be possible for the parties to alternate between the options each of them favors. In an alternating scheme, neither side forsakes his preferred option, but each is allowed to enjoy it at a different time. For example, the couple in the prior example might go to the mountains this year and the seashore next year. Alternating schemes will be more integrative than simple compromise when the options being sought cannot be divided into parts without excessive loss of utility. For example, one week at the seashore and one week in the mountains may not be satisfying to husband or wife if such a compromise requires disruptive travel in the middle of a vacation.

(3) Logrolling. Bargainers can often discover integrative potential in a situation if they are willing to engage in logrolling, which involves the development of tradeoffs—i.e., exchanges of concessions on issues of differing importance to the bargainers. Each bargainer gets his way on one issue in exchange for making a concession on another of lesser importance to himself. A difference in priorities will facilitate logrolling so long as it is not viewed as indicative of a basic dissensus in values. Such dissensus may lead to a sense of outrage, which can preclude the development or acceptance of an integrative option even when an objective analysis would reveal considerable potential for logrolling.

Sometimes logrolling leads to the adoption of an already known alternative. But often considerable creativity is required. For instance, suppose that the husband favors a mountain vacation primarily because of the opportunity for hunting and fishing, and the wife favors the seashore primarily because she wants to swim and get a suntan. Successful logrolling may require the parties to think of a third location that would satisfy both sets of needs—e.g., a Canadian park with beaches, streams, and woodlands. Finding such a novel solution would require a thorough analysis of the needs and values at stake on both sides, so as to uncover the true issues underlying the stated preferences, plus some creative thinking.

Logrolling in Sequential Agendas

Tradeoffs can often be arranged when two or more issues are considered simultaneously, and there is logrolling potential. (By "logrolling potential" is meant the existence of issues of differing importance to the two parties.) It is much more difficult to arrange tradeoffs in sequential agendas, where the issues are considered one at a time (Froman and Cohen, 1970; Schulz, 1976; Walker and Thibaut, 1971; Yukl et al., 1976). Instead, bargainers tend to compromise on each issue as it comes up, thereby achieving less overall satisfaction than would be derived from an exchange of concessions.

Research by Kelley (1966) suggests that bargainers will increasingly opt for simultaneous consideration of issues when they repeatedly face a choice between simultaneous and sequential consideration. But such a choice is frequently not available; sequential agendas are often hard to avoid. Either the issues are too complex to be handled simultaneously, or they arise and must be resolved at different times, as in any interpersonal relationship that persists over a period of time.[2] Hence, it is important to inquire about the conditions under which bargainers are likely to achieve integrative solutions in sequential agendas that have logrolling potential.

We assume that mutual responsiveness (Pruitt, 1972) constitutes one such condition, where on any given issue the party with the weaker needs gives in to the one with the stronger needs. Assuming that one party has stronger needs on issue A and the other on a later issue B, mutual responsiveness will produce a result that is tantamount to logrolling even though the two issues may not be connected in the minds of the bargainers. The result will certainly be more integrative than if they had compromised on each issue separately.

Research by Morgan and Sawyer (1967) suggests that friends are more responsive to one another's needs than are strangers. Hence, friends should be more likely to achieve integrative solutions in sequential agendas. The same might be thought to apply to married couples and other kin, though this proposition was not supported in a study by Schulz (1976) which compared married couples with mixed-sex stranger dyads. Conceivably, the issues used in Schulz's bargaining task were not sufficiently compelling to bring out a difference between the two kinds of dyads.

Another source of responsiveness is *reciprocity,* the desire to repay the other party for a past favor or favors. Reciprocity can contribute to the development of an integrative solution in a sequential agenda if one party makes an initial concession. The other may feel some obligation to reciprocate this favor with a return concession, which may elicit a further concession from the first, and so on. Of course, such a chain of concessions must have a beginning. The starting mechanism in a sequence of concessions often involves one party's *trust* that the other will concede at a later time.

Substitutes for trust are sometimes available when trust itself is weak, including the reversible concession that can be withdrawn if the other fails to reciprocate (Deutsch, 1958). Strong norms often exist that interdict the withdrawal of firm concessions. But there are ways of phrasing concessions that permit their reversal if they are not reciprocated, called "sign language" by Peters (1955). For example, a bargainer may say about an issue early in the agenda, "This one looks easy to resolve—let's go on to the next." By this, he or she means, "I'll give in on this issue if you'll reciprocate on a later one."

One ground rule that would seem to encourage the development of concession sequences is to agree at the beginning of negotiation that nothing is approved until all issues have been thoroughly discussed (Walton and McKersie, 1965). This rule reverses the norm against withdrawing concessions and, hence, presumably makes it easier for a bargainer to make the first concession. Such a rule is sometimes adopted by mutual consent at the beginning of a formal negotiation.

The analysis and theory to be presented in the remainder of this chapter will focus on the unitary bargaining incident; though we believe that some of what will be said can be applied to sequential agendas as well.

OVERVIEW

This chapter will present a theory of integrative bargaining that has been developed by the authors on the basis of a series of empirical studies. The theory rests on a distinction between the strategies used in an attempt to reach agreement (the *means* of bargaining) and the goals and aspirations sought (the *ends* of bargaining). We will argue that the discovery of integrative alternatives requires that bargainers be flexible with respect to means, trying out many options and alternatives, but rigid with respect to ends, maintaining high goals and aspirations unless and until they prove unworkable.

We will begin by examining several bargaining strategies that emerge from our research. Factors that determine choice of strategy will then be explored. Next, we will move to a consideration of the role of aspirations and goals in the process of integrative bargaining. Combining insights derived from our research, we will examine bargaining in terms of a two-dimensional model based on the means-ends distinction.

The theory to be presented and the research upon which it is based deal primarily with relations between members of dyads. Nevertheless, our aim is to construct a broader theory, and we believe that many of these principles apply to multilateral bargaining as well. Hence, after the theory has been presented, there will be a section on integrative bargaining in groups.

METHODOLOGY

Results from five completed studies (two reported in Pruitt and Lewis, 1975; Schulz et al., 1974; and two unpublished experiments) and two in progress will be discussed frequently in this and later sections. Hence, we will describe our methodology at this point.

The task involves a simulated negotiation between buyer and seller in a wholesale market. Pairs of subjects, taking the roles of buyer and seller, must agree on prices for three commodities: iron, sulphur, and coal.[3] As is so often the case in multi-issue negotiation, these commodities have differing importance for the two bargainers. Hence, in order to find the more integrative agreements, it is necessary to develop tradeoffs, with each bargainer making substantial concessions on the commodity of least personal importance.

The profit schedules given to buyer and seller are shown in Table 5.1. They list nine prices, represented schematically by the letters A to I. Next to each price on the seller's sheet are the profits he or she obtains by selling each commodity at that price. Next to each price on the buyer's sheet are his profits for reselling each commodity if it is purchased at that price. The reader will note that the buyer receives his highest profits on iron and the seller on coal. Hence, the most integrative agreements involve a larger seller concession on iron and a large buyer concession on coal—in other words, a low price on iron and a high price on coal. Compromise agreements are also possible, in which the bargainers make roughly equal concessions on all three commodities. Compare, for example, the tradeoff A-E-I, which yields $2,600 to each party with the compromise E-E-E, which yields only $2,000 apiece.

We operationally define the integrativeness of an agreement as the total of the individual profits of the two parties. The profit schedules are so constructed that a larger difference in price between coal and iron implies a greater joint profit, the price of sulphur being immaterial to joint profit.

In most of our studies, the bargainers meet face to face. They can say anything they want to each other but they may not show each other their profit schedules. All sessions are tape-recorded.

As part of a post-session interview, subjects are asked to indicate which of the three commodities is most and which is least valuable to their counterpart. Responses to this question serve as a measure of insight into task structure. For coding the discussions between our bargainers, we have developed a series of indices, which we view as "windows" into the process of integrative bargaining. Correlations between these indices and joint profit are always computed on an averaged within-cell basis, so as to eliminate the variance due to manipulations imposed by the experimenter.

We believe that our task simulates major features of the negotiation conference. Many process variables described by other theorists and observers of actual negotiation are free to vary or can be manipulated in our setting. Hence, we have been able to test, and in some sense validate, several hypotheses drawn from the literature. In doing so, we have often refined and clarified concepts developed by others. Furthermore, our capacity to observe the processes immediately and compute correlations over many comparable cases has encouraged concept-formation, especially in the realm of strategies that increase or diminish joint profits.

However, there are a number of limitations, or potential limitations, to this method:

(1) Events and moves in arenas other than the negotiation conference cannot occur. Hence, such processes as the building of power, soliciting third-party participation, and cloakroom conferences are not involved. These can be important for the outcome of bargaining.

TABLE 5.1
Buyer and Seller Profit Sheets

	BUYER						SELLER					
	Iron		Sulphur		Coal		Iron		Sulphur		Coal	
	Price	Profit	Price	Profit	Price	Profit	Price	Profit	Price	Profit	Price	Profit
	A	$2,000	A	$1,200	A	$800	A	$000	A	$ 000	A	$ 000
	B	$1,750	B	$1,050	B	$700	B	$100	B	$ 150	B	$ 250
	C	$1,500	C	$ 900	C	$600	C	$200	C	$ 300	C	$ 500
	D	$1,250	D	$ 750	D	$500	D	$300	D	$ 450	D	$ 750
	E	$1,000	E	$ 600	E	$400	E	$400	E	$ 600	E	$1,000
	F	$ 750	F	$ 450	F	$300	F	$500	F	$ 750	F	$1,250
	G	$ 500	G	$ 300	G	$200	G	$600	G	$ 900	G	$1,500
	H	$ 250	H	$ 150	H	$100	H	$700	H	$1,050	H	$1,750
	I	$ 000	I	$ 000	I	$000	I	$800	I	$1,200	I	$2,000

Note: Prices are referred to by letters. The dollar numbers listed under each commodity indicate the profit to be made on that commodity at the particular price.

(2) The explicit laboratory setting, absence of deeply felt incentives, numerical displays, etc., are potential threats to generality. Hence, we cannot confidently generalize novel findings until we have replicated them successfully in other settings.

(3) The issues upon which tradeoffs are based are known from the first in our setting, as are (in principle) all the possible options. Hence, our results are more relevant to the later stages of bargaining, after issues and options have been crystallized, than to the more fluid, earlier stages.

(4) Our student subjects are amateur bargainers. Hence, some of the perspectives and strategies used by professionals will seldom be found here—e.g., elaborate signals of the kind described by Pruitt (1971) and Peters (1955).

Despite these limitations, we believe our task provides a heuristic setting for developing, clarifying, and refining concepts. Theory development, in our view, requires the constant interchange of laboratory and field methodology in which concepts derived in one setting are put to a test in the other.[4] The ideas presented in this chapter are preliminary, subject to the refinement that additional research and generality studies will provide.

BARGAINING STRATEGIES

The Distributive Strategy

Bargainers often rely on what Walton and McKersie (1965) call the distributive strategy. The aim of this strategy is to elicit concessions from the other bargainer. This can be accomplished by either lowering the subjective probability of success he attaches to certain options (e.g., through the use of commitment tactics), lowering the utility he attaches to these options (e.g., through threats), or changing his attitudes (e.g., through persuasive arguments).

In all of our studies, we have found inverse correlations (averaging -.36) between joint profit and measures of distributive behavior. These measures have included the use of threats, demands, positional commitments, status slurs, and extraneous arguments for one's offers.

There is clearly an incompatibility between the distributive strategy and integrative bargaining. The problem is not that distributive bargainers are unwilling to make concessions. Our distributive subjects are perfectly able to move in the direction of compromise, and they fail to reach agreement only when a compromise does not satisfy their levels of aspiration. Rather, it seems that they cannot find or do not take seriously the more integrative options.

Why should this be? Perhaps the assumption of a competitive (win/lose) reward structure that often underlies distributive behavior makes it hard for them to visualize the possibility that both parties can win. They see only two options before them, holding firm or giving in. Perhaps the heightened stress inherent in competition reduces their flexibility and creativity (Deutsch, 1973; North et al., 1964). Or perhaps the goal of distributive behavior—pulling the other party toward one's preferred position—is incompatible with the openness and flexibility that constitute the core of the strategies that lead to the adoption of integrative options.

One wonders why so many people in and out of the laboratory are so quick to adopt the distributive interpretation of bargaining. In part, the answer may lie in the tendency of many bargainers to imitate the other party's apparent level of distributive behavior. Threats tend to elicit counter-threats (Hornstein, 1965), and bargainers are less willing to make concessions to the extent that the other party's demands seem excessive in light of his constraints (Liebert et al., 1968). This suggests that a Prisoner's Dilemma reward structure may underlie decisions about whether or not to adopt a distributive strategy. If so, bargaining would naturally gravitate toward a distributive approach, because it requires only one party to move the interaction in that direction, while the firm resolve of both parties is needed to avoid such movement.

Information Exchange

When we place the two profit schedules shown in Table 5.1 side by side in front of individual subjects, most of them have little difficulty in finding the most integrative options. They quickly discover that the two bargainers have complementary priorities and that a mutually profitable tradeoff is available. But in our usual procedure, where subjects are able to see only their own profit schedules, such insights are more difficult to achieve. This latter procedure more closely models the real world, where values and priorities are a private matter.

It is, of course, possible for bargainers to talk about their values and priorities and thus encourage insight into the joint reward structure. Indeed Walton and McKersie (1965) have argued that integrative bargaining proceeds *mainly* through such information-exchange. In several of our studies, we have tested this position, which draws heavily on Dewey's (1933) theory of rational problem-solving. We have usually employed two measures of information exchange: asking for information about the other's profit schedule, and giving truthful information about one's own schedule. These indices are always highly correlated with each other across dyads.

On the whole, our results do not support Walton and McKersie's exclusive emphasis on information exchange. Under most conditions, we find relatively little information exchange and only moderate, though always positive (averaging .20), relationships between measures of this phenomenon and joint profit. Yet integrative solutions are often found, suggesting that integrative processes other than explicit information exchange are often at work. It would be foolish to argue that information exchange cannot lead to integrative solutions. But we believe that it is not the only and possibly not the most important route.

We have found two conditions under which information exchange *is* predictive of outcome. One (Schulz et al., 1974) involved a team orientation, where bargainers were told to act as if they were members of the same organization and were paid for joint profits. Here we found a good deal of information exchange and a high correlation ($r = .93$) between this variable and joint profit. The other involved subjects who were high in cognitive complexity, as measured by the Streufert and Driver (1967) technique. These subjects engaged in no more information exchange than their less complex compatriots. But they seemed to be able to use the information more effectively to achieve highly integrative solutions ($r = .54$).

The first of these results suggests that fairly large amounts of information are necessary before the average person can gain insight into the joint reward structure. The second suggests that there are people with a superior capacity to process information who need less information to gain insight.

A note of caution must now be sounded. While information exchange can under some conditions lead to integrative agreements, it can actually be counter-productive under others. For example, where there is a good deal of value dissensus, it can lead to a sense of shock and outrage about the other bargainer's perspectives. This is likely to induce distributive behavior and thus preclude the development or acceptance of an integrative option, even where an objective analysis would reveal considerable logrolling potential (Druckman and Zechmeister, 1973). Another problem can arise when information exchange reveals the existence of an option that offers equal profit to the two bargainers (Yukl, 1974b). The norm of equal division can make this option seem so attractive that a premature agreement will be reached, precluding the search for better prospects. In such circumstances, information exchange should be avoided and other strategies employed for the attainment of integrative agreements.

So far, the discussion has dealt with direct information exchange, in which the bargainers talk to one another about their needs and values and their priorities among the issues. In our most recent study, we have examined an indirect form of information exchange that seems to yield more reliable insights into the other bargainer's profit schedule than what he says about this schedule. This involves statements that compare two actual or potential package offers—for example, "I prefer ACD to BCC" or "A and C are O.K. on iron and sulphur, but F is too low on coal." This "comparative" information exchange was strongly correlated with insight[5] ($r = .54$) and moderately correlated with joint profit ($r = .37$), while direct information exchange was quite unrelated to both variables ($r = .12$ and $.13$). One possible explanation for these results lies in the fact that comparative information was more common than direct information. Hence, enough subjects may have been above some information threshold to yield a sizable correlation. It is also possible that bargainers are better able to process comparative information and find it more credible. A final decision about the importance of comparative information exchange must await further research.

Heuristic Trial and Error

The alternatives to information exchange are a set of response-based (as opposed to "information-based") tactics, that can be described in terms of the way bargainers make proposals to one another. We call them collectively "heuristic trial and error." They involve trial and error in the sense that bargainers who employ them frequently vary their proposals in search of an option upon which both parties can agree. They are heuristic in the sense that they employ one or another fruitful technique for deciding what alternative to propose.

Our measures of heuristic trial and error are usually much more closely related to joint profit than to insight. Hence, it appears that these tactics ordinarily lead to solution without insight.

Both heuristic trial and error and comparative information exchange can be used under circumstances where it is difficult or unwise to talk frankly about values and priorities: For example, where communication is not possible, where frank communication may reveal disruptive value dissensus, where constituents are listening, or where trust is not strong enough for people to feel that they can safely reveal intimate information about their motives.

All of the tactics to be described in this section have one element in common—frequent variation of proposals. In an effort to capture this element, we have devised two variation indices: One reflects the number of different package offers proposed; (e.g., A-B-A, F-G-C); the other reflects the frequency of suggestions about more general approaches that can be taken by the two bargainers. Both indices are invariably positively related to joint outcome, with correlations averaging .28. This suggests the importance for integrative bargaining of frequent variations in what is being proposed.

Three types of response-based tactics will now be described:

Systematic concession-making. Kelley and Schenitzki (1972) have described a tactic that involves maintaining one's level of aspiration while frequently varying one's proposal. A bargainer must start out aspiring to a high profit for himself and propose as many options as he can think of that will provide that level of profit. Only when he has exhausted all possibilities should he reduce his level of aspiration. He should then try out all options at this new level before descending to the next, and so on. These authors have shown, in a logically tight theoretical derivation, that systematic use of this strategy by one or both bargainers leads to agreement on an option which has no rival that is better for both parties. They have also demonstrated the value of this strategy in an empirical study that used the Siegel and Fouraker (1960) price-quantity simulation, with bargaining accomplished by note-passing.

We have also used a measure of systematic concession-making in our studies. It reflects the proportion of times an offer is changed in such a way that its value stays within $200 of the previous proposal and a concession on one issue is coupled with an increased demand on another. For example, if the buyer proposed BCD and then followed this with a proposal of ACE or CCC, his second offer would be considered a systematic concession.

This index has been positively related to joint profit in all of our studies, with an average correlation of .31. Correlations between this index and insight into the other party's profit schedule are ordinarily considerably lower, thus supporting the notion that this strategy usually succeeds without an understanding of the joint profit structure. These results add to the external validity of the Kelley/Schenitzki findings by showing that the effect generalizes to face-to-face conversational negotiation, where information exchange might have been thought to be the preferred mode of integrative bargaining.

Concessions on low-priority issues. Another reasonable principle to follow in generating integrative offers is to concede on issues of low priority to oneself while holding firm on high-priority issues. If the other party's priorities for the two are reversed, as in the case of iron and coal in Table 5.1, this strategy will cause the party using it to propose an integrative tradeoff. Furthermore, its use may help the other party to gain insight into the first party's priority rankings among the issues.

Schulz et al. (1974) used a low-priority concession (LPC) index, which consisted of the proportion of new offers in which a bargainer conceded further on his low-priority commodity than on the other two commodities. In a condition where the bargainers could communicate only by passing notes, this index was strongly related to joint outcome ($r = .51$) and weakly but positively related to insight ($r = .32$), as would be expected from the theoretical analysis just presented. Furthermore, bargainers who had been given a team orientation used this strategy more vigorously than did those who had been told to consider only their own needs (an individualistic orientation) *and* made higher joint profits despite the fact that they could not talk to one another. This suggests that making concessions on one's low-priority issues may be a good strategy to choose when bargainers want to develop high joint profits but are not able to exchange information with one another. The use of this strategy is also productive of joint outcome when bargainers can communicate freely with each other, with correlations averaging .30 over the five studies where LPC was measured.[6]

It is interesting to note that Kelley and Schenitzki (1972), in a condition where bargainers could not talk, got a result that was the opposite of ours. They found that, unlike the individualistic orientation, the team orientation *reduced* joint outcome. The major apparent difference between their study and ours lies in the bargaining task employed. The Siegel and Fouraker task, which they used, does not entail issues of differing priority, such as our iron and coal. Hence, there is no way to construct integrative agreements by means of logrolling. Rather, such agreements are to be found at arbitrary locations in a complex matrix of price and quantity. As a result, the strategy of making concessions on low-priority issues, which was so important in our situation, cannot be implemented in theirs.

The only effective strategy in the Siegel and Fouraker task would appear to be the one involving systematic concession-making. Kelley and Schenitzki presented evidence that the team orientation disrupts the use of this strategy. Their team-oriented bargainers jumped around in search of a mutually acceptable option, in contrast to individualistically oriented bargainers, who systematically explored the available options at each successive level of aspiration. This may account for the fact that the team orientation led to reduced joint profit in their study. However, it is difficult to know what to think about these results inasmuch as Schulz et al. found no evidence of reduced use of the systematic concession strategy under the team orientation.

Requesting the other party's reaction. In all of our studies, we have found a positive relationship between joint outcome and the frequency with which the bargainers ask each other's reactions to the latest offer (with an average correlation of .29). There are two possible interpretations of this finding: One is that the feedback achieved from such a request is useful for devising a new offer that will be more to the liking of the other party than was the prior offer. The other is that such a request encourages the listener to believe that the speaker is trying to find a jointly acceptable solution and thus encourages integrative, problem-oriented behavior from the listener.

Possible Limitations of Heuristic Trial and Error

As with any trial-and-error procedure, heuristic trial and error is most likely to succeed where the more integrative options are either (a) among those whose identities are initially known (even though the fact that they are integrative is not known) or (b) easily constructable out of known parts. Our experimental task represents such a situation. There are other situations in which integrative options can be developed only by reconceptualizing the issues and seeking totally new approaches. Insight into the joint reward structure is likely to be particularly important in such situations. Hence, some form of information exchange is likely to be needed, along with, or instead of, heuristic trial and error.

ORIENTATIONS UNDERLYING CHOICE OF STRATEGY

The strategy adopted by a bargainer reflects in part his or her orientation toward the other bargainer. We have already mentioned the team orientation, involving a goal of maximizing joint profits. Our results suggest that this orientation produces information exchange in situations where bargainers can communicate verbally and concessions on low-priority issues in situations where they cannot.

We have also investigated a *problem-solving orientation,* in which people have the goal of finding a mutually acceptable solution. This orientation bears some resemblance to responsiveness in that the other's needs are taken into account. But it is really quite different, since a genuine interest in the other's welfare need not be present. Rather, the other is helped as a means of reaching agreement. To produce this orientation, we tell our subjects to treat the situation as a solvable problem, in which they seek to maximize their own profits while keeping the other bargainer's needs in mind. In two studies, we have contrasted this orientation with an individualistic one, in which bargainers are instructed only to maximize their own profits.

Our results suggest that the problem-solving orientation reduces the incidence of distributive behavior and increases reliance on information exchange and heuristic trial and error. Hence, it produces more integrative agreements. As in Deutsch's (1958) early research on the Prisoner's Dilemma, we found that the individualistic orientation has no systematic impact on the choice of strategy. Some dyads whose members are given this orientation move in the direction of distributive behavior and reach relatively nonintegrative agreements. Others show signs of spontaneously adopting a problem-solving orientation and achieve relatively integrative agreements.

In our thinking, we tend to contrast the problem-solving orientation not with the individualistic orientation but with what we call the "win/lose orientation." This orientation derives from the belief that gains for one party can be achieved only at the expense of the other party. Hence, it has the aim of eliciting concessions from the other bargainer and leads to the adoption of distributive tactics. We view the win/lose orientation as antithetical to the development of integrative agreements.

Results of our most recent study (Magenau et al., 1975) suggest that *trust* is another important antecedent of strategic choice. Trust was manipulated in two ways: In the high-trust condition, we presented the problem-solving orientation, while the subjects were together in the same room and also gave each bargainer a questionnaire that the other had allegedly filled out showing him to be a highly cooperative type. In the low-trust condition, problem-solving instructions were presented separately to each subject, and the false questionnaire portrayed the other bargainer as a highly competitive type. Limit was also manipulated.

Interactions between trust and limit were found, such that the most information was exchanged under a combination of high limit and high trust, and the most distributive behavior was exhibited under a combination of high limit and low trust. These results can be interpreted if we assume that higher limits discourage bargainers from expecting that a solution can be achieved by means of a simple compromise and encourage them to try to influence the other bargainer. When the other is trusted, it seems safe to provide him with information about one's own profit levels, in search of a jointly acceptable solution. When he is not trusted, distributive measures seem to be the best possible means of influence.

Conditions Affecting Orientation

Relatively little is known about the origins of win/lose and problem-solving orientations, so we shall have to rely mainly on speculation in this section.

We would expect a win/lose orientation to develop because of such factors as anger, perception that the other is a threat (Walton and McKersie, 1965), past competition with the other, and the discovery of evidence that both parties cannot succeed simultaneously (Deutsch, 1973; Druckman, 1968). Analogously, it can be argued that a problem-solving orientation will be encouraged by positive feelings, interdependence, kinship, a perception of value congruence or common fate, and apprehension about the development of a conflict spiral. Conceivably the development of a problem-solving orientation also mediates the success of superordinate goals in resolving conflicts (Sherif et al., 1961).

Karrass (1970) has suggested that a pattern of early success in resolving issues in a sequential agenda sets a tone for bargaining that can make it easier to solve later issues. Perhaps such a pattern succeeds because it produces a problem-solving orientation.

Milgram (1974) and Gahagan (1970) have found that it is easier to impose costs on another person when he is at a distance than when he is close at hand. This suggests that physical intimacy may discourage distributive behavior and encourage problem-solving and, hence, the development of integrative solutions. This speculation receives some support from the finding that bargainers take more flexible positions and concede more rapidly when they are face to face than when they are at a distance (Bavelas et al., 1963; Morley and Stephenson, 1969, 1970; Vitz and Kite, 1970). But a recently completed study by Lewis and Fry (1975) suggests that the situation is more complex than one might think. All of their subjects were seated at the same distance from one another, but in some cases they were visually separated by a barrier. They employed *more* distributive behavior and reached *less* integrative agreements when they could see each other than when they could not. Within-cell correlations suggest that the barrier inhibits two forms of nonverbal distributive behavior, staring at the other bargainer and physically invading his territory.

The findings by Bavelas and others on the effect of distance are difficult to interpret because unidimensional tasks were employed—i.e., tasks that restrict bargainers to a set of options on a single dimension. Hence, it is hard to know whether these findings can be generalized to situations with integrative potential. Similar interpretational problems arise with respect to many other results in the bargaining literature. For example, it has been found (Druckman et al., 1972; Teger and Morchan, 1972; Benton, 1972) that representatives who are accountable to their constituents make fewer concessions per unit of time than do representatives who are not accountable and negotiators who are bargaining on their own behalf. But it is not clear whether the fact of being an accountable representative produces a win/lose orientation or a high, inflexible level of aspiration. If the former, accountable representatives will be poor at integrative bargaining; if the latter, results to be discussed shortly suggest that they may be good at it. There is clearly a research frontier here.

Strategies for Inducing Problem-Solving

In the discussion of strategies and orientations so far, we have mainly examined the case in which both bargainers take the same approach. This is a reasonable focus because, as was mentioned earlier, there is a tendency for bargainers to end up adopting a distributive strategy if either starts this way. But suppose one party is behaving distributively while the other wants to shift to joint problem-solving. What can the second party do to change the approach of the first?

Distributive behavior often represents backlash—i.e., is a defensive reaction to a sense of threat. Hence, it can often be reduced by removing perceived threat. For example, Deutsch (1973) suggests that the other party should be reassured that he and his values are viewed as legitimate. Bach and Wyden (1968) recommend "elegant fighting," in which the other's weaknesses are not exploited and he is not forced to make maximal concessions. Walton (1965) suggests that an effort be made to demonstrate trust in the other party. Gibb (1968) argues that one should avoid appearing to evaluate or feel superior to the other party. Kimmel (1975) suggests the importance of performing favors that are viewed as above and beyond the normal call of duty.

Rapoport (1960) has developed a three-step program for reducing defensiveness in debates. He argues that debators resist changing their views because they feel that the adversary is not taking these views seriously. Hence, one must first "convey to the opponent that he has been heard and understood," for example, by engaging in role reversal, which involves verbalizing one's understanding of the other's position. Second, one must communicate to the other party that one has found a "region of validity" in his position—i.e., some portion of his position that one can accept. Finally, one must subtly encourage the other to make the first two steps himself. These proposals are not explicitly oriented toward bargaining but seem relevant whenever bargaining involves a discussion of substantive issues.

In a study designed to test the effectiveness of Rapoport's first step, Johnson (1971) found that accurate role reversal encouraged the other bargainer to make concessions. However, as always with unidimensional bargaining studies, it is not clear whether this effect was due to the development of a problem-solving orientation or to lowered aspirations. Johnson also found that *warm* role reversal (where the other party's views are paraphrased in a friendly manner) made the other party like the actor better but also strengthened the other's commitment to his own position. Conceivably, these results amount to the adoption of a problem-solving orientation along with a high level of aspiration—a combination of conditions which we will argue is highly promotive of integrative agreements.

In an effort to test the effectiveness of Rapoport's second "region of validity" step, Druckman (1968) formed study pairs, composed of a member of each of the two opposing teams, and instructed them to seek "areas of greater or lesser agreement" in their positions. This condition did not contribute to ease of agreement in comparison with a condition in which the issues were discussed informally *within* the teams. However, Rapoport's proposals are aimed at relieving defensiveness in bargaining, and it is not clear that Druckman's procedure allowed such defensiveness to develop since the bargainers did not present their positions to each other before the intervention.

A broader perspective on strategic behavior can be achieved if we view the problem-solving orientation as the cooperative (C) choice in a Prisoner's Dilemma game and the win/lose orientation as the noncooperative (D) choice. Such a perspective is proposed by Walton and McKersie (1965) and makes sense in light of the tendency bargainers have to imitate one another's level of distributive behavior. Research on the Prisoner's Dilemma shows that the other party is most likely to cooperate when one adopts a *matching strategy*, reacting cooperatively to his cooperative behavior and noncooperatively to his noncooperative behavior (Solomon, 1960; Wrightsman et al., 1972). This is essentially a recommendation for the carrot and the stick. To translate this into the terms of integrative bargaining theory, the "carrot" can be viewed as problem-solving behavior and the "stick" as distributive behavior. Recent research (Deutsch, 1973) suggests further that the "stick" part of this strategy will elicit more constructive reactions if it involves behavior that the other party can clearly label as defensive rather than aggressive.

There is one major problem with the matching strategy; namely, that the other party will never experience the "carrot" if he starts and remains distributive in his approach. Indeed, research by Kelley and Stahelski (1970) indicates that he may well adopt the self-righteous belief that he himself is only responding defensively. This means that some sort of *starting mechanism* will often be needed to elicit initial cooperative behavior, which can then be rewarded.

A possible starting mechanism is included in Osgood's GRIT strategy. Osgood (1962) suggests that an individual who seeks cooperation should himself be cooperative for a period of time and then switch to a matching strategy. Osgood's basic theory of conflict regards distributive behavior as defensive in motivation, so he recommends initial reassuring moves, such as partial, unilateral disarmament. But the GRIT strategy may also be applicable to the case in which the other party (or a potentially dominant faction thereof) has been behaving distributively for selfish or competitive reasons, provided that he now views distributive behavior as counter-productive and secretly wishes that both parties were engaged in joint problem-solving. In this case, almost any credible sign of cooperative intent should be enough to alter his behavior.

One advantage of the GRIT proposal is that it takes into account the fact that the other party may be slow to reciprocate initial cooperation because of deep-seated suspicions or failure to understand the value of reciprocity. Hence, the user of the GRIT strategy is advised to (a) remain noncontingently cooperative for a period of time, (b) explain why he has suddenly become cooperative, and (c) invite reciprocation.

Pilisuk and Skolnik (1968) claim to have tested the Osgood proposal with results that were only weakly supportive. But in their study, the GRIT strategy was imposed at the very beginning of interaction, before patterns of behavior had had a chance to develop. Since the GRIT strategy is designed to ameliorate a situation in which the other party is locked into a pattern of distributive behavior, it is not clear that the requisite prior conditions were present.

Resolving the Dilemmas of Bargaining

So far in this chapter we have treated the win/lose and problem-solving orientations as relatively incompatible. In other words, we have implied that it is hard for an individual to embrace both simultaneously. The data from our research tend to support this position, since we often find an inverse correlation between indices of the two kinds of orientation. There are several ways of explaining this incompatibility. One is that strategies involving openness and variety do not mesh well with those involving an effort to become committed to an option that is highly favorable to oneself. Another is that it is psychologically difficult to be both hard and soft at the same time, to seek the other's defeat while genuinely trying to cooperate. Since in most bargaining situations there are incentives for both competition and cooperation, bargainers often experience a dilemma (Kelley, 1966; Walton, 1965; Walton and McKersie, 1965).

How can this dilemma be overcome in such a way as to encourage integrative bargaining? One way is for bargainers to avoid distributive behavior and defend their interests by adopting and maintaining a high level of aspiration. This is the approach of "flexible rigidity," about which more will be said later. But forsaking distributive goals may not always be practical, since they often seem quite promising. Another approach is to *insulate* distributive from problem-solving episodes. Insulation takes two general forms: differential role assignment and sequencing (Walton, 1965).

Differential role assignment is often found on both sides of a dispute. One set of bargainers drawn from both sides (the so-called "black hats") is engaged in distributive sparring, while another set (the so-called "white hats") is quietly exploring possible integrative agreements. Such a phenomenon has been uncovered in interviews with State Department personnel (Pruitt, 1964). Differential role assignment is possible only where both sides consist of more than one individual, thus permitting a division of labor. Often the black hats are prominent in the formal negotiations while the white hats meet informally on the side—e.g., at a local bar.

Sequencing involves a transition from one mode to the other. A two-stage process, moving from distributive to problem-solving behavior, has been described as typical of labor/management negotiation (Douglas, 1962; Stevens, 1963). Problems of coordination presumably occur at the point of transition between stages, since neither party will ordinarily be willing to forsake distributive behavior until the other seems willing to do so. Osgood's GRIT strategy may be useful at this juncture. Also, Pruitt (1971) has suggested several forms of *indirect communication* that can facilitate coordination—namely, signalling, engaging in informal conferences, and communicating through mediators and intermediaries.

Walton and McKersie (1965) argue that a reverse sequence makes more sense from the viewpoint of a rational bargainer. First one engages in problem-solving to find the best possible options, and then one bargains distributively to achieve as much as possible for oneself. But they also question the likelihood of finding such a sequence, because distributive tactics are hard to sustain after a problem-solving episode. A possible example of such a sequence (which also involves differential role assignment) can be seen in the Soviet-American arms control negotiations, where scientists have often talked informally at first and diplomats have followed with formal bargaining (Newhouse, 1973). This example involves a combination of sequencing and differential role assignment. Such a combination is especially common in the first sequence mentioned, with the black hats beginning negotiation and the white hats finishing it. Little is known about the conditions that encourage insulation or determine the form it takes.

GOAL-SETTING

While the problem-solving orientation and the strategies it elicits often contribute to the development of integrative agreements, they generally are not enough. It is usually also necessary for both parties to develop and maintain ambitious goals with respect to their own welfare (Follett, 1940). In other words, they must have high levels of aspiration concerning the issues under consideration and, because integrative agreements are often slow to develop, be willing to *maintain* these aspirations over a reasonable period of time. This means that integrative bargaining will often require participants to experience, at least temporarily, some degree of conflict in their relationship.

It might be argued that an exception to this principle is found in relationships where one party (or both) is genuinely responsive to the other's needs—in the sense of actively seeking to help the other. This can happen when there is real affection, a sense of obligation, or a team orientation. Then all that may be needed is for one party to pose the issue, interview the other concerning his needs, and try to solve the problem of how best to integrate these needs with his own. As was mentioned earlier, responsiveness (if it is mutual) is often instrumental in the development of integrative tradeoffs in sequential agendas. But in the case of a single issue or simultaneous consideration of several issues, there are many other ways in which integrative agreements can be reached, all requiring that the participants actively defend their own interests. In such situations, the societal ideal of responsiveness is probably much less influential than most people imagine or would like. Indeed, this ideal can be dysfunctional, as when people believe in the ideal but are not able to achieve it in their relationship. Members of such dyads need (but may be reluctant, for sentimental or ideological reasons, to engage in) a more frankly conflictful mode of interaction.

The importance of aspirations can be seen in four of our studies where goal-setting was manipulated by giving limits to both parties (either high [$2,300] or low [$2,000]). High limits essentially encourage the development and maintenance of high aspirations, below which their profits were not supposed to drop. The dollar values assigned to high and low limits were not chosen arbitrarily. As the reader can see in Table 5.1, a simple compromise (E-E-E) is feasible in the low-limits condition, while high limits force the bargainers either to find an integrative tradeoff or to discontinue negotiation.

As was expected, we have found that agreements are more integrative when limits are higher. But this favorable trend is balanced, under the typical individualistic orientation, by the fact that nearly one-half of the dyads fail to reach agreement. These dyads resort to distributive behavior and are consequently unable to locate an option that satisfies the aspirations of both parties.

The key to success seems to lie in a combination of high limits and a problem-solving orientation. The high aspirations associated with high limits presumably provide the motivation to keep looking for more suitable options, while the problem-solving orientation provides the right approach for finding such options. Where limits and/or aspirations are low, agreement can usually be reached without developing or locating the more integrative alternatives. Hence, there is little reason to look beyond obvious options, and integrative solutions are often not forthcoming. While a problem-solving orientation may make such solutions a little more likely, our research suggests that it is not very effective in and of itself.

High limits and aspirations have received some bad press in the empirical literature on bargaining because they can slow down the bargaining process and increase the risk of no agreement (Pruitt, 1976). This viewpoint results from the fact that most past experiments have employed unidimensional tasks that lack integrative potential. Even where there is integrative potential, bargainers can, of course, go too far in the direction of adopting and maintaining high aspirations and thereby lose valuable time and/or alienate the other party to the point of withdrawal. Hence, realism must temper the necessary idealism that goes into goal-setting. It is necessary to be willing to alter goals if and when they prove unworkable.

In the setting of realistic goals and the making of concessions with respect to them, the ideal of integrative bargaining will be served best if each bargainer can distinguish clearly between issues of greater and lesser personal importance. This allows him or her to adopt the strategy of holding firm on high-priority issues while conceding on low-priority issues. It encourages the development of trade-offs; it also contributes to valid information exchange.

Unfortunately, people often have difficulty gaining insight into their own priorities. Indeed, research by Balke et al. (1973) suggests that this is true even of professional negotiators. These authors propose a method for helping a bargainer clarify his priorities among several issues. First, he ranks a set of hypothetical package offers. These rankings are then fed into a computer, which uses them to determine how strongly he feels about each issue. Finally, he is apprised of the results of this analysis. (See also the Brehmer and Hammond chapter in this volume.)

In situations where integrative potential exists and bargainers take a problem-solving orientation, conditions that enhance level of aspiration should be positively correlated (up to a point) with the joint outcome obtained in agreement. For example, it is known that high time pressure produces a drop in level of aspiration (Pruitt and Drews, 1969; Yukl, 1974a). It follows that fewer integrative agreements will be reached under greater time pressure, a prediction that has been verified by Yukl et a. (1976).

For aspirations to rise, people must be aware of their own interests and have some faith in the possibility of furthering them. Such awareness and faith often develop in cohesive groups of people with common interests who discuss their situation with one another. Explicit "consciousness-raising" discussions can contribute to such a development. Aspirations are particularly likely to rise when such groups view themselves as part of a broader social movement, making common cause with similar groups in other locations (Kriesberg, 1973).

Such group effects can contribute to joint outcome provided that, as aspirations rise, a problem-solving orientation is maintained by both parties. But here there is a substantial dilemma, because cohesive groups that partake of a social movement are frequently quite distributive in outlook and engender a similar orientation (commonly called "backlash") on the other side.

One solution to this dilemma is to fully or partially insulate group-induced militancy from the bargaining process. As was mentioned earlier, insulation takes two forms, sequencing and differential role assignment. Differential role assignment might involve using as negotiators nonmilitant personnel who are allowed to explore possible agreements with their counterparts in private and away from the surveillance of the group. The negotiators would then be required to seek group approval of the final agreement, so as to ensure that basic aspirations had been met. Sequencing would involve delaying negotiation until after the period of group-building, when distributive militancy is typically at its peak. Thus, for example, the kind of integrative bargaining one sees today in labor/management relations was not so feasible in earlier times when labor unions were being formed. The earlier, more militant stage was probably essential for consciousness-raising and the building of aspirations. But the more integrative conflict episodes came somewhat later.

FLEXIBLE RIGIDITY

Combining insights derived from different facets of our research, it appears useful to categorize the behavior of bargainers along two dimensions: flexibility of means and flexibility of ends. The first dimension is, in part, determined by orientation, and it concerns the extent to which bargainers are willing to explore many options in a search for mutually acceptable alternatives. The second dimension is determined by aspirations and concerns the degree to which bargainers set and maintain high goals. The interaction between these two dimensions can be seen in Figure 5.1, where, in order to simplify the analysis, each dimension is assumed to take either a high or a low value, and both bargainers are assumed to have adopted the same approach.

Our findings suggest that integrative agreements are most likely to emerge when bargaining falls into quadrant I and bargainers demonstrate what might be called *flexible rigidity* in their behavior. While remaining relatively rigid with respect to ends (i.e., goals or aspirations)—holding fast to them over a

Flexibility of Means

		High	Low
Flexibility of Ends	Low	integrative bargaining I	distributive behavior II
	High	premature concession III	compromise IV

FIGURE 5.1 The Flexible Rigidity Model

period of time—they must be flexible with respect to means, trying out various options in search of one that satisfies both sides. Such flexibility can be achieved by means of either information exchange or heuristic trial and error.

Quadrant II describes distributive bargaining, in which the bargainers are rigid with respect to *both* means and ends. Rather than exploring many options, each side attempts to persuade the other to accept his position by means of distributive tactics.

Quadrant III describes a pattern of behavior likely to lead to premature concessions. While the bargainers demonstrate needed flexibility with respect to means, their flexibility with respect to goals makes it likely that agreement will be reached before the boundaries of the situation are fully explored.

In Quadrant IV, while the bargainers are unwilling to try out many approaches to the problem, they are willing to lower their aspirations or goals when agreement is not forthcoming. Compromise agreements based on norms or existing precedents are a likely result.

The concept of flexible rigidity is especially important because people often do not distinguish between means and ends in their approach to bargaining. Sometimes they feel they should take a "hard" approach, and they end up in Quadrant II. At other times, they favor an undifferentiated, "soft" stance and end up in Quadrant III. The reason for taking a hard approach on ends and a soft approach on means, while quite logical, is often not clear in practice.

THE IMPORTANCE OF CONFLICT

In the last two sections, we have endorsed as a precondition for integrative bargaining the maintenance of individual aspirations during joint decision-making. Inevitably this means that each party is making demands on the other while resisting the other's demands. In other words, it means that integrative bargaining commonly emerges from social conflict. In this analysis, conflict is not viewed as a cause of integrative bargaining but as an often-necessary concomitant.

In talking about conflict, we are not, of course, referring to the kind of knock-down-drag-out battles that undermine the problem-solving orientation, stop people from listening to each other, and make them uncreative and repetitive. Such angry conflicts may sometimes be antecedent to the development of a necessary level of aspiration or the conviction that bargaining is necessary. But they cannot themselves produce integrative solutions. Rather, we are talking about what are commonly called "vigorous discussions," "mild arguments," "negotiation," "jockeying for position," etc.

The points just made suggest that people who try too hard to avoid conflict often end up not fully exploiting the integrative potential of their situation. Conflict avoidance can take many forms, including the following:

(a) Submission—in which one party makes a decision and the other follows it.

(b) Denial—in which one or both parties come to believe that there are no differences between them. When problems arise, discussion shifts to points of agreement, as if this will somehow make the disagreement go away.

(c) Withdrawal—where one or both parties turn to some alternative activity or means of need satisfaction. Withdrawal will be encouraged to the extent that the alternative, individualistic activity looks feasible and attractive, and it will be discouraged to the extent that bargaining seems to offer the possibility of a profitable agreement.

(d) Norm-following—in which parties resolve the problems that divide them by adopting ready-made and time-honored solutions instead of trying to develop new approaches. Since norms typically represent the result of earlier joint problem-solving, they are sometimes capable of leading people to integrative agreements. But they often do not quite fit the situation and, because they seem to be the "right approach," can block the discovery of more integrative solutions. Certain kinds of fairness norms seem particularly problematic in this respect since they are likely to encourage compromise rather than the development of integrative agreements.

Willingness to face conflict and engage in bargaining is probably greater to the extent that both parties are equal in power. When they are unequal, the more powerful is likely to avoid bargaining because of a belief that he can or should be able to dominate the other, and the less powerful is likely to follow suit out of fear of reprisal or because of a sense of hopelessness about achieving an equitable agreement. This prediction is supported by the experimental research of Thibaut and Faucheux (1965) and by Bach's clinical observations (Bach and Wyden, 1968). On the international scene, one can argue that serious efforts to resolve the differences between the United States and the USSR and between Egypt and Israel came only after a rough military balance had been achieved and jointly recognized.

While equal power seems to encourage bargaining, the road to this condition is fraught with danger. As the less powerful party builds his strength, the more powerful party may become frightened and resentful, leading to a backlash. Following in the steps of Alinsky (1971), Deutsch (1973) has suggested several ways of building power that are legitimate and relatively nonthreatening. Another potential pitfall in the pursuit of equal power is the anger and resentment that is likely to be felt by the less-powerful party whenever this pursuit meets with frustration. Such emotions can lead to adventuristic policies that invite a further backlash from the more powerful party. The radical black and student movements of the late 1960s seem to have been victims of such a backlash.

Certain individuals are more likely to avoid conflict than others. Bach (Bach and Wyden, 1968; Bach and Goldberg, 1974) describes these individuals as "aggression phobics." Such people subscribe to the belief that anger is best left unexpressed and that fighting is never worth the hassle. The closest they get to strife is when some of them criticize others for initiating arguments, thereby further diminishing the incidence of creative conflict in their lives. Bach describes group therapeutic methods for encouraging aggression phobics to argue more with their spouses. (He also discusses techniques for toning down angry exchanges by the other kind of married couple, who engage in nonproductive, knock-down-drag-out battles.)

Little is known about the characteristics of people who are conflict-phobic. Conceivably this trait is related to persuasibility. If so, we would expect people with a high need for affiliation and with low self-confidence to be poor integrative bargainers. Common folklore might lead one to expect women to be more conflict-phobic than men. Terhune (1970) reviews literature which suggests that women tend to seek compromise and avoid competition more often than men. But the research literature is not really consistent on this point.

Patton and Giffin (1973) argue that conflict is more common among people who feel greater trust toward and comfort with one another. Distrust and discomfort lead to conflict avoidance because of fear that the already fragile relationship will be further disrupted. This generalization would seem to apply more to informal bargaining among individuals who are dependent on one another than to formal bargaining between representatives of organizations.

BARGAINING IN GROUPS

In the prior discussion, we have focused on bargaining in the dyad. Yet we believe that most of our analysis can be applied to larger groups as well.

Groups

The topic most closely related to bargaining in the group literature is referred to as "group problem-solving" (see Kelley and Thibaut, 1969). Research on this topic has usually involved decisions as to how to reach a common goal rather than how to integrate opposing goals and values. Yet some of the principles developed in this research seem applicable to integrative bargaining in groups.

Our analysis suggests that the quality of group problem-solving will suffer to the extent that group members are unwilling or unable to confront the differences that exist between them. Such unwillingness may result from hierarchical power structures (Maier and Hoffman, 1960), in which the few dominate the many, or from group norms that discourage the expression of conflict (Bion, 1959; Stock and Thelen, 1958).

Many groups use a rule of majority decision when they encounter differences of opinion. Like other norms, this rule is often capable of resolving controversy, yet is dysfunctional since it inhibits the development of an integrative agreement (Maier and Solem, 1952). At a minimum, the positions of minority members should be heard before a decision is made. Better still from the viewpoint of integrative bargaining would be a norm that makes voting the last resort, to be used only after a real attempt has been made to achieve unanimity. Such a norm might seem overly costly in time. Yet it should be noted that business meetings in the Society of Friends (Quakers) have traditionally been run on a principle of unanimity, often with considerable efficiency.

Group Cohesiveness

The relationship between cohesiveness and integrative bargaining is problematic. On the one hand, Back (1951) has shown that the members of more cohesive groups feel freer to express doubts and reservations about one another's arguments and yet are more capable of reaching a joint decision. This sounds like flexible rigidity. On the other hand, Janis (1972) has warned against cohesiveness in his theory of groupthink, arguing that in highly cohesive groups there is a tendency to suppress doubts and arguments that challenge the existing or emerging group consensus. Unfortunately, Back's study was performed on dyads, where it is not possible to have at the same time dissent and an emerging group consensus. Hence, research is needed to determine whether (and under what conditions) his results apply to larger groups. It may also be useful to distinguish between the concepts of attraction toward the group (cohesion) and security in the group (idiosyncrasy credit). Groupthink may occur whenever members are highly attracted to a group but are insecure about how others feel about them. Flexible rigidity may be the product of high attraction in conjunction with a general sense of security.

Whether or not Janis is right about the dysfunctional effects of cohesiveness, his concept of groupthink seems important. Groupthink occurs when people protect the group consensus by failing to voice their doubts, disciplining others who do so, and preventing others from receiving dissonant information. He suggests the following ways of avoiding groupthink: Encourage members to discuss the issues with trusted associates away from the group; invite one or two outside experts to each group meeting; have the leader of the group abstain from stating his or her own position at the outset of the meeting; encourage free expression of reservations and doubts; assign one or more members the role of devil's advocate to challenge the majority view; and hold special meetings after a preliminary consensus has been reached in order to permit members to express their remaining doubts. Though these suggestions are intended to improve group problem-solving, most of them also seem to hold promise as means for helping groups engage in the sort of conflict that is essential for the development of a more integrative consensus.

SUMMARY AND CONCLUSIONS

On the basis of our research findings, we have argued that integrative bargaining requires individuals to demonstrate *flexible rigidity* in their behavior. While remaining relatively rigid with respect to goals, bargainers should be flexible with respect to the means they use to seek agreement. Our process analysis suggests that flexibility of means can be achieved by either (a) heuristic trial and error—a response-based strategy for seeking the other party's reactions to a large variety of tentatively advanced options and general proposals, or (b) information exchange, in which bargainers ask for information about the needs and values of others (and provide valid information about their own). The distributive strategy, with its use of threats, positional commitments, and arguments about why the other should concede, amounts to rigidity with respect to means. Hence it blocks the development of integrative agreements.

So long as individuals maintain a problem-solving orientation, involving readiness to seek a mutually acceptable option, heuristic trial and error and/or information exchange are likely to predominate. But a problem-solving orientation is usually not enough. Consistent with the principle of flexible rigidity, the discovery of integrative alternatives also requires individuals to set and maintain high aspirations unless and until these aspirations prove unworkable.

In addition to discussing the bargaining behavior of dyads, we have also examined briefly the applicability of the flexible rigidity concept to multilateral bargaining in groups.

Our ideas are based largely on research using a laboratory simulation of the negotiation conference. We believe the laboratory provides a heuristic setting for the development, clarification, and testing of concepts. But in the broader sense, theory development requires the constant interplay of both laboratory and field methodologies. Hence, our theory should best be viewed as preliminary, subject to the refinements that additional laboratory *and* field research will provide.

NOTES

1. First used by Walton and McKersie (1965).

2. In this discussion, the term "agenda" has been extended to embrace any sequence of encounters involving divergent interests between two or more parties. For example, it might cover a year's worth of decision-making for a married couple.

3. In some of our studies, we have substituted household appliances for these commodities.

4. The viewpoint stated here is largely derived from Kelman (1968).

5. The insight measure was weighted by confidence and was scored only for bargainers who indicated that they had achieved their insight during the bargaining.

6. Interpretation of the correlations just cited is tricky in that movement toward an integrative solution for other reasons could conceivably produce a heightened LPC. To rule out this possibility, we have looked at LPC in the first two offers for protocols in which both parties make at least four offers. We have found that bargainers who concede more at first on their low-priority commodity end up with higher joint profit, suggesting that some element of LPC is causally related to integrative bargaining.

REFERENCES

ALINSKY, S. (1971) Rules for Radicals. New York: Random House.
BACH, G. R. and H. GOLDBERG (1974) Creative Aggression. Garden City, N.Y.: Doubleday.
BACH, G. R. and P. WYDEN (1968) The Intimate Enemy. New York: Avon.
BACK, K. W. (1951) "Influence through social communication." J. of Abnormal and Social Psychology 46: 9-23.
BALKE, W. M., K. R. HAMMOND, and G. D. MEYER (1973) "An alternate approach to labor-management relations." Administrative Sci. Q. 18: 311-327.
BAVELAS, A., T. G. BELDEN, E. S. GLENN, J. ORLANSKY, J. W. SCHWARTZ, and H. W. SINAIKO (1963) Teleconferencing: Summary of a Preliminary Research Project. Washington, D.C.: Institute for Defense Analyses.
BENTON, A. A. (1972) "Accountability and negotiations between group representatives." Proceedings of the 80th Annual Convention of the American Psychological Association: 227-228.
BION, W. R. (1959) Experiences in Groups. New York: Basic Books.
DEUTSCH, M. (1958) "Trust and suspicion." J. of Conflict Resolution 2: 265-279.
——— (1973) The Resolution of Conflict. New Haven, Conn.: Yale Univ. Press.
DEWEY, J. (1933) How We Think. Lexington, Mass.: D. C. Heath.
DOUGLAS, A. (1962) Industrial Peacemaking. New York: Columbia Univ. Press.
DRUCKMAN, D. (1968) "Prenegotiation experience and dyadic conflict resolution in a bargaining situation." J. of Experimental Social Psychology 4: 367-383.
——— and K. ZECHMEISTER (1973) "Conflict of interest and value dissensus: Propositions in the sociology of conflict." Human Relations 26: 449-466.
DRUCKMAN, D., D. SOLOMON, and K. ZECHMEISTER (1972) "Effects of representational role obligations on the process of children's distribution of resources." Sociometry 35: 387-410.
FESTINGER, L. (1950) "Informal social communication." Psych. Rev. 57: 271-282.
FOLLETT, M. P. (1940) "Constructive conflict," in H. C. Metcalf and L. Urwick (eds.) Dynamic Administration: The Collected Papers of Mary Parker Follett. New York: Harper: 30-49.
FROMAN, L. A., Jr. and M. D. COHEN (1970) "Compromise and logroll: Comparing the efficiency of two bargaining processes." Behavioral Sci. 15: 180-183.
GAHAGAN, J. P. (1970) "Social contact and communication in the Prisoner's Dilemma game." Presented at the Annual Meeting of the Eastern Psychological Association.
GIBB, J. R. (1968) "Defensive communication," in W. G. Bennis et al. (eds.) Interpersonal Dynamics. Homewood, Ill.: Dorsey.
HORNSTEIN, H. (1965) "The effects of different magnitudes of threat upon interpersonal bargaining." J. of Experimental Social Psychology 1: 282-293.
JANIS, I. L. (1972) Victims of Groupthink. Boston: Houghton Mifflin.

JOHNSON, D. W. (1971) "Effects of warmth of interaction, accuracy of understanding and the proposal of compromises on listener's behavior." J. of Counseling Psychology 18: 207-216.

KARRASS, C. L. (1970) The Negotiating Game. New York: Thomas Y. Crowell.

KELLEY, H. H. (1966) "A classroom study of the dilemmas in interpersonal negotiations," in K. Archibald (ed.), Strategic Interaction and Conflict. Berkeley, Calif.: Institute of International Studies, University of California.

——— and D.P. SCHENITZKI (1972) "Bargaining," in C.G. McClintock (ed.) Experimental Social Psychology. New York: Holt, Rinehart & Winston.

KELLEY, H. H. and A. J. STAHELSKI (1970) "Social interaction basis of cooperators' and competitors' beliefs about others." J. of Personality and Social Psychology 16: 66-91.

KELLEY, H. H., and J. W. THIBAUT (1969) "Group problem solving," in G. Lindzey and E. Aronson (eds.) Handbook of Social Psychology. Vol. 4. Reading, Mass.: Addison-Wesley.

KELMAN, H. C. (1968) A Time to Speak. San Francisco: Jossey-Bass.

KIMMEL, M. J. (1975) "Distinguishing trusting orientations from game behavior in the Prisoners' Dilemma." Presented at the American Psychological Association Convention.

KRIESBERG, L. (1973) The Sociology of Social Conflicts. Englewood Cliffs, N.J.: Prentice-Hall.

LEWIS, S.A. and R. FRY (1975) "The effects of orientation and visual isolation on integrative bargaining." Unpublished manuscript, Wayne State University.

LIEBERT, R.M., W.P. SMITH, M. KEIFFER, and J.H. HILL (1968) "The effects of information and magnitude of initial offer on interpersonal negotiation." J. of Experimental Social Psychology. 4: 431-441.

LOTT, A. and B. LOTT (1965) "Group cohesiveness as interpersonal attraction: A review of relationships between antecedent and consequent variables." Psych. Bull. 64: 259-309.

MAGENAU, J., D. G. PRUITT, I. KONAR, and M. J. KIMMEL (1975) "The impact of trust on integrative bargaining." Presented at the Eastern Psychological Association Convention.

MAIER, N. F. and L. R. HOFFMAN (1960) "Quality of first and second solutions in group problem solving." J. of Applied Psychology 44: 278-283.

MAIER, N. F. and A. R. SOLEM (1952) "The contribution of a discussion leader to the quality of group thinking: The effective use of minority opinions." Human Relations 5: 277-288.

MILGRAM, S. (1974) Obedience to Authority. New York: Harper & Row.

MORGAN, W. R. and J. SAWYER (1967) "Bargaining, expectations, and the preference for equality over equity." J. of Personality and Social Psychology 6: 139-149.

MORLEY, I. E. and G. M. STEPHENSON (1969) "Interpersonal and inter-party exchange: A laboratory simulation of an industrial negotiation at the plant level." British J. of Psychology 60: 543-545.

——— (1970) "Formality in experimental negotiations: A validation study." British J. of Psychology 61: 383-384.

NEWHOUSE, J. (1973) Cold Dawn: The Story of Salt. New York: Holt, Rinehart & Winston.

NORTH, R. C., R. A. BRODY, and O. A. HOLSTI (1964) "Some empirical data on the conflict spiral." Peace Research Society (International) Papers 1: 1-14.

OSGOOD, C. E. (1962) An Alternative to War or Surrender. Urbana, Ill.: Univ. of Illinois Press.

PATTON, B. R. and K. GIFFIN (1973) Problem-Solving Group Interaction. New York: Harper & Row.

PETERS, E. (1955) Strategy and Tactics in Labor Negotiations. New London, Conn.: National Foremen's Institute.

PILISUK, M. and P. SKOLNICK (1968) "Inducing trust: A test of the Osgood proposal." J. of Personality and Social Psychology 8: 121-133.

PRUITT, D. G. (1964) Problem Solving in the Department of State. (Social Science Foundation and Department of International Relations Monograph Series in World Affairs). Denver, Colo.: University of Denver.

——— (1971) "Indirect communication and the search for agreement in negotiation." J. of Applied Social Psychology 1: 205-239.

——— (1972) "Methods for resolving differences of interest: A theoretical analysis." J. of Social Issues 28: 133-154.

——— (1976) "Power and bargaining," in B. Seidenberg and A. Snadowsky (eds.) Social Psychology. New York: Free Press.

——— and J. L. DREWS (1969) "The effect of time pressure on the reaction to a concession in negotiation." J. of Experimental Social Psychology 5: 43-60.

PRUITT, D. G. and S. A. LEWIS (1975) "Development of integrative solutions in bilateral negotiation." J. of Personality and Social Psychology 31: 621-633.

RAPOPORT, A. (1960) Fights, Games, and Debates. Ann Arbor: Univ. of Michigan Press.

SCHULZ, J. W. (1976) "Integrative bargaining in couples: The effects of normative structure." Unpublished doctoral dissertation, State University of New York at Buffalo.

——— D. G. PRUITT, and S. A. LEWIS (1974) "The effects of communication and orientation on integrative bargaining." Presented at the 45th Eastern Psychological Association Convention, Philadelphia.

SEN, A. K. (1970) Collective Choice and Individual Values. New York: Holden-Day.

SHERIF, M., O. J. HARVEY, B. J. WHITE, W. R. HOOD, and C. W. SHERIF (1961) Intergroup Conflict and Cooperation. Norman, Okla.: Institute of Group Relations.

SIEGEL, S. and L. E. FOURAKER (1960) Bargaining and Group Decision Making. New York: McGraw-Hill.

SOLOMON, L. (1960) "The influence of some types of power relationships and game strategies upon the development of interpersonal trust." J. of Abnormal and Social Psychology 61: 223-230.

STEVENS, C. M. (1963) Strategy and Collective Bargaining Negotiation. New York: McGraw-Hill.

STOCK, D. and H. A. THELEN (1958) Emotional Dynamics and Group Culture. Washington, D.C.: National Training Laboratory.

STREUFERT, S. and M. DRIVER (1967) "Impression formation as a measure of the complexity of conceptual structure." Education and Psych. Measurement 27: 1025-1039.

TANNENBAUM, A. S. (1968) Control in Organizations. New York: McGraw-Hill.

TEGER, A. I. and R. MORCHAN (1972) "The agent, team, and the individual factors in negotiations." Unpublished manuscript, State University of New York at Buffalo.

TERHUNE, K. W. (1970) "The effects of personality in cooperation and conflict," in P. Swingle (ed.) The Structure of Conflict. New York: Academic Press.

THIBAUT, J. and C. FAUCHEUX (1965) "The development of contractual norms in a bargaining situation under two types of stress." J. of Experimental Social Psychology 1: 89-102.

VITZ, P. C. and W. R. KITE (1970) "Factors affecting conflict and negotiation within an alliance." J. of Experimental Social Psychology 6: 233-247.

WALKER, W. L. and J. W. THIBAUT (1971) "An experimental examination of pre-trial conference techniques." Minnesota Law Rev. 55: 1113-1137.

WALTON, R. E. (1965) "Two strategies of social change and their dilemmas." J. of Applied Behavioral Science 1: 167-179.

――― and R. B. McKERSIE (1965) A Behavioral Theory of Labor Negotiation. New York: McGraw-Hill.

WRIGHTSMAN, L. S., Jr., J. O'CONNOR, and N. J. BAKER [eds.] (1972) Cooperation and Competition. Belmont, Calif.: Brooks/Cole.

YUKL, G. (1974a) "The effects of situational variables and opponent concessions on a bargainer's perception, aspirations and concessions." J. of Personality and Social Psychology 29: 227-236.

――― (1974b) "A review of laboratory research on two party negotiation." Unpublished manuscript, University of Akron.

YUKL, G. A., M. P. MALONE, B. HAYSLIP, Jr. and T. A. PAMIN (1976) "The effects of time pressure and issue settlement order on integrative bargaining." Sociometry 39: 277-280.

Chapter 6

THE ROLE OF DEBATE IN NEGOTIATION

CHARLES WALCOTT
P. TERRENCE HOPMANN
and
TIMOTHY D. KING

Department of Political Science
University of Minnesota

Most negotiations are, to some extent, exercises in persuasive debate: "mutual campaign(s) of education toward a mutual appreciation and adjustment of the perceptions and preferences of several or all of the parties concerned" (Deutsch, 1968: 131).[1] At the same time, few negotiations are *exclusively* debates. Rather, processes of persuasion coexist with processes of bargaining. The latter tend to be concerned with gaining advantage and reaching solutions independently of changes in negotiators' attitudes or beliefs regarding substantive issues. This embedding of debate in a context that includes, and is often dominated by, bargaining makes the empirical analysis of debate in negotiation a challenging task both conceptually and methodologically.

The role of debate in negotiation processes varies widely. First, when analyzing any particular case, one must ask whether the debate is being pursued "seriously." For example, when diplomats debate an issue such as on-site inspection in connection with a proposed treaty governing nuclear testing, they will seem to be trying sincerely to persuade one another that their respective positions are technically correct, politically acceptable, and so on. In fact, they may feel genuinely capable of persuading one another on such matters. Or they may be merely showing intransigence while waiting for

AUTHORS' NOTE: The authors acknowledge the valuable support of the Harold Scott Quigley Center of International Studies, the Office of International Programs, and the Graduate School Research Fund, all at the University of Minnesota.

a weakening of another party's position and hoping for a change not in their adversaries' beliefs, but simply in their bargaining strategy. An analysis of debate as distinguished from bargaining must assume serious intent to persuade. In actual cases, though, this determination is often difficult to make.

Even granting seriousness, the purposes and consequences of debate will vary. Ordinary persuasive debate entails attempting to bring an adversary's views into line with one's own, and in this sense debate is a competitive activity. The debater's aim is to improve his or her position in a final settlement, at the expense of the other party or parties. However, debate may be pursued also as a device for facilitating joint problem-solving and promoting the attainment of "integrative" agreements. (See the discussion by Pruitt and Lewis in the previous chapter.) Whether debate has primarily competitive or cooperative implications may depend upon both the initial intentions of the negotiating parties and the manner in which the debate is approached. In this chapter, the problem will be examined, with particular attention to evidence pertaining to the possible role of debate in cooperative problem-solving within the context of negotiation.

We will also be concerned with questions of method. While processes of conflict and bargaining can be analyzed using abstract models or scenarios for interactive behavior (e.g., the Prisoner's Dilemma matrix), debate is a verbal activity that requires a relatively complex substantive context (i.e., something worth debating about) in order to take place. This suggests that debate must be observed either in very realistic laboratory settings, such as simulations, or outside the laboratory, in situ. Research of this sort raises some interesting questions with regard to design and measurement. We will discuss these questions and review work, including our own, that has been done in this area.

TECHNIQUES OF DEBATE: SELF-PRESENTATION AND BILATERAL FOCUS

When debate is approached competitively, it typically follows a straightforward format. Each debater outlines his position and the reasons for it, attempting to counter or mitigate arguments of a similar nature made by others. One may or may not attack another directly, but in any event primary emphasis is apt to be placed on the presentation, explanation, and defense of one's own position. This technique may be labeled "self-presentation." The debater who uses it is normally assumed to be seeking to maximize his or her own gain from negotiation, rather than to find a novel solution to the joint problem under negotiation, or to reach some agreement per se.

In contrast to the above, it has been argued, most notably by Rapoport (1960, 1964), that debate can make a unique contribution to problem-solving and conflict resolution in negotiations if it is pursued properly. In this view, conflict is often grounded in misunderstanding. Such misunderstanding is not (or is not limited to) merely factual disagreement, nor is it simply a result of ambiguous communication. It stems from basically different images of reality held by the parties to a dispute or negotiation. These images may have their sources in cultural differences, in different individual or collective learning experiences, or in different ideologies, and, as Rapoport suggests, they are reinforced by the "blindness of involvement" in one's own particular experiences or point of view. Rapoport's is a complex and speculative analysis, but it reduces to the basic proposition that parties to disputes do not understand one another adequately and, moreover, are typically unaware of that fact. This, Rapoport suggests, produces a psychological set that is inimical to the development of trust, problem-solving, and thus conflict resolution.

In order to overcome failure of understanding, Rapoport (1964: 176) has recommended a strategy of constructive debate that involves:

(1) the ability and willingness of each participant to state the position of the opponent to the opponent's satisfaction (exchange of roles);
(2) the ability and willingness of each participant to state the conditions under which the opponent's position is valid or has merit; and
(3) the ability and willingness of each opponent to assume that in many respects the opponent is like himself—that is, that a common ground exists where the opponents share common values, and each is aware of this common ground and perhaps of the circumstances that have led the opponent to the position he holds (empathy).

It should be noted that only the first two of these involve overt behavior—i.e., the making of particular kinds of statements. And only these two—role reversal and exploration of the region of validity—have been amenable to direct experimental manipulation and observation. The third requirement, empathy, depends upon a negotiator's good will and determination to attempt the technique, or it is a product of meeting the first two requirements.

Following Druckman (1968, 1973), we will refer to this technique, or variants of it, as "bilateral focus." It differs from self-presentation not only in its method but in its purposes. While this makes comparisons between the two techniques hazardous, they have nonetheless been undertaken, usually with the purpose of discovering whether bilateral focus does in fact produce results that differ substantially from those occurring through self-presentation. This research has tended strongly to deal with dependent variables that indicate conflict resolution (e.g., the attainment of agreement or the development of positive mutual attitudes) but not with those that reflect the outcomes of competition (e.g., a negotiator's winnings relative to those of another negotiator). In reviewing this comparative literature, we will therefore separate those studies that focus primarily on conflict resolution from those concerned, at least in part, with competition.

Debate as Conflict Resolution

Johnson (1967) contrasted self-presentation with a technique of role reversal in which each member of a negotiating dyad was instructed to present the viewpoint of the other member early in the negotiation. Self-presenters were instructed to both present their own position and rebut that of the other. The issue, a hypothetical court case, was presented in one of two forms. In the "compatible" condition, though subjects were given to believe that the positions were incompatible, there actually was no necessary conflict between them. An agreement could be reached if this misunderstanding could be cleared up. In the "incompatible" condition, the positions were mutually exclusive, and agreement could be reached only if at least one subject would yield. Thus, bilateral focus was examined both under conditions that closely reflected Rapoport's view of the source of conflict (misunderstanding) and under conditions that did not.

Johnson found that bilateral focus, as predicted, led to a greater objective understanding of the opponent's position than did self-presentation. However, only in the compatible condition did reversing roles lead to a greater perception that *the opponent* understood one's own position better. In the incompatible condition, self-presenters felt that they were better understood.

With respect to the achievement of agreement, there appeared to be no significant difference between role reversal and self-presentation. Increased understanding of the opponent's position thus did not have an identifiable effect on the propensity to reach agreement.

Johnson also had all role reversers rated by observers on the adequacy of their performance. This permitted analysis to be done on highly able subjects alone and produced a finding that was not apparent when all subjects were analyzed. Here, role reversal produced significantly more perception of similarity of positions under the compatible condition than did self-presentation, but significantly less perception of similarity of positions under the incompatible condition. The same finding held with respect to perceived "similarity as people."

Thus, Johnson demonstrated a relationship between bilateral focus and the kind of attitude change that one might expect would facilitate agreement, but this relationship was qualified by both the adequacy of role reversal and the compatibility of initial positions. The former qualification seems reasonable enough, and it suggests that the production of bilateral focus may not be easy. The latter qualification is more interesting. In effect, it suggests that Rapoport's approach has merit, but only when Rapoport's initial assumption—that conflict arises out of misunderstanding—is conceded. Where positions were "objectively" incompatible, role reversal led to heightened perceptions of dissimilarity and even a sense of not being well understood.

Muney and Deutsch (1968) examined the effects of role reversal in a manner similar to that used by Johnson. Their specific technique differed somewhat, however. Subjects were instructed to literally play the role of the other, and act as if they sincerely believed the other's point of view. However, subjects were not fully informed, prior to role reversal, of the other's positions and supporting arguments, which casts some doubt on the effectiveness of this particular version of the technique.

Muney and Deutsch instructed dyads holding opposing views to either role-reverse or self-present in discussions of euthanasia or of teachers' strikes, with the goal of reaching a mutually agreeable joint recommendation. Perhaps their most striking finding was that role reversers obtained not more, but fewer agreements on both issues than did self-presenters.

Again, as in Johnson's (1967) study, both skill in role reversal and the nature of the issue under debate were found to be important, and these two variables interacted significantly. On the strike issue, skillful role reversers experienced a positive attitude change and feelings of acquired insight into the other's position. However, in discussions of euthanasia, effective role reversers felt less understood by their opponents. Overall, while both procedures produced evidence of positive attitude change, role reversal tended to work better in the teachers' strike debates, while self-presentation was more successful when euthanasia was debated. In effect, the data from the strike debate resembled those from Johnson's compatible condition, while the data from the debate on euthanasia resembled those from the incompatible condition. Since Muney and Deutsch found that more agreements were reached regarding strikes while more opinion change occurred concerning euthanasia, we may infer that initial opinions on the euthanasia issue were more divergent (i.e., less compatible) than those on the strike issue. Thus, the findings of Muney and Deutsch may be viewed as confirming the rather qualified support for Rapoport's thesis found in Johnson's data.

Hammond et al. (1966: 352) used procedures very similar to Rapoport's techniques in operationalizing bilateral focus. Their procedures consisted of:

(1) restating accurately the other person's position;
(2) stating reasons for agreement with some specific points in the person's argument;
(3) either exploring the area of disagreement, or making a positive statement of one's own position.

The experimental procedures used by Hammond et al. were relatively complex. (See also the chapter by Brehmer and Hammond in this volume.) The problems involved estimating the level of "democratic institutions" in hypothetical nations, based upon stimulus cues supplied by the experimenters. Subjects were trained to evaluate the cues differently, however. One group's training involved tasks where the cue variable "state control" accounted for 98 percent of the variance in the criterion variable (in a nonlinear manner), while the other cue variable, "free election," was randomly related to the criterion. For the other group, "free elections" accounted for 98 percent of the variance (in a linear manner), while "state control" was randomly related to the criterion.

Dyads consisting of one subject trained in each manner were then given new cases to judge. Each subject recorded an individual judgment, then the two discussed their differences until a joint decision could be reached. Each subject then recorded a private judgment which was not revealed to the other. Finally, the experimenter reported the correct answer, and another case was introduced. Each member of each pair was trained in either the bilateral focus procedure or in self-presentation. Five pairs consisted of two subjects trained in bilateral focus, five contained two self-presenters, and ten contained one of each.

The basic finding was that there were no significant differences between methods of debate (bilateral focus and self-presentation) with respect to either amount of cognitive change or amount of compromise. Agreements could not be used as a dependent variable since all pairs (evidently) reached agreement on all cases.

One can speculate that the constraints of the experiment may have contributed to these findings. Overt compromise, at least, was required of all subjects. The feedback from the experimenter in the form of correct answers may have provided strong enough cues to override any differential effects of method of presentation. Under such circumstances, perhaps, failure to find significant differences between bilateral focus and self-presentation should not be surprising. Nonetheless, the evidence that bilateral focus, under conditions of "objective" disagreement, does not produce a greater disposition toward compromise than does self-presentation is consistent with the other findings reviewed to this point.

Druckman (1968) examined the effects of using bilateral focus procedures prior to actual negotiation. Using a complex labor-management simulation, Druckman employed four prenegotiation conditions: unilateral discussion (labor or management groups discussed the issues among themselves); unilateral position-formation (the groups were instructed to formulate positions and strategies); bilateral study (subjects from both groups discussed the issues and were instructed to try to gain an understanding of the opposing point of view); and control (subjects were familiarized with the issues, but did not discuss them). Individuals from labor and management then negotiated in pairs, each pair consisting of subjects from the same prenegotiation condition. No role-reversal procedures were required during the actual negotiation.

Druckman found that prenegotiation issue-formation tended to inhibit agreement. However, he did not find evidence that would suggest that bilateral study was superior to unilateral focus in producing agreement. Thus Druckman's findings fit the pattern of results reviewed above, in which bilateral focus fails, on the whole, to produce significantly more actual agreement than does self-presentation.

Johnson (1971b) examined the intervening effects of warmth of interaction, accuracy of understanding, and the proposal of compromises in a study that used the basic model of Johnson's earlier (1967) study, except that one member of each pair was a confederate of the experimenter and was responsible for manipulating the above variables, and only the incompatible condition was used. Only the confederate role reversed, and role reversal was used in all pairs. Johnson found that accurate role reversal produced more agreements than did inaccurate role reversal, but that the proposal of compromises was even more strongly related to the attainment of agreement. Warmth of interaction was unrelated to agreement, but was related to positive attitudes and perceptions of similarity.

Conclusions

While Rapoport's argument for the use of bilateral focus techniques in debate is in many ways compelling, our review of experimental findings to date reveals little empirical support for it. Specifically, our reading of the evidence suggests the following conclusions (see also Johnson, 1971c):

(1) The hypothesis that bilateral focus is superior in general to self-presentation as a means of inducing agreement is not supported. Johnson (1967) and Druckman (1968) have found no significant difference, while Muney and Deutsch (1968) found self-presentation more effective.

(2) There is evidence that bilateral focus may be effective in producing attitudinal changes (e.g., assumptions of similarity) and cognitive changes (e.g., greater understanding of the opponent's position), which may be associated with conflict resolution (Johnson, 1967; Muney and Deutsch, 1968; but see also Hammond et al., 1966).

(2a) The positive effects of bilateral focus may be stronger or more consistent when the issue under negotiation is such that the two positions are potentially compatible. Johnson's (1967) findings suggest this, and those of Muney and Deutsch (1968) can be interpreted in this way.

(2b) Under incompatible conditions, bilateral focus may serve to sharpen the perceptions of incompatibility, inhibiting positive attitudinal change (Johnson, 1967; and perhaps Muney and Deutsch, 1968). In particular, bilateral focus may be less effective than self-presentation in producing a feeling that one has been understood.

(3) Several additional factors affect the successful use of bilateral focus techniques (see Druckman, 1971). These include the "adequacy" with which the behavior is performed (Johnson, 1967; Muney and Deutsch, 1968), the proposal of compromises (Johnson, 1971b), and perceived warmth of interaction (Johnson, 1971b).

These conclusions must be viewed with caution, since they derive from only a few studies. Moreover, as we have noted, the operational definitions of bilateral focus used in the various studies have differed, which makes comparison among them difficult. Finally, these conclusions reflect an exclusive concern with conflict resolution. Debate, as we have suggested above, is also potentially relevant to determining the outcome of a competitive interaction. We now turn to that issue.

Debate as Competition

The consequences of bilateral focus for the determination of winners and losers in negotiation have barely been explored. However, Johnson (1971a) has provided some preliminary, suggestive evidence. Using a confederate as one member of each negotiating dyad, and using only the incompatible condition (see Johnson, 1967), Johnson explored the consequences of unilaterally role reversing and of listening to one's opponent unilaterally role reverse.

Johnson found that engaging in role reversal tended to produce the greatest increase in knowledge of the opponent's position. Listening to role reversal fared worst in these respects, generally producing fewer results than self-presentation, which in turn fared worse than role reversal. Although listeners perceived that their (role-reversing) opponent accepted them as persons and felt warmly toward them, the attitudes of listeners toward the issues under debate tended to be reinforced rather than modified. Perhaps, as Johnson speculates, unilateral role reversal suggests to the listener that it is the role reverser who is open to persuasion.

The implication of this finding is that unilateral role reversal would be a bad strategy in a mixed-motive negotiation, since one would be inviting exploitation. However, in Johnson's study, there are no data on the amount of substantive change made in the positions of the parties, so we cannot tell how they actually fared. This argument would not apply, of course, to bilateral role reversal, but it does suggest that bilateral role reversal may have to be planned in advance, since a second role reversal is perhaps not a likely response to an unplanned, unilateral gesture of this sort.

Johnson and Dustin (1970) compared the consequences of listening to role reversal for individualistically and competitively oriented subjects. Using a confederate as the role reverser in each dyad, and using both the compatible and the incompatible conditions (Johnson, 1967), they found an interaction between individual orientation and compatibility of positions. In the incompatible condition, competitively oriented subjects perceived more similarity between their own and their opponent's basic opinions and beliefs than did individualistically oriented subjects; in the compatible condition, the reverse was true.

If role reversal (or a similar procedure aimed at producing a bilateral focus) is to be used, either unilaterally or with an expectation of reciprocity, its effects apparently will vary with the listener's definition of the situation, as well as with the compatibility of initial positions. Whether such definitions of the situation can in turn be affected by bilateral focus techniques remains a subject for investigation, though the evidence reviewed above, that bilateral focus can render more positive one's attitudes toward one's opponents, can be seen as encouraging in that regard.

That most of the research done on the effects of bilateral focus has concentrated on conflict resolution is understandable and appropriate in view of Rapoport's (1960, 1964) emphasis in that direction. However, since negotiation is a mixed-motive activity, it will be necessary to give more attention to the consequences (defined in terms of winning and losing) of the use of techniques that are designed to induce cooperation.

BILATERAL FOCUS, INTEGRATIVE BARGAINING, AND VERBAL INTERACTION

While research on bilateral focus may have concentrated too little on competitive consequences, there is a sense in which a paradigm of competition may have been too influential in these efforts. In the design of problems for negotiation, and in the adoption simply of "agreement" as a criterion of conflict resolution, investigators may have inadvertently limited the options available to their negotiating subjects and thus precluded the possibility of "integrative" bargaining (Walton and McKersie, 1965; see also the Pruitt and Lewis chapter in this volume).

"Integrative" bargaining is a process by which negotiators seek to maximize joint utility, often through finding nonobvious solutions to their common problems. It is not clear that the problems employed in the experiments that involved bilateral focus permitted integrative, as opposed to "distributive" (compromise), solutions. To the extent that they did not, an important possible consequence of bilateral focus procedures may have been overlooked. Even if the problems negotiated in these experiments did permit some degree of integrative bargaining, it cannot be determined from the data presented whether any such behavior actually occurred.

A partial exception to the above criticism is the work Johnson has done with compatible issues, where the initial disagreement is due essentially to misunderstanding. The solution to this is certainly not to be found through distributive bargaining, but rather through the kind of communication and problem-oriented debate that is characteristic of attempts at integrative bargaining. However, the solution of Johnson's compatible-issue problem does not call for a very high level of this type of skill, since once the nature of the problem is recognized, a solution should flow almost automatically. Still, it may be noteworthy that role reversal fared best in comparison to self-presentation under the compatible condition (Johnson, 1967).

In addition to the nature of the issues debated, the experiments dealing with bilateral focus show another limitation. These studies use a sequence of events in which bilateral focus procedures (role reversal, etc.) are first employed, then bargaining begins without any necessary continuation of the bilateral focus procedures. To some extent, of course, bilateral focus procedures and normal bargaining are mutually exclusive. Walton and McKersie have noted that this is the case for problem-solving (integrative) and normal (distributive) bargaining, and bilateral focus procedures closely resemble Walton and McKersie's conception of problem-solving (see Walton and McKersie, 1966), whatever may be the causal linkages between them. Problem-solving (and bilateral focus) tend to involve sharing of perspectives and information in the context of a cooperative search for jointly acceptable solutions. Bargaining, on the other hand, places a premium on concealing one's true preference structure, withholding some kinds of information, and using tactics of manipulation. That an opponent who understands one's true preferences will tend to profit thereby in hard bargaining has been demonstrated, in the context of simulated out-of-court litigation, by Reiches and Harral (1974).

However, the fact that problem-solving, or bilateral focus procedures, and hard bargaining are not apt to occur simultaneously, or to be closely intermingled, does not imply that a particular sequence must always be followed. While it may often be true that the optimal time for creating bilateral focus is early, when issues and attitudes are still being defined, there are several factors that might mitigate the effectiveness of such procedures at that stage. For instance, a general failure of bilateral focus to induce agreement may result from the fact that the negotiators know that hard bargaining will follow, and as a result they withhold a full commitment to bilateral focus. On the incentives involved in competitive bargaining (and perhaps the excitement of the prospect, especially in laboratory situations) may tend to override any predisposition toward integrative, problem-solving behavior at the outset of negotiations. It is possible that, under some circumstances, attempts to create a bilateral focus near the middle or the end of a negotiation might prove relatively more successful. For example, the experience of deadlock and frustration might dispose negotiators more favorably toward problem-solving.[2]

There are basically two ways to observe bilateral focus-oriented behavior that occurs other than at the beginning of negotiation. One is to instruct subjects (or confederates) to begin to reverse roles, etc., at some different point in the negotiations. The other is simply to observe a great deal of negotiation and debate, looking for instances of bilateral focus and somehow recording and analyzing them (see the previous chapter by Pruitt and Lewis, for a similar approach to integrative bargaining). Neither of these approaches rules out the implementation of bilateral focus at the outset of negotiations as well. However, both, but especially the latter, direct attention (a) to the possibility that some of the more interesting questions about bilateral focus concern the conditions under which it may arise "spontaneously" during negotiations, and (b) what might be its consequences under such circumstances. The approach of waiting for spontaneous bilateral focus also permits observation of the phenomenon outside the laboratory, in situ.

To deal with debate, whether as conflict resolution or as competition, in an unstructured setting requires methods different from those previously employed. Specifically, some kind of interaction or content analysis instrument is needed in order that data can be created out of negotiators' debates. In the rest of this chapter, we will review efforts along this line, with particular attention to our own ongoing research.

INTERACTION ANALYSIS OF DEBATE

Though negotiation is essentially verbal interaction, the bulk of empirical literature concerning it does not deal directly with words. Much of the work on bargaining behavior has dealt with nonverbal interaction, such as the choosing of rows and columns in a Prisoner's Dilemma matrix. In many other studies, verbal behavior has been permitted, but it has not been recorded or analyzed systematically. Most of the studies discussed above fall in this category: Verbal interaction occurs, but what is measured is the *outcome* of that interaction (agreement, attitude change, etc.), not the content or patterning of the interaction itself. Such procedures as noting the "adequacy" of role reversal are steps in the direction of content analysis, but modest ones.

Examples of Interaction Analysis

The negotiation literature does contain a few examples of the use of interaction analysis to examine verbal behavior. Landsberger (1955.) employed Bales' Interaction Process Analysis system (Bales, 1952) to study collective bargaining in situ. He found patterns of "phase movement" (Bales and Strodtbeck, 1951) in these groups and a relationship between the strength of such patterns and success. McGrath and Julian (1963) likewise worked with Bales' system, albeit a modified version, to investigate role structure and the phasing of activities in laboratory negotiating triads. Barber (1966) has used the Bales system to examine the behavior of Connecticut Boards of Finance, transplanted to the laboratory, while Walcott (1971) has used the same system to study budget-making behavior in a simple, three-person simulation.

Bales system, however, is more suitable for the analysis of essentially cooperative behavior than for mixed-motive negotiation. It does not allow for the coding of manipulative behavior (e.g., threats, promises, commitments) or for the clear identification of concessions or other position changes. Even integrative bargaining and bilateral focus procedures take place within a bargaining context, and the context, as well as the relatively cooperative interactions, must be accounted for. Nonetheless, the exact manner in which all of this is done can vary considerably, the suitability of any particular approach being dependent on the problem under investigation.

One extremely interesting system is that developed by Zechmeister and Druckman (1973). Although it was not used in the analysis of techniques of debate, it would seem to be quite applicable in that area. Zechmeister and Druckman coded tape recordings of laboratory subjects who were negotiating a simulated conflict of interest as follows:

> (A) Cognitive statements: descriptive statements; factual, without expression of preference.
>   (1) Similar to other's position or expressed opinion.
>   (2) Different from other's position or expressed opinion.
>   (3) Neutral with respect to other's position or expressed opinion.
>
> (B) Value statements: preferential statements; support for or opposition to evaluative positions or statements.
>   (1) Similar to other's position.
>   (2) Different from other's position.
>   (3) Neutral with respect to other's position.

Each sentence was coded either Cognitive or Value. However, the designations Similar, Different, or Neutral were applied only to sequences, defined as uninterrupted speeches. The following measures were thus derived and used in analysis:

> % sentences Cognitive
> % sentences Value
> % sequences revealing Cognitive Differences
> % sequences revealing Cognitive Similarities
> % sequences revealing Value Differences
> % sequences revealing Value Similarities

Zechmeister and Druckman used this instrument rather tentatively, coding tapes from only a sample of negotiating dyads. Their findings, however, provide an excellent illustration of the potential utility of this type of approach in the study of debate. A significant relationship was found between type of interest conflict (all-or-none versus divisible payoff) and both percentage of value arguments and percentage of cognitive arguments; the all-or-none condition produced a significantly greater percentage of the former and a significantly smaller percentage of the latter. Moreover, participants in the all-or-none condition used value arguments to indicate disagreement far more often than did those in the condition where payoff could be distributed. These findings are of interest not only because they demonstrate the utility of the coding system in general, but because the types of conflict represented resemble Johnson's (1967) compatible/incompatible distinction. The theoretical orientation implicit in the coding instrument might provide very useful insights into the processes of attitude change and resistance documented in the role-reversal studies.

Zechmeister and Druckman also examined the differences in debate content between subjects who played the roles of representatives of an ideology and those who did not. They found that the ideological role-identification led to the use of more cognitive arguments revealing differences and a greater percentage of arguments revealing differences, per se. Again, developing ways of exploring the development and maintainence of ideological positions in debate is highly relevant to a further assessment of the consequences of bilateral focus and self-presentation.

Another system that illustrates the application of interaction analysis to a particular problem or theoretical focus is that of Pruitt and his colleagues, which was developed for analyzing distributive and integrative bargaining (see the Pruitt and Lewis chapter in this volume). These investigators have focused on variables hypothesized to correlate with integrative bargaining, such as information exchange and various forms of heuristic trial and error. The close relationship between the concerns of this research and those of research into techniques of debate has been stressed above. Obviously the Pruitt methodology has considerable potential for contributing to the latter.

Bargaining Process Analysis

Walcott and Hopmann (1975) have developed an interaction analysis system that is intended to deal with bargaining and competitive debate. The system, called Bargaining Process Analysis (BPA), owes much to the conceptualizations of Schelling (1960), as well as to Bales (1952). All verbal behavior of negotiators is coded as falling into one of thirteen categories. These categories are organized into five groups, as follows:

(1) Substantive behavior (initiations, accommodations, retractions)
(2) Strategic behavior (commitments, threats, promises)
(3) Task behavior (agreements, disagreements, questions, answers)
(4) Affective behavior (positive, negative)
(5) Procedural behavior (subject changes, etc.)

The categories of the BPA are designed to provide a set of conceptual building blocks which may have theoretical importance singly and which also can be combined to form composite variables. For example, variables such as the following can be constructed:

(1) Soft bargaining strategies: proportion of initiations, accommodations, and promises, over a given period.
(2) Hard bargaining strategies: proportion of retractions, commitments, and threats, over a given period.
(3) Relative hardness (softness) of strategy: ratio of hard to soft strategies, over a given period.
(4) Task orientation: ratio of task-oriented behavior to affect-oriented behavior, over a given period.
(5) Quality of task behavior: ratio of agreements to disagreements, over a given period.

(6) Quality of affective behavior: ratio of positive to negative affect, over a given period.

The BPA instrument was designed to be applied both to the behavior of subjects in a laboratory setting and to transcripts of "real-world" negotiations. Examples of each are discussed by Hopmann and Walcott in Chapter 10 of this volume. The data discussed there do not bear directly on the main concern of the present chapter—techniques of debate. Indeed, the BPA is probably not as well adapted to detection of the component behaviors of debating techniques as is the Zechmeister and Druckman (1973) system, discussed above. However, since debate in negotiation occurs within a mixed-motive framework that certainly includes bargaining behavior, and since there are clearly important relationships between debating and bargaining behavior, the BPA would seem to have something to offer for the study of debate.

Application to the Study of Bilateral Focus

The above contention is supported in a study by King (1976), which combined elements of the Zechmeister-Druckman and Walcott-Hopmann approaches to interaction analysis and applied them to an investigation of the effects of role reversal in international negotiation. While this study represents only a first attempt at the integration of such systems and the theoretical points of view that underlie them, it does suggest the promise of this approach.

King's substantive focus was on negotiations that took place during 1962 and 1963 and culminated in the partial nuclear test ban treaty. Specifically he sought to determine whether these negotiations were characterized by the use of debate procedures. Working from transcripts of negotiations in the Eighteen-Nation Disarmament Conference, King isolated, judgmentally, all instances of self-presentation and role reversal by the United States, the Soviet Union, and the United Kingdom. He defined role reversal generously as all "restatements of the positions of an opponent who is present" (1976: 10), excluding verbatim repetition of others' statements. King also isolated all statements charging another actor with a misstatement of one's position. From these measures, he constructed two indices, a role-reversal score and a misunderstanding score. The former was defined as the number of restatements of one's opponents' positions, divided by the number of statements and restatements of one's own and one's allies' positions. The latter was defined as the number of allegations that another party had misunderstood one, divided by the number of role-reversal statements made by that party. A misunderstanding score was computed for the Soviet Union and the West (United States plus United Kingdom), limiting the measurement of misunderstanding to interactions between these opponents. Separate role-reversal scores were assigned to each of the three major powers for their behavior toward each of their opponents and toward the nonaligned nations present.

Further pursuing the Rapoport (1964) model of constructive debate. King sought to operationalize the concept of exploration of the region of validity of an opponent's position. Here, he used a procedure derived from Zechmeister and Druckman's (1973) work, computing a "perceived similarity" score for each of the major powers vis-à-vis their opponents, for each substantive issue under negotiation. The perceived similarity score was defined as the number of statements indicating similarity divided by the total number of statements indicating similarity or dissimilarity.

King also attempted to deal with the final criterion proposed by Rapoport (1964), the induction of assumptions of similarity. As a measure of this, King chose the positive affect variable used in the Bargaining Process Analysis. This variable was coded with regard to the general issue of each country's view of its own and its opponents' contribution to the success of the negotiations. A positive affect score was developed for each of the three countries studied, with respect to the affect that each directed toward its opponents and itself. The score was simply the proportion of positive affect to total affect.

These data have not yet been analyzed to the fullest extent, but King (1976) has developed a preliminary analysis that is indicative of the potential of this approach. Among the findings are the following:

(1) Each party stated its own position more often than it stated anyone else's. The United States was most prominent in this respect, stating its own position a little more than twice as often as it stated its opponents' positions. At the other end of the spectrum was Britain, somewhat of a "third party" in these negotiations, with nearly equal numbers of statements of own and of opponents' positions. None of the three major negotiating teams restated the positions of the nonaligned nations (not coded as "opponents") in more than about 15 percent of the total statements and restatements of position.

(2) The United States and the Soviet Union were far more active in substantive discussions than was the United Kingdom.

(3) The West felt itself misunderstood much more often than did the Soviets. Alleged misunderstandings were concentrated on the issue of on-site test inspections. It is noteworthy that that issue was not resolved in these negotiations.

(4) Each of the three major powers perceived dissimilarities in positions more often than similarities. Perceived similarity scores for the full negotiating period were less than 25 percent for each of the parties. However, closer analysis indicated that perceived similarity scores did improve (to about 50 percent) following substantial (though sometimes gradual) modifications of position by one or several of the negotiating parties. Data also showed that for all three major negotiators, perception of similarity between their positions and those of the eight nonaligned participants was nearly total. King suggests that a lack of corrective feedback from the nonaligned

negotiators may have accounted for this. On the other hand, it might also have been a desire on the part of the major powers to interpret ambiguous stimuli (the neutrals' positions) in a manner designed to maximize the appearance of agreement between themselves and the nonaligned states.

(5) No negotiating party expressed much positive affect toward its opponents. The United States was high in this regard with 7 percent; the Soviet Union, low with 1 percent. Even more strikingly, each country was 100 percent positive about itself. The Soviets expressed affect more than twice as often as did the United States and United Kingdom combined.

While King's analysis at this point merely suggests the directions in which interaction analysis of debate in negotiation might go, it at least establishes the value of such measurement for precise description (in this regard, see also Hopmann, 1974), and, along with the other efforts noted above, contributes to our optimism about the hypothesis-testing capability of this type of research.

CONCLUSION

It is difficult, and perhaps inappropriate, to try to reach firm conclusions about a field of research that has not been extensively developed, but that may be beginning to open up. Studies of debate in the context of negotiation have not been numerous, nor have applications of interaction or content analysis to negotiations. And the convergence of these has been rarer still. Therefore, it is much too early to claim to see the "wave" of the future. Nonetheless, one can speculate upon some of the directions that this research is most likely to take, provided that some of its apparent promise is fulfilled.

The virtues of the laboratory, such as observational access and the ability to control, are substantial. The laboratory will remain a valuable site for those kinds of research that cannot be conducted elsewhere and an important source of hypothesis development and refined testing. However, negotiation is accessible in situ, and it seems probable that more research will deal directly with the "real world." Given either the availability of transcripts or personal access, interaction measurements can be taken, and analyses performed that are similar to those discussed by Hopmann and Walcott (in Chapter 10 of this volume), or those illustrated in such diverse attempts to deal with "real" negotiations as Barber (1966), Hopmann (1974), or Druckman et al. (1974). Our efforts at establishing the degree of correspondence between negotiations in the laboratory and negotiations in situ represent one effort to bridge the gap between these two settings by generating comparable data.

The analytic possibilities of interaction analysis have barely been explored to date. While examinations of "phase movement," for instance, have been important in the literature associated with Bales' approach (see Landsberger, 1955), there has been little explicit concern with phasing in the rest of the literature noted above. For example, despite the importance of the question as to the likely or appropriate timing of efforts to induce bilateral focus, we have little relevant evidence. On the other hand, Hopmann's (1974) study of the stages through which the negotiations on the seabed treaty passed represents a beginning in this regard.

Analytic efforts thus far have also tended toward aggregation, perhaps too much so. While the proportion of one type of behavior to another within a given time period may be a good indicator of some system characteristic (such variables, of course, have worked well in analyses), it is possible that sometimes such analyses might prove misleading. For instance, will it usually be the case that ten threats, or ten attempts at role reversal, will be ten times as significant or effective as one? Perhaps. But it may be also that context affects the meaning of such gestures considerably and that there might be a point of diminishing return (for instance, if threats should become routine). No doubt the meaning of such behaviors also varies from one negotiation setting to another, depending upon the norms and relationships, the individuals, and the issues involved.

Sensitivity to such possibilities my lead to some emphasis on microanalysis—i.e., examining closely each instance of a particular type of behavior (such as a role reversal or an attempt to threaten or promise) within a given time or issue frame, and looking for similarities and differences among the antecedent and subsequent behaviors surrounding these events. The patterns so discovered, if any, could then be compared across issues, settings, environmental states, etc. To date, there has been no such analysis, and the prospects for it remain a matter of speculation.

At present, interaction analysis of debate in both laboratory and field settings appears a promising line of research, but hardly a proven one. There is a great deal of room for the development of technique, the elaboration of theory, and the creative combination of existing tools. The questions involved are interesting and significant, practically as well as intellectually, and we anticipate that much progress will be made in the relatively near future.

NOTES

1. This is a reference to persuasive debate, as distinguished from forensic debate. The latter involves attempts to impress parties external to the debate itself. While there is no doubt that much debate that is apparently persuasive in intent is actually aimed in part or entirely at third parties (disarmament negotiations, for instance), we will not deal with that aspect of debate in this chapter.

2. Our impression, based on transcripts and extensive interviewing of diplomats by Hopmann, is that phasing and timing may vary from one negotiation to another in the international context. However, we do not have hard data on phases that would confirm or refute this at the present time.

REFERENCES

BALES, R. F. (1952) "Some uniformities of behavior in small social systems," in G. E. Swanson et al. (eds.) Readings in Social Psychology. New York: Holt, Rinehart & Winston.

——— and F. L. STRODTBECK (1951) "Phases in group problem solving." J. of Abnormal and Social Psychology 46: 485-495.

BARBER, J. D. (1966) Power in Committees. Chicago: Rand McNally.

DEUTSCH, K. (1968) The Analysis of International Relations. Englewood Cliffs, N.J.: Prentice-Hall.

DRUCKMAN, D. (1968) "Prenegotiation experience and dyadic conflict resolution in a bargaining situation." J. of Experimental Social Psychology 4: 367-383.

——— (1971) "The influence of the situation in inter-party conflict." J. of Conflict Resolution 15: 523-544.

——— (1973) Human Factors in International Neagotiations: Social Psychological Aspects of International Conflict. Beverly Hills, Calif.: Sage Publications.

———, R. ROZELLE, R. KRAUSE, and R. MAHONEY (1974) "Power and utilities in an interreligious council: a situational approach to. interparty decision-making," in J. Tedeschi (ed.) Perspectives on Social Power. Chicago: Aldine.

HAMMOND, K. R., F. J. TODD, M. WILKINS, and T. O. MITCHELL (1966) "Cognitive conflict between persons: Application of the 'lens-model' paradigm." J. of Experimental Social Psychology 2: 343-360.

HOPMANN, P. T. (1974) "Bargaining in arms control negotiations: The seabeds denuclearization treaty." International Organization 28: 313-343.

JOHNSON, D. W. (1967) "The use of role-reversal in intergroup competition." J. of Personality and Social Psychology 7: 135-142.

——— (1971a) "The effectiveness of role-reversal: The actor or the listener." Psych. Reports 28: 275-282.

——— (1971b) "Effects of warmth of interaction, accuracy of understanding, and the proposal of compromises on listener's behavior." J. of Counseling Psychology 18: 207-216.

——— (1971c) "Role reversal: A summary and review of the research." International J. of Group Tensions 1: 318-334.

——— and R. DUSTIN (1970) "The initiation of cooperation through role reversal." J. of Social Psychology 82: 193-203.

KING, T. D. (1976) "Role reversal debates in international negotiations: the partial test ban case." Presented at the 17th Annual Meeting of the International Studies Association, Toronto.

LANDSBERGER, H. A. (1955) "Interaction process analysis of the mediation of labor-management disputes." J. of Abnormal and Social Psychology 51: 552-559.

McGRATH, J. E. and J. W. JULIAN (1963) "Interaction process and task outcome in experimentally-created negotiation groups." J. of Psychological Studies 14: 117-138.

MUNEY, B. F. and M. DEUTSCH (1968) "The effects of role-reversal during the discussion of opposing viewpoints." J. of Conflict Resolution 12: 345-356.

RAPOPORT, A. (1960) Fights, Games, and Debates. Ann Arbor: Univ. of Michigan Press.

——— (1964) Strategy and Conscience. New York: Harper & Row.

REICHES, N. A. and H. B. HARRAL (1974) "Argument in negotiation: A theoretical and empirical approach." Speech Monographs 41: 36-48.

SCHELLING, T. C. (1960) The Strategy of Conflict. New York: Oxford Univ. Press.

WALCOTT, C. (1971) "Incrementalism and rationality: An experimental study of budgetary decision-making." Experimental Study of Politics 1 (December): 1-34.

––– and P. T. HOPMANN (1975) "Interaction analysis and bargaining behavior." Experimental Study of Politics 4 (February): 1-19.

WALTON, R. E. and R. B. McKERSIE (1965) A Behavioral Theory of Labor Negotiation. New York: McGraw-Hill.

––– (1966) "Behavioral dilemmas in mixed-motive decision making." Behavioral Sci. 11: 370-384.

ZECHMEISTER, K. and D. DRUCKMAN (1973) "Determinants of resolving a conflict of interest: A simulation of political decision-making." J. of Conflict Resolution 17: 63-88.

Chapter 7

MEASURES OF LAST RESORT:
COERCION AND AGGRESSION IN BARGAINING

JAMES T. TEDESCHI
State University of New York, Albany

THOMAS V. BONOMA
University of Pittsburgh

THE BARGAINING CONTEXT

Bargaining, as it has been studied in the social sciences, is generally an underarticulated conceptualization of the interaction situation it is intended to represent. There is agreement that bargaining is a type of social conflict in which participants attempt to settle an issue of resource redistribution (e.g., Messé, 1971) or, as Webster defines it, to arrange "what each gives or receives in a transaction between them." And, as with all conflicts (cf. Deutsch, 1973), it is generally recognized that the parties to bargaining will attempt—through their offers or through other, more esoteric machinations—to use various forms of social influence in order to gain a maximally favorable exchange rate vis-à-vis their opposite numbers. But beyond these characterizations, there has been no generally accepted explication of how bargaining interactions differ from other kinds of conflict, or indeed just what unique characteristics define a bargaining interaction (e.g., Rubin and Brown, 1975).

Since the nature and definition of bargaining as a particular type of conflict is closely tied to the influence modes that can be applied as bargaining levers, we first try to explicate our understanding of the bargaining

AUTHORS' NOTE: The order of the authors' names does not reflect their relative contributions, which were equal.

relationship in order to establish a common frame for analysis. In this way, we hope to show why coercion and aggression are "measures of last resort" in bargaining and why an understanding of their operation is essential to conflict resolution and management. Given the initial perspective, the rest of this chapter examines what is known about the social psychology of threats and aggression and their use in bargaining.

Bargaining as a System

There is a fundamental difference between those conflicts where resource exchange is the major focus and those in which the main goal of an individual is to get rewards without giving up anything in return. Voluntary resource exchange is one of the factors that distinguish bargaining from other kinds of conflict situations. The basic transactional problem of bargaining is to find a mutually endorsable agreement on exchange rates.

Bargaining usually does not occur unless each of the parties believes he or she can gain something from making an agreement. If one of the parties believes he is much more powerful than the other, he may try to coerce the weaker party into giving up resources without receiving anything in return. Hence the bargaining situation requires that the parties not be too asymmetrical in power. However, the lower limits of this necessary equivalence between interactants are not clear. Even when a strong legitimate authority confronts relatively weak protestors, bargaining can still take place if the latter can offer cessation of physical disruptions or institutional processes in return for something the government is willing to concede (Gamson, 1975).

When parties to bargaining are about equal in their relative strengths regarding an issue, coercion and escalation of conflict become counterproductive for both, since the inconsiderable resources of the other means probable retaliation and, hence, high costs. Norm-formation and rule-setting may occur as protective measures as each participant agrees to give up the use of his (usually damaging) capabilities (Brickman, 1974; Thibaut and Faucheux, 1965). Thus, the means that can be used to influence the exchange rates are limited and constitute an initial and often implicit first-stage bargaining agreement in the situation.

Norms are often developed to help ease the difficulty of reaching solutions to bargaining. Such rules include equity (cf. Cook, 1975), reciprocity (Gouldner, 1960), equality (Vinacke, 1959), and social welfare (Morgan and Sawyer, 1967) norms. In addition, other social conduct norms may be developed, including the familiar but uninvestigated offer-then-counteroffer sequencing rule for participants. The entire bargaining sequence may be capped by a formal or informal agreement known as a contract, which is itself a rule that binds the parties to an agreed-upon rate of exchange.

Bargaining and Social Influence

Most theories of bargaining assume that each party will try to maximize his gains from the encounter. Influence tactics, such as persuasion, promises, and threats, may be used to induce the opponent to agree to the source's preferred exchange rate. As a consequence, two countervailing forces are in constant operation during bargaining interactions. On the one hand, influence tactics are used to affect bargaining outcomes and help the source get his way; on the other hand, there is the restraining force of norms that keeps the conflict from escalating coercively and thereby producing excessive costs to both parties.

Influence is exerted in order to convince the target of the merits of a commodity or to derogate it. It can be used (a) to affect the probability estimations of future consequences associated with either concluding an agreement or failing to do so, (b) to sweeten the value of an agreement (by promising some added value), and (c) to make refusal to agree more costly to the target (by threatening some added costs). Coercion is usually not a preferred mode of influence because of the obvious dangers of escalation. It is introduced only when it appears that something of great value will be lost by failure to gain agreement when there is great disparity in power between the bargainers—for example, when "bargaining" is simply a cover for a more unequal interaction mode. That is, the use of coercive power is usually the influence mode of last resort in bargaining.

Bargaining and Coercion

Certainly coercion is not the only remedy for resolving conflicts. If it were, all life on this planet would have long ago ceased to exist. All kinds of tactics and strategies have been invented for the purpose of getting others to do what one wants. In addition, third parties can be prevailed upon (bribed, threatened, persuaded, manipulated) to intervene and gain the acquiescence of recalcitrant targets. Ecological, environmental, and other indirect influence controls can be used to totally reconstruct the reality and value systems of those who can be placed in an institutional setting.

We will largely ignore the richer context that characterizes most human relationships—including bargaining ones—to focus on the use of coercive power in conflict situations. Principles underlying the target's responses to threats and punishments are fairly well established. However, much less is known about the conditions under which coercion is used and what its relationship is to aggression as it occurs in bargaining.

THE NATURE OF COERCIVE POWER

Threats are verbal or nonverbal communications by a source of influence indicating that he intends to harm a target at a specific time in the future; sometimes the conditions under which he intends to inflict this harm are specified, and sometimes not. Whether any particular communication from one party to another can be considered a threat could be determined operationally by a panel of cultural peers or by a participant-observer scientist who shares the bargainer's phenomenology. Idiosyncratic factors of communication (e.g., "kidding") associated with the source, or unique target-valuing mechanisms (e.g., masochism) may mislead the scientist who indiscriminately tries to apply principles of coercive power to interactions that are not so characterized by participants. Nevertheless, it is possible to construct a general typology of threats and punishments that will be suitable for categorizing particular instances whenever the general conditions of coercion are satisfied. Such a typology has some importance for bargainers who are contemplating coercion since different subtypes of coercive power intuitively seem to elicit different reactions by the target and selective employment by the source.

Types of Threats

A communication from a source that indicates an intention to punish a target may take a noncontingent or a contingent form. A noncontingent threat simply asserts "I will do [not do] y," where y is a source action perceived as detrimental by the target. A contingent threat takes the form "If you do [do not do] x, I will do [not do] y," where x is some target action and y a punisher. The contingent threat provides the target with an opportunity (or at least the *appearance* of one) to avoid the stipulated punishment; the noncontingent message does not do so, but is simply a self-prediction by the source. Noncontingent threats seem to be more indicative of hostility in the source, since they give the target no "out" by complying, and they are more likely to promote revolution, preemptive aggression, or some other self-protective response by the target (Milburn, 1974).

As we shall point out at some length later, the course of conflict will be greatly affected by whether a coercive action is perceived as offensive or defensive in character. To some extent the way a threat is phrased (see Fisher, 1969) indicates whether the source is taking an offensive or a defensive action. Schelling (1966) has distinguished between compellent threats, which require that a target perform specific actions to avoid a threatened punishment, and deterrent threats, which order the target not to do something. Compellent threats are usually perceived as more offensive, hostile, and constraining because the threatened party must make one particular response and forego all other responses; deterrent threats forbid only one particular behavior and by omission allow the target to do anything else he wishes.

Types of Punishment

There are many ways in which people can harm one another, ranging from a frown or sarcastic answer to a violent physical attack. Intuition suggests that these punishments can be placed into a simple typology. They may take the form of noxious stimulation, deprivation of existing resources, deprivation of expected gains, and social punishments.

Noxious stimulation refers to any external event that creates an unpleasant sensation for the target individual. It may be the unpleasant taste of a chemical substance like quinine or the enforced restriction of body movement over a period of time. Alternatively, a target may be deprived of some resources and hence suffer punishment. Wartime loss of territory by a nation, or a citizen's fine for violation of a traffic ordinance are examples of resource deprivation. Resources may include almost anything possessed and valued by the target, including money, candy, land, oil, love, or any number of other physically or psychologically important commodities or relationships.

Expected gain deprivation is usually associated with perceived injustice, exploitation, and anger; it often produces volatile reactions on the part of the target. For whatever reason, the target has been led to expect rewards, and at the last minute they are withdrawn (deliberately or not). Despite the risk in using this type of punishment, a source is tempted because this form of coercive power can be exercised with little investment of valuable influence resources.

Social punishments are seen as harmful because they damage the target's self-concept or the impression he tries to maintain in the eyes of others. Expressions of dislike, name-calling, exclusion, expatriation, or excommunication reflect on an individual's character as well as on his desirability in the eyes of others. Signs of disapproval, such as postural slouching or failure to smile at a joke can be experienced as social punishment; in the same category, but at a higher level of intensity, is the social punishment resulting from having the "wrong" skin color or a disease like leprosy which requires cultural exclusion.

Of course, contingent or noncontingent, compellent or deterrent threats can refer to any or all of these types of punishment. Presumably, the effectiveness of contingent threats in gaining compliance depends, in addition to other factors, on the intensity and quality of the punishment threatened.

FACTORS AFFECTING COMPLIANCE BY A TARGET

A target person, who has been threatened during a conflict or bargaining sequence, has essentially two choices: to comply with the threatener's demands, or to defy them. Of course, he can also counterattack, try to run away, retreat into his own subjective world, deny the threat, pretend he could not understand it, and so on. But each of these responses can be thought of as consistent with, though not identical to, noncompliance. The "hard-nosed" source will usually interpret them as noncompliant actions.

When making up his mind about this binary choice, the target weighs the probability that the source will punish noncompliance, considers the negative utility of the punishment, and compares these factors with similar computations associated with a compliant action. Though it is unlikely that real-life targets actually perform any such computations in a rigorous sense, still the probabilities and values associated with coercive influence attempts can be described by various combination rules and models, such as the subjective expected utility variant of behavioral decision theory. Then if it is assumed that real-life targets act *as if* they were maximizing (or satisficing) the subjective expected utilities associated with the alternatives in their choice set (in this case, compliance versus noncompliance), these models can well be used to predict a target's reaction to threats. Since the most important of these relationships can be described in plain English without the customary mathematical jargon, we elect that option and recommend to the interested reader more complete treatments elsewhere (e.g., Lee, 1971; Pollard and Mitchell, 1972; and Tedeschi et al., 1973).

The target's tendency to comply with or defy the threatener, other things being equal, depends on his estimates of the probability of being punished for noncompliance. Source and target characteristics are hypothesized to reliably distort, change, and otherwise bias the subjective cognitive assessments the target makes about this probability. Subjective probability estimates serve as the major predictors in the present theory, although some consideration is also given to values or utilities. Of course it will be necessary to tie this hypothetical process to both antecedent and consequent conditions. This can be done by stating the exact relations between source and target characteristics and the direction of bias in estimations, and the consequent effects they have on behavior.

Credibility and Believability

Social psychologists have not always been careful to distinguish between the objective truthfulness or credibility of a communicator and the subjective believability of a message to a target individual. A source's credibility reflects the reliability of his communications in the history of his interactions with the target. Frequent failure to back up threats with punishing deeds produces low credibility, and consistent punishment of noncompliance leads to high credibility.

Believability is the target's perception that the consequences and contingencies stipulated in a specific message will probably occur. A current message has no credibility because the events it foretells have not yet had a chance to occur, but the target may or may not believe what it forecasts. In general, the higher the source's threat credibility, the more likely the target is to believe his current message, and, hence, compliance is more probable (Bonoma and Tedeschi, 1973; Bonoma et al., 1972). Of course, many other factors besides source credibility affect the believability of a message and subsequent compliance. These include source characteristics, presentation styles, and characteristics of the target.

A particular threat may not be believed even though the source has established high credibility by having consistently punished noncompliance in the past. A child may not believe his father's threats in the grocery store or at grandmother's house despite the fact that he knows his father consistently punishes disobedience at home. Thus, credibility may be perceived as relevant only to particular situations. Conversely, the target may believe the threats of a low-credibility source when he appears to be very angry or desperate.

Source credibility can be operationalized and measured. The source's credibility is affected only when a target refuses to comply with the threatener's demands. Successful threats do not enable the source to carry out punishment because the target does what he is told. Hence, threat credibility is measured by the proportion of times the source actually punished noncompliance with his demands over the entire history of threat interactions with the target.

It is not known whether a target maintains a separate index for each kind of message sent to him by a source (say, promises, warnings, and recommendations, in addition to threats), or whether he develops an overall estimate of a source's credibility across various influence modes. Suppose the source usually backs up his threats: Will the target believe his subsequent promises? The rhetoric of foreign policy decision makers in the United States suggests that they believe it is important to back up threats in order to maintain the believability of promises.

There is some recent and rather surprising evidence on this question. Heilman (1974) manipulated a source's reputation by providing students with information that the person with whom they were to interact had sent either a threat or a promise to a prior subject and either had kept her word or had not. Whichever message (threat or promise) the source had allegedly sent to a prior person, she sent the opposite message to the subject. Measures of believability (but not behavioral compliance) were obtained. The threats were more believable when the source had kept her previous promise, but there was no transfer from a threat to a promise. Schlenker et al. (1974) have found almost identical results when compliance measures were obtained in the context of a Prisoner's Dilemma game.

The need for more research regarding the generalization of credibilities is evident when the discussion is broadened to other modes of influence that can be used during bargaining. We do not know whether the credibilities of warnings and recommendations generalize to promises and threats (or vice versa), nor is it known whether observations of a source's credibility with others affect the believability of messages sent to the target. Furthermore, many messages take on a complex form. For example, Druckman et al. (1972) have noted that bargaining offers are often interpreted as simultaneously communicating a promise of further concessions and the threat to terminate bargaining. Perhaps the target combines the promise and threat credibilities in some way to arrive at an overall credibility estimation.

Source Characteristics, Believability, and Compliance

Who a source of influence is, what he or she is like, what resources he possesses, the scope of his legitimate authority, and the intentions attributed to him by a target all affect the believability of threats. Source characteristics may be considered bases of power because they contribute to the believability of communications and, hence, to successful influence. The empirical work reviewed by Carson (1969), Giffin (1967), and by Tedeschi et al. (1973) has provided support for the view that legitimate authority, expertise, control over resources, perceived trustworthiness, and attraction are source characteristics that affect the way a target responds to influence attempts.

Legitimacy and status. Role positions in human groups and institutions are formalized in order to coordinate activities and distribute authority. A person's perception that another has been given legitimate authority is referred to as status. Although status is often imputed to a source because of his formal role, it may also be inferred from symbolic cues, such as the uniform of a police officer (cf. Bickman, 1971). Status is sometimes given to a person in exchange for his significant contribution to achieving group goals (Homans, 1961). The considerable degree of obedience that legitimate authorities elicit from subordinates even when the behavior requested is antinormative has been demonstrated experimentally by Milgram (1974) and historically by both Adolf Eichmann and Lt. William Calley.

High status contributes to the believability of a source's communications and, hence, to the effectiveness of his threats in gaining compliance from a target. Faley and Tedeschi (1971) recruited high- and low-status ROTC students and gave them the role of the target of threats in a Prisoner's Dilemma game. Low-status cadets believed they were playing either a high-status cadet or another low-status cadet. High-status cadets believed they were playing a status equal or a status inferior. Low-status targets were more compliant when the source was of high rather than low status, and high-status targets were defiant of threats sent by a low-status source. Unexpectedly, high-status targets were just as compliant with a status equal as were low-status targets with the threats of a high-status source. The old saying that rank has its privileges was confirmed not only vertically but also horizontally. Persons of high status have much to gain from each other and probably have too much to lose by maintaining hostilities—a characteristic of bargaining interactions generally.

Expertise and compliance. One of the best-established social-psychological principles is that an expert is superior to a nonexpert in gaining conformity to his persuasive communications. Expertise enhances the effectiveness of warnings and recommendations (cf. McGuire, 1969). A source's reputation for expertise apparently leads others to assume that his credibility is high, since it would be difficult to acquire such a reputation if his recommendations and predictions were almost always wrong. The scope of influence of an expert is usually assumed to be confined to the area of his special competence, but little empirical evidence is available on this question. Does expertise, for example, directly affect the believability of threats? If the expert's reputation is based on his truthfulness, perhaps he feels constrained to back up his threats also; or at least target persons may believe that experts are constrained to be truthful. In either case, the believability of an expert's threats should be greater than those of a nonexpert. Tedeschi et al. (1975) found that an expert did receive more compliance to threats of low credibility than did a nonexpert. However, the expert's area of competence was that of controlled violence and could have been perceived by subjects as directly relevant to using and enforcing threats. There is little reason to believe that a carpenter's or a psychology professor's threats should be generally more believable than those of others, especially when these individuals are operating outside their traditional sphere of control (e.g., with apprentices or students).

Resource control of the source. If a source's threats are to be believable, he must be perceived as having the means to administer the relevant punishments. A union threatening to go out on strike must have sufficient membership backing (i.e., votes) and funds or else management will not believe the threat. Sometimes people attempt to promote the impression that they have resources when they do not. Bluffing, when combined with secrecy, implies more power than the source actually possesses; the combination of threats and secrecy may also tempt others to seek out a test of strength (Coser, 1956).

There are relations between information management and resource control other than fostering confusion in one's opposite number (cf. Druckman, 1973: 44-47). When constituencies are involved as third parties to negotiations, intranegotiation secrecy may have the valuable function of facilitating agreements between groups or nations, since the parties' constituents cannot see, and hence cannot object to, the "valuable" home resources being traded away for "insufficient" concessions from the opponent. Constituency complications in considering negotiation processes themselves notwithstanding, there are also frequently intended uncertainties about whether or not resources on the agenda for bargaining are possessed by the interactants, or more frequently, in what form and amount these are possessed.

The successful concealment of own-payoffs from resource trades tends to have contradictory effects on negotiation success. In varying settings, resource concealment sometimes deadlocks negotiations and other times provokes large concessions due to an opponent's ignorance (cf. Walton and McKersie, 1965). Sometimes a bargainer may promote a resource in his possession as valuable when actually he considers it to be a liability.

Possession of an abundance of relevant resources enhances the believability of a source's threats and, hence, contributes to their success. This is a distinct factor in the continued momentum of the arms race between East and West. The psychological bargaining advantage that a stockpile of nuclear and conventional weapons provides is considered to be worth the extraordinary cost. However, there is some danger in possessing great resources. Nacci et al. (1975) found that, holding punishment magnitude constant, a threatener gains less compliance when he has greater-magnitude threats than when he has only lower-level threats if the former uses less power than he could and the latter uses all that he has. The implication is that the use of low-level threats by a source with great resources reveals a lack of resolve or commitment to the value that is in conflict.

In a study supporting Teddy Roosevelt's admonition to "speak softly but carry a big stick," Lindskold and Bennett (1973) had a confederate transmit twenty noncontingent promises of cooperation to subjects during play in a Prisoner's Dilemma game. The source could display only a promise in one condition but could also display a contingent threat in a second condition. In the latter condition, the source actually used the threat only once, at the outset of play. Subjects were more cooperative with a promisor who could also threaten them.

Perceived intentions and compliance. The believability of a source's threats is affected by the intentions attributed to him by a target. As early as 1864, Lord Robert Cecil recognized the important relationship between capability and intent when he wrote that "a nation which is known to be willing, as well as able, to defend itself will probably escape attack." This basic notion has reappeared throughout the history of political science and particularly in the areas of bargaining and deterrence. Singer (1958, 1963) has proposed a model of international relations in which he defined prestige as a multiplicative function of the resources controlled by a source and the intentions attributed to him by the target. Japan, for example, although possessing enormous economic resources, is thought to have neither the capability (e.g., nuclear weapons) nor the hostile intentions that would render her a threat to the U.S.-bloc nations. Russia, on the other hand, has both high capabilities and (supposedly) clear resolve regarding their use if necessary. China, which has only a limited military capability outside its own borders, is perceived as very powerful by those who attribute hostile intentions to her.

Osgood et al. (1957) have found that observers tend to use evaluative (good-bad) and potency (strong-weak) dimensions in forming impressions of others. A person who is consistently cooperative and rewarding is perceived as good and impotent, while a person who frequently attempts exploitation and administers punishments is perceived as bad but potent. Komorita and Brenner (1968) found that a bargainer who yields the most is viewed by his opponent as good but weak, while a bargainer who yields the least is perceived as bad but strong. Similar reactions to persons who use threats and promises have been found. A threatener who consistently punishes defiance by a target is perceived as bad and potent, but he is viewed as good and impotent if he seldom punishes defiance. Conversely, a promisor who consistently rewards compliance is perceived as good and impotent, but he is viewed as bad and potent if he seldom fulfills his promises by rewarding compliance.

If harm-doing causes an observer to view the actor as bad and potent, one can ask whether the reverse also occurs. That is, would a bad and potent person be expected by others to do harm? Smith et al. (1976) manipulated the connotative impressions of a stranger and then asked subjects to predict how they would react in a number of hypothetical situations. An impression of a good, impotent person led the subjects to predict lack of resolve in backing up threats, consistent fulfillment of promises, unwillingness to lie for a friend, and readiness to help strangers; a bad, potent image led to just the opposite predictions.

Extrapolation to bargaining situations of these effects of first impressions is congruent with existing theory (Bartos, 1970). Bargainers who appear "tough" (bad and potent) may gain a more favorable exchange rate than those who appear "soft" (good and impotent). In this regard, it is important to note that bargaining situations, like other conflicts, have a number of part-behaviors comprising their "settings," which have nothing to do with their offers or other influence gestures, but may affect the attributions or impressions of others. Prenegotiation variables, seating arrangements, and so on can all be manipulated as subtle but powerful indicators of intentions, or what Horai and Tedeschi (1975) have called "resoluteness."

The kind of threat issued by a source may affect the degree of hostile or exploitative intentions attributed to him (Schelling, 1966). Compellent threats, which specify actions the target must perform, should be perceived as more hostile, coercive, and exploitative than deterrent threats, which specify an action the target must not perform. A hostile and exploitative threatener should be perceived as having greater resolve to follow through in his use of coercion by punishing noncompliance, and, hence, his threats should be more believable. In a test of Schelling's hypothesis, Schlenker et al. (1970) placed subjects in the position of targets of one of two kinds of threats in a Prisoner's Dilemma game: (1) a compellent threat that demanded a cooperative choice from subjects, or (2) a deterrent threat that told subjects not to make the competitive choice. Since in the Prisoner's Dilemma game the subject can make only one of two choices, telling him to make the cooperative choice and telling him not to make the competitive choice amount to the same thing. Nevertheless, subjects evaluated the compellent threatener more negatively and complied with his threats more often than with those of the deterrent threatener. It may be concluded tentatively that perceived hostility and exploitativeness do contribute to the effectiveness of threats.

Attractiveness of the source. A target's response to a source's threat depends to some extent on the quality of their relationship. The target may believe that a friend will be reluctant to harm him, but may be all too ready to believe that an enemy would relish the opportunity to do harm. On the basis of these assumptions Tedeschi et al. (1975) predicted that targets would be more likely to comply with the threats of a disliked than of a liked source. In an experiment designed to test this hypothesis, subjects were induced to like or dislike a confederate, who was then provided with coercive power in a Prisoner's Dilemma game. The confederate punished noncompliance either 10 or 90 percent of the time. Results indicated that subjects who disliked the source complied equally often whether the threats were low or high in credibility. Even when a disliked source showed a reluctance to back up threats, target subjects still complied frequently. On the other hand, when subjects liked the source, they were realistic in their appraisal of the situation and complied more often with the high- than with the low-credibility threatener. Liking apparently does not cause an optimistic bias by undermining the threatener's credibility.

While Tedeschi and his colleagues have shown that positive attraction does not seem to mediate any "discounting" of an influencer's power, Druckman and Bonoma (1976) have demonstrated a deleterious effect of mutual positive attraction on the bargaining process itself when compared with the performance of bargainers who did not like each other. They had eighth-graders bargain with an attitudinally similar (high-attraction) or dissimilar (low-attraction) opponent in a bilateral monopoly game. Buyers who were highly attracted to a simulated opponent required significantly more trials to reach agreement with the liked seller than did dissimilar (nonattracted) buyers, and a higher proportion of deadlocks occurred in the high-similarity condition. Additional data analyses indicated that high-attraction subjects facing a "tough," nonconcessionary opponent experienced a disconfirmation of their cooperative expectancies as a result of the attractive opponent's behavior and "got tough" themselves during the last phases of bargaining, a behavioral pattern which resulted in deadlock. In essence, Druckman and Bonoma found that positive attraction toward an opponent may inhibit the bargaining process and agreement, and a "healthy disrespect" for one's opponent may facilitate it.

From these two findings—one on reactions to coercive power and the other on the course of bargaining itself—it can only be concluded that straightforward generalizations from considerations of liking or attitude similarity to the bargaining situation are not possible without close consideration of other aspects of the bargaining context, including other areas of the opponent's behavior.

Commitment Tactics

Certain influence tactics are important in affecting the believability of a communication, and, hence, bargaining outcomes. Schelling (1966) has examined the tactic of committing oneself to a particular position in negotiation. A commitment, within the context of bargaining, is essentially a move by one negotiator designed to take the interaction out of a bargaining mode and put it into some other interactional system (force, fait accompli, etc.). For example, giving another nation "one final offer" of allowing them to withdraw from an occupation has the following communicational values:

(1) It serves to communicate source's intent that coercive actions will be taken if withdrawal is not instigated.
(2) It places the initiative for whether or not bargaining will deteriorate into the hands of the target by giving him the "last-clear-chance" choice to avoid confrontation.
(3) It intensifies the conflict by reducing the alternative choice options open to both parties.
(4) Whether it succeeds or fails, the character of the interaction is changed irrevocably.

As Schelling points out (1966: 51 ff.), both nations and individuals have limitations on the things that they can get exceptionally concerned about during interaction; making bids for resoluteness by burning one's bridges behind oneself *necessitates* a win-lose situation in which one of the two parties must back down or both will sustain high losses. Essentially, then, commitment tactics are extremely high-risk maneuvers in which one party to the bargaining trades the possibility of achieving a mutually favorable exchange ratio for the potential of getting a very favorable outcome from the interaction by converting it from a mixed-motive to zero-sum situation.

Schelling also rightly points out that failures of commitment in one area of bargaining promote the loss of credibility with regard to other areas as well (see above for experimental evidence). This is most easily seen in international interaction, where the "domino" theory is an embodiment of the notion that if we do not display resolve in one country, we will lose others as well. Brinkmanship, salami tactics, and "trip wire" deterrence are all examples of commitments made at the international level. The strike is an example at the corporate or organizational level. And, such moves as walking away from the bargaining table and violating bargaining norms about force are examples of commitment tactics at the level of interpersonal negotiations. Perhaps the most widely familiar example of interpersonal commitment is "making him an offer he can't refuse."

Target Characteristics and Compliance

Social psychologists have not found that personality traits have much to do with the target's reaction to threats, or to bargaining behavior in general (Druckman, 1973). Self-esteem has long been associated with compliance with persuasive communications and conformity pressures, but there has been little interest in examining it in relation to coercive power. Presumably an individual's self-evaluation indicates his bias regarding his own expectations of rewards and punishments. High-self-esteem persons generally believe they will be accepted, approved of, and rewarded by others, while low-self-esteem persons expect to be rejected, disapproved of, and punished. Cohen (1959) stressed the ways in which these expectations can affect behavioral styles. High-self-esteem persons are active in self-defense in anticipation of the harm others are apt to do to them. Lindskold and Tedeschi (1971) found some support for these notions. High-self-esteem children were more compliant to both promises and threats than low-self-esteem children under conditions where compliance led to better outcomes than did defiance. That is, low-self-esteem persons tended to act in a self-destructive manner.

Interpersonal trust, defined as a tendency to rely on the communications of strangers, has not been directly related to bargaining behavior (Rotter, 1967). However, some hints exist from related work that suggest preliminary hypotheses. Though the critical test has not been made with threats, Schlenker et al. (1973) found that high-trust subjects (as identified by paper-and-pencil tests) were more cooperative in response to promises than were low-trust subjects. Bonoma (1976) found that high-trust decision makers were reliably less rational than low-trust actors when the task was one of making uncertain decisions and the criterion of rationality was that of subjective expected utility.

The conflict literature also shows reliable differences in behavior between males and females (cf. Terhune, 1970; Bonoma and Tedeschi, 1973; Tedeschi et al., 1973). The conflict behavior of males seems predictable by even the most rudimentary cost-gain models in decision theory (e.g., expected value), while that of females seems to be guided more by cost-independent norms of social inclusion and concern for self-presentation. However, some caution should be exercised in making or interpreting this generalization. Evidence found by Howe and Zanna (1975) and Bonoma and Schlenker (1975) suggests that males and femals show strong behavioral differences only on male role-appropriate tasks, like bargaining games, and that these results may well reverse themselves when decisions are placed in a female-appropriate context. Bonoma and Schlenker, for example, report that it is male decision makers who behave "irrationally" when a decision task of estimating minimum subjective expected utilities (SEUs) for female actors in risky dilemmas is used. The old saw of feminine irrationality may have to be modified and some new teeth for male irrationality added. Again, contextual factors seem to be the key.

Finally, a most powerful characteristic of parties to bargaining is encompassed by the term "motivational orientation," which refers to the cooperative or competitive attitudes, perceptions, or "set" which the interactants bring to negotiations (Rubin and Brown, 1975: 201-213). Kelley and Stahelski (1970a, 1970b), for example, found that subjects with cooperative motivational orientations more accurately perceived the intentions of their opponents, showed more variance in their predictions of how a "typical" person would behave in a Prisoner's Dilemma game, and chose cooperatively more often themselves (especially when the other also chose cooperatively) than did subjects who had a competitive motivational orientation. They interpreted their results as supporting a "triangle" hypothesis, in which cooperatively oriented subjects responded to either cooperatively or competitively oriented opponents with reciprocal cooperation or competition, but competitively oriented subjects responded to the behavior of others competitively regardless of motivational orientation.

McClintock (1972) separated subjects with a purely competitive orientation from those with an individualistic motivation as regards bargaining behavior; he found that subjects concerned with "relative gain maximization," or "beating" the other guy, were more competitive than those concerned more with maximizing their own gains and less with defeating others.

THE EXERCISE OF COERCIVE POWER

Before initiating any influence attempts, a potential source must somehow gauge his chances of success in gaining what he wants from potential targets in the environment. Often there is more than one other person who has what is desired, and the questions must be answered of who will be selected as a target and how the source will proceed to influence him (cf. Lasswell et al., 1952). The choice of a particular target from all of those available who possess the value sought is assumed to be a simple comparison; the target who maximizes the source's utilities will be selected. Utilities can be maximized in at least two ways: (a) a target might be preferable because he has more of the desired resource, or (b) target's "possession style" of the resource might lead source to believe that only low costs will be incurred in gaining it. Thus, police departments commonly recommend to citizens that they lock their autos. Locked autos are equally stealable by professional thieves but more costly in time, and hence they increase the probabilities of detection.

Once a target has been selected from those available, the source must go on to decide what influence mode to use in order to gain compliance. There are clear differences between the probabilities that coercion versus bribery will elicit compliance (Tedeschi and Lindskold, 1976), and also differences in the relative costs incurred by the source, while using one or another influence mode. We have discussed these issues at length elsewhere (Tedeschi et al., 1973); basically, the source will choose the influence mode that is most likely to elicit compliance (given the particular nature of the target) and that costs least to use.

The source must consider three types of costs before making a decision to attempt influence. Fixed costs are those that are known beforehand and are incurred voluntarily by the source so he can use a particular influence tactic. Costs that may be incurred, but are contingent on what the target does, can be referred to as opportunity costs (Harsanyi, 1962). Finally, there are costs that may be imposed on a potential source of influence by the target. These target-imposed costs tend to balance the advantages of threats when only opportunity costs are considered, thus detracting from the desirability of using coercion. In general, the greater the probability and amount of costs expected for using coercive power, the less it will be used.

Tedeschi et al. (1970) found that the type of costs had effects on how a source used coercive power. In one condition, the target was said to have retaliatory power, which he used to partially "get even" each time the subject punished him. In another condition, the exact same number of points in penalties were deducted from a subject's totals each time he punished the confederate and were labelled as automatically imposed opportunity costs incurred for the use of punishment power. In the human retaliation case, the target was punished reliably less often than in the opportunity-costs condition, even though the magnitude of cost was the same. We theorized that this occurred because, in the subjects' minds, the opportunity costs were more "certain" than was the other's retaliation, which was open to choice and, hence, possible nonuse.

Factors Eliciting the Use of Coercion

A distinction must be made between the defensive and offensive uses of coercion both because persons react differently to them and because social psychologists tend to study only the former and inappropriately overgeneralize the principles found to the latter. In most societies, the individual is taught to defend himself, is not disapproved of for striking someone who physically assaults him, and is not held legally responsible even for killing another if it is in self-defense. Defensive coercion is elicited by norms of reciprocity and equity and is amplified by physiological arousal states in the actor. The offensive use of coercion is generally disapproved and resisted, and in many instances it is illegal and merits punishment of the source. Nevertheless, if a person cannot persuade, bribe, manipulate, or otherwise induce another person to comply with his wishes during bargaining, and compliance is sufficiently important to him, then his power may ultimately depend on his ability to threaten, restrain, immobilize, injure, punish, or destroy the target. To paraphrase Clausewitz' definition of war as merely an extension of diplomacy, it may be said that the exercise of coercive power is a means of gaining compliance that is used when other means fail. Of course, we want to know why, when, how, and against whom coercive means will be employed.

Negative reciprocity and negative equity. The negative norm of reciprocity may be defined in terms of two minimal demands: (1) harm those who harm you; and (2) do not help those who harm you (Gouldner, 1960). This normative demand to extract "an eye for an eye" requires a person to retaliate. This is a defensive norm and restricts the actor to making his response in proportion. The probability and the degree of retaliation depend on the magnitude of the attack, the characteristics of the attacker and the victim, and the degree of legitimization or justification for the first attack. Experiments have consistently shown that the degree of retaliation by subjects is proportional to the amount of provocation (Berkowitz and Green, 1962; Helm et al., 1972).

When persons have access to different resources and capabilities, a question may arise with respect to what constitutes equivalence across types of punishment. McDaniel et al. (1971) investigated this problem by providing two modes of rating: points and shocks. Within each mode the confederate gave the subject a positive rating of 2 (points or shocks) or a negative rating of 6. Subjects did more harm to the confederate when he had done more harm to them. However, they gave him a more negative rating when they could retaliate in kind than when they were forced to retaliate in a different mode. Difficulty in deciding what constituted equivalence when counterattack was made in a different mode apparently led subjects to err on the side of underpayment; overpayment runs the risk of escalation.

The capability, attractiveness, and sex of a provoker affect the probability and degree of retaliation administered by his victim. Shortell et al. (1970) found that an opponent's ability to do great harm tempered the intensity of the subjects' retaliatory behavior. The effects of liking on level of retaliation probability depend on a number of factors, such as the degree of legitimacy of the attacker's behavior and the arousal state of the person attacked. Thus, while Hendrick and Taylor (1971) found no relationship of liking to amount of retaliation, Stapleton et al. (1975) found a tendency of subjects to lower the level of retaliation against a liked person as compared to a disliked person. Krauss (1966) also found that attracted persons were less likely to use coercion against one another in a bargaining situation than persons who did not like one another.

Conflict intensity. The degree of conflict between two persons has important effects on the modes of influence that each directs toward the other. Intense conflict in which the goals are incompatible, interdependent, and vital to each party breeds suspicions regarding motives and trustworthiness and reduces the effectiveness of positive modes of influence, such as promises, persuasion, or moral exhortations. Threats are easier to believe under these circumstances, and it is the tendency of each party to view himself as defending against the intrusions of the other. Deutsch et al. (1971) manipulated the size of conflict in a bargaining game and found a direct relationship between the size of conflict and the amount of coercion used by subjects.

Scarcity of resources is the basis of most conflicts between people. Rights to hunting or fishing areas, control over strategic territories, rivalry for mates, control over which television program will be viewed, and many other situations present persons with conflicts of greater or lesser intensity. In such situations, the individual has only three choices: (1) withdraw and allow the other person to have what he wants; (2) seek conflict-resolution through bargaining and compromise; or (3) attempt to make the other person withdraw. The more intense the conflict, the more likely it is that threats and punishments will be used.

Druckman (1973) has pointed to an important bifurcation in conflict types and distinguishes interest from value conflict (see also the Druckman et al. chapter in this volume). The above discussion exemplifies interest conflicts, in which the subject of dispute is actually the control or redistribution of scarce resources. In conflicts over values, there is often a basic disparity in the way in which bargaining participants view the world. Hammond (1965) refers to this as "cognitive conflict." Druckman reports that it is probably to be expected that conflicts of value will generally achieve more intensity and will be harder to resolve than will conflicts of interests.

The most commonly occurring conflicts at the international level, of course, are those in which both means and values are implicated. Kahn (1960, 1962) and Rapoport (e.g., 1964) have offered typologies of the nature of perception of such "mixed" conflicts as regards intensity and effects. For Kahn, international escalation consists of offensive military actions taken in response to anticipated or actual hostile actions of an opposing nation; a sort of "implicit bargaining in force" occurs, with the winner being he who is willing to progress further up the increments of force toward nuclear holocaust in any confrontation (e.g., the Cuban missile crisis). Thus, Kahn's "escalation ladder" represents a typology of military force incursions ranging from the "don't rock the boat" threshold of declarations, economic gestures, and political moves during international crises through the critical "no nuclear use" threshold of conventional force demonstrations and clashes plus nuclear ultimate, to the "city targeting" threshold of counter-value use of thermonuclear devices against the population of the opposing nation. Rapoport has distinguished those crises over whose consideration national actors fall into the "zero-sum" trap (that is, they construe the problem in win-lose terms) from those that are considered in a more problem-solving or bargaining mode. He claims the former kind of thinking is always associated with perceptions of more intense conflict and serves especially well as an example that it is more the construction that we place on a given crisis than any "objective" situation that determines conflict intensity. Pruitt (1965) implies distrust in the development of threat perception and consequently perceptions of conflict intensity, and "responsiveness" (noncoercive employment of resources for cooperative interaction) in the reduction of threat perception and conflict intensity.

Self-presentation and identity. According to Toch (1969), an advertised desire or willingness to fight is a way of promoting a tough and masculine self-image. The machismo promoter acts to provoke others into fighting him. It is not necessary for him to win all of the fights; the important thing is to show that he has "guts." The reputation gained by the self-image promoter may cause others to defer to his demands since even the strong may back down before the fury of a weaker person unless the stakes are clearly worth it. The tought self-image promotor builds a reputation that lends credibility to his threats and enhances the effectiveness of his coercive-influence attempts. Some commentators have interpreted the recovery of the American container ship *Mayaguez* by the U.S. Marines as a welcome opportunity in the wake of the Vietnam disaster for a display of machismo by Secretary of State Kissinger, who was interested in signalling to the North Koreans his resolve to support the South Koreans and, hence, deter an attack by the former.

When a person has been embarrassed or humiliated by another person, he may try to restore a positive self-image by establishing his superiority in controlling or defeating a third party. Brown (1968) found American males who had earlier been subjected to humiliating defeat in front of an audience to be quite ready to resort to exploitation and coercion in a bargaining game, even at cost to themselves, for the purpose of saving face. Seventy-five percent of the retaliators reported that they did so to "avoid looking foolish." Holmes (1971) probably created concern among male subjects about how they were being evaluated when he had them suck on a baby's bottle, a pacifier, a breast shield, and a baby's rattle. As compared to subjects who were not previously embarrassed, subjects who had engaged in sucking objects later were willing to accept stronger electric shocks. Presumably, their willingness to accept high shock intensities was meant to re-establish themselves as tough, courageous, masculine types.

These personal concerns for face also occur in bargaining situations. Iklé (1964: 76) has emphasized the role of reputation, firmness, bluff, and other "face" considerations in international negotiations, noting that "bargaining strength depends not so much on what these [reputational] attributes really are as on what others believe them to be." To avoid a test of strength when it is appropriate or when one's bluff has been called is to admit strategic inferiority; to be "called" on one's commitment to an action, and then to have the choice of backing down, acknowledging publicly that one does not back up one's words, or rejoining the bargaining effort and accepting a less-than-satisfactory agreement is really no choice at all. Face considerations demand the unsatisfactory agreement rather than the public broadcast of an unfulfilled commitment (see the Brown chapter in this volume).

Inequity and relative deprivation. Distribution norms (see Adams, 1965) refer to fair or just solutions to the allocation of rewards, the core problem of bargaining. According to Pruitt (1972: 144), a norm of equality proposes that "people should have equal basic rights, that they should begin a contest with equal resources, and that they should divide benefits equally." Another rule of fairness is the norm of equity, also referred to as a principle of distributive justice. The norm of equity specifies that each individual should receive a share of rewards, based on the contribution each makes in acquiring the resources to be allocated. Hence, each group member should receive a share of the rewards offered by the group, in proportion to his relative contribution to the group (Homans, 1961). Regardless of which allocation norm the individual supports, he will feel relatively deprived and angry when he gets less than the amount he considers to be his fair share of the rewards (cf. Gurr, 1970).

The general literature on equity maintenance in bargaining is not reviewed here since it has been covered elsewhere (Adams, 1964; Leventhal, 1976). By way of summary, however, it can be said that equity-seeking and adjustment are among the main tasks of those seeking to bargain, for the question of a suitable exchange ratio is functionally identical with a resolution of the "inputs-to-outputs" problem addressed by equity theorists. Leventhal (1976) has provided an especially good account of current research on equity maintenance in organizational life, and his essay serves to alert us that bargaining outcomes (equitable or not) may not be interpreted apart from the context in which they occur. Thus, while equitable bargaining agreements "ensure that recipients whose behavior is most useful have greatest access to essential resources" (1976: 96) within the organization, reinforce these participants, and punish less-useful organizational functionaries, there are a number of dysfunctional effects of adhering to a strictly equitable allocation norm. Among these are (a) discouragement of members who are developing but are currently performing poorly and (b) maximizing the likelihood of overt conflict between "haves" and "have-nots." It is implicit in every "equitable" bargaining contract concluded between two or more participants within a multiple-populated context that others not so rewarded will feel deprived and, hence, inequitably treated (Stouffer et al., 1949).

Given an interactant's dissatisfaction with the disaffection either of his bargaining partner, as a result of a sensed inequity in exchange, or of others who form his social environment, as a result of observing their relative successes from negotiation, coercion will be more readily sought as a mechanism to restore a balance or at least to destroy the favored position of others.

Time perspective. There are two ways in which time perspective may determine whether a source will use coercion against others. Where compliance by a target person is required quickly and other means of influence are deemed too slow to produce the behavior, coercion will be used. The United States did not want to experience a long delay in gaining the release of the *Mayaguez* and its crew from the Cambodian government, and so it passed up slower diplomatic tactics in favor of direct military intervention. When the source wants to control the timing of the target's responses (which cannot be done using modes of influence that leave the decision as to how and when to respond up to the target), coercive power is likely to be used.

A second way in which time can play a role in the source's behavior is through a contraction of time perception in which the future consequences of action are not considered. Melges and Harris (1970) identify three conditions that predispose a person to ignore future costs and to attack those who appear responsible for his inability to achieve goals: (1) a felt need to take some action quickly; (2) a focus on the present to the exclusion of the future;

and (3) an egocentric view of the situation that precludes empathy and even dehumanizes the opponent. All of these conditions are likely to occur during very intense conflicts or in crisis situations.

At the interpersonal level, Druckman (1973), as well as Rubin and Brown (1975), have summarized the effects of time pressure during bargaining. The collective findings appear to indicate that (a) moderate time pressures, when applied to both bargainers equally in the form of a deadline or penalties, promote reaching agreement and making the concessions necessary to do so, but (b) result in worse individual outcomes for bargainers under pressure than for bargainers not under pressure. At the international level, the literature is replete with anecdotes and descriptive suggestions that time pressures may have negative effects on the goodness of bargaining outcomes; it has been suggested (J. Coffey, personal communication), for example, that the United States made more concessions to reach the SALT accord than it otherwise might have considered because the draft of the treaty was being finalized during the plane trip to the negotiations. The effects of severe time pressures are not clear, but these probably function, like any noncontingent threat, to promote deadlock.

COERCIVE POWER, PERCEIVED AGGRESSION, AND BARGAINING

Within or outside bargaining interactions, it is important to separate conceptually an actor's use of coercion from the observer's labelling of him. While not all coercive acts are labelled as aggressive by observers, labelling has consequences for both the actor and the observer. The process of labelling an actor as aggressive is associated with assigning responsibility to him and evaluating him negatively, and it implies a willingness by the observer to support retributive actions. The bargainer who would use coercion is usually aware that being labelled as aggressive is associated with retribution, and so he tries to justify his use of coercion to prevent observers from so labelling him. In this way, the bargaining context, which is antithetical to many overt coercive or aggressive moves by its very structure and the functional equivalence (and harm-doing capacity) of its participants, may support a large variety of coercive actions (including "covert operations," "dirty tricks," and so on) that have an aggressive intent but are designed so as not to earn an aggressive label.

Since being labelled implies that the actor will incur costs involving negative evaluations, as well as reactions by others, the anticipation of being so labelled is probably a powerful inhibitor of the use of coercive power. Yet the gains may outweigh the costs, or the actor may seek some excuse to justify his planned actions to avoid the costs. Once he has been labelled as aggressive, the actor may engage in one of a number of possible post-transgression responses designed to convince the observer that he has mis-labelled the actor or to mitigate the negative reaction of the observer.

Post-transgression responses often are successful in lessening the degree of punishment assigned to a transgressor because he is believed to be less likely to repeat the action and appears to be more amenable to rehabilitation. For example, Schwartz et al. (1975) found that expression of remorse is an effective post-transgression strategy in mitigating punishment. Expressions of guilt, self-criticism, and self-punitive behavior also tend to alleviate or to mitigate the degree of punishment administered to a transgressor (Aronfreed, 1970). The actor may also make restitution to the injured party as an expression of remorse or to indicate lack of intention to do harm (Berscheid and Walster, 1967). Another strategy that might be adopted by a transgressor is to derogate his victim and hence suggest that he deserved what he got (Glass, 1964).

Post-transgression responses may be applied in bargaining, which is often an especially dangerous interaction situation in which to use coercion; the probability of retaliation from a "functionally equivalent" opponent is apt to be high. A bargainer who uses coercion is more likely to suffer retaliation when he is judged by observers to be offensive and aggressive. Actions labelled as aggressive also cause others to form defensive coalitions against the individual. In addition, certain norm-maintenance agencies ensure that the rules of bargaining are followed (e.g., the legal system in consumer behavior). Hence, the bargainer may follow his coercive acts with attempts to manipulate the impressions of his opposite number (Tedeschi et al., 1973), or of any audience, to ensure that coercive actions are not judged as offensive, anti-normative, or aggressive. He may refer to the coercion as "dictated" by the circumstances, the other's behavior, or some other precipitating factors. When labelled as aggressive, the bargainer will engage in a number of gestures designed to defuse the possible response of the strong "other."

COERCIVE POWER AND BARGAINING TACTICS

Threats, though risky, may be effective in bringing an adversary to a bargaining agreement. Consider how threats affect the target's utility schedule. If the target does not accept the source's offer, he stands some chance of being punished. If the target is punished, he will be worse off than before the bargaining process started. Punishments lower the status-quo point of the target. As a consequence, he should be eager to reach agreement just to get even. Unless he can regain his losses through an agreement, the target must withdraw from the interaction with a net loss. The problem for the would-be coercive bargainer is that he or she cannot be certain just how the opposite number will seek to avoid such losses. One way, we imply here, would be to accept a less-favorable exchange rate and a "worse" agreement. Another way is the reciprocal imposition of costs on the coercer through coercive retribution. The dangers of escalation, of coercive reciprocity, constitute the major risk for the coercive negotiation.

An escalation of conflict is usually likely to occur when one party punishes the other. By failing to retaliate against a threat, an individual may leave the impression that he is weak and compliant, thereby inviting further attacks against himself. Even if the target is subjectively willing to accede to a powerful adversary's demands, he may still openly defy the threatener because of his fear that the threatener would be encouraged to make even greater demands in the future. Appeasement consists of yielding to a threatener's demands for a change in the status quo.

Resistance not only is a matter of momentary defense but may also serve to deter future attempts to coerce the person. Though one cannot out-muscle a more powerful opponent, a target may threaten great-enough costs that it would not be worthwhile for the opponent to pursue his objectives through coercive means. Allowing a threat to go unchallenged also causes the target to lose self-esteem. We have already seen that people are willing to pay a price to save face. All of these considerations work against the success of coercion in bargaining situations.

Bonoma and Tedeschi (1974) found that deliberate escalation, which consisted of raising the punishment "ante" for the target's noncompliance with each successive threat, was the most effective compliance gainer in the short run. However, accommodative escalation, where the threatener used the stick of punishment combined with the carrot of joint rewards for compliance, elicited maximal target-compliance in the long run. A policy of complete and total disarmament coupled with other conciliatory behavior was less effective in resolving conflict, but was no worse than the least effective escalatory strategy studied.

When the intensity of conflict is sufficiently high, and an escalatory cycle can be foreseen as providing no advantage for either side, a strategy for defusing the situation may be sought. One such strategy is to limit the areas of disagreement and to fractionate issues (Fisher, 1969). Slicing a big issue into smaller ones makes it possible to focus attention on each smaller issue one at a time or to trade off so that a party gains an advantage on one issue and accepts a disadvantage on another. These tactics have been instrumental in bringing about the arms control negotiations in Geneva between the United States and the Soviet Union. The complementary strategy of aggregating issues can also be used to good advantage for bargaining agreement and conflict resolution. One instance that can be cited is that of logrolling, or systematically trading off bundles of issues that are desirable to another but not important to self for bundles of other issues not important to alter but of concern to ego. The U.S. Senate is said to function through such tradeoffs.

Another strategy for reducing the amount of conflict between parties is to attempt to build liking and trust between them. Osgood (1962) suggested a strategy called GRIT (graduated reciprocation in tension-reduction), the purpose of which is to reduce hostilities and establish a bond of trust between contending parties. GRIT consists of a series of small, unilateral, preannounced, conciliatory initiatives. Failure to announce benevolent or cooperative actions invites exploitation (Solomon, 1960), and asymmetry of power vitiates the effectiveness of conciliatory gestures (Tedeschi et al., 1969). But when equals in power pre-announce and take unilateral initiatives (while maintaining a firm stance with regard to any attempts by the adversary to exploit the display of good will) and invite reciprocation, the GRIT strategy often appears to work.

CONCLUSIONS AND IMPLICATIONS

Our analysis of the "state of the art" regarding coercion theory and research reveals some notable and regrettable shortcomings that limit practical recommendations and normative prescriptions. For example, the great bulk of social-psychological research on coercion has been devoted to analyses of the factors that produce behavioral compliance, attitude change, obedience to authority, conformity to social pressure, imitation of models, and so on. This is not the place to examine the reasons for such a focus on the activities of the weak to the exclusion of those of the strong (cf. Pilisuk, 1973), but certainly we must direct more attention in the future to the source of influence. Even the study of leadership has concentrated on a leader's reactions to influence from others or on how he obtains a position of leadership in the first place, but almost nothing has been done about the factors explaining the occupant's exercise of influence per se (see Kipnis, 1974, for an exception). However, it is clear that a logical analysis of the bargaining situation and context, when combined with the substantial amount that is known about coercive power use and response in other conflict settings, allows preliminary prescription as well as prediction. In particular, the propositions to be noted are these:

(1) The bargaining interaction system is one in which individuals, groups, or nations that are "functionally equivalent" regarding some issue or topic attempt to work out an exchange ratio through which one set of utilities can be shown to correspond with another. Without this functional equivalence, bargaining will not occur, and some other interaction system (e.g., coercive or bribing conflicts) will obtain.

(2) Because of this structure and context, the bargaining situation tends to be a rule-rich, norm-laden one, in which equally strong participants endorse mutual behavior patterns and constraints designed to reduce the probability of inflicting serious and mutual losses on one another, and, hence, of having mutually unprofitable interaction.

(3) Coercion is usually the major subject of such normative prohibitions, and, hence, the use of coercion in bargaining is a "measure of last resort"–a high-risk influence gesture that always carries attendant risks of retaliation, retribution, and costly escalation.

(4) The rules of coercion are identical within and outside bargaining contexts; credibilities, magnitudes of punishment, believability, target characteristics, and source characteristics all affect the influence and compliance process in predictable and established ways.

(5) Coercion is more probably invoked when (a) negative norms of reciprocity or equity are aroused, (b) conflicts are intense, (c) issues of "face-maintenance" or impression-management come to the fore through bargaining performance, or, (d) inequity through relative deprivation is aroused.

(6) However, because of its risks, great care must be taken when using coercion in bargaining to make sure that the attributions arising from its use judge the actor as defensively motivated and nonaggressive. These conditions are fulfilled when the coercive action is seen as (a) unintended, (b) not meant to punish or be used for selfish purposes, or (c) supported by the situational norms.

(7) Bargainers will act to defuse possible retaliatory gestures from their opposite numbers following the use of coercive means by expressing guilt, self-criticism, or a number of other face-maintenance gestures designed to defuse potentially counter-aggressive responses.

(8) Finally, there is a dilemma for the recipient of coercive gestures during bargaining. By retaliating, he or she runs the serious risk of conflict escalation; by not retaliating, he or she runs the risk of attributions of weakness, further incursions, and more aggression. If the latter persists, the bargaining relations will eventually disintegrate due to the lack of perceived functional equivalence between the parties.

REFERENCES

ADAMS, J. S. (1965) "Inequity in social exchange," in L. Berkowitz (ed.) Advances in Experimental Social Psychology. Vol. 2. New York: Academic Press.

ARONFREED, J. (1970) "The socialization of altruistic and sympathetic behavior: Some theoretical and experimental analyses," in J. Macaulay and L. Berkowitz (eds.) Altruism and Helping Behavior: Social Psychological Studies of Antecedents and Consequents. New York: Academic Press.

BARTOS, O. J. (1970) "Determinants and consequences of toughness," in P. Swingle (ed.) The Structure of Conflict. New York: Academic Press.

BERKOWITZ, L. and J. A. GREEN (1962) "The stimulus qualities of the scapegoat." J. of Abnormal and Social Psychology 64: 293-301.

BERSCHEID, E. and E. WALSTER (1967) "When does a harm-doer compensate a victim?" J. of Personality and Social Psychology 6: 435-441.

BICKMAN, L. (1971) "Effect of different uniforms on obedience in field situations." Proceedings of the 78th Annual Meeting of the American Psychological Association: 359-360.

BONOMA, T. V. (1976) "Locus of control, trust, and decision making under uncertainty." Unpublished manuscript, University of Pittsburgh.

———and B. R. SCHLENKER (1975) "An empirical assessment of the hedonic calculus." Unpublished manuscript, Institute for Juvenile Research, Chicago.

BONOMA, T. V. and J. T. TEDESCHI (1973) "Some effects of source behavior on target's compliance to threats." Behavioral Sci. 18: 34-41.
——— (1974) "The relative efficacies of escalation and deescalation for compliance-gaining in two party conflicts. Social Behavior and Personality 2: 212-218.
——— and S. LINDSKOLD (1972) "A note regarding an expected value model of social power." Behavioral Sci. 17: 221-228.
BRICKMAN, P. (1974) "Rule structures and conflict relationships," in P. Brickman (ed.) Social Conflict. Lexington, Mass.: D. C. Heath.
BROWN, B. R. (1968) "The effects of need to maintain face in interpersonal bargaining." J. of Experimental Social Psychology 4: 107-122.
CARSON, R. C. (1969) Interaction Concepts of Personality. Chicago: Aldine.
COHEN, A. R. (1959) "Some implications of self-esteem for social influence," in C. I. Hovland and I. L. Janis (eds.) Personality and Persuasibility. New Haven: Yale University Press.
COOK, K. S. (1975) "Expectations, evaluations, and equity." Amer. Soc. Rev. 40: 372-388.
COSER, L. A. (1956) The Functions of Social Conflict. New York: Free Press.
DEUTSCH, M. (1973) The Resolution of Conflict. New Haven: Yale University Press.
———, D. CANAVAN, and J. RUBIN (1971) "The effects of size of conflict and sex of experimenter upon interpersonal bargaining." J. of Experimental Social Psychology 7: 258-267.
DEUTSCH, M. and R. M. KRAUSS (1960) "The effect of threat upon interpersonal bargaining." J. of Abnormal and Social Psychology 61: 181-189.
DRUCKMAN, D. (1973) Human factors in international negotiations: Social psychological aspects of international conflict. Beverly Hills: Sage Professional Papers in International Studies, Vol. 2.
——— and T. V. BONOMA (1976) "Determinants of bargaining behavior in a bilateral monopoly situation: II. Opponent's concession rate and similarity." Behavioral Sci. 21: 252-262.
DRUCKMAN, D. K. ZECHMEISTER, and D. SOLOMON (1972) "Determinants of bargaining behavior in a bilateral monopoly situation: Opponent's concession rate and relative defensibility." Behavioral Sci. 17: 514-531.
FALEY, T. E. and J. T. TEDESCHI (1971) "Status and reactions to threats. J. of Personality and Social Psychology 17: 192-199.
FISHER, R. (1969) International Conflict for Beginners. New York: Harper & Row.
GAMSON, W. A. (1975) The strategy of Social Protest. Homewood, Ill.: Dorsey.
GIFFIN, K. (1967) "The contribution of studies of source credibility to a theory of interpersonal trust in the communication process." Psych. Bull. 68: 104-120.
GLASS, D. C. (1964) "Changes in liking as a means of reducing cognitive discrepancies between self-esteem and aggression." J. of Personality 32: 531-549.
GOULDNER, A. W. (1960) "The norm of reciprocity: A preliminary statement." Amer. Soc. Rev. 25: 161-178.
GURR, T. R. (1970) Why Men Rebel. Princeton, N.J.: Princeton University Press.
HAMMOND, K. R. (1965) "New directions in research on conflict resolution." J. of Social Issues 11: 44-66.
HARSANYI, J. C. (1962) "Measurement of social power, opportunity costs, and the theory of two-person bargaining games." Behavioral Sci. 7: 67-80.
HEILMAN, M. E. (1974) "Threats and promises: Reputational consequences and transfer of credibility." J. of Experimental Social Psychology 10: 310-324.
HELM, B., T. V. BONOMA, and J. T. TEDESCHI (1972) "Reciprocity for harm done." J. of Social Psychology 87: 89-98.

HENDRICK, C. and S. P. TAYLOR (1971) "Effects of belief similarity and aggression on attraction and counteraggression." J. of Personality and Social Psychology 1: 342-349.

HOLMES, D. S. (1971) "Compensation for ego threat: Two experiments." J. of Personality and Social Psychology 18: 234-237.

HOMANS, G. C. (1961) Social Behavior: Its Elementary Forms. New York: Harcourt.

HORAI, J. and J. T. TEDESCHI (1975) "Compliance and the use of threats and promises after a power reversal." Behavioral Sci. 20: 117-124.

HOWE, R. G. and M. P. ZANNA (1975) "Sex-appropriateness of the task and achievement behavior." Presented at the annual meetings of the Eastern Psychological Association, New York City.

IKLE, F. C. (1964) How Nations Negotiate. New York: Harper & Row.

KAHN, H. (1960) On Thermonuclear War. Princeton, N.J.: Princeton University Press.

––– (1962) On Escalation: Metaphors and Scenarios. New York: Praeger.

KELLEY, H. H. and A. J. STAHELSKI (1970a) "Errors in perception of intentions in a mixed-motive game." J. of Experimental Social Psychology 6: 379-400.

––– (1970b) "Social interaction basis of cooperators' and competitors' beliefs about others." J. of Personality and Social Psychology 16: 66-91.

KIPNIS, D. (1974) "The powerholder," in J. T. Tedeschi (ed.) Perspectives on Social Power. Chicago: Aldine.

KOMORITA, S. S. and A. R. BRENNER (1968) "Bargaining and concession-making under bilateral monopoly." J. of Personality and Social Psychology 9: 15-20.

KRAUSS, R. M. (1966) "Structural and attitudinal factors in interpersonal bargaining." J. of Experimental Social Psychology 2: 42-55.

LASSWELL, H. D., D. LERNER, and I. SOLA POOL (1952) The Comparative Study of Symbols. Stanford, Calif.: Stanford University Press.

LEE, W. J. (1971) Decision Theory and Human Behavior. New York: John Wiley.

LEVENTHAL, G. S. (1976) "The distribution of rewards and resources in groups and organizations," in L. Berkowitz and E. Walster (eds.) Advances in Experimental Social Psychology. Vol. 9. New York: Academic Press.

LINDSKOLD, S. and R. BENNETT (1973) "Attributing trust and conciliatory intent from coercive power capability." J. of Personality and Social Psychology, 28: 180-186.

LINKDSKOLD, S. and J. T. TEDESCHI (1971) "Self-esteem and sex as factors affecting influenceability." British J. of Social and Clinical Psychology 10: 114-122.

McCLINTOCK, C. (1972) "Social motives—A set of propositions." Behavioral Sci. 17: 438-454.

McGUIRE, W. J. (1969) "The nature of attitudes and attitude change," in G. Lindzey and E. Aronson (eds.) Handbook of Social Psychology. Vol. III. Reading, Mass.: Addison-Wesley.

MELGES, F. T. and R. F. HARRIS (1970) "Anger and attack: A cybernetic model of violence," in D. E. Daniels et al. (eds.) Violence and the Struggle for Existence. Boston: Little, Brown.

MESSE, L. A. (1971) "Equity in bilateral bargaining." J. of Personality and Social Psychology 17: 287-291.

MILBURN, T. W. (1974) "When do threats provoke violent responses?" Presented at the 82nd Annual Meeting of the American Psychological Association, New Orleans.

MILGRAM, S. (1974) Obedience to Authority. New York: Harper.

MORGAN, W. R. and J. SAWYER (1967) "Bargaining, expectations, and the preference for equality over equity." J. of Personality and Social Psychology 6: 139-149.

NACCI, P., G. GAES, and J. T. TEDESCHI (1975) "Capability and use of resources as they affect compliance to threats." Unpublished manuscript, State University of New York at Albany.

OSGOOD, C. E. (1962) An Alternative to War or Surrender. Urbana: Univ. of Illinois Press.

———, G. J. SUCI, and P. H. TANNENBAUM (1957) The Measurement of Meaning. Urbana: Univ. of Illinois Press.

PILISUK, M. (1973) "Fact and fiction in the utilization of social science knowledge." J. of Social Issues 29: 123–132.

POLLARD, W. E. and T. R. MITCHELL (1972) "A decision theory analysis of social power." Psych. Bull. 78: 433-466.

PRUITT, D. G. (1972) "Methods for resolving differences of interest: A theoretical analysis." J. of Social Issues 28: 133-154.

——— (1965) "Definition of the situation as a determinant of international action," in H. Kelman (ed.) International Behavior: A Social-Psychological Analysis. New York: Hol. 91–432.

RAPOPORT, A. (1964) "Critique of strategic thinking," in R. Fisher (ed.) International Conflict and Behavioral Science. New York: Basic Books.

ROTTER, J. B. (1967) "A new scale for the measurement of interpersonal trust." J. of Personality 35: 651-665.

RUBIN, J. and B. BROWN (1975) Social Psychology of Bargaining and Negotiation. New York: Academic Press.

SCHELLING, T. C. (1966) Arms and Influence. New Haven: Yale University Press.

SCHLENKER, B. R., T. V. BONOMA, J. T. TEDESCHI, and W. P. PIVNICK (1970) "Compliance to threats as a function of the wording of the threat and the exploitativeness of the threatener." Sociometry 33: 394-408.

SCHLENKER, B. R., P. NACCI, B. HELM, and J. T. TEDESCHI (1974) "Reactions to coercive and reward power: The effects of switching influence modes on target compliance." Unpublished manuscript, University of Florida.

SCHWARTZ, G., T. KANE, J. JOSEPH, and J. T. TEDESCHI (1975) "The effects of remorse on reactions to a harm-doer." Unpublished manuscript, State University of New York at Albany.

SHORTELL, J. R., F. EPSTEIN, and F. P. TAYLOR (1970) "Instigation to aggression as a function of degree of defeat and the capacity for massive retaliation." J. of Personality 38: 313–328.

SINGER, J. D. (1958) "Threat-perception and the armament-tension dilemma. J. of Conflict Resolutions 2: 90–105.

——— (1963) "International influence: A formal model." Amer. Pol. Sci. Rev. 57: 420-430.

SMITH, R. B. III, R. C. BROWN, Jr., and J. T. TEDESCHI (1976) "First impressions and expectations for social behavior." Unpublished manuscript, State University of New York at Albany.

SOLOMON, L. (1960) "The influence of some types of power relationships and game strategies on the development of interpersonal trust." J. of Abnormal and Social Psychology 61: 223-230.

STAPLETON, R. E., B. L. NELSON, V. T. FRANCONERE, and J. T. TEDESCHI (1975) "The effects of harm-doing on interpersonal attraction. J. of Social Psychology 96: 109–120.

STOUFFER, S. A., E. A. SUCHMAN, L. C. DEVINNEY, S. A. STAR, and R. M. WILLIAMS, Jr. (1949) The American Soldier: Adjustment During Army Life. Princeton, N. J.: Princeton University Press.

TEDESCHI, J. T. and S. LINDSKOLD (1976) Social Psychology: Interdependence, Interaction, and Influence. New York: John Wiley.

TEDESCHI, J. T., T. V. BONOMA and H. NOVINSON (1970) "Behavior of a threatener: Retaliation vs. fixed opportunity costs." J. of Conflict Resolution 14: 69-76.

TEDESCHI, J. T., B. R. SCHLENKER, and T. V. BONOMA (1973) Conflict, Power, and Games: The Experimental Study of Interpersonal Relations. Chicago: Aldine.

——— (1975) "Compliance to threats as a function of source attractiveness and esteem." Sociometry 38: 81-98.

TEDESCHI, J. T., S. LINDSKOLD, J. HORAI, and J. GAHAGAN (1969) "Social power and the credibility of promises." J. of Personality and Social Psychology 13: 253-261.

TERHUNE, K. W. (1970) "The effects of personality on cooperation and conflict," in P. Swingle (ed.) The Structure of Conflict. New York: Academic Press.

THIBAUT, J. and C. FAUCHEUX (1965) "The development of contractual norms in a bargaining situation under two kinds of stress." J. of Experimental Social Psychology 1: 89-102.

TOCH, H. (1969) Violent Men: An Inquiry Into the Psychology of Violence. Chicago: Aldine.

VINACKE, W. E. (1959) "Sex roles in a three-person game." Sociometry 22: 343-360.

WALTON, R. E. and R. B. McKERSIE (1965) A Behavioral Theory of Labor Negotiations. New York: McGraw-Hill.

PART III

INFLUENCES: CONDITIONS AND BACKGROUND FACTORS

EDITOR'S INTRODUCTION

The behavioral scientist defines his or her task as one of identifying and isolating the causes of behavior. His imputations of causal relations are based on empirical evidence. But the types of variables chosen for analysis are delimited by his discipline. The social psychologist, as behavioral scientist, concentrates on factors that are related to the actor and his immediate situation. When he turns his attention to negotiating *behavior, the social psychologist focuses on influences that are regarded as conditions and background factors. Examples of such conditions include negotiating sites, audiences, time pressures, external events, consequences of outcomes, and number and size of negotiating teams. Background factors include culture, attitudes and personalities of team members, and role constraints determined by bureaucratic structures and processes. A subset of these types of influences is represented in the chapters in this section.*

The contributors to this section present analyses of the effects of (a) personality variables, (b) audiences and constituencies, and (c) stresses caused by external events. This set of variables can be divided into the categories of person, role, and situation. In their chapter, Hermann and Kogan attempt to isolate the independent and interactive effects of eight personality variables on behavior in the Prisoner's Dilemma game. The subtle effects found by these investigators could lead to a reconsideration of the impact of personality. The few consistent relationships obtained in earlier studies may have been due to the small number of variables included in the designs. The Hermann and Kogan evidence suggests that different personality variables influence different aspects of negotiating behavior. Such effects can be observed only if a large number of personality and behavioral variables are included in the study.

But there are compelling reasons to suspect that, for many negotiating situations, personality effects are negligible. Negotiators are also role-incumbents whose performances are evaluated by well-defined constituencies; and they are held accountable to these constituencies for the outcomes of the deliberations. Under such circumstances, the effects of negotiators' personalities may be minimized. This is the case especially when the negotiation is being monitored. Brown's chapter elaborates the implications of these negotiating imperatives, with special attention being paid to the importance of face-maintenance motives.

Another effect of performance evaluation is increased tension. Negotiators operate in stressful environments. For this reason, it would be important to document the effects of stress or tension on negotiating behavior. An attempt to do this has been made by Hopmann and Walcott. Their studies demonstrate the dysfunctional effects on negotiation processes and outcomes of increased tension caused by external events. But this is not a simple stimulus-response relationship. Intervening social-psychological processes are suggested by the authors' review of related literature that demonstrates the effects of stress on both cognitive and group structure.

The chapters in this section represent advances—in the form of new findings and insights—in our understanding of the determinants of negotiating behavior. These discoveries are derived from meticulous analyses of experimental data and/or from frameworks designed for organizing and interpreting the results of numerous studies. The analyses have yielded important findings. The frameworks have served to consolidate diverse findings. These two types of efforts are complementary. Both are necessary for moving us from pre-theoretical formulations to the development of a theory that would specify more precisely the interrelationships among person, role, and situational factors. We await the further work that will provide the passage.

Chapter 8

EFFECTS OF NEGOTIATORS' PERSONALITIES
ON NEGOTIATING BEHAVIOR

MARGARET G. HERMANN

Ohio State University

and

NATHAN KOGAN

New School for Social Research

LITERATURE REVIEW

To date, experimental research on the effect of personality on negotiating behavior is generally discouraging. Recent reviews of this literature (e.g., Baxter, 1972; Terhune, 1970) show only a few personality variables for which there are more significant than nonsignificant relationships, and these few variables are generally in studies yet to be replicated. As Terhune (1970: 199) indicates: "Personality effects have been sufficiently elusive to render the overall results equivocal."

A closer examination of this experimental research, however, suggests that there are at least three different ways in which personality characteristics may affect negotiating behavior which are often confounded in the literature. Personality may be related to initial orientation to the negotiations; strategies and other process variables may be influenced by personality; and the mix of

AUTHORS' NOTE: The research reported in this chapter was supported by a grant (DAHC 12-67-63) from the Advanced Research Projects Agency to the second author (then affiliated with the Educational Testing Service). We are grateful to Guillermo Maseero for aiding in the collection of the data and Henrietta Gallagher for help with the data analysis.

the opposing negotiators' personality characteristics may affect the outcome of the negotiations. The inconsistent results reported in summaries of the literature may simply reflect unwarranted comparisons among these three approaches. These alternative approaches to the study of personality and negotiating behavior may be explicated in more detail by referring to an experimental paradigm that is often used in the research—the Prisoner's Dilemma (PD).

One type of PD study involves only one trial. Generally the subject in the one-trial PD indicates his or her choice from a payoff matrix as well as his or her expectation of an opponent's choice. There is no actual feedback of the opponent's response. The question at issue is: How does the subject define or view the situation? Single-trial studies investigate the relationship between personality characteristics and orientation to (rather than behavior in) the PD. In examining personality characteristics in single-trial PDs, we are in effect exploring what subjects with four different orientations are like. In other words, how do subjects with a cooperative orientation (choose to cooperate, expect cooperation) differ from those with an apprehensive orientation (choose to cooperate, but expect competition), from those with an exploitative orientation (choose to compete, but expect cooperation), and from those with a defensive or competitive orientation (choose to compete, expect competition)? In sum, the researcher explores the question of whether these four ways of structuring the environment are differentially related to personality variables.

When there is interaction between opponents in the PD, there is no longer only one subject but two to consider. The focus of attention switches from the personality characteristics of the single subject to the personality characteristics of the pair of opponents. The mix of the personality characteristics of the members of the dyad becomes important; the opponents become dependent on each other's predispositions and predilections. In the multitrial PD, we are interested in exploring the effect of the joint personality characteristics of the dyad on behavior.[1]

The personality characteristics of single subjects become relevant in multitrial PDs when we examine process variables as opposed to outcome variables. Similar outcomes can be attained by different processes. The particular way in which a subject chooses to respond to an opponent—(a) the subject's strategy, (b) perceptions of his/her opponent, (c) choices following specific kinds of plays—may be influenced by his/her personality characteristics.

These three ways of relating personality variables to behavior in the PD have parallels in more complex negotiation situations. How negotiators define their negotiating situation (their orientation) can influence the kind of strategy they use in a negotiation (see Druckman, 1971; Terhune, 1968; Wrightsman, 1966). One determinant of definitions of the situation is the personal characteristics of the negotiators. The issue of coordination in negotiation focuses on the interaction between negotiators. In the bargaining process, each negotiator is influenced by and responds to the behavior of an opposite number. Whether the outcome of the negotiations is agreement or deadlock depends on the ability of the negotiators "to coordinate their intentions and concession-making functions" (Druckman, 1976: 423). The similarities and differences between the personality characteristics of the negotiators may affect the extent of coordination and the form that coordination assumes. With regard to personality-process relationships, Douglas (1957: 77) has argued that the personality characteristics of negotiators have a greater effect during the second stage of the bargaining process, when it is important for negotiators "to assay the rapid conversations going on in the environment and to improvise adaptive behaviors on the spot." What the negotiator does at this stage is probably, in part, a function of his or her personality.

The purpose of the present chapter is to explore these three ways in which personality may have an impact on negotiating behavior. We pose the following questions: (1) How do personality characteristics relate to general orientation toward the negotiation situation? (2) Are the personality characteristics of negotiators related to process variables (e.g., strategy, perceptions of opponent)? (3) Does focusing on the interplay of the personality characteristics of opposing negotiators suggest that personality is related to negotiation outcomes?

Eight personality characteristics are examined in this chapter. These eight characteristics were chosen because each has been used in more than one experimental studies concerned with these traits that have examined orientation, process variables, or dyads. For each personality variable, the table indicates the direction of any relationship with a negotiation variable reported as significant in a particular experimental study, the number of trials belligerence in interpersonal relations. Table 8.1 presents a review of the experimental studies concerned with these traits that have examined orientation, process variables, or dyads. For each personality variable, the table indicates the direction of any relationship with a negotiation variable reported as significant in a particular experimental study, the number of trials used in that study, and whether the study examined orientation, process variables, or dyads. Since most of the studies in Table 8.1 used the PD as the experimental negotiation setting, the relationships reported are with cooperative orientation, cooperative behavior, and various types of cooperative strategies.

An examination of Table 8.1 shows that twenty-six (79 percent) of the thirty-three studies that looked at subjects' orientations, process variables, or dyads found significant relationships for these eight personality characteristics; in contrast, only six (33 percent) of the eighteen studies that did not use these research strategies found significant relationships. (Among the eighteen

TABLE 8.1
Previous Negotiation Research Examining Eight Personality Characteristics

Personality Characteristic	Focus of Study			
	Cooperative Orientation	Cooperative Strategy or Process	Dyadic Cooperation	Other[a]
Anxiety		Tedeschi, Burrill, and Gahagan (1969)[b] – 100 trials, -.54 with forgiveness[e]		Baxter (1973)[b] – 30 trials, n.s.[c]; Wrightsman et al. (1967)[b] – multitrial[d], -.42 for 90% cooperative strategy
Authoritarianism	Ashmore (1969) – 1 trial, significant negative relationship[d]; Berkowitz (1968) – 1 trial, significant X^2 (negative relationship); Deutsch (1960) – 1 trial, -.50; Wrightsman (1966) – 1 trial, $t=1.99$ (negative relationship)	Gahagan et al. (1967) – multitrial[d], n.s.	Slack and Cook (1973) – 100 trials, metamorphic game, negative relationship; Wilson and Robinson (1968) – 20 trials, n.s.	Bixenstine and O'Reilly (1966) – 30 trials, -.30; Klein and Solomon (1966)[b] – 30 trials, n.s.; McKeown et al. (1967)[b] – multitrial, n.s.; Wrightsman et al. (1969) – multitrial[d], n.s.
Cognitive Complexity	Driver (1976) – Inter-Nation Simulation, significant positive relationship	Nardin (1968) – 60 trials, n.s.; Phelan and Richardson (1969)[b] – 60 trials, $F=4.38$ (positive relationship), relationship more dramatic across time; Pilisuk et al. (1965) – 55	Nydegger (1974) – 60 trials, $X^2=11.71$ (positive relationship); Pilisuk et al. (1965) – 55 trials, significant positive relationship	Larson, Moffit and Preston (1968) – multitrial[d], .55

TABLE 8.1 (Continued)

		Focus of Study		
Personality Characteristic	Cooperative Orientation	Cooperative Strategy or Process	Dyadic Cooperation	Other[a]
		trials, subjects classified on basis of lock-in on a particular strategy; Streufert, Streufert, and Castore (1968) – Tactical and Negotiation Game, leadership strategies		Uejio and Wrightsman (1967) – 50 trials, n.s.; Wrightsman et al. (1969) – multitrial[d], n.s.
Tendency toward Conciliation	Ashmore (1969) – 1 trial, significant positive relationship[d]; Wrightsman (1966) – 1 trial, $F=3.77$ (Exp. I), $F=3.40$ (Exp. II) (positive relationship)	Tedeschi, Heister, and Gahagan (1969) – 100 trials, .30 with martyrdom[e]	Shure et al. (1966) – multitrial[d], significant positive relationship	
Dogmatism		Gahagan et al. (1967) – multitrial[d], significant positive relationship with repentance[e]	Druckman (1967) – bargaining simulation, significant negative relationship	Downing et al. (1968) – n.s.[d]; Larson, Moffit, and Preston (1968) – multitrial, n.s.
Risk-Avoidance	Crow and Noel (1976) – Algonian Exercise, $F=9.27$ (positive relationship); Sherman (1967, 1968) – 10 paired-matrix	Pilisuk et al. (1965) – 55 trials, n.s.; Harnett, Cummings, and Hughes (1968) – price negotiation simulation, more willingness to yield,	Crowne (1966) – 20 trials $t=3.39$ (positive relationship); Pilisuk et al. (1965) – 55 trials, n.s.; Shure et al. (1966) multitrial[d],	Dolbear and Lave (1966)[b] – 13 trials, n.s.

TABLE 8.1 (Continued)

Personality Characteristic	Cooperative Orientation	Focus of Study Cooperative Strategy or Process	Dyadic Cooperation	Other[a]
	situation, significant positive relationship	particularly if little information	significant positive relationship	
Self-Esteem		Pilisuk et al. (1965) – 55 trials, n.s.; Tedeschi, Heister and Gahagan (1969) – 100 trials, -.41 with trustworthiness[e]	Pilisuk et al. (1965) – 55 trials, n.s.	Faucheux and Moscovici (1968)[b] – 50 trials, n.s.; Klein and Solomon (1966)[b] – 30 trials, n.s.; Larson, Moffit, and Preston (1968) – multitrial[d], -.40; Williams, Steele, and Tedeschi (1969) – 300 trials, .30
Suspiciousness	Shure et al. (1969)[b] – 1 trial, significant negative relationship			Arnstein and Feigenbaum (1967) – 24 trials, -.70; Klein and Solomon (1966)[b] – 15 trials, n.s.

Note: If the number of trials is indicated, the experimental paradigm used in the study was the PD; otherwise, the particular experimental paradigm is listed.
[a] These studies often examined the realtionship between a personality characteristic for one subject and his (her) cooperative behavior.
[b] Subjects played against programmed opponent or simulated partner.
[c] The abbreviation n.s. stands for "not significant."
[d] Study unavailable to authors; information gleaned from following secondary sources — Baxter (1972), Kelley and Stahelski (1970), Rubin and Brown (1975), or Terhune (1970).
[e] Forgiveness — subject cooperates following trial in which he (she) cooperated and opponent competed; martyrdom — subject cooperates after trial involving mutual competition; repentance — subject cooperates after having chosen competitive response while opponent was cooperative; trustworthiness — subject cooperates after trial of mutual cooperation.

[252]

studies classified as "other" in Table 8.1, the predominant strategy was to examine how a subject's personality influenced his/her behavior, regardless of the personality of the opponent.) With regard to the three research strategies, all eleven studies exploring orientation found a significant relationship; eight (67 percent) of the twelve studies that looked at process variables reported a significant relationship; and seven (70 percent) of the ten studies examining dyads found a significant relationship. Table 8.1 lends some support to the worthwhileness of the present undertaking.

Propositions

What do the studies reported in Table 8.1 suggest about the relationships between the eight personality characteristics and negotiating behavior when we examine orientation, process variables, and dyads? Because the emphasis in these studies is on cooperation as a dependent variable, this discussion of the propositions gleaned from the research will be couched in similar terms.

(1) The more anxious a negotiator is, the less cooperative (more competitive) is his/her orientation to a negotiating situation and the less cooperative is his/her negotiating behavior. Baxter (1973) and Tedeschi, Burrill, and Gahagan (1969) suggest that highly anxious persons are likely be more cautious and conservative in an interpersonal situation. They expect the worst and try to minimize their losses by adopting a competitive strategy. Such behavior is likely to be most apparent when both of the opposing negotiators are highly anxious.[2]

(2) The less authoritarian a negotiator is, the more cooperative is his/her orientation to a negotiating situation and the more cooperative is his/her negotiating behavior. The more cooperative orientation of the low authoritarian is suggested by the four studies in Table 8.1 that examined authoritarianism and orientation (Ashmore, 1969; Berkowitz, 1968; Deutsch, 1960; Wrightsman, 1966). Kelley and Stahelski (1970), in reviewing the authoritarianism literature that is relevant to interpersonal interaction, propose that low authoritarians have an egalitarian orientation to the world (all people are seen as equally deserving) and thus are more cooperative in interpersonal affairs; high authoritarians, according to Kelley and Stahelski, have an egoistic orientation (self-interest is what the world is all about) and thus are more competitive in dealing with others. Moreover, the authors suggest that the orientation of the high authoritarian "could well lead to treating the mixed-motive game as a setting in which one proves his forcefulness by establishing a rivalry framework for the relationship within which one attempts to overcome and outdo the opponent" (Kelley and Stahelski, 1970: 88). The least cooperation will probably occur when high and low authoritarians are paired. The low authoritarian, who may easily be exploited at the beginning of the relationship, may overreact and match or better the competitiveness of the high authoritarian. Along this line, Slack and Cook (1973) report that dyads

composed of high and low authoritarians produced the most competitive environments in an experimental conflict situation.

(3) The more cognitively complex a negotiator is, the more cooperative is his/her orientation to a negotiating situation and the more cooperative is his/her negotiating behavior. In Table 8.1 six of the seven studies examining cognitive complexity support this proposition. In discussing their results, Phelan and Richardson (1969) indicate that less cognitively complex subjects made responses that were aimed at increasing their opponents' losses while more cognitively complex subjects focused on attaining an equal distribution of the payoffs with their opponents. This generally cooperative outlook of cognitively complex individuals is supported in other literature on cognitive complexity. Harvey et al. (1961) note that cognitively complex persons tend to persist in decision-making tasks until they find an *acceptable* resolution to the problem. Driver (1976) found that in an inter-nation simulation cognitively complex decision makers sought a cooperative solution to conflicts. Moreover, the leadership research of Streufert et al. (1968) indicates that cognitively complex leaders show more consideration in interpersonal relations than less cognitively complex leaders and are able to tolerate interpersonal conflict better than less cognitively complex leaders. The most cooperative behavior is expected from dyads where both members are cognitively complex.

(4) The greater a negotiator's tendency toward conciliation as opposed to belligerence in interpersonal relations, the more cooperative is his/her orientation to a negotiating situation and the more cooperative is his/her negotiating behavior. The Ashmore (1969) and Wrightsman (1966) studies in Table 8.1 lend support to the orientation part of this hypothesis. Shure and Meeker (1965: 11) have described the conciliatory person as "responding to the needy and less fortunate . . . with understanding, help, and friendliness. They urge admitting their own wrongs, and refuse to use threats or belligerent means . . . . Instead they advise a diplomatic and constructive response guided by considerations of humanitarianism and cooperation." Such individuals have a generally favorable view of and reaction to people. Research by Shure et al, (1966) in a bargaining situation suggests that, whereas dyads composed of conciliatory persons will be the most cooperative, mixed dyads composed of a more conciliatory and a less conciliatory person will be the least cooperative. The more conciliatory individual appears to overreact to the competitiveness of the less conciliatory opponent.

(5) The more dogmatic a negotiator is, the more cooperative is his/her orientation to a negotiating situation and the more cooperative is his/her negotiating behavior. The direction of the present proposition is based on the following rationale. It has been found in a variety of situations that dogmatic individuals are dependent on authority figures to indicate the appropriate goals for them (see Vacchiano et al., 1969). Moreover, dogmatic persons have

a need to receive support, encouragement, and understanding from such significant others (Vacchiano et al., 1968). If the goal of the negotiation task, as explained by an authority figure (e.g., an experimenter, a reference group), is to earn as much money as possible, as is often the case in the PD, that goal can be integrated with the need for positive feedback by cooperation, particularly if one's opponent has tended to be cooperative. (The direction of this proposition probably depends on the nature of the payoff matrix. Note the results for dyads reported in Druckman, 1967, for a bargaining simulation.) Given the general inflexibility and resistance to change of the more dogmatic individual (see Vacchiano et al., 1969), once such subjects have selected a cooperative strategy, they can be expected to pursue it tenaciously. Most cooperation then will probably occur for dyads that are composed of highly dogmatic persons.

(6) The greater a negotiator's desire to avoid taking risks, the more cooperative is his/her orientation to a negotiating situation and the more cooperative is his/her negotiating behavior. Five of the eight studies in Table 8.1 indicate a significant positive relationship between risk-avoidance and cooperation. Individuals who are risk-avoiders are described by Shure and Meeker (1965: 12) as "unadventuresome" and "unwilling to expose themselves to dangers or hazard risks of either a material or physical character." Crowne (1966) suggests that such individuals are more interested in reaching bargaining agreements than in using a competitive strategy, and bargaining agreements are more likely to occur if cooperative goals prevail over competitive ones. Miller and Swanson (1960) indicate that the parents of risk-avoidant persons emphasize the importance of being accepted and of finding and maintaining a niche for oneself in the interlocking roles that exist in present complex social organizations. Paralleling Crowne's (1966) findings, we propose that dyads with both members risk-avoidant will show the most cooperation; dyads with both members low in risk-avoidance will be the least cooperative.

(7) The more self-esteem a negotiator has, the less cooperative (more competitive) is his/her orientation to a negotiating situation and the less cooperative is his/her negotiating behavior. Persons high in self-esteem are assumed to have confidence in themselves, to expect success rather than failure in encounters with the environment. As Pepitone (1964) has proposed, persons high in self-esteem take advantage of the situations in which they find themselves, behaving so as to ensure themselves of the reward they feel they deserve. Faucheux and Moscovici (1968) suggest that high-self-esteem persons act competitively because they think they probably deserve more on the average than do their opponents, and they intend to manipulate their opponents to guarantee themselves success. On the basis of this rationale, the most cooperation will probably occur in dyads where both members are low in

self-esteem; the least cooperation will occur in dyads where both members are high in self-esteem.

(8) The more suspicious a negotiator is, the less cooperative (more competitive) is his/her orientation to a negotiating situation and the less cooperative is his/her negotiating behavior. Shure and Meeker (1965) propose that persons who are highly suspicious are distrustful of others, selfish, excitable, and likely to project hostility upon others. Such individuals will probably suspect the motives of any person in an interpersonal encounter and will expect the worst. As a result, they may try to beat the others at their own game (cf. Scott and Lyman, 1968). Dyads with both members high in suspiciousness are expected to be the least cooperative. Of particular interest is the behavior of the more suspicious individual in a mixed dyad who is interacting with an essentially trusting person. Given enough time, the trusting member may convince the suspicious partner that his motives are worthy of confidence, leading to a highly cooperative set of decisions.

If we put persons with these eight characteristics into a negotiating situation and examine their orientations, strategies, and interactive behavior, do we find support for these propositions? In other words, does personality appear to have an effect on negotiators' orientations, the processes they choose to make use of, and the ways they interact and interrelate with their opponents? The rest of this chapter describes a study that was designed to explore these questions. The study uses the Prisoner's Dilemma (PD) as the negotiating situation. Admittedly the PD does not represent the complex negotiation setting we perceive in the SALT negotiations or a labor-management dispute. However, as Rubin and Brown (1975: 20-25) have noted, the PD does have some of the characteristics usually found in bargaining or negotiation situations: (1) two parties, (2) involved in a conflict of interest on an issue, (3) who are focusing on resolving the conflict, and (4) who have several possible alternatives to pursue, (5) with the outcome depending on the interaction and choices of the parties. If we are right to find support for the impact of personality on orientation, process variables, and dyadic behavior in a minimal negotiating situation like the PD, we begin to learn at what point in the more complex negotiation setting to start to examine the relationship between the personalities of the negotiators and their negotiating behavior.

RELATING PERSONALITY AND NEGOTIATING BEHAVIOR

Method

Procedure. The subjects were 108 undergraduate men from Princeton University who volunteered to participate in the study. They earned a minimum of $3.00 for the two hours involved in the study. The maximum amount earned was determined by winnings from the PD.

Subjects spent the first hour answering questionnaire items that were intended to assess the personality variables. The questionnaire contained one scale for each of the eight personality variables. The subjects were told that they were helping in the development of a questionnaire by responding to the items and were paid $1.50 when they completed the inventory.

The last questionnaire item presented the subjects with the payoff matrix they would be using later in the research (see Figure 8.1). After describing the consequences of the various choices, the subject was asked to assume that he had an opponent and to indicate what choice he would make were he to have to announce his choice before his opponent. After marking his choice, the subject had to state why he chose it. In light of his choice, the subject was requested to guess his opponent's choice and the reasons for the opponent's choice. A final question asked whether subjects had had any previous experience using payoff matrices of this sort and, if so, to describe the experience.

After finishing the questionnaire and receiving their money for completing that part of the study, all subjects were instructed as to how the PD worked. Subjects were then told that: (a) they had been randomly paired with another student not in the room with them who would serve as the other party in the PD; (b) there would be a series of trials in which both members of a pair would make simultaneous decisions and record their choices on the apparatus provided; and (c) they were to keep a record of their earnings since each member of a pair would know the other's responses. The subjects were further instructed that their goal was to make as much money as they could because their winnings would constitute their earnings for the second part of the study. After these instructions, subjects were taken to individual booths, where they were asked to read over the instructions for the PD once more. They were also asked to keep the doors to the booths closed and not to communicate verbally with their opponent, who was next door.

In the booth, each subject had a box on which there were one red and one green button and two rows of lights—one green light and one red light in each row. Each subject had a copy of the payoff matrix and a sheet on which to record his earnings and to cumulate them. At the sound of a buzzer (every 30 seconds), the subject was instructed to push either the red or the green button. Pushing the red button indicated a cooperative response, pushing the green button indicated a competitive response (see Figure 8.1). When the opponent made a decision, the choices of both were illuminated on the top of the box—the red and green lights immediately above the subject's choice buttons showing his response, the top lights indicating his opponent's responses. The subject was asked to note which cell of the payoff matrix had been selected, given his response and that of his opponent, and to record the amount of money he should receive on his earnings record, adding this amount to previous amounts. As the trials proceeded, the subject's responses were also independently recorded on an Esterline Angus 20 pen recorder.

This equipment plus the buzzer and timer were located in a room that was separated from the subject booths.

In all there were thirty trials of the PD. The payoff matrix (see Figure 8.1) is the standard PD used by Pruitt (1967) in studying the decomposed PD. Pruitt found that the level of cooperation across twenty trials for this matrix remained relatively constant at about 50 percent. With regard to the payoffs in the matrix, if both members of the dyad chose to cooperate, they each received $.12; if both members of the dyad chose to compete, they each received $.06; if one chose to compete and the other to cooperate, the payoff was $.18 and nothing, respectively. As noted earlier, the choice of a·red button on the apparatus indicated a cooperative response; the choice of a green button indicated a competitive response.

After the last trial, the subjects were asked to indicate whether they had used a strategy in responding to the PD and, if so, to describe their strategy.

Personality measures. The following personality scales were used to assess the eight personality characteristics.

Anxiety: The Alpert and Haber (1960) anxiety scale was used to measure anxiety. This scale assesses situational anxiety—more specifically, anxiety occurring in a test-taking or evaluative setting.

Authoritarianism: The Clayton and Jackson (1961) F-scale was used to measure authoritarianism. This twenty-eight item, true-false scale contains fourteen items that are tentatively worded (e.g., "probably few people have

FIGURE 8.1
Payoff Matrix

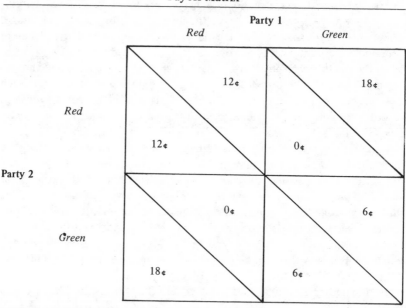

learned important things through suffering") and fourteen items that are extemely worded (e.g., "no sane, normal person could ever think of hurting a close friend or relative").

Cognitive complexity: A twenty-two item, true-false attitude questionnaire developed by Barron (1953) was used to measure cognitive complexity.

Tendency toward conciliation: An eighteen item scale developed by Shure and Meeker (1965) to assess conciliation versus belligerence in interpersonal relations was used to measure subjects' tendency toward conciliation. This scale, as well as those assessing risk-avoidance and suspiciousness, were developed for use in negotiation research.

Dogmatism: A twenty item shortened version of the Rokeach (1960) Dogmatism Scale was used to assess this personality variable.

Risk-avoidance: A nineteen item scale developed by Shure and Meeker (1965) to measure unwillingness to take risks was used.

Self-esteem: Self-esteem was measured by the ten items from the Janis and Field (1959) personality questionnaire that assess feelings of inadequacy in social settings.

Suspiciousness: A seventeen item scale developed by Shure and Meeker (1965) to measure suspiciousness versus trust was used to assess this variable.

Dependent variables. Orientation to PD: As was noted earlier, the last item in the questionnaire asked the subjects to indicate their response and that of a fictional opponent to the payoff matrix that was subsequently used in the study. The subjects' responses were considered as indicating a cooperative orientation to the PD if they chose a red response and a competitive orientation if they chose a green response. Moreover, subjects were considered to be expecting an opponent to be cooperative if they indicated that the opponent would choose a red response and as expecting an opponent to be competitive if they indicated that the opponent would choose a green response. These two types of responses were divided into a fourfold classification that indicated the subject's general orientation to the PD. Possible psychological interpretations of the four orientations are: cooperative (choose to cooperate, expect cooperation), apprehensive (choose to cooperate, expect competition), exploitative (choose to compete, expect cooperation), and competitive (choose to compete, expect competition). Alternative psychological interpretations have been proposed for the apprehensive and the competitive orientations (see, for example, Terhune, 1968). The apprehensive orientation could also be considered as an altruistic orientation; the competitive orientation could also be viewed as a defensive orientation.

Cooperative behavior: From the experimenter's records, the percentage of red or cooperative responses was determined for each subject for each block of ten trials.

Process variables: The two types of process variables that we examined were "perceived own strategy" and "stochastic variables."

(1) **Perceived own strategy:** After the last trial (Trial 30). subjects were asked to indicate whether they were using a strategy and, if they were, to describe the strategy. The item was open-ended. Subjects' responses were classified as indicating either a focus on self-interests or on mutual interests. The coding scheme for examining strategies described by Terhune (1968) was followed in the present study. A focus on self-interests meant that the subject said that: (a) he wanted to achieve the largest amount of money, (b) he did not trust his partner, and played accordingly, (c) he wanted to exploit what seemed like a gullible opponent, or (d) he acted so as to achieve the best odds for himself. A focus on mutual interests meant that the subject said that: (a) he was trying to get as much money as possible for both himself and his opponent, (b) he was interested in achieving mutual cooperation, (c) he hoped that by choosing a cooperative response he could communicate to his opponent the value of mutual cooperation, or (d) he was choosing a competitive response in order to alert his opponent to the dangers inherent in being competitive and the value of cooperation.

(2) **Stochastic variables:** Rapoport and Chammah (1965) have developed a series of variables based on the probability of a subject making a cooperative response after each of four prior dyadic conditions. Of interest are the relative amounts of time that a subject spends: (a) following a cooperative choice on the part of both himself and his opponent with another cooperative response (the subject's propensity to be trustworthy), (b) following a cooperative choice on his part, but a competitive choice by his opponent, with another cooperative response (the subject's propensity to be forgiving), (c) following a competitive choice on his part, but a cooperative choice by his opponent, with a cooperative response (the subject's propensity for being repentant), and (d) following a competitive choice on the part of both himself and his opponent with a cooperative response (the subject's propensity to be a martyr).

Results

Correlations among personality measures. Examining the intercorrelations among the personality measures showed eight significant relationships. These were: anxiety/self-esteem ($-.32$), authoritarianism/cognitive complexity ($-.45$), authoritarianism/dogmatism ($.33$), authoritarianism/suspiciousness ($.24$), tendency toward conciliation/risk-avoidance ($.22$), tendency toward conciliation/suspiciousness ($-.34$), dogmatism/suspiciousness ($.34$), and self-esteem/suspiciousness ($-.26$). None of the other correlations exceeded $.19$. The magnitudes of the correlations indicated no serious overlap among the measures; that is, no measure was so similar to another as to indicate that it should be dropped from the analysis.

Personality and orientation. Table 8.2 presents data for the personality variables by type of orientation. None of the subjects chose a cooperative response when they expected a competitive response from an opponent. Only

TABLE 8.2
Mean Scores for Personality Variables by Type of Orientation to the PD

Orientation to PD[a]	Anxiety	Authoritarianism	Cognitive Complexity	Personality Variables Tendency to be Conciliative	Dogmatism	Risk-Avoidance	Self-Esteem	Suspiciousness
Cooperative (Cooperate, Expect Opponent to Cooperate) (N = 26)	52.88	18.31	13.27	57.77	6.42	38.23	20.38	39.58
Exploitative (Compete, Expect Opponent to Cooperate) (N = 33)	47.24	17.45	14.12	50.58	6.42	37.21	21.09	40.48
Competitive (Compete, Expect Opponent to Compete) (N = 48)	49.35	18.38	12.29	54.54	7.48	38.02	23.10	35.81
	$F = 2.75$ $df = 2/104$ $p = .07$	$F = 0.67$ $df = 2/104$ n.s.	$F = 3.76$ $df = 2/104$ $p = .03$	$F = 2.48$ $df = 2/104$ $p = .09$	$F = 1.86$ $df = 2/104$ n.s.	$F = 0.18$ $df = 2/104$ n.s.	$F = 3.66$ $df = 2/104$ $p = .03$	$F = 2.22$ $df = 2/104$ n.s.

[a] One of the subjects failed to complete these questions so the total N here is 107.

three orientations—cooperative (cooperate, expect cooperation), exploitative (compete, expect cooperation), competitive (compete, expect competition)—are represented in the data. Some 76 percent of the subjects indicated that they would compete, while the expectation of the opponent's behavior was more evenly divided between cooperation (55 percent) and competition (45 percent).

The results of an unweighted-means analysis of variance were significant for two of the personality variables—cognitive complexity and self-esteem. For two other variables—anxiety and tendency to be conciliative—the results approached significance ($p < .10$).

With regard to cognitive complexity, subjects with an exploitative orientation were more cognitively complex than were subjects with the other two orientations. Subjects with a competitive orientation were lowest in cognitive complexity. A comparison among means suggests that the important difference is between those who expected competition and those who expected cooperation. Subjects who expected cooperation were more cognitively complex than those who expected competition ($F = 5.87$, df = 1/104, $p < .05$).

As the means for self-esteem in Table 8.2 indicate, subjects with a competitive orientation had the highest self-esteem. Subjects with exploitative and cooperative orientations were, respectively, intermediate and lowest in self-esteem. As in the case of cognitive complexity, a difference was found between subjects in their expectation of the opponent's behavior. A comparison of means shows that subjects who expected competition from their opponents had higher self-esteem than those expecting cooperation ($F = 7.17$, df = 1/104, $p < .01$).

Highest anxiety scores were found for subjects with a cooperative orientation; lowest anxiety scores were obtained for those with an exploitative orientation. A comparison among means shows that the difference among orientations centered on the subject's choice. Subjects who said they would cooperate were more anxious than were subjects who said they would compete ($F = 4.83$, df = 1/104, $p < .05$).

As might be expected, subjects with a cooperative orientation were the most conciliative. Interestingly, however, subjects with an exploitative orientation, rather than those with a competitive orientation, were least conciliatory. A comparison among the means suggests that the subject's choice is important once there is an expectation that the opponent will be cooperative. Under these circumstances, subjects who chose to cooperate were more conciliative than were those who chose to compete ($F = 4.85$, df = 1/104, $p < .05$).

In sum, the results suggest something about the kinds of people who favored each orientation. Subjects with a cooperative orientation were high in anxiety, moderate in cognitive complexity, high in conciliation, and low in self-esteem. Subjects with an exploitative orientation were low in anxiety, high in cognitive complexity, low in conciliation, and moderate in self-esteem. Subjects with a competitive orientation were moderate in anxiety, low in cognitive complexity, moderate in conciliation, and high in self-esteem. The findings for tendency to be conciliative and self-esteem lend support to the propositions suggested earlier; those for anxiety and cognitive complexity are contrary to the propositions.

An important question concerns the relationship between orientation and behavior. Is orientation related to the subjects' subsequent behavior in the PD? An examination of the subjects' responses in the first trial indicated a close parallel to orientation ($X^2 = 61.25$, df = 2, p < .01). Some 91 percent (44) of the subjects with a competitive orientation made a competitive response, while 92 percent (24) of the subjects with a cooperative orientation made a cooperative response. Of the subjects with an exploitative orientation, 85 percent (28) made a competitive response. As Table 8.3·indicates, orientation had an effect on behavior across the first ten trials, at least for subjects with cooperative and competitive orientations. Subjects with an exploitative orientation became more cooperative than their orientation would suggest. Differences among orientations began to disappear, however, in trials ·11-20; and by trials 21-30, subjects with all three orientations showed about the same rate of cooperation. Orientation appears to have been important in the initial trials but to have diminished in importance as a history of interaction between opponents developed. In other words, only behavior that was proximate in time to the assessment of orientation was affected by orientation.

Personality and process variables. Perceived own strategy: When subjects' statements about their strategies were classified as denoting a focus on self- or mutual interests, some 36 percent (39) of the subjects indicated a focus on self-interests, while 64 percent (69) indicated a focus on mutual interests. An examination of the impact of personality on perceived own strategy revealed an effect for authoritarianism and self-esteem. Subjects whose strategy focused on their own self-interests were more authoritarian than were subjects whose strategy focused on mutual interests (t = 2.12, p < .05). Moreover, subjects with a self-interest strategy were higher in self-esteem than were subjects with a mutual-interest strategy (t = 1.92, p < .10). These results lend

TABLE 8.3

Mean Rate of Cooperation by Blocks of Ten Trials for Subjects with Three Orientations

	Trials		
Orientation	*1 - 10*	*11 - 20*	*21 - 30*
Cooperative	.65	.65	.73
Exploitative	.67	.70	.74
Competitive	.52	.63	.72
	$F = 2.39$;	F < 1;	F < 1;
	$df = 2/104$;	n.s.	n.s.
	$p < .10$		

support to the propositions advanced earlier for these two traits. None of the tests for the other six personality variables was significant or approached significance.

Stochastic variables: The results found in relating the personality variables to Rapoport and Chammah's (1965) stochastic variables were disappointing. Only three (9 percent) of the thirty-two possible correlations were significant, i.e., equal to or more than .20. Anxiety was positively associated (.24) with forgiveness (a subject's tendency to follow a cooperative response on his own part, and a competitive response by his opponent, with a cooperative response). Anxiety was negatively associated (-.20) with repentance (a subject's tendency to follow a competitive choice on his own part, but a cooperative choice on his opponent's part, with a cooperative response). Cognitive complexity was also negatively associated (-.20) with repentance. None of the other correlations exceeded .11.

Dyadic analysis. To perform the dyadic analysis, the subjects' scores on each of the eight personality variables were divided at the median. Subjects were considered to be high on a variable if their scores were above the median on that variable, and low if their scores were below the median on that variable. Each pair of opponents (or dyad) could then be classified as homogeneously high on a particular personality characteristic, homogeneously low on the trait, or heterogeneous (high, low; or low, high) on the trait. Eight 3 x 3 analyses of variance, using unweighted means, were performed with this classification of dyads and with the three blocks of ten trials as independent variables and the rate of cooperation in the PD as the dependent variable. In determining the rate of cooperation for a dyad, the rates of cooperation for each opponent were averaged.

For two of the personality variables—suspiciousness and anxiety—there were significant or near-significant ($p < .10$) main effects for type of dyad (for suspiciousness, $F = 3.28$, $df = 2/51$, $p < .05$;. for anxiety $F = 3.15$, $df = 2/51$, $p < .10$). The mean rates of cooperation for suspiciousness for the three types of dyads were: high, high (HH) = .51; low, high, or high, low (LH) = .69; and low, low (LL) = .74. The means for anxiety were: HH = .54; LH = .68; and LL = .77. These results support the propositions from the literature on suspiciousness and anxiety.

For five of the personality variables, there was a significant type of dyad by trial interaction. These variables were cognitive complexity, tendency to be conciliative, dogmatism, risk-avoidance, and suspiciousness. Table 8.4 presents the mean rates of cooperation for these five variables among the three types of dyads by blocks of ten trials.

As Table 8.4 shows, personality generally had more of an effect on cooperative behavior in the later trials, i.e., after opponents had interacted for a while. The data show that the discrepancy between the HH and LL dyads in rate of cooperation became larger over time for most of these

TABLE 8.4

Mean Rate of Cooperation Among Types of Dyads by Blocks of Ten Trials for Five Personality Variables
(Decimals Omitted)

PERSONALITY VARIABLE

Type of Dyad	Cognitive Complexity				Tendency to be Conciliative				Dogmatism				Risk-Avoidance				Suspiciousness			
			Trials				Trials				Trials				Trials				Trials	
	Dyad N	1-10	11-20	21-30	Dyad N	1-10	11-20	21-30	Dyad N	1-10	11-20	21-30	Dyad N	1-10	11-20	21-30	Dyad N	1-10	11-20	21-30
Low Low	14	58	52	61	13	58	70	65	12	62	58	61	17	61	67	69	11	60	79	82
Low High (High Low)	25	61	70	79	27	58	58	73	28	58	66	78	22	65	64	73	33	63	66	78
High High	15	62	73	75	14	66	78	81	14	63	73	74	15	53	68	78	10	50	54	49
	$F=2.47, df=4/102,$ $p<.05$				$F=3.34, df=4/102,$ $p<.05$				$F=3.56, df=4/102$ $p<.01$				$F=2.74, df=4/102,$ $p<.05$				$F=3.99, df=4/102,$ $p<.01$			

variables. Moreover, the heterogeneous dyads tended to behave like one or the other of the homogeneous types of dyads.

The most dramatic pattern is that for suspiciousness. Dyads high in suspiciousness maintained a 50 percent level of cooperation across trials, whereas dyads low on suspiciousness started with 60 percent cooperation and increased to 82 percent cooperation across trials. Interestingly, those dyads with one opponent high and one opponent low in suspiciousness mimicked the low-suspiciousness rather than the high-suspiciousness dyads. The behavior of the less-suspicious opponent seems to have mollified the suspiciousness of the highly suspicious opponent.

For only one of the five personality variables—risk-avoidance—did the HH and LL dyads change positions in rates of cooperation across trials. Dyads with a high fear of risk showed the lowest rate of initial cooperation (trials 1-10), but their rates increased rapidly thereafter so that by trials 21-30 they showed the most cooperation. Although low risk-avoidant dyads also increased in cooperation across trials, they did so more slowly. Their rate of cooperation was the lowest of the three types of dyads in trials 21-30.

In general, the direction of the differences between dyad types is consistent with the propositions presented earlier for HH and LL dyads. The behavior of the mixed dyads, however, is not as extreme as expected for tendency to be conciliative and suspiciousness, but is more extreme than expected for dogmatism. A relevant question to ask about the mixed or heterogeneous dyads concerns which member of the dyad succeeds in influencing the other? In other words, which of the homogeneous dyads does the behavior of the mixed dyad resemble most closely? For cognitive complexity and dogmatism, Table 8.4 indicates that the member high in the trait influenced the behavior of the dyad. For suspiciousness, the member low in the trait influenced the behavior of the dyad. For two of the traits—conciliation and risk-avoidance—at one time the low member of the dyad was influential, at another time the high member of the dyad was influential. In the case of these two variables, thirty trials may not have been enough to achieve some kind of power equilibrium.

Also of interest is the amount of change among the homogeneous dyads. An examination of the cooperative behavior of the HH and LL dyads in Table 8.4 shows that change was greater in one type of homogeneous dyad than in the other. Members of dyads manifesting considerable behavioral change appear more sensitive to one another's behavior than do members of homogeneous dyads showing little change. From Table 8.4, we note that HH dyads changed to a greater extent than did LL dyads for cognitive complexity, tendency to be conciliative, dogmatism, and risk-avoidance; for suspiciousness, the LL dyads changed more than did the HH dyads. Moreover, while the homogeneous dyads indicating change showed a linear increase over blocks of trials, the homogeneous dyads with little change exhibited curvilinear patterns of cooperation over blocks of trials. For the latter, the greatest change occurred in trials 11-20. There was a return to original behavior in trials 21-30. Attempts on the part of the members of these dyads to be sensitive to their opponent's behavior actually seem to have reinforced their original predilections, with the result that they decided to "leave well enough alone."[3]

CONSIDERATIONS IN RELATING PERSONALITY
TO NEGOTIATING BEHAVIOR

The results suggest more complexity in the relationship between personality and negotiating behavior than was anticipated. Four of the eight personality variables were related to specific orientations to the PD. Although these orientations were relevant to behavior early in the bargaining process, they became less important as the opponents developed a history of interaction. What became important for ascertaining the pattern of this interaction was a knowledge of the mix of personality characteristics of the opponents engaged in bargaining. Six of the eight personality variables showed significant main or interaction effects in the dyadic analysis.

Our results suggest support for Terhune's (1970) contention that personality has an effect on initial behavior and subsequent interactive (reaction) behavior in interpersonal settings such as negotiations. Personality can influence initial behavior because individuals may have little to rely on but their predispositions and past experiences in defining the situation. However, once interaction is under way, the personality and behavior of the opponent become important. Each opponent reacts, in turn, to the other. The mesh of the predispositions of the opponents can help determine how each perceives the other's moves and intentions and how sensitive each will be to the other's behavior.

Apfelbaum (1974) and Rubin and Brown (1975) have focused on interpersonal sensitivity ("interpersonal reactivity" for Apfelbaum; "interpersonal orientation" for Rubin and Brown) as an important determinant of behavior in an interpersonal setting such as is represented by a bargaining and negotiation situation. Apfelbaum (1974) argues that when a member of an interacting dyad perceives that the other's behavior is contingent on his own, an interdependence develops between actors; each can influence and be influenced by the other. Rubin and Brown (1975), on the basis of a review of bargaining studies, propose that this interpersonal sensitivity is more typical of some types of persons than of others. Individuals who are high (low) on particular traits are interpersonally oriented; individuals who are low (high) on the same traits are not. The present research suggests that interpersonal sensitivity depends on the personality characteristics of *both* members of a dyad. Dyads with characteristics suggestive of an interpersonal orientation (such as cognitive complexity and tendency to be conciliative in the present study) exhibit more interpersonal sensitivity and change their original behavior during the course of the interaction.[4]

What characteristics seem to suggest different degrees of interpersonal sensitivity? These are the characteristics that had significant type of dyad by trial interactions; They appear to be of two kinds. Traits such as tendency to be conciliative and suspiciousness involve others in their definition. Each indicates the nature of an individual's reaction to others and, hence, is suggestive of the *interpersonal style* of the individual. These characteristics imply interpersonal sensitivity directly. The other kind of characteristic involved in the significant interactions focuses on how individuals gather information from others in their environment. Three traits—cognitive complexity, dogmatism, and risk-avoidance—fit into this category. Cognitive complexity concerns the complexity or detail to which an individual is atuned in processing information; dogmatism refers to flexibility or the capacity to accept new ideas; risk-avoidance involves a heightened sensitivity to the element of costs when processing information. All three characteristics suggest something about an individual's *decision style*. They indicate sensitivity to the information cues that are present in an interpersonal interaction. Thus, an individual's characteristic ways of dealing with others—interpersonal style—and his characteristic ways of processing information—decision style— seem to affect how sensitive he will be in an interpersonal, decision-making setting such as the PD.

How does this discussion bear on negotiations in general? As was noted at the beginning of this chapter, we realize that the PD paradigm used in the present research contains only a bare minimum of the characteristics considered important in defining a negotiation or bargaining situation. There was no verbal communication among bargainers, no way to opt out of the bargaining relationship, no outside parties that the bargainers represented, and no intangible issues to be negotiated (see Nemeth, 1972; Rubin and Brown, 1975). Thus what we are going to say at this point is merely suggestive and needs to be explored further in a field setting or a more complex experimental bargaining paradigm. Our results provide some leads as to how negotiators' personalities affect their negotiating behavior.

One determinant of a negotiator's initial orientation to a negotiating situation is his personality. His predispositions and expectations about the other side's behavior can be affected by his personality characteristics. The strength of this relationship between personality and initial definition of the situation probably depends on the constraints imposed upon the negotiator by the party that he represents. The less constrained the negotiator, the more likely his personality is to influence the initial definition of the situation. When a negotiator enters into bargaining with a representative of the other side, a stage of exploration begins as each learns about the positions and intentions of the other and the constraints on him. If the negotiators are not too greatly constrained by the parties they represent and if they have characteristics that make them interpersonally sensitive to each other, the give and take necessary for reaching agreement can occur. If, however, the negotiators' characteristics make them less interpersonally sensitive, they will be less aware of the opportunities for give and take with the opponent. Either a deadlock or decidedly slow progress toward agreement can be expected. Such outcomes become more probable when the less sensitive negotiators are severely constrained by the parties they represent.

For the less interpersonally sensitive negotiator, initial predispositions are likely to remain important throughout the negotiations. What cues they do perceive from their environment are interpreted as supporting their predispositions. If initial predispositions are toward agreement or cooperation, the lack of sensitivity may have less effect on the negotiation outcome than it would if the initial orientations are toward nonsettlement or settlement *only* under certain feasible conditions. When negotiators differ in their interpersonal sensitivity (e.g., one is high, and the other is low), the more sensitive party will probably be responsible for any movement in the negotiations. Progress toward agreement in this case, however, may be slow and not without serious consequences, such as abrupt terminations and threatened strikes, as the more sensitive negotiator tries to influence the behavior of his less sensitive opponent.

One of the personality characteristics in the present study—anxiety—showed significant or near-significant effects in the orientation, process, and dyadic analyses. High scores on anxiety were related to a cooperative orientation, to forgiveness, and—with both members of the dyad highly anxious—to a .54 rate of cooperation (the lowest among the dyads for anxiety). Low scores on anxiety were related to an exploitative orientation, to repentance, and—with both members of the dyad low in anxiety—to a .77 rate of cooperation (the highest among the dyads for anxiety). In effect, anxiety was relevant to both the initial and the interactive phases of the PD. In the present study, the kind of anxiety that was assessed was anxiety in an evaluative setting. The particular scale used to measure anxiety (Alpert and Haber, 1960) focuses on anxiety in a test-taking or evaluative situation. Participation in a psychological experiment like the present study is likely to arouse such anxiety since one expects to have his or her performance evaluated. Moreover, knowledge that one is interacting with another person in the PD leaves open the possibility that they too are evaluating one's performance. Negotiators in "real-world" settings also are evaluated. If they are representing other parties, their behavior is scrutinized by these parties. How well is the negotiator upholding the party's position? How accurate a perception of the opponent does he have? The opposing negotiators evaluate one another's behavior as they try to determine what the next steps in the negotiations might be. In a sense, negotiators act in a fishbowl; everyone is interested in their performance. Thus, evaluation anxiety seems an important personality characteristic to consider in future research on negotiation.

By mixing modes of analysis, by doing research on one personality characteristic at a time, by not thinking about characteristics of the negotiation situation in choosing personality characteristics to study, and by lack of replication, previous experimental research relating personality to negotiating behavior has shown few concrete results. Instead of negating the effect of personality on negotiations, however, as some are proposing, we need to be more thoughtful now about which kinds of personality characteristics can affect bargaining and under what conditions and where in the negotiation process they can have an effect. We hope that this chapter is a move in that direction.

Although the chapter has focused on research using contrived negotiation situations, techniques are available to allow us to assess the personality characteristics of actual negotiators on the basis of their statements. For example, one of the present authors (Hermann, 1976) has used content analysis to examine how the coping behaviors of the four major participants in the 1965-1966 New York City transit negotiations influenced what happened in the bargaining. The main sources of data for this study were film clips from interviews with the participants immediately after the negotiation sessions. Techniques such as content analysis permit us to move from the laboratory to the field. We can take the propositions found in the laboratory and begin to explore them in an actual negotiation situation. However, as we go from the laboratory to the field, the negotiations that we are examining become more complex. Therefore, it would seem to be a more prudent use of research time and funds to consider how personality characteristics interact with role characteristics and situational phenomena in affecting negotiations rather than how personality by itself is important. Druckman (1976) with his discussion of the interrelationship of person, role, and situation in international negotiations and Rubin and Brown (1975) with their three-factor model of interdependence in bargaining have provided us with some first steps in this direction.

NOTES

1. In this discussion and what follows (unless otherwise indicated), we are assuming a nonprogrammed opponent. We presume that there is an opportunity for each opponent to try to influence the other.

2. Unless otherwise noted in this discussion of propositions, a statement suggesting extreme behavior for one of the homogeneous dyads (both members either high or low on a particular characteristic) presupposes that mixed dyads will manifest a moderate degree of the behavior, while the other type of homogeneous dyad will show the opposite extreme of the behavior.

3. Some information can be gained from our data on another oft-used method of analyzing the effects of personality on behavior in an experimental negotiation situation—that is, examining the relationship between each subject's personality scores and his/her rate of cooperation in the PD (see note a to Table 8.1). Intercorrelations between personality scores and rate of cooperation during trials 1-10, 11-20, and 21-30 showed little relationship. None of the correlations exceeded .17.

4. The reader should keep in mind throughout this discussion that the subjects in the present study interacted with a nonprogrammed opponent. The behavior of each member of a dyad was contingent on the other's behavior; there was an opportunity for each to try to influence the other. Thus, neither member of the dyad had more control over the relationship than the other. Relations were symmetrical. Based on Apfelbaum's (1974) discussion of interpersonal reactivity, our results might have been different if we had used a programmed opponent or an asymmetrical power situation. We are arguing that, to a certain extent, persons low in interpersonal sensitivity act as if they were in a noncontingent relationship, paying little attention to their opponent's behavior or their own influence on the opponent.

REFERENCES

ALPERT, R. and R. N. HABER (1960) "Anxiety in academic achievement situations." J. of Abnormal and Social Psychology 61: 207-215.

APFELBAUM, E. (1974) "On conflicts and bargaining." Advances in Experimental Social Psychology 7: 103-156.

ASHMORE, R. D. (1969) "Personality-attitude variables and characteristics of the protagonist as determinants of trust in the Prisoner's Dilemma." Unpublished manuscript.

ARNSTEIN, F. and K. D. FEIGENBAUM (1967) "Relationship of three motives to choice in the Prisoner's Dilemma." Psych. Reports 20: 751-755.

BARRON, F. (1953) "Complexity-simplicity as a personality dimension." J. of Abnormal and Social Psychology 48: 163-172.

BARTOS, O. J. (1967) "How predictable are negotiations?" J. of Conflict Resolution 11: 481-496.

BAXTER, G. W., Jr. (1972) "Personality and attitudinal characteristics and cooperation in two-person games: A review," pp. 97-103 in L. S. Wrightsman et al. (eds.) Cooperation and Competition: Readings on Mixed-Motive Games. Belmont, Calif.: Brooks/Cole.

——— (1973) "Prejudiced liberals? Race and information effects in a two-person game." J. of Conflict Resolution 17: 131-161.

BERKOWITZ, N. H. (1968) "Alternative measures of authoritarianism, response sets, and predictions in a two-person game." J. of Social Psychology 74: 233-242.

BIXENSTINE, V. E. and E. F. O'REILLY, Jr. (1966) "Money versus electric shock as payoff in a Prisoner's Dilemma game." Psych. Record 16: 251-264.

CLAYTON, M. B. and D. N. JACKSON (1961) "Equivalence range, acquiescence, and overgeneralization." Educ. and Psych. Measurement 21: 371-382.

CROW, W. J. and R. C. NOEL (1976) "An experiment in simulated historical decision making," pp. 385-405 in M. G. Hermann (ed.) A Psychological Examination of Political Leaders. New York: Free Press.

CROWNE, D. P. (1966) "Family orientation, level of aspiration, and interpersonal bargaining." J. of Personality and Social Psychology 3: 641-645.

DEUTSCH, M. (1960) "Trust, trustworthiness, and the F-scale." J. of Abnormal and Social Psychology 61: 138-140.

DOLBEAR, F. T., Jr. and L. B. LAVE (1966) "Risk orientation as a predictor in the Prisoner's Dilemma." J. of Conflict Resolution 10: 506-515.

DOUGLAS, A. (1957) "The peaceful settlement of industrial and intergroup disputes." J. of Conflict Resolution 1: 69-81.

DOWNING, L. L., W. HASTINGS, T. RYWICK, and A. KAHN (1968) "Profit vs. social motives in the Prisoner's Dilemma game." Presented at the meeting of the Mid-western Psychological Association, Chicago, May.

DRIVER, M. J. (1976) "Individual differences as determinants of aggression in the Inter-Nation Simulation," pp. 337-353 in M.G. Hermann (ed.) A Psychological Examination of Political Leaders. New York: Free Press.

DRUCKMAN, D. (1967) "Dogmatism, prenegotiation experience, and simulated group Inter-Nation Simulation." pp. 337-353 in M. G. Hermann (ed.) A Psychological Examination of Political Leaders. New York: Free Press.

——— (1971) "The influence of the situation in interparty conflict." J. of Conflict Resolution 15: 523-554.

——— (1976) "The person, role, and situation in international negotiations." pp. 409-456 in M. G. Hermann (ed.) A Psychological Examination of Political Leaders. New York: Free Press.

FAUCHEUX, C. and S. MOSCOVICI (1968) "Self-esteem and exploitative behavior in a game against chance and nature." J. of Personality and Social Psychology 8: 83-88.

GAHAGAN, J. P., J. HORAI, S. BERGER, and J. T. TEDESCHI (1967) "Status and authoritarianism in the Prisoner's Dilemma game." Presented at the meeting of the Southeastern Psychological Association, Atlanta, April.

HARNETT, D. L., L. L. CUMMINGS, and G. D. HUGHES (1968) "The influence of risk-taking propensity on bargaining behavior." Behavioral Sci. 13: 91-101.

HARVEY, O. J., D. E. HUNT, and H. M. SCHRODER (1961) Conceptual Systems and Personality Organization. New York: John Wiley.

HERMANN, M. G. (1976) "Verbal behavior of negotiators in periods of high and low stress: The 1965-66 New York City transit negotiations," pp. 356-382 in M. G. Hermann (ed.) A Psychological Examination of Political Leaders: Free Press.

JANIS, I. L. and P. B. FIELD (1959) "A behavioral assessment of persuasibility: Consistency of individual differences." pp. 29-55 in C. I. Hovland and I. L. Janis (eds.), Personality and Persuasibility. New Haven, Conn.: Yale Univ. Press.

KELLEY, A. H. and A. J. STAHELSKI (1970) "Social interaction bases of cooperators' and competitors' beliefs about others." J. of Personality and Social Psychology 16: 66-91.

KLEIN, E. B. and L. SOLOMON (1966) "Agreement response tendency and behavioral submission in schizophrenics." Psych. Reports 18: 499-509.

LARSON, K. S., J. W. MOFFITT, and R. PRESTON (1968) "The relationship of some personality variables to non-zero sum game behavior." Presented at the meeting of the Western Psychological Association, San Diego, March.

McKEOWN, C. D., J. P. GAHAGAN, and J. T. TEDESCHI (1967) "The effect of prior power strategy on behavior after a shift of power." J. of Experimental Research in Personality 2: 226-233.

MILLER, D. R. and G. E. SWANSON (1960) Inner Conflict and Defense. New York: Holt.

NARDIN, T. (1968) "Communication and the effects of threats in strategic interaction." Peace Research Society Papers 9: 69-85.

NEMETH, C. (1972) "A critical analysis of research utilizing the Prisoner's Dilemma paradigm for the study of bargaining." Advances in Experimental Social Psychology 6: 203-234.

NYDEGGER, R. V. (1974) "Information processing complexity and gaming behavior: The Prisoner's Dilemma." Behavioral Sci. 19: 204-210.

PEPITONE, A. (1964) Attraction and Hostility. New York: Atherton.

PHELAN, J. G. and E. RICHARDSON (1969) "Cognitive complexity, strategy of the other player, and two-person game behavior." J. of Psychology 71: 205-215.

PILISUK, M., P. POTTER, A. RAPOPORT, and J. A. WINTER (1965) "War hawks and peace doves: Alternate resolutions of experimental conflicts." J. of Conflict Resolution 9: 491-508.

PRUITT, D. G. (1967) "Reward structure and cooperation: The decomposed Prisoner's Dilemma game." J. of Personality and Social Psychology 7: 21-27.

RAPOPORT, A. N. and A. M. CHAMMAH (1965) Prisoner's Dilemma: A Study in Conflict and Cooperation. Ann Arbor: Univ. of Michigan Press.

ROKEACH, M. (1960) The Open and Closed Mind. New York: Basic Books.

RUBIN, J. Z. and B. R. BROWN (1975) The Social Psychology of Bargaining and Negotiation. New York: Academic Press.

SCOTT, M. B. and S. M. LYMAN (1968) "Paranoia, homosexuality, and game theory." J. of Health and Social Behavior 9: 179-187.

SHERMAN, R. (1967) "Individual attitude toward risk and choice between Prisoner's Dilemma games." J. of Psychology 66: 291-298.

――― (1968) "Personality and strategic choice." J. of Psychology 70: 191-197.

SHURE, G. H. and R. J. MEEKER (1965) A Personality/Attitude Schedule for Use in Experimental Bargaining Studies. Santa Monica, Calif.: Systems Development Corporation, Report TM-2543.

―――, W. H. MOORE, Jr., and H. H. KELLEY (1966) Computer Studies of Bargaining Behavior: The Role of Threat in Bargaining. Santa Monica, Calif.: Systems Development Corporation, SP 2916.

SLACK, B. D. and J. O. COOK (1973) "Authoritarian behavior in a conflict situation." J. of Personality and Social Psychology 25: 130-136.

STREUFERT, S., S. C. STREUFERT, and C. H. CASTORE (1968) "Leadership in negotiations and the complexity of conceptual structure." J. of Applied Psychology 52: 218-223.

TEDESCHI, J. T., D. BURRILL, and J. P. GAHAGAN (1969) "Social desirability, manifest anxiety, and social power." J. of Social Psychology 77: 231-239.

TEDESCHI, J. I., D. S. HIESTER, and J. P. GAHAGAN (1969) "Trust and the Prisoner's Dilemma game." J. of Social Psychology 79: 43-50.

TERHUNE, K. W. (1968) "Motives, situation, and interpersonal conflict within Prisoner's Dilemma." J. of Personality and Social Psychology Monograph Supplement 8: 1-24.

――― (1970) "The effects of personality in cooperation and conflict," pp. 193-234 in P. Swingle (ed.) The Structure of Conflict. New York: Academic Press.

UEJIO, C. K. and L. S. WRIGHTSMAN (1967) "Ethnic-group differences in the relationship of trusting attitudes to cooperative behavior." Psych. Reports 20: 563-571.

VACCHIANO, R. B., P. S. STRAUSS, and L. HOCHMAN (1969) "The open and closed mind: A review of dogmatism." Psych. Bull. 71: 261-273.

VACCHIANO, R. B., P. S. STRAUSS, and D. C. SCHIFFMAN (1968) "Personality correlates of dogmatism." Psych. Bull. 72: 83-85.

WALTON, R. E. and R. B. McKERSIE (1965) A Behavioral Theory of Labor Negotiations. New York: McGraw-Hill.

WILLIAMS, C. D., M. W. STEELE, and J. T. TEDESCHI (1969): "Motivational correlates of strategy choices in the Prisoner's Dilemma game." J. of Social Psychology 79: 211-217.

WILSON, W. and C. ROBINSON (1968) "Selective intergroup bias in both authoritarians and non-authoritarians after playing a modified Prisoner's Dilemma game." Perceptual and Motor Skills 27: 1051-1058.

WRIGHTSMAN, L. S. (1966) "Personality and attitudinal correlates of trusting and trustworthy behaviors in a two-person game." J. of Personality and Social Psychology 4: 328-332.

———, G. W. BAXTER, L. BILSKY, and R. H. NELSON (1969) "Effects of information about other player and other player's game behavior upon cooperation in a mixed-motive game." Presented at the meeting of the Western Psychological Association, Vancouver, B.C., June.

WRIGHTSMAN, L. S., D. DAVIS, W. LUCKER, R. BRUININKS, J. EVANS, R. WILDE, D. PAULSON, and G. CLARK (1967) "Effects of other person's race and strategy upon cooperative behavior in a Prisoner's Dilemma game." Presented at the meeting of the Midwestern Psychological Association, Chicago, May.

Chapter 9

FACE-SAVING AND FACE-RESTORATION
IN NEGOTIATION

BERT R. BROWN

Department of Psychology
Rutgers University

Among the most troublesome kinds of problems that arise in negotiation are the intangible issues related to loss of face. In some instances, protecting against loss of face becomes so central an issue that it "swamps" the importance of the tangible issues at stake and generates intense conflicts that can impede progress toward agreement and increase substantially the costs of conflict resolution. In general, such issues may arise as spin-offs of one or more of the tangible issues in dispute, from the history of the relationship between the parties to the conflict, and/or as a result of certain situational factors.

Through daily exposure to mass-media reports of international and labor-management negotiations, and perhaps through some of our interpersonal negotiations, too, we become aware of, or involved in, disputes deadlocked over issues that threaten one or more of the participants with loss of face. Regrettably, we have seen instances in which the costliness of these kinds of deadlocks has been assessed in terms of the loss of human lives, the widespread destruction of property, and the severe economic hardships sometimes suffered by individuals or groups dependent upon the outcomes of these negotiations for their subsistence. Especially disturbing is the recurrence of such conflicts in many areas where negotiation is relied upon as a primary instrument of conflict resolution. Prominent examples of situations where face has played an important role are the 1951 Korean cease-fire negotiations at Kaesong and Panmunjom, the 1972 Paris-Vietnam peace talks, the continuing Mideast truce negotiations, and numerous disputes occurring each year in the United States in private industry, public education, and state and local government collective bargaining (for a more detailed analysis of the effects of face in these illustrative cases, see Rubin and Brown, 1975).

Although the importance of face in negotiation has been discussed in general terms by several authors (see Schelling, 1963; Stevens, 1963; Iklé, 1964; Swingle, 1970; Gallo, 1972; Deutsch, 1969, 1973; Rubin and Brown, 1975), it has been the focus of only a limited number of systematic empirical studies (see Brown, 1968; Pruitt and Johnson, 1970; Johnson, 1971; Johnson and Tullar, 1972; Tjosvold, 1974; Brown and Garland, 1976). More characteristically, investigators studying related aspects of negotiation have introduced "face-saving" as an explanatory concept in interpreting their findings (see Deutsch and Krauss, 1962; Borah, 1963; Hornstein, 1965; Berger and Tedeschi, 1969; Podell and Knapp, 1969; Bonoma et al., 1970; Schlenker et al., 1970; Benton and Druckman, 1973; Druckman and Bonoma, 1976). Although these interpretations are often highly suggestive, they do not usually contain empirical evidence about the specific mechanisms that regulate this kind of behavior or about its effects on the negotiation process.

Through an integration of previous conceptual analyses and related empirical research, this chapter explores fundamental reasons why face-maintenance motives tend to influence the negotiation process. Also examined are several forms of behavior that may be engendered by such motives, as well as mechanisms that may function as "regulators" and "targeters." It is hoped that this kind of integration will broaden our understanding of the mechanics of face-maintenance in negotiation, stimulate further research, and perhaps be of constructive value to practitioners.

DEFINITIONS: FACE-SAVING AND FACE-RESTORATION

In an early laboratory investigation of the effects of face in interpersonal bargaining, Brown (1968), drawing largely on prior conceptualizations by Deutsch and Krauss (1962) and Goffman (1955, 1959), suggested that pressures to maintain face are apt to become heightened in "aggressive" or adversary relationships and that individuals may sometimes engage in such behavior at high cost to themselves. Brown proposed that face-maintenance— the desire to project an image of capability and strength, or conversely to avoid projecting an image of incapability, weakness, or foolishness—is a culturally induced motive that is heightened by threats to face, and that such threats are likely to result in attempts to either save or restore lost face. In negotiation, it was pointed out, threats to face may be experienced as a result of unwarranted intimidation or insult, unfair reduction of one's outcomes, or other events causing public humiliation—events that are perceived by a negotiator as casting doubt, or as having the potential for casting doubt, on his capability, strength, status, prestige, or reputation in the eyes of salient others. Accordingly, *face-saving* was conceptualized as anticipatory and pre-ventative, and as becoming evident when A attempts to prevent, forestall, or block actions by B that A supposes could cause him to look foolish, weak, or incapable. In contrast, *face-restoration* was conceptualized as reparative of damage already done and as reflected in attempts by A to seek redress from B, whom A believes has already caused him to look foolish, weak, or incapable.

FUNDAMENTAL REASONS FOR
FACE-MAINTENANCE IN NEGOTIATION

There are two general explanations for the salience of face-maintenance motives in negotiation. One is a "structural" reason, suggested by Stevens' (1963) analysis of an "inherent paradox" of negotiation. Although Stevens focused primarily on collective bargaining, the paradox that he describes probably arises in many other areas, too. Briefly, this paradox grows out of a *necessity* for yielding in order to reach agreement, on the one hand, and the *strategic value* of not yielding, or at least of minimizing such behavior, in order to increase one's outcome, on the other hand. Stevens' paradox brings to light a fundamental bind in which negotiators often find themselves: To be effective, they must normally be firm without appearing too rigid, and, at the same time, they must be willing to yield without appearing too conciliatory. This parallels the "bargainers' dilemma" outlined by Podell and Knapp (1969: 512): " . . . how to offer a concession while retaining the appearance of being unyielding, so as not to weaken one's bargaining position."

Kelley (1966) has suggested that determining how firm or how yielding to be in negotiation is often a difficult and exacting task and that negotiators may therefore "err" or overshoot in either direction. The consequences of such errors may be perilous. By being too firm and fostering an impression of rigidity, one may (1) forego timely opportunities to reach agreement, (2) cause oneself to be seen as unfair or as unwilling to negotiate in good faith, or (3) cause the opposing party to become exceedingly tough and resistant. All of these effects may turn out to be contrary to one's best interests; in some instances, they may even lead to costly breakdowns of negotiations. On the other hand, the consequences of being too conciliatory—of yielding too much or too readily—may be equally perilous. In this case, one may (1) create an impression of being overly anxious to reach agreement, or (2) cause oneself to be seen as willing to settle for less than one might otherwise be expected to seek. Either effect could work against one's best interests because the opposing party, particularly if inclined to be rapacious, could be led to view one as weak and perhaps vulnerable to exploitation.

Since there is often some degree of uncertainty in negotiation as to whether an opposing party will seize a competitive advantage afforded him, firmness is necessary but normally this must be tempered with some demonstrable willingness to yield or to compromise. However, because yielding may possibly project an impression of weakness or vulnerability, such behavior may be accompanied by some concern for dispelling these kinds of impressions and for maintaining instead an image of strength, even though it may be costly to do so. Thus from the perspective of Stevens' paradox, the contradictory needs for yielding and, at the same time, for minimizing such behavior may be viewed as building pressures toward face-maintenance into the structure of negotiation.

Deutsch and Krauss (1962) suggest another explanation for face-maintenance motives in negotiation. They point out that there is a wide-spread tendency in our society to resist undeserved intimidation in order to guard against the loss of self-esteem and of social approval that ordinarily results from uncontested acquiescence to such treatment. Inherent in their analysis is the assumption that negotiation represents a microcosm of our broader social milieu and that negotiating behavior is therefore regulated by societal norms that place a positive value on displays of strength and a negative value on expressions of weakness' or undue deference, particularly in competitive situations. And because of the special importance of demonstrating one's capability and strength in negotiation, this is an arena in which many of our underlying cultural attitudes about the adversity of being seen as weak or vulnerable are especially likely to be played out.

Both the structural and the normative viewpoints lead to the general conclusion that face-maintenance motives and their behavioral expressions ought to be commonplace in negotiation. But, beyond this, they also bring several important and, in some cases, unexplored questions into clearer perspective. Among these are: (1) What specific forms of negotiation behavior may be engendered by such motives? (2) What mechanisms may regulate the occurrence of these types of behavior? (3) Who, besides the other negotiator(s) in the exchange may become the "targets" of such behavior? (4) What mechanisms may be involved in the targeting of such behavior and may thereby be capable of shifting it from one target to another? Each of these questions is explored below.

SPECIFIC EXPRESSIONS

Face-Saving

As was pointed out in the "Definitions" section above, an essential characteristic of face-saving behavior is that it is *anticipatory* and *preventative*. It is thus future-oriented and offensive. It reflects actions designed to hide, soften, ward off, prevent, or block the future disclosure of information and to control the occurrence of future events that one expects will foster an appearance of weakness or vulnerability, particularly when it is presumed that such events will impair one's image or the image of those whom one represents. Specific behaviors keyed to this purpose in negotiation may take many forms, including verbal statements and actions of a more definitive nature.

Verbal expressions. Recent research findings reported by Hewitt and Stokes (1975) reveal that, in the course of social interaction, statements made to others may be prefaced with a variety of "disclaimers," often used to prevent future embarrassment that one suspects may result from revealing ineptness or vulnerability. Broadly speaking, these findings are corroborated by evidence on embarrassment reported by Brown and Garland (1970) and by Goffman's (1959) conceptual analysis of "frontal" aspects of self-presentation. More specifically, Hewitt and Stokes suggest that "hedging" and "credentialing" disclaimers often underlie use of the following kinds of statements: "I'm no expert, but . . ." "I really haven't thought this through very well, but. . . ." "I know what I'm going to say sounds crazy, but. . . ." Such statements, they feel, are often made in order to avoid damaging one's "identity" in a listener's eyes, to avoid being typed as ignorant or prejudiced, or to avoid seeming to lack a sufficient grasp of facts or reality.

These are illustrations of the broad range of disclaimers that negotiators may use in phrasing their proposals, demands, concessions, or other statements as aids in protecting them from being seen as weak, foolish, ignorant, etc. In general, disclaimers used for face-saving purposes are future-oriented, conditional, and often tentative; they attempt to minimize or soften the possible negative effects of proposals or other statements. For example: "It's not that I (we) can't–but . . . ." "I know this proposal may (seem, sound, look) _____ , but. . . ." "I'm (we're) not (disorganized, in disagreement, unprepared, etc.), it's just that I'm (we're). . . ." "It may look like I'm (we're) _____ but. . . ." "Well, perhaps I (we) could rethink. . . ." As Hewitt and Stokes point out, "If a disclaimer is successful, the listener concedes that the speaker may have a good point and does not label him or her as foolish, dumb, uninformed or generally worthless" (1975: 254).

Along similar lines, negotiators may also couch their statements in terms that are tentative or vague so as to permit later modification, should this become desirable. In this connection, Iklé (1964) describes the strategy of "hedging against failure," which, he points out, is commonly used by international negotiators. This may involve omitting or avoiding discussion of specific issues, withholding certain information, exhortations of magnanimity, morality, or the enormity of one's sacrifices when making concessions. Or it may take the form of bluffing or other types of deception in order to ward off anticipated damage to one's personal or national "image" or reputation arising from the disclosure of information that one feels would reflect poorly on him or expose his vulnerabilities.[1]

In general terms, there are several kinds of factors that may have a considerable potential for damaging one's image of capability and/or strength when disclosed to an opposing negotiator, including: unpreparedness; poorly conceived proposals or demands; inconsistencies or "irrational" elements in one's position; lack of sufficient commitment to a position that one is advocating; inability or apparent lack of resources to defend a position that one has taken; and indications of a disorganized or splintered negotiating team or constituency. The major point to be emphasized here is that, although many of the verbal devices that have been outlined may be used for other strategic purposes also, they may be viewed as attempts at face-saving when used to prevent indications of weakness or vulnerability from being transmitted to others.

Face-saving actions. Beyond using strictly verbal devices for face-saving purposes, negotiators may engage in a broad range of additional activities. Such actions may or may not be accompanied by verbal pronouncements. The primary purpose of these kinds of actions is similarly to prevent potential sources of weakness or incapability from becoming evident to others, particularly when there is seen to be a risk that such disclosure may cast one (or those whom he represents) in a negative light and thereby increase his vulnerability. Again, such actions are future-oriented and offensive. They tend to arise out of concerns with protecting, increasing, and/or demonstrating one's strength or resources, or at a minimum, with establishing or improving internal security so that unpreparedness, disorganization, turmoil, etc., may be prevented from becoming evident to others. Specific actions keyed to this purpose in negotiation may include allocating, mobilizing, or deploying resources of various sorts; staging demonstrations or other public displays of military or other kinds of strength and taking pre-emptive actions, provided such actions are designed to minimize, hide, or camouflage sources of anticipated weakness or other liabilities. Short of these "large-scale" types of actions, negotiators may take more limited ones also. These include taking a hard line—refusing to make or making only small concessions. Or they may attempt to forestall negotiations by holding unduly lengthy caucuses, procrastinating, persevering on specific procedural or substantive issues by introducing irrelevancies, distractions, and side issues, or by otherwise attempting to prevent adverse information or indications of weakness from "leaking out." It is to be emphasized again that these are suggestive of a much broader range of options available. Many of these may be adopted for other strategic purposes, too, but they are most clearly keyed to face-saving when the underlying motive is to keep weakness hidden from others who are expected to exploit it for its competitive advantage.

For empirical corroboration of some of these generalizations, the evidence is scant, but there is some that is available to us. Perhaps the clearest is found in the results of an experiment conducted by Pruitt and Johnson (1970), who found that subjects making concessions under heightened (as compared to lessened) time pressure experienced more pronounced feelings of personal weakness as a result of conceding. Moreover, subjects who made concessions in accordance with a mediator's suggestion were apparently able to dispel their feelings of personal weakness by passing much of the responsibility for their concessions on to him. Additional findings reported by Johnson and Tullar (1972) and Podell and Knapp (1969), using simulated labor-management disputes, and by McKersie et al. (1965), who conducted a field study of contract negotiations in the automotive industry, corroborate the view that making concessions or engaging in other forms of yielding is likely to be resisted because of the implications that it carries for feelings of personal weakness. Also, conceptual analyses of third-party involvement in collective bargaining (Kerr, 1954; Kressel, 1972) and of the conduct of labor-management and international negotiation (Stevens, 1963; Fisher, 1969: Iklé, 1964) address this problem. These sources provide a considerable amount of anecdotal evidence suggesting that unless these kinds of concerns can be ameliorated, yielding and related forms of conciliatory behavior are apt to be resisted and/or accompanied by face-saving actions.

Face-Restoration

An essential characteristic of face-restoration behavior is that it is designed to repair damaged or lost face. It is post facto; it occurs in response to events that have already transpired. Thus, it is past-oriented and defensive. It reflects actions designed to re-establish or reassert one's capability and/or strength *after* one feels they have been damaged. Again, such actions may occur on a verbal or an action level, or they may include elements of both.

Verbal expressions. Illustrations of the kinds of verbal statements keyed to face-restoration include qualified or hedged retractions or modifications of erroneous, misinformed, or otherwise inappropriate statements that are thought to have caused one to look weak, foolish, etc. Many of the disclaimers outlined in the previous section, when expressed in the past tense, may be used for face-restoration purposes. Or doggedly holding to and refusing to alter previously made statements known to be incorrect, minimizing one's outward commitment to previously stated positions, and minimizing the impact of previous events may be used for similar purposes. In addition, Iklé (1964) points out that international negotiators sometimes issue warnings or threats of future actions in response to events experienced as derisive or otherwise inappropriate in terms of their personal or "national" prestige or reputation. However, he also suggests that although threats are sometimes used for these purposes, warnings are more likely to occur because they often require a lesser commitment to future enactment than do threats. Thus, warnings of future resistance or noncooperativeness, of future refusals to yield, or of future reprisals may be used in order to reassert one's capability and strength after being threatened. Such warnings may be stated forthrightly, or they may be veiled by innuendo. Again it is important to note that any of these kinds of statements may be made for a variety of other strategic purposes also, but they most clearly reflect attempts to restore lost face when they are used to reassert one's capability and strength *after* those are thought to have been damaged.

Face-restoration actions. Many of the verbal statements used for purposes of face-restoration may be translated into more definitive actions. In this connection, the results of several laboratory investigations using the Acme-Bolt Trucking game, the Prisoner's Dilemma, and Siegel and Fouraker's (1960) bilateral monopoly bargaining situation are suggestive of some of the specific kinds of behavior that negotiators may adopt for purposes of restoring lost face. Briefly, Deutsch and Krauss (1962) reported that the *use of threat* tended to produce threat-counterthreat-aggression cycles that severely curtailed bargaining effectiveness. It was explained that an underlying motive behind the subjects' use of threat in these circumstances was their concern with repairing damage to their self-esteem and "social face," as a result of their intimidation by the opposing party. The implication here is that threat was probably frequently adopted as a response in order to reassert capability and strength after they had been challenged by the other. Accompanying evidence, particularly in the form of verbatim transcripts of subjects' conversations during the exchange, generally supports this interpretation. Furthermore, data that reflect bargaining outcomes in this condition suggest that, in choosing to respond in this manner, subjects not only inflicted losses on the opposing party, but did so at substantial costs to themselves.

Additional findings reported by Borah (1963), Brown (1968), and Deutsch et al. (1971) provide further support for the contention that threats may be used in order to reassert one's capability and strength. The results of these studies also suggest that related forms of behavior, such as *imposing retaliatory penalties, obstruction, resistance to threat, and other displays of strength,* often involving costs to self, may be adopted for similar purposes. Investigations using the Prisoner's Dilemma game reveal a similar pattern. Here, Schlenker et al. (1970) attributed *increased retaliation* against a threatening other to subjects' concerns with reasserting themselves; Berger and Tedeschi (1969) suggested that *aggression* against one who had caused subjects to experience humiliation may have been grounded in similar concerns; Bonoma et al. (1970) attributed subjects' *refusals to disclose their intentions* to a previously exploitative other to similar concerns; and Tedeschi et al. (1971) explained subjects' *deception* (i.e., not living up to their previously announced intentions) of a previously exploitative other on these grounds.

In summary, the evidence considered thus far suggests that face-maintenance motives may lead to a variety of forms of negotiation behavior and that these may be restricted to verbal expressions, may involve more direct types of action, or may include elements of both. Furthermore, the evidence also suggests that specific behavioral expressions of this motive are apt to reflect negotiators' defensive responses to prior threats to face or offensive responses to anticipated future ones. We turn next to an examination of several mechanisms that may function as situational regulators of these kinds of behavior.

SITUATIONAL REGULATORS OF
FACE-SAVING AND FACE-RESTORATION

It has been proposed that face-maintenance is a social motive that, when activated or heightened by the occurrence of certain events, may call forth any of a variety of responses keyed to the prevention or restoration of lost face. The research evidence and conceptual analyses that have been examined suggest that foremost among the kinds of "events" that may threaten a negotiator's face are those stemming from: (1) the opposing party's actions, and (2) the influence of a variety of other salient social referents. We shall also consider how instigation by any of these sources may be affected by the availability of appropriate means for carrying out such behavior and by the relative gains/costs in doing so.

The Opposing Party as Regulator

Perhaps the most readily apparent regulator of face-saving and face-restoration in negotiation is the opposing party. It is through his overt or anticipated actions, or through information that one obtains about him, that face-maintenance concerns and ensuing defensive or offensive responses may be called forth.

As a rule, if an opposing party acts in ways that in fact threaten, or are experienced as threatening, or as having the potential for threatening one's face through inappropriate or unjust intimidation, then (holding aside for the moment other considerations, such as the availability of specific mechanisms for carrying out such action, its "costs," etc.), the threatened party's response is likely to be guided by face-maintenance motives and to result in attempts either to prevent or to repair lost face. This general assertion is supported by empirical evidence suggesting that threats to face may be experienced when one is exposed to another who (1) makes bids or proposals that reflect excessive self-interest, refuses to make or makes "negative" concessions (Brown and Garland, 1976); (2) issues threats frequently and with a high probability of carrying them out (Horai and Tedeschi, 1969; Bonoma et al., 1970); (3) penalizes him severely (Brown, 1968; Tedeschi et al., 1971); or (4) is unduly deceptive (Tedeschi et al., 1971).

In all of these studies, subjects were exposed to a competitively programmed confederate who, they probably had reason to believe, was like themselves in terms of age, status, etc. Given their probable perceptions of similarity, these subjects may well have experienced the confederate's behavior as highly unjust and intimidating, and therefore as necessitating reassertion of their capability and strength. This kind of effect has been discussed by

Homans (1961), from the standpoint of the adverse affective and inter-personal consequences of distributive "injustice," and by Kelley (1965), in terms more directly related to the status perceptions of subjects in bargaining experiments. Also, it has been observed in experiments conducted by Borah (1963), Hornstein (1965), and Druckman and Bonoma (1976).

There is also evidence to suggest that, short of actually being intimidated, similar motives and responses may be engendered when a negotiator faces another who makes indirect claims to the *right* to intimidate him. Such claims may also be conveyed to one as incidental effects of specific actions taken by the other party (e.g., demanding a highly inequitable share of the available outcome, making insufficient concessions, "nonnegotiable" demands, threats, etc.), or may be engendered by information available to one about the other's status claims, intentions, expectations, etc. In this connection, Kelley (1965) points out that threats may communicate the threatener's implicit assump-tion that he has the right to threaten and to expect a deferential response from the threatened party. However, if the threatener's assumption is not shared by his target, there is a strong likelihood that the expected deference may be supplanted by resistance. This is supported by the results of Borah's (1963) experiment, which indicated that unacceptable claims to superiority made by an opposing party are likely to increase one's competitiveness and resistance to yielding in order to contest the other's illegitimate status claims. Presumably, acquiescence to such claims may adversely affect one's self-image or may be felt to provide grounds for causing the opposing party and/or other salient social referents to view one as weak.

In summary, the evidence examined suggests that if an opposing negotia-tor, through a variety of either direct or indirect actions, behaves in a way that causes one to experience unjust intimidation, then this is apt to increase one's face-maintenance motives and to call forth specific responses designed to assert or reassert one's capability and strength.

Other Social Referents as Regulators

Let us now consider how a referent other than an opposing party may regulate face-saving and face-restoration behavior. This calls for an expansion of one rather limited aspect of Brown's (1968) distinction between these types of behavior—namely, its emphasis on the other negotiator (B) in the exchange as both the "instigator" and the "target" of A's face-maintenance concerns. Although Brown's findings, together with many everyday experi-ences, inform us that the opposing party is indeed likely to be a frequent instigator and target, journalistic and other reports of negotiations conducted in many areas reveal that a host of additional social referents may serve similar functions too.

Focusing on instigators (targets and targeting mechanisms will be con-sidered in a later section), we have seen that: (1) constituencies or their subgroups sometimes create conditions that threaten a representative's face; (2) various "publics" not directly involved in a negotiation may provide this kind of impetus; and (3) third parties, such as mediators or arbitrators, may either appeal to a negotiator's image or intervene in ways that have implications for it. Moreover, the terms "constituencies" and "publics" may be extended to cover a broad range of possibilities, including referents that need not be present at a negotiation site and may be only vaguely defined or identified in a negotiator's mind, but may nevertheless instigate face-saving and face-restoration actions. In addition, referents that at first glance seem rather "nonpersonal" may function in this manner, too. For example, Iklé (1964) points out that diplomats sometimes become concerned as to how their actions will look "in the eyes of history." Additional, seemingly nonpersonal, referents include "the law," "business," "government," etc.

Through what mechanisms may these kinds of referents regulate face-saving and face-restoration behavior? In considering this question, it is useful to view referents such as constituencies and publics as *audiences* (even if they are nonpresent, nonclearly identified, or nonpersonal), provided that a negotiator supposes that they (1) are interested in events occurring during the proceedings or the outcomes, (2) have access to information about these events, and (3) are scrutinizing or evaluating his behavior. To the extent that these conditions exist, a negotiator may become concerned with his image in an audience's eyes, and may therefore be said to attach salience to it. Such concerns may exist for various reasons, but generally these are grounded in the material and/or psychological rewards or punishments that an audience may tender. In the case of "nonpersonal" referents, salience may nevertheless involve a negotiator's concern with how he will look to personalized elements, such as "future historians," prominent figures or groups within the legal or business community, etc. Such referents may be rather abstract and need not be directly involved in the situation at hand.

Beyond the assumptions that a negotiator makes about an audience's interest, access to information, and scrutiny of his behavior, the nature of his "linkage" to that audience may also influence its salience to him (see Woolbert, 1916, for an insightful analysis of audience linkage). In this regard, evidence reported by Hermann and Kogan (1968), Lamm and Kogan (1970), Vidmar (1971), Druckman, Solomon, and Zechmeister (1972), and Benton and Druckman (1974) suggests that representational role obligations may markedly affect negotiators' actions and may also increase their concerns with their appearance or image in the eyes of those whom they represent. Additional findings reported by Gruder (1971), Gruder and Rosen (1971), Benton (1972), and Klimoski and Ash (1974) suggest that increased "accountability" to constituents is apt to heighten these effects. Evidence reported by Organ (1971) and Druckman et al. (1976) suggests that being able to monitor the proceedings and to provide feedback is also apt to add to a constituency's salience and to a negotiator's concerns with his appearance in its eyes. Rubin and Brown (1975) have summarized the evidence bearing on these kinds of linkages in terms of pressures toward face-maintenance. They have suggested that constituencies, which are usually at least fairly salient to negotiators, may use representational role obligations for gaining loyalty, commitment, and advocacy from their representatives. This form of leverage, they suggest, is dependent on accountability, which in turn provides a basis for constituencies to use positive and negative evaluation as mechanisms for controlling their representatives' behavior.

A primary mechanism for the transmission of positive or negative evaluation in negotiation is audience feedback. To the extent that an audience is salient to a negotiator, its feedback may also serve as a prime regulator of his face-maintenance motives and ensuing actions. The results of two experiments (Brown, 1968; Brown and Garland, 1976) illuminate several specific aspects of audience feedback that may regulate face-saving and face-restoration behavior.

Subjects in both of these experiments were treated exploitatively by a programmed confederate during an initial period of negotiation. Then they either received or did not receive feedback from an observing audience before continuing the negotiation session. In the earlier experiment, the audience feedback was largely evaluative, focusing on the "image" that audience members had formed of subjects in light of their prior exploitation by the confederate. In one condition, the feedback informed subjects that they had been "suckered"—caused to look weak and foolish for allowing the others to exploit them. In a second condition, subjects were informed that they were seen as gentlemanly and fair in view of the others' exploitativeness. In a third condition, no feedback was provided, though subjects still believed that the audience members were observing them. Placing oneself in the shoes of subjects in the feedback conditions, one surmises that the messages they received probably went beyond simply providing positive or negative evaluation and also provided cues about the audience's (1) definition of the situation, (2) expectations for "appropriate" negotiation behavior, and (3) preferences for norms. Although subjects in these conditions were free to determine their own manner of responding to the confederate, the feedback received from the audience put pressure on them to adopt its definition of the situation and its preferences and thereby regulated their face-restoration behavior. In contrast, in the "no feedback" condition, where subjects had no explicit indication of the audience's views on these matters, they were left to their own devices, so to speak, and adopted a "cultural" definition of the situation akin to that described by Deutsch and Krauss (1962). These subjects engaged in significantly more face-restoration than subjects who received the supportive audience feedback, but significantly less than those who believed the audience saw them as weak and foolish.

In a more recent experiment involving a similar paradigm (Brown and Garland, 1976), subjects were engaged in a bilateral monopoly bargaining session with a confederate, whose offers resulted in outcomes unfavorable to them and who stubbornly refused to yield throughout the session. Before making their final offers, subjects either received feedback from a group of "constituents" with whom they had met earlier and who were thought to be observing the proceedings, or they received no feedback. Subjects believed their constituents were dependent on them for their outcomes and that if no agreement could be reached in the session, all outcomes/would be forfeited In one condition, the constituents demanded that the representative make a concession so that they would at least obtain a nominal outcome rather than none at all. In a second condition, the subjects were informed that if they declined to concede they would be seen as more interested in saving face before the opposing party than in working toward their constituents' best interests. Subjects in a third condition received no constituency feedback. The results revealed that subjects in this last condition conceded significantly less often than those in the "straightforward demand" condition, who conceded significantly less often than those receiving the "threat to face" feedback. Post-experimental questionnaire data revealed that a prominent motive among subjects not receiving feedback was their desire to reassert their strength to the confederate, while subjects in the "threat to face" condition became less concerned with this, but significantly more concerned with looking strong to their constituents.

Taken together, the results of these studies suggest that feedback transmitted to negotiators by salient audiences, whether they are outcome- or non-outcome-dependent, for purposes of evaluating or influencing their behavior, may also play an important part in regulating their face-maintenance motives and resulting actions. Such effects, it has been proposed, may be attributable to components of an audience's feedback that, if only implicitly, suggest its definition of the situation, its expectations for a negotiator's behavior, the norms it may favor, and perhaps, too, the sanctions that it may bring to bear on a negotiator for failing to accede to its wishes.

Availability of Appropriate Mechanisms as Regulator

Although unjust intimidation by an opposing party and instigation by other referents may do much to fuel face-maintenance motives, their translation into specific face-saving or face-restoration efforts depends, in part, upon the availability of appropriate mechanisms or procedures for their enactment. Availability and appropriateness may be influenced by "prominence," prior use, and/or endorsement of certain actions by salient referents. Prominence refers to features of the negotiation situation that draw attention to themselves by virtue of physical configuration, uniqueness, or precedent (Schelling, 1963). Willis and Joseph (1959) and Benton and Druckman (1973) provide evidence indicating that structural prominence may indeed affect solutions chosen by negotiators. An overview of several different types of negotiation experiments suggests that these factors may also influence face-saving or face-restoration efforts.

Prominent and readily available mechanisms for asserting strength in the Acme-Bolt Trucking game include use of the barriers, obstruction, and refusing to yield in order to block the other player's progress. These mechanisms are often used either when an opposing party behaves unduly competitively or when any of a variety of situation or relational factors cause one to anticipate such events. In related terms, Kelley (1965) and Borah (1963) have contended that this particular bargaining task may induce a gamelike frame of mind, prompting the use of "devious" methods (e.g., using the barriers in conjunction with the alternate pathways) for purposes of trickery and deception. Although this strategy may indeed be viewed as devious, it nonetheless employs a procedure that stands out by virtue of its physical configuration and availability and is highly conducive to asserting or reasserting one's capability and strength. Furthermore, the use of these mechanisms for face-saving or face-restoration purposes may be reinforced by "precedent"—i.e., prior use by the opposing party—(Deutsch and Krauss, 1962); or by feedback received from salient referents endorsing certain behavior or norms (Brown, 1968).

Similar mechanisms exist in the Prisoner's Dilemma game, particularly the message-modified version employed by Tedeschi and his associates. In the standard version of this game (without messages or other forms of communication), mechanisms available for asserting strength are limited to selecting the B choice on any given trial or to patterning one's B choices for this purpose. However, in the message-modified version there are several additional mechanisms that are both prominent and readily available. These include refusing to disclose one's intentions, failing to fulfill one's previously announced intentions and sending either threat or punishment messages. The results of numerous experiments using the message-modified format reveal that subjects often respond to a highly competitive confederate by using one or more of these mechanisms for face-saving or face-restoration purposes, and this interpretation has often been made by these investigators.

In the bilateral monopoly type of bargaining situation, prominent and readily available mechanisms for asserting or reasserting capability and strength involve several aspects of concession-making. These include: (1) the willingness/unwillingness to concede, (2) the size or magnitude of concessions, and (3) their timing or sequencing. The results of a number of experiments (e.g., Podell and Knapp, 1969; Pruitt and Johnson, 1970; Johnson and Tullar, 1972; Druckman, Zechmeister, and Solomon, 1972; Brown and Garland, 1976; Druckman and Bonoma, 1976) suggest that willingness to concede and concession size are apt to be affected materially by subjects' concerns with looking strong when threats to face are experienced. In general, such concerns: (1) may either be grounded in subjects' feelings about themselves or may spring from attributions they suppose salient others may make about them, and (2) may be heightened, either by an opposing party whose actions are seen as unduly competitive, or by the existence of situational or relational circumstances that intensify their face-maintenance motives.

Costs as Regulators

Further evidence suggests that using readily available and appropriate mechanisms or procedures in responding to threats to face is apt to be controlled by the relative costs—both material and psychological—of doing so. In general, this evidence suggests that several different kinds of costs may be involved. These include: (1) evaluation costs, (2) status costs, and (3) vulnerability costs.

Evaluation costs. Pruitt's (1971) contention that negotiators are motivated to minimize both position loss and image loss, together with Benton and Druckman's (1974) conceptualization of a constituency's *monitoring* and *feedback* functions, suggest that negotiators may be expected to seek positive evaluations from salient referents (or at least to avoid negative ones) and, therefore, to consider the evaluation costs of their actions. This reasoning is generally consistent with research findings indicating that negotiators are apt to accede to constituency directives or preferences, especially as accountability is strengthened and there are increased pressures to "prove" themselves or to "please" their constituents (e.g., Frey and Adams, 1972; Benton and Druckman, 1974; Wall, 1975, 1976).

Evaluation costs refer to the image losses that a negotiator supposes he may incur in the eyes of a salient referent as a result of engaging in specific actions. Acting in accord with a referent's preferences would thus serve to minimize such costs. In the absence of specific information, negotiators are apt to attribute preferences to salient audiences and to act accordingly (Benton and Druckman, 1974).

The results of two experiments provide insight into how evaluation costs may be transmitted and how they may regulate a negotiator's face-maintenance efforts. In Brown's (1968) Trucking game experiment (described earlier) subjects chastized for being "suckered" were indirectly encouraged to reassert their strength in order to restore face lost to the confederate. Using the gate to penalize him was a prominent mechanism for pursuing this objective. Too, its prior use by the confederate and the audience feedback established its appropriateness for this purpose. For these subjects, the material costs of retaliating were overridden by the evaluation costs of nonretaliation. In contrast, the supportive feedback, commending subjects for their gentlemanliness and fairness in the face of the confederate's onslaught, encouraged nonretaliation. Here the evaluation costs of retaliating out-weighed the gains to be derived from doing so.

In the Brown and Garland (1976) experiment, also described previously, the constituency demand that was coupled with a threat-to-face for failure to act appropriately, clearly and emphatically indicated that group's preference and strongly suggested that failure to accede would result in a negative evaluation. Subjects receiving this directive heeded it more often than did those in the remaining conditions. The "threat-to-face" feedback thus height-ened the evaluation costs of not acceding in comparison to the remaining conditions. These findings suggest that the adoption of mechanisms or pro-cedures that are available and appropriately used for purposes of saving or restoring lost face may be fostered or curtailed by the evaluation costs of either acting in this manner or failing to do so.

Status costs. Status costs refer to the degree to which a negotiator's actions (or inactions) may place him in a position of inferiority to the opposing party. As Harsanyi (1966) and Rubin and Brown (1975) have pointed out, being in a position of inferiority has adverse implications for the amount of deference to be shown toward another and, through norms of distributive justice, for the proportion of outcomes that one may expect. Furthermore, as Deutsch and Krauss (1962) have suggested, showing defer-ence toward another who has no legitimate right to expect it often involves a loss of face. For these reasons, negotiators may be expected to go to considerable lengths to avoid showing deference toward another whose power or use of power is viewed as nonlegitimate.

The results of several experiments provide insight into how status costs may regulate the use of various procedures for face-maintenance purposes. Borah (1963) found that "time lost in standoffs," an indicator of a prom-inent and readily available form of resistance in the modified version of the Trucking game that he used, was heightened when subjects within each pair believed that the opposing person had made claims of being "superior," and each felt that the other's claims were unjustified. Here the status costs of yielding to someone who inappropriately considered himself to be superior and probably also expected to be treated deferentially were heightened by the implication that yielding would amount to accepting the other's superior-ity and, hence, one's own inferiority. As a result, the status costs of yielding were greater than the tangible gains that might have resulted from nonresis-tance and induced resistance in order both to contest the other's false claims and to assert status equality.

Status costs also played an important part in inducing subjects to use a readily available mechanism for face-restoration purposes in Hornstein's (1965) message-modified bilateral monopoly bargaining experiment. Subjects were randomly assigned to conditions in which "threat potential" (TP), the capability of threatening and penalizing each other, was varied along two dimensions—the amount and the equality of its distribution within pairs. On the basis of a "deterrence" rationale, Hornstein expected that weaker bargainers would yield to their stronger counterparts more often than the latter would yield to the former. However, this did not occur. Instead, particularly as the disparity in TP within pairs decreased, weaker bargainers frequently responded to threats made by stronger bargainers with counterthreats, using a mechanism that was both readily available and appropriate for such purposes because of its prior use by the opposing party. Post-experimental questionnaire data suggested that many subjects could not accept arbitrary assignment to a weaker position because they perceived themselves and the other bargainer primarily as students and therefore as status equals. Hornstein explained that the weaker TP bargainers were probably affronted by the others' inappropriate use of threat, and that the status costs of deference were therefore sufficient to outweigh both the economic gains that might result from such behavior and the economic costs of using the counterthreat mechanism in order to restore lost face.

Similarly, findings reported by Tjosvold (1974) indicate that, when a high-powered bargainer is intimidated by another whom he sees as less powerful, he will probably experience a threat to face, which is likely to lead to increased competitiveness and/or resistance for face-restoration purposes. Here, too, the status costs of permitting inappropriate intimidation to remain uncontested outweighed the material costs of engaging in such behavior.

In general, these findings suggest that if the status costs of failing to assert or reassert one's strength exceed the material and/or psychological gains from acting deferentially, then negotiators are likely to use available and appropriate mechanisms for this purpose. That is, if the costs to be incurred by acquiescing to illegitimate threats to one's status are sufficient, then one may be expected to challenge the party making the illegitimate status claims.

One may wonder about the degree to which status costs regulate face-saving or face-restoration efforts in negotiations outside the research laboratory. For instance, it might seem that status costs are much less important when there are large differences in military capability. One need only look at the records of the early Vietnam peace talks in Paris to find evidence of the regulating effects of status costs on face-saving and face-restoration efforts by the United States and the North Vietnamese over the issues of recognition and participation of the Viet Cong in the negotiations (see Rubin and Brown, 1975, for evidence related to this dispute).

Vulnerability costs. Another consideration often involved in responding to threats to face are the vulnerability costs of specific face-saving or face-restoration actions. Vulnerability costs arise from the risk that one's own actions may elicit damaging responses from the opposing party or may have other adverse consequences. In general, the higher the vulnerability costs of any given course of action, the less the likelihood that such action will be taken. Thus, there are circumstances in which vulnerability costs may override the psychological gains of acting to save or restore lost face. This is particularly likely to occur when (1) opposing negotiators each have high deterrent capability, and an intimidating response to a threat to face may induce the threatener to use his deterrent force with injurious results, and (2) power is distributed asymmetrically, and the weaker party, though affronted by the stronger, remains apprehensive about intimidating him because the latter's command of resources leaves him vulnerable to future injurious sanctions (see also Snyder, 1960; Milburn, 1961; Schelling, 1963).

Additional evidence (Brown, 1968) suggests that vulnerability costs may also arise from circumstances that have a high potential for further loss of face as a result of engaging in actions whose purpose is to save or restore previously lost face. Apparently, allowing one's face-saving actions to be publicly visible is itself a negatively valued form of social behavior that increases vulnerability to further negative evaluation. Often this occurs in circumstances where it is anticipated that salient social referents, such as audiences or constituencies, may become informed of the self-inflicted costs that negotiators may be willing to bear in their attempts to maintain face.

In general, the research evidence cited above suggests that the use of available and appropriate procedures for purposes of saving or restoring lost face may be limited, made covert, delayed, or dropped when the vulnerability costs of acting in this way exceed its gains.

TARGETS AND TARGETING MECHANISMS

As was pointed out earlier, the potential targets of face-maintenance efforts are numerous. Besides the opposing party, these include various kinds of audiences, constituencies, or their subgroups, "publics," and even third parties. Accountability to such referents often subjects negotiators to face-maintenance pressures. Also, where there is differential accountability to opposing constituency factions or to other divided groups, conflicting face-maintenance pressures may be experienced. This occurs frequently across a wide spectrum of negotiation arenas.

Students of the negotiation process have commented and provided considerable anecdotal evidence about face-maintenance pressures (Schelling, 1963; Stevens, 1963; Iklé, 1964; Sawyer and Guetzkow, 1965; Lieberman, 1971; Rubin and Brown, 1975). However, there has been little systematic thought or empirical investigation focused on specific mechanisms or conditions under which various individuals or groups may become face-maintenance targets. Instead, analysis has been limited to rather general expositions about the pros and cons of "open" versus "secret" negotiations, public visibility, public opinion, managing one's constituency, and so on.

Targeting Mechanisms

The analysis and empirical evidence presented bring into focus three kinds of targeting mechanisms. These are (1) an opposing negotiator's actions, (2) an audience's or constituency's feedback or directives, and (3) a third party's interventions. Through such mechanisms, any of these referents may target a recipient's face-saving or face-restoration efforts toward itself or toward an alternate referent. This implies that face-maintenance efforts may be shifted away from one referent and "re-targeted" toward another during negotiation.

The opposing party as targeter. An opposing negotiator may target a recipient's face-maintenance efforts in at least two ways. Because the first (direct targeting by the opposing party toward himself) has already been discussed, we shall simply reiterate the conclusion drawn earlier. If one negotiator anticipates or experiences another's actions toward him as threatening, he is likely to make face-saving or face-restoration efforts toward the instigator. This is subject to control by the cost and availability of appropriate means for taking such action. Here the recipient's response is targeted directly toward the instigator, who is viewed as the source of the threat and the referent in whose eyes face must be maintained.

Situations also arise where one negotiator's actions increase a recipient's concerns with face in the eyes of an alternate referent, such as his constituency, the public at large, or segments of these groups. Such situations may be brought about intentionally, as when one side attempts to discredit or impair the other's face or reputation in the eyes of an alternate referent, or they may occur unintentionally. In these instances, one may have to prevent or mend a tarnished image in the eyes of a referent other than the instigator. Here a negotiator faces the problem of deciding which among several referents is to be the target of his face-maintenance efforts. Accordingly, such efforts may be wholly or partially diverted from the instigator to another referent. These kinds of situations arise frequently in collective bargaining and in negotiations between hostile nations.

Little is known about the mechanisms involved in the targeting of negotiators' face-maintenance activities by an opposing party to referents other than himself, or about the determinants of recipients' responses in such situations. However, the results of investigations conducted by Brown (1968), Frey and Adams (1972), Wall (1975, 1976), and Brown and Garland (1976) suggest that concerns with one's image in the eyes of an alternate referent may outweigh similar concerns vis-à-vis the opposing party provided that (1) the alternate referent is sufficiently salient, (2) the recipient feels sufficiently accountable to it, and (3) the evaluation costs of failing to accede to the alternate's definition of proper face exceed the gains to be derived from acting to maintain face in the eyes of the opposing party.

Audience feedback as targeter. It was pointed out above that communicational inputs from salient audiences or constituencies during negotiation may call forth or heighten a negotiator's face-maintenance concerns and may also regulate the frequency, timing, magnitude, etc. of related actions. However, an audience's or constituency's communications may also target or retarget a negotiator's face-saving or face-restoration actions toward itself or toward alternate referents. For instance, constituency communications that are critical or nonsupportive of a negotiator or that reflect distrust of him may heighten his concerns with maintaining face in its eyes, or in the eyes of the opposing side, various constituency subgroups, the public at large, etc. (Brown, 1968; Frey and Adams, 1972; Wall, 1975, 1976; Brown and Garland, 1976). Or a militant constituent subgroup may foster the impression that a representative is unable either to control or to speak authoritatively on behalf of the whole constituency, thereby threatening his face in the eyes of the opposing party. Evidence obtained in some of the investigations cited above indicates that in response to these kinds of constituency communications, a negotiator is apt to behave more competitively toward the opposing party in order to "prove himself" to his constituents. Or, as results obtained by Brown and Garland (1976) and Wall (1976) indicate, negotiators may be induced, for similar reasons, to behave more cooperatively upon receiving cooperative directives. In some instances, opposing negotiators have even been known to "collude" with one another as a result of mutual concerns with keeping their images or reputations from being damaged in the eyes of their respective constituencies or other onlookers (Kerr, 1954; Lieberman, 1971).

As was suggested earlier, the capability of a salient audience's communications to target or re-target a negotiator's face-maintenance efforts probably arises from indications (either implicit or explicit) that one has failed to fulfill certain expectations or preferences and is therefore subject to negative evaluation and sanctions. Such communications may also suggest actions to be taken toward itself or specified others in order to avoid or minimize negative evaluation. Thus, efforts to prevent or restore lost face may be targeted toward a given referent, or re-targeted from one to another, by messages from salient audiences to whom one is accountable, provided that the gains to be derived from pursuing this objective override the costs and that appropriate means are available.

Third party as targeter. Through their interventions, third parties, such as mediators, arbitrators, and informal intermediaries, may either diminish or intensify face-maintenance concerns and target or re-target them toward themselves or alternate referents. These capabilities sometimes prove to be highly useful tools for facilitating movement toward agreement.

Many third-party interventions indirectly affect face-maintenance concerns. For example, Rubin and Brown (1975) point out that "structural" interventions related to site selection, arrangement, and utilization often have implications for audience visibility and may either limit or foster communicational inputs. We have seen how these conditions may affect face-maintenance concerns and actions. Furthermore, since salient audiences may target face-maintenance concerns toward other referents, structural interventions affecting audience involvement may indirectly affect these concerns vis-à-vis the opposing party and other referents.

Walton (1969) and Rubin and Brown (1975) have pointed out that negotiations conducted on one side's "territory" may engender disputes over situational power. Research conducted by Martindale (1971) supports this viewpoint. Interventions relevant to site selection may either short-circuit or fuel such disputes and may thereby heighten or diminish issues of face arising from unacceptable claims for special privilege associated with territorial dominance. Similarly, calling for private rather than joint sessions at certain times may also affect face-maintenance concerns. By separating opposing sides during periods of intense conflict, the likelihood that insult or other affronts will occur may be reduced. Pressing for informal rather than formal sessions may have similar "cooling down" effects, as a result of changing the "social climate" or setting of the negotiation.[2]

SUMMARY AND CONCLUSIONS

The central points made in this chapter are as follows:

(1) Face-maintenance motives are commonplace in negotiation, due to fundamental aspects of this activity and cultural norms related to demonstrating one's capability and strength.

(2) Threats to face may be experienced as a result of a variety of events occurring in negotiation.

(3) Face-saving and face-restoration efforts may take a variety of different forms, including verbal and larger-scale actions.

(4) Face-saving and face-restoration efforts may be regulated by:

(a) the behavior of the opposing party and the involvement of other salient referents, such as constituencies and other types of audiences;

(b) the availability of appropriate mechanisms and the costs of using them for these purposes.

(5) A wide range of salient referents may become "targets" of face-maintenance efforts.

(6) A salient referent may target or re-target face-maintenance efforts toward itself or toward alternate referents.

(7) Third parties, such as mediators, may strategically target or re-target face-maintenance efforts in order to facilitate movement toward agreement.

In general, the analysis in this chapter suggests that actions taken for face-maintenance purposes are highly susceptible to situational influence. It also reveals the lack of empirical research focusing directly on the mechanisms that influence this kind of behavior. Considering that negotiation is such a widely used instrument of conflict resolution, further research in the areas outlined above is clearly called for. Although there is a need for continued laboratory research in order to identify the specific mechanisms involved, research in naturalistic settings is also needed for refinement and to account for unique constraints operating in different negotiatioñ arenas. This might be accomplished through systematic observation, perhaps coupled with examination of transcripts or other records, and interviews with negotiators, third parties, and constituent members.

Several intriguing questions that deserve further research are brought to light by this chapter: How may face-maintenance motives be channelled toward more constructive ends? What factors may mitigate the targeting capabilities of third parties, constituencies, and other referents? What factors may cause one referent to dominate another when a negotiator is faced with a potential loss of face in the eyes of two or more referents who are making conflicting demands on him?

In addition, the chapter suggests several questions of a more practical nature: May negotiators be trained to respond more constructively to threats to face? May mechanisms be developed for improving constituency feedback and directives? May third parties be trained to utilize face-maintenance concerns more productively?

NOTES

1. Iklé's observation is supported by the empirical evidence reported by Deutsch and Krauss (1962) and Terhune (1968) as well as by the early studies of Newcomb (1947) and Thibaut and Coules (1952) on "autistic hostility." Further support can be found in the transcripts of the negotiations between the United States and North Vietnam (Halberstam, 1969), and in reports of the 1973 Mideast cease-fire accords (Golan, 1976; Kalb and Kalb, 1974).

2. Other functions served by third-parties include: (a) expanding existing communication channels; (b) reformulating issues and generating alternative solutions; (c) targeting face-maintenance concerns toward specific referents or the public at-large; (d) retargeting face-maintenance concerns toward himself by publicly espousing the wisdom of making a certain proposal; and (e) raising the costs of conflict by creating evaluation pressures. Each of these functions is designed to affect communication between the opposing sides. Some of them may bring about a reassessment of the gains and costs of acting to maintain a favorable image in the eyes of one referent as compared to another.

REFERENCES

BENTON, A. A. (1972) "Accountability and negotiations between group representatives." Proceedings of the 80th Annual Convention of the American Psychological Association 7: 227-228.

——— and D. DRUCKMAN (1974) "Constituent's bargaining orientation and intergroup negotiations." J. of Applied Social Psychology 4: 141-150.

——— (1973) "Salient solutions and the bargaining behavior of representatives and nonrepresentatives." International J. of Group Tensions 3: 28-39.

BERGER, S. E. and J. TEDESCHI (1969) "Aggressive behavior of delinquent, dependent, and 'normal' white and black boys in social conflicts." J. of Experimental Social Psychology 5: 352-370.

BONOMA, T., B. SCHLENKER, R. SMITH, and J. TEDESCHI (1970) "Source prestige and target reactions to threats." Psychonomic Sci. 19: 111-113.

BORAH, L. A. (1963) "The effects of threat in bargaining: Critical and experimental analysis." J. of Abnormal and Social Psychology 66: 37-44.

BROWN, B. R. (1968) "The effects of need to maintain face on interpersonal bargaining." J. of Experimental Social Psychology 4: 107-122.

——— and H. GARLAND (1976) "Constituency communication, concession-making and face-saving in a bilateral monopoly bargaining situation." Unpublished manuscript, New Brunswick, New Jersey: Rutgers University.

——— (1970) "Face-saving following experimentally induced embarrassment." J. of Experimental Social Psychology 6: 255-271.

DEUTSCH, M. (1973) The Resolution of Conflict. New Haven, Conn.: Yale Univ. Press.

——— (1969) "Conflicts: Productive and destructive." J. of Social Issues 25: 7-41.

———, D. CANAVAN, and J. RUBIN (1971) "The effects of size of conflict and sex of experimenter upon interpersonal bargaining." J. of Experimental Social Psychology 7: 258-267.

DEUTSCH, M. and R. KRAUSS (1962) "Studies of interpersonal bargaining." J. of Conflict Resolution 6: 52-76.

DRUCKMAN, D. and T. BONOMA (1976) "Determinants of bargaining behavior in a bilateral monopoly situation II: Opponent's concession rate and similarity." Behavioral Sci. 21: 252-262.

DRUCKMAN, D., D. SOLOMON, and K. ZECHMEISTER (1972) "Effects of representational role obligations on the process of children's distribution of resources." Sociometry 35: 387-410.

DRUCKMAN, D., K. ZECHMEISTER, and D. SOLOMON (1972) "Determinants of bargaining behavior in a bilateral monopoly situation: Opponent's concession rate and relative defensibility." Behavioral Sci. 17: 514-531.

DRUCKMAN, D., A. BENTON, I. ALI, and J. S. BAGUR (1976) "Cultural differences in bargaining behavior: India, Argentina, and the United States." J. of Conflict Resolution 20: 413-452.

FISHER, R. (1969) International Conflict for Beginners. New York: Harper.

FREY, R. L. and J. S. ADAMS (1972) "The negotiator's dilemma: Simultaneous in-group and out-group conflict." J. of Experimental Social Psychology 8: 331-346.

GAHAGAN, J., J. TEDESCHI, T. FALEY, and S. LINDSKOLD (1970) "Patterns of punishment and reactions to threats." J. of Social Psychology 80: 115-116.

GALLO, P. (1972) "Prisoners of our own dilemma?" pp. 43-49 in L. Wrightsman et al. (eds.) Cooperation and Competition: Readings on Mixed-Motive Games. California: Brooks Cole.

GOFFMAN, E. (1959) The Presentation of Self in Everyday Life. Garden City, N.Y.: Doubleday.

——— (1955) "On face work." Psychiatry 18: 213-231.

GOLAN, M. (1976) The Secret Conversations of Henry Kissinger. New York: Bantam Books.

GRUDER, C. (1971) "Relations with opponent and partner in mixed-motive bargaining." J. of Conflict Resolution 3: 403-416.

——— and N. ROSEN (1971) "Effects of intragroup relations on intergroup bargaining." International J. of Group Tensions 1: 301-317.

HALBERSTAM, D. (1969) The Best and the Brightest. New York: Random House.

HARSANYI, J. (1966) "A bargaining model for social status in informal groups and formal organizations." Behavioral Sci. 11: 357-369.

HERMANN, M. and N. KOGAN (1968) "Negotiations in leader and delegate groups." J. of Conflict Resolution 12: 332-344.

HEWITT, J. and R. STOKES (1975) "Disclaimers." Amer. Soc. Rev. 40 (February): 1-11.

HOMANS, G. (1961) Social Behavior: Its Elementary Forms. New York: Harcourt.

HORAI, J. and J. TEDESCHI (1969) "Effects of credibility and magnitude of punishment on compliance to threats." J. of Personality and Social Psychology 12: 164-169.

HORNSTEIN, H. (1965) "The effects of different magnitudes of threat upon interpersonal bargaining." J. of Experimental Social Psychology 1: 282-293.

IKLÉ, F. (1964) How Nations Negotiate. New York: Harper & Row.

JOHNSON, D. (1971) "Compliance, deterrent threats and the need to maintain face." Presented at Eastern Psychological Association meetings.

——— and W. TULLAR (1972) "Style of third party intervention, face-saving and bargaining behavior." J. of Experimental Social Psychology 8: 319-330.

KALB, M. and B. KALB (1974) Kissinger. Boston: Little, Brown.

KELLEY, H. (1966) "A classroom study of the dilemmas in interpersonal negotiations," in K. Archibald (ed.) Strategic Interaction and Conflict: Original Papers and Discussion. Berkeley, Calif.: Institute of International Studies.

——— (1965) "Experimental studies of threats in interpersonal negotiations." J. of Conflict Resolution 9: 79-105.

KERR, C. (1954) "Industrial conflict and its resolution." Amer. J. of Sociology 60: 230-245.

KLIMOSKI, R. and R. ASH (1974) "Accountability and negotiator behavior." Organizational Behavior and Human Performance 11: 409-425.

KRESSEL, K. (1972) Labor Mediation: An Exploratory Survey. New York: Association of Labor Mediation Agencies.

LAMM, H. and N. KOGAN (1970) "Risk taking in the context of intergroup negotiation." J. of Experimental Social Psychology 6: 351-363.

LIEBERMAN, M. (1971) "Negotiations with members of your own team." School Management 15: 10-11.

MARTINDALE, D. (1971) "Territorial dominance behavior in dyadic verbal interactions." Proceedings of the seventy-ninth Annual Convention of the American Psychological Association 6: 305-306.

McKERSIE, R., C. PERRY, and R. WALTON (1965) "Intraorganizational bargaining in labor negotiations." J. of Conflict Resolution 9: 463-481.

MILBURN, T. (1961) "The concept of deterrence." J. of Social Issues 3: 3-11.

NEWCOMB, T. (1947) "Autistic hostility and social reality." Human Relations 1: 69-86.

ORGAN, D. (1971) "Some variables affecting boundary role behavior." Sociometry 34: 524-537.

PODELL, J. and W. KNAPP (1969) "The effect of mediation on the perceived firmness of the opponent." J. of Conflict Resolution 13: 511-520.

PRUITT, D. (1971) "Indirect communication and the search for agreement in negotiation." J. of Applied Social Psychology 1: 205-239.

——— and D. JOHNSON (1970) "Mediation as an aid to face-saving in negotiation." J. of Personality and Social Psychology 14: 239-246.

RUBIN, J. and B. BROWN (1975) The Social Psychology of Bargaining and Negotiation. New York: Academic Press.

SAWYER, J. and H. GUETZKOW (1965) "Bargaining and negotiation in international relations," in H. Kelman (ed.) International Behavior: A Social-Psychological Analysis. New York: Holt.

SCHELLING, T. C. (1963) The Strategy of Conflict, New York: Oxford Univ. Press.

SCHLENKER, T., T. BONOMA, J. TEDESCHI and W. PIVNICK (1970) "Complaince to threats as a function of the wording of the threat and the exploitativeness of the threatener," Sociometry 33: 394-408.

SIEGEL, S. and L. FOURAKER (1960) Bargaining and Group Decision Making: Experiments in Bilateral Monopoly. New York: McGraw-Hill.

SNYDER, G. (1960) "Deterrence and power." J. of Conflict Resolution 4: 163-178.

STEVENS, C. (1963) Strategy and Collective Bargaining Negotiation. New York: McGraw-Hill.

SWINGLE, P. (Ed.) (1970) The Structure of Conflict. New York: Academic Press.

TEDESCHI, J., T. BONOMA, and R. C. BROWN (1971) "A paradigm for the study of coercive power." J. of Conflict Resolution 15: 197-223.

TERHUNE, K. (1968) "Motives, situation and interpersonal conflict within prisoner's dilemma." J. of Personality and Social Psychology Monograph Supplement 8: 1-24.

THIBAUT, J. and J. COULES (1952) "The role of communication in the reduction of interpersonal hostility." J. of Abnormal and Social Psychology 47: 770-777.

TJOSVOLD, D. (1974) "Threat as a low-power person's strategy in bargaining: Social face and tangible outcomes." International J. of Group Tensions 4: 494-510.

VIDMAR, N. (1971) "Effects of representational roles and mediators on negotiation effectiveness." J. of Personality and Social Psychology 17: 48-58.

WALL, J. (1976) "A representative's bargaining: The effects of constituent directives, constituent trust and expectation of future negotiation." Unpublished manuscript. Bloomington: Indiana University.

--- (1975) "Effects of constituent trust and representative bargaining orientation on intergroup bargaining." J. of Personality and Social Psychology 31: 1004-1012.

WALTON, R. (1969) Interpersonal Peacemaking: Confrontations and Third Party Consultation. Reading, Mass.: Addison-Wesley.

WILLIS, R. and M. JOSEPH (1959) "Bargaining behavior. I. 'Prominence' as a predictor of the outcome of games of agreement." J. of Conflict Resolution 3: 102-113. 102-113.

WOOLBERT, C. (1916) "The audience." Psych. Monographs 21: 37-54.

Chapter 10

THE IMPACT OF EXTERNAL

STRESSES AND TENSIONS ON NEGOTIATIONS

P. TERRENCE HOPMANN
and
CHARLES WALCOTT

Department of Political Science
University of Minnesota

Recent research and writing on international negotiations has emphasized the point that negotiations must be viewed as a process occurring within a larger social system (Walton and McKersie, 1965: 3-4). This means in part that events occurring during the negotiations may be affected by the state of the system in which they are embedded and may have an effect on future states of that system (Druckman, 1973: 80-81). Furthermore, this approach to the analysis of negotiations has emphasized the effect that stresses and tensions emanating from the environment may have on both the processes and the outcomes of negotiations. A fundamental linkage between the environment and negotiations at the international level has been hypothesized by Druckman (1973: 81) as follows:

> Overreaction (e.g., by increasing a nuclear arsenal) might increase the long-term stability by preserving the balance of power, but this is acquired at the price of increases in the tension level. A high level of tension in the system may also lead to an overreaction which is reflected in a breakdown of ongoing negotiations, and so on. An underreaction to another nation's provocations, on the other hand, may

AUTHORS' NOTE: The authors acknowledge the valuable support of the Harold Scott Quigley Center of International Studies, the Office of International Programs, and the Graduate School Research Fund, all at the University of Minnesota. They would also like to thank Timothy King for his assistance in the preparation of this chapter.

[301]

result in short-term stability through a decrease in the level of tension (see Pruitt, 1969). Under such conditions, mediational mechanisms are likely to be resorted to as techniques for resolving issues that the parties cannot resolve themselves. A reduced level of tension in the system is also likely to produce underreactions initiating a cycle which may lead to the resolution of such issues as, "What are the 'appropriate' conditions for disarmament?" (see Osgood, 1962).

In this chapter we shall explore this relationship. Sawyer and Guetzkow (1965: 511-513) have noted that research on the subject of international negotiations has taken place in three types of methodological environments—namely, "game experimentation," "simulation," and "research 'in situ'." Thus, this chapter will begin with a review of some of the evidence obtained from laboratory experiments about the effects of stresses and tensions on individual and group behavior. This may suggest hypotheses to be applied at the level of international negotiations. We shall then examine a tentative effort to bridge the gap between laboratory research and "real world" research through a simulation of the test ban negotiations. Finally, some of the hypotheses derived from the laboratory studies will be applied to an analysis of negotiations in the Eighteen-Nation Disarmament Conference in 1962-1963, which led to the Partial Nuclear Test Ban Treaty.

LABORATORY RESEARCH

The Effects of Stresses and Tensions on Individual Performance

A substantial amount of research in laboratories indicates that stresses and tensions have some systematic effects on the behavior and performance of individuals. Some of the findings from this research may be applicable to the performance of negotiators. The most common and consistent finding seems to be that stress generally has a curvilinear effect on individual performance. At fairly low levels below some threshold, increases in stress may facilitate performance, especially if the behavior is relatively uncomplicated or has been well learned. On the other hand, after the threshold is crossed, an increase in stress is generally associated with a decrease in a number of aspects of individual performance, especially for more complex tasks (Milburn, 1972: 264; Kretch and Crutchfield, 1958: 392).

One of the most common effects of stress on the individual appears to be on perceptions. For example, Postman and Bruner (1948: 314) found that stress tended to produce an increased "primitivation" of perceptual organization. They noted particularly (1948: 322) that the "selection of percepts from a complex field became less adequate and sense is less well differentiated from nonsense." They further remarked that the maladaptive nature of the responses under stress often tended to take the form of aggressive behavior.

A second effect of stress is that it increases intolerance of ambiguity. A study by Smock (1955) found that individuals who were placed under stress took longer than control groups did to identify ambiguous symbols and often tended to respond before enough information was available. Thus the subjects were unable to withhold their responses to ambiguous symbols until further information was made available to them that would have provided more fully structured cues as a basis for more adequate responses.

A third, and perhaps related, effect of stress is that it tends to enhance cognitive rigidity. For example, Pally (1955) compared the effects of threat, operationalized as success or failure in problem-solving, upon the cognitive rigidity of subjects, defined as their ability to shift quickly to new solutions to a problem. He concluded that, under conditions of tension or threat, there was "a difficulty or inability to respond to a changed situation appropriately" (Pally, 1955: 352). He also suggested that this response was similar to the one observed in clinical studies of persons in a variety of pathological states.

Fourth, stress has been found to be associated with a reduced ability to perform well in problem-solving tasks. Ray (1965) has even learned that this applies under conditions of relatively mild stress, contrary to the most general formulation of the curvilinear relationship suggested above. Thus, Ray (1965: 234) discovered that, above very minimal levels, stress produced "increasing inhibition of problem-solving, the effect being greater with complex problems."

In short, the general conclusion of this research seems to be that stress is dysfunctional for individuals, especially in ways that are likely to increase their hostility and rigidity when they are engaged in negotiations. Of course, it is important to keep in mind that in most of these experiments stress was induced in the laboratory by frustrating the subjects in their performance of assigned tasks, which may be somewhat different from stress that is generated by external actors or events. Nevertheless, stress consistently tended to make individuals more rigid, more intolerant of ambiguous situations, more likely to oversimplify their perceptions, and less effective in problem-solving. All of these consequences are likely to be dysfunctional for negotiations, since negotiations often involve complex situations that do not lend themselves readily to oversimplification (at least not without enhancing the prospects of stalemate) and that require tolerance of the ambiguity inherent in such complex situations. Furthermore, negotiators must be able to perceive accurately the situation and the behavior of other actors, and they must be able to solve complex problems quickly and effectively in order to arrive at agreements. The research just cited seems to indicate that increases in stress are likely to have negative effects on the perceptions, attitudes, and behaviors of negotiators and thereby to detract from both the process and the outcome of negotiations.

The Effects of Stresses and Tensions on Group Performance

Another related line of research examines the impact of stress on the behavior of groups. This research is relevant since we conceive of a negotiating conference as a process of group interaction. Although negotiators may be serving as representatives of external entities, such as labor unions, management, nation-states, or whatever, they nevertheless interact with their counterparts as part of a group, so that the dynamics of group interaction may affect their behavior.

In a classic study, Lanzetta (1955) examined the effects of stress on three aspects of group behavior: i.e., group properties (e.g., cohesiveness), interactional patterns (e.g., agreeing-disagreeing behaviors), and individual characteristics (e.g., striving for group recognition and leadership). One finding from this study was that increased stress tends to increase the cohesiveness of a group. In general, group friction declined, competition for leadership was reduced, and cooperativeness and friendliness of interaction increased. However, there are some significant limitations to generalizing from this result to the case of negotiations. In this experiment, the stress could be perceived as being generated from without. In many negotiations, however, the action of one of the actors or of his constituents is perceived as the cause of stress. In addition, the groups in this experiment were essentially task-oriented and were involved in cooperative problem-solving. By contrast, in most negotiations the relationship among the actors is essentially mixed-motive and involves a combination of common and conflicting interests. When the interests of the group are essentially cooperative, stress may be integrative, as this study suggests. On the other hand, when the interests of the group are of a mixed-motive character, then we would speculate, on theoretical grounds, that there is a much greater chance that stress will produce increased friction and conflict within the group. As Coser (1956: 93) has observed, "If a group is lacking in basic consensus, outside threat leads not to increased cohesion, but to general apathy, and the group is consequently threatened with disintegration."

Other findings of Lanzetta's study, however, were consistent with the general results of the research on individuals. In particular, he found that an increase in stress produced initially a decrease in talkativeness, but that higher levels of stress produced an increase in verbosity, which the author felt is generally distracting. There was a similar curvilinear relationship between productivity and stress and between morale and stress, since both productivity and morale tended to increase under moderate levels of stress and to fall off significantly under higher levels.

Unfortunately, we don't know of any studies that investigate directly the impact of stress on mixed-motive groups. However, a study by Krauss (1966) of bargaining in mixed-motive groups deals with the impact on group behavior of the situational structure and of attitudinal structure, and the results of this study are of direct relevance to our central concern in this chapter. The principal focus of the study is on the issue of balance between the structure of the situation (which may be competitive or cooperative) and the interpersonal attitudinal sets of the negotiators (which may be positive or negative); it also examines the effects of the strength of anchoring of the attitudinal set as an intervening variable.

Krauss found that when attitudinal anchoring was strong, positive attitudinal orientations tended to result in more effective bargaining, but that negative attitudes were associated with less effective bargaining. Under these conditions, there was no significant difference in bargaining effectiveness (defined as joint payoffs to both parties) between the competitive and the cooperative structure of the situation. Thus, in this instance, behavior seemed to be modified to become consistent with the strongly anchored attitudes, as is suggested by theories of cognitive balance. On the other hand, when the attitudinal anchoring was weak, the difference between the positive and the negative attitudinal conditions was small in terms of bargaining effectiveness, but a cooperative structure produced significantly more effective bargaining than did a conflictual structure. In this case, attitudinal change tended to occur to restore consistency with the structure of the situation; and subsequent behavior was also consistent with this initial structure.

Although the Krauss study does not deal directly with the effects of stress, it does seem to have several interesting implications. A major cause of external stress in most negotiations is likely to be the competitive nature of the interactions among actors. That is, competition in the external environment is likely to produce tension and anxiety for the negotiators and also to affect their attitudes. Of course, the linkage between the situational structure and stress, though plausible, is at this time largely untested, and further laboratory research on this issue is clearly required. However, if this relationship may be assumed to exist, then the study by Krauss would certainly tend to indicate that this kind of external or environmental conflict and tension would probably have a disruptive effect on negotiations and would reduce payoffs to the actors. This specific relationship will be explored more fully later in this chapter.

In evaluating the laboratory research concerning the effects of stresses and tensions on individuals and on problem-solving groups, we find some suggestions about the possible effects of tensions on negotiations. Before we can generalize more fully from this research to "real-world" negotiations, we shall need further research on the effects of stresses and tensions upon mixed-motive rather than primarily cooperative groups. In addition, even the laboratory research that has been done to date on bargaining in mixed-motive groups has tended to concentrate on overly simple models, such as the Prisoner's Dilemma (PD) paradigm (see Rapoport, 1960: 173-177), in which the effects of external stresses and tensions could not be studied adequately.

For example, in most laboratory games based on the PD paradigm, payoffs are provided to players after each round of play. Yet most real-world bargaining problems do not involve discrete bargaining moves that are followed by payoffs and then followed by another set of moves, and so forth. Rather, most bargaining situations found in international politics have at least one primary, identifiable payoff occuring at the end of the interaction or after a rather lengthy series of interactions. This payoff is preceded by considerable verbal bargaining, where strategies and tactics somewhat analogous to the laboratory bargaining may be used, but where the objective is to affect the probabilities and utilities associated with perceived possible solutions to the overall problem (the end-game or "meta-game" solution), rather than to secure rewards in the short run. This suggests a further limitation of laboratory studies that are based on the PD paradigm—namely, that they overlook an essential aspect of most real-world negotiations: the verbal interactions that take place between negotiators. In Chapter 6, some means by which this deficiency might be at least partially overcome were suggested.

In spite of the limitations of laboratory studies, we have derived several hypotheses from the research reviewed above that may be of considerable heuristic value in our analysis of the effects of stresses and tensions on international negotiations:

(1) Stress, at least above some particular thresholds, tends to affect the cognitive and perceptual behavior of individuals by reducing perceptual differentiation, lessening tolerance of ambiguity, increasing cognitive rigidity, and curtailing problem-solving abilities.

(2) Stress, at least above some threshold, tends to increase group cohesiveness when the source of the threat is external to the group or its constituents.

(3) Stress, at least above a particular threshold, tends to detract from the ability of groups to solve problems effectively.

(4) External competition among members of a group tends to detract from the ability of the group to reach agreement in bargaining unless strong countervailing positive attitudes are generated.

SIMULATION RESEARCH

Theoretical Foundations

The second level of research on international negotiations suggested by Sawyer and Guetzkow (1965) involved simulations—that is, experiments in a laboratory under partially controlled conditions where an explicit effort is made to replicate (i.e., to simulate) some of the essential features of the referent world. The authors (Hopmann and Walcott, 1975) have developed such a simulation, which was designed to test hypotheses about the effects of stresses and tensions in a situation such as that which existed during the negotiations leading up to the Partial Nuclear Test Ban Treaty of 1963. This simulation was based theoretically on the laboratory studies reviewed above and on some more or less impressionistic theory developed by political scientists who have studied international negotiations, especially in the area of arms control.

Perhaps the most comprehensive work on negotiations by a political scientist is that of Iklé (1964), who notes that negotiations are affected by the general climate of relations among the participating nations outside of negotiations, although the relationship between these two sets of factors may be mutually reinforcing. Iklé (1964: 88) concludes that "a change in foreign relations from hostility to friendship (or vice versa) is normally accompanied by a change in negotiating style." Iklé has also noted that there are three general tactics that may contribute to the tension level within negotiations. The first is a warning issued by one party to others about the natural consequences that are likely to follow from the noncompliance of the others. The second is a threat, in which one party indicates that it will undertake specific negative actions if the other parties fail to comply with its demands. In the threat, unlike the warning, execution of the action remains directly under the control of the threatener; on the other hand, the warning concerns events or actions that will occur without regard to any specific actions by the actor applying it. The third tactic involves the use of commitments: One party tries to indicate that it cannot compromise its negotiating position. Thus, implicit in the commitment is the message that the failure of others to accept agreement at the point where the original party has committed itself will lead to a stalemate. Although all three tactics may be used to induce other parties to accept agreements on terms desired by the actor who uses them, they also are likely to increase tensions within the negotiations because of fear of the consequences that may result from any of these tactics.

In addition to these sources of tensions that may originate within the negotiations, tensions may be projected into the negotiations from the international environment. Druckman (1973: 58) has observed:

> Stress may also be caused by the level of tension in the international system. High levels of tension in the system may lead a nation to overreact to provocations made by another nation, leading to a breakdown in negotiations, and increasing the level of system tension. The spiral is reversed for low levels of system tension, with a nation underreacting to provocations from another, allowing them to pursue deliberations and to broach such sensitive issues as the conditions for disarmament.

With particular reference to negotiations on disarmament, Singer (1962) has noted that three general approaches have been taken to the interaction between environmental tensions and disarmament negotiations. The first is called the "tensions first" approach and asserts that negotiations on disarmament are not likely to be successful until international tensions have been resolved. According to this approach, nations are not likely to trust one another to abide by an agreement as long as tensions continue to exist. The second, called the "political settlements first" approach, assumes that settlement of nondisarmament issues must precede agreement on disarmament issues, since armaments are only a symptom and not a cause of conflict. This approach is typified by the "linkage" theory, which is held, for example, by Secretary of State Kissinger. According to Kissinger's biographers (Kalb and Kalb, 1974: 102), the Secretary felt that "every problem between the United States and the Soviet Union was linked with every other problem; and progress on one would affect progress on all." The third, which Singer calls the "armaments first" approach, contends that armaments themselves make a significant contribution to international tensions, and that these tensions feed back and make negotiations more difficult. Thus, it is not clear that tensions can be done away with until some agreement is reached to reduce or eliminate the arms that are at least a partial cause of those tensions. Some effort must be made to limit arms even though tensions may still be present. In this view, which is similar in some ways to Osgood's (1962) concept of Graduated Reciprocal Initiative in Tension-reduction (GRIT), agreement itself on some issues under negotiation may reduce tensions and thus enhance the prospects for further agreement.

In addition to the three approaches suggested by Singer, a fourth position has appeared in recent years, primarily in policy-making circles within the United States government. This position contends that external tensions may actually be useful in attaining agreements because they can be used to reinforce threats, warnings, or commitments. In other words, tensions may intensify the expected negative consequences if agreements are not reached, while their reduction may be held out as a possible consequence of agreement and, hence, as an incentive to agree. Thus, for example, in spite of the fact that it may produce increased tensions, the expansion of armaments programs has been justified in recent years because it may also serve as a "bargaining chip" to increase the probability of agreements in the Strategic Arms Limitations Talks (SALT) or in the negotiations on Mutual (Balanced) Force Reductions in Europe.

There have been relatively few empirical studies of this relationship. Jensen (1962) has studied early postwar Soviet-American disarmament negotiations, in which he observed a curvilinear relationship between international tensions and agreement within negotiations. He concluded that concessions decreased during periods of both high and low international tension. On the other hand, Hopmann (1972) has found a generally positive correlation between a reduction of international conflict and enhanced agreement in the negotiations on the Partial Nuclear Test Ban Treaty of 1963.

Therefore, on the basis both of laboratory studies and of some evidence from international relations, we find ourselves in general agreement with the following proposition identified by Druckman (1973: 58-59):

The higher the level of tension in the international system, the more likely will one nation's negotiator overreact to provocations made by the other nation's negotiator; overreactions to provocations are likely to lead to a breakdown in the negotiations.

The lower the level of tension in the international system, the more likely will one nation's negotiator underreact to another's provocations; underreactions to provocations are likely to facilitate negotiation or lead parties to seek mediational mechanisms for resolving their differences on such vital issues as disarmament.

Experimental Design

The authors (Hopmann and Walcott, 1976) have examined the impact of changes in the external environment on the negotiation process and on outcomes in a simulated arms control negotiation. Three hypothetical nations, including two "great powers" (Algo and Omne) and one minor power allied to Algo (Utro), participated in the negotiation. Although the events were hypothetical, they paralleled in a general way the events and conditions leading up to the Partial Nuclear Test Ban Treaty of 1963. Furthermore, the structure and resources of the three countries were patterned roughly after those of the United States (Algo), the Soviet Union (Omne), and the United Kingdom (Utro).

The simulation scenario presented the three negotiators representing each of these countries with a central problem (a comprehensive ban on testing a fictitious chemical weapon). The problem was intended to elicit bargaining and also to produce stress and frustration since the positions of the great powers were incompatible on that issue. The scenario did permit the negotiators to decompose the issue, however, and to reach agreement on a more limited ban on the testing of this weapon in the field, though not in the laboratory. The basic purpose of this simulation was to determine under what conditions negotiators could arrive at this "solution" within a fixed length of time, and we were particularly interested in observing the effect of an increase and a decrease in tensions between nations outside the negotiations on their ability to attain this solution.

The roles of the negotiators for each of the three nations were played by undergraduate students. The basic problem which they faced was to define the issues under negotiation clearly in such a way as to exclude mutually incompatible positions and to identify the area of "bargaining space" within which their positions overlapped. The general design of the experiment involved the interactions among the following variables:

(I) Independent Variable: Changes in systemic tension levels—benign, neutral, and malign.
(II) Intervening Variables: The bargaining process:
    (a) Attitudes—perceptions of friendliness and hostility.
    (b) Bargaining strategies:

    (1) hard and soft bargaining;
    (2) commitments.
  (c) Bargaining styles:
    (1) positive and negative affect;
    (2) task behavior—agreements and disagreements;
    (3) task-orientation and affect-orientation.
(III) Dependent Variable—Negotiation outcomes:
  (a) Attainment of solutions.
  (b) Agreement scores.

The independent variable—change in the level of external tensions—was manipulated by means of a news bulletin introduced midway through the negotiation session. In one-third of the runs (the benign condition) the bulletin announced a tension reducing agreement on nondisarmament matters among the countries, in another one-third of the runs (the malign condition) it announced the onset of a crisis which produced increased political tensions and the threat of war, and a final one-third of the runs (the neutral condition) had no news bulletin introduced, so that these runs served as control groups. Thus there were three experimental conditions, and eight sessions were run under each. The intervening variables were measured primarily through a system called Bargaining Process Analysis (Walcott and Hopmann, 1975), discussed in Chapter 6 of this volume. The dependent variable was operationalized in two different ways. First, the groups were divided dichotomously into those which successfully achieved a written and signed "treaty" banning field tests and those which failed to do so. Second, a system for scoring peripheral agreements in terms of their importance in the scenario was developed, and this provided an indicator of the *level* of agreement achieved.

Hypotheses and Results

    The central hypothesis in this study posited a direct relationship between the independent variable, the change in international tension, and the dependent variable, the outcome of the negotiations. This hypothesis may be stated as follows:

> Malign interventions from the external environment will reduce the level of agreement in negotiations, and benign interventions from the external environment will increase the level of agreement in negotiations.

    For each condition the number of solutions reached (out of eight possible) and the average agreement scores are listed in Table 10.1. It is clear from the table that the number of solutions was considerably less in the malign condition (13 percent) than in either the benign condition (63 percent) or the neutral condition (63 percent). The average agreement scores were also lower in the malign condition (1.38) than in the benign (6.00) or the neutral (5.50) conditions. The differences between the malign condition and the other two were significant, although the benign condition did not produce significantly better outcomes than the neutral runs. The hypothesis thus must be modified somewhat since the malign condition clearly had a negative effect on the negotiations, while the benign condition did not produce the positive impact relative to the control groups which we had expected.

Additional analyses also suggested that this basic relationship was perhaps influenced by some mediating variables which linked the independent and dependent variables. First, perceptions of friendship and hostility tended to mediate for the dyad involving Omne and Utro. That is, in the malign condition Omne tended to perceive the minor actor, Utro, as being more hostile, and Utro in return perceived Omne as less friendly. In turn, Omne's perception of Utro on the friendliness-hostility dimension was positively correlated with the level of agreement reached, and Utro's perception of Omne was also significantly related to outcomes. The attitudinal linkage was less significant for the "great power" dyad between Algo and Omne. This does seem to suggest that mutual friendliness between the "outsider," namely Omne which had no ally in these negotiations, and Utro which often served as a kind of mediator, may have been particularly influential in producing agreement.

Second, bargaining strategies appeared to be an important intervening variable for the two major actors. For these two countries, bargaining strategies tended to be softer in the benign condition compared to the malign one and in the neutral runs relative to the malign condition. Furthermore, soft strategies tended to be pursued more often in runs in which the solution was achieved and when the level of agreement was highest. Similarly, the two major actors were significantly more likely to employ commitments in the

TABLE 10.1

Summary of Results for the Three Manipulated Conditions of the International Environment: Agreement Scores and Attainment of a Solution

	Benign Environment	Malign Environment	Neutral Environment
	0	0	0
	0	0	0
	4	0	3
	5*	0	5*
	7*	0	7*
	10*	1	7*
	11*	3	9*
	11*	7*	13*
Average Agreement Score	6.00	1.38	5.50
Number of Solutions	5 (63%)	1 (13%)	5 (63%)

ANOVA: $F_{2,21}$ = 3.30 (.10 > p > .05)
Note: Attainment of solution is indicated by *.

malign condition than when tensions were relaxed, and the use of such commitments was negatively associated with the level of agreement attained. Therefore, in general the malign condition seemed to generate tougher bargaining strategies and especially the use of commitments, and these in turn tended to detract from the outcome of the negotiations.

Third, we examined the mediating role of affect, ranging from positive to negative. Again, we found this variable to be significant for the dyad of Algo and Omne. The malign environment tended to produce more negative affect than either the benign intervention or the neutral condition. To complete the linkage, negative affect was found to be associated with a lower probability of reaching a solution and with a lower agreement score. Therefore, the increased conflict in the system structure seemed to generate more negative attitudes, where strong anchoring of attitudes had not previously existed, and these attitudes in turn detracted from the overall outcome, a finding which is quite consistent with the Krauss (1966) study cited earlier.

Fourth, task-oriented behavior, defined here as a proportion of agreements relative to disagreements on specific issues, was also found to intervene between the environment and the outcomes. Across all three dyads combined, the malign environment tended to provoke more disagreements relative to agreements when compared with the benign and neutral conditions. The runs which failed to reach final agreement tended to be characterized by a significantly higher proportion of disagreements than those leading to successful outcomes, and task-orientation was highly correlated with agreement scores across all dyads combined.

Fifth, we failed to obtain significant results involving the proportion of task-oriented behavior relative to affect-oriented behavior. Although we had predicted that the malign condition would increase the emotional level of the negotiations and that this would detract from the outcomes, this prediction was not supported by the data.

The overall result of this simulation study was to suggest that the negotiation process consists of a set of tightly interrelated variables, most of which may be affected by changes in the level of external tension and have a significant impact on the outcome of negotiations. Thus, we found that increased tensions in the external environment seemed to increase significantly: (1) the amount of hostility in mutual perceptions, (2) the proportion of "hard" relative to "soft" bargaining strategies, (3) the employment of commitments, (4) the ratio of negative to positive affect, and (5) the ratio of disagreements to agreements in substantive issues under negotiation. In turn, we found that these increasingly hostile attitudes and perceptions and the toughening of bargaining positions appeared to detract significantly from the ability of the negotiators to arrive at successful agreements.

Perhaps the most interesting implication of this study is to be drawn from the finding that increased tensions generally produced negative results in both the negotiation process and the outcomes, whereas the reduced tensions failed to exert any significant positive effect relative to the control groups. This seems to indicate that negotiations are affected by tension, but that these effects are clearly evidenced only when fairly high levels of stress and tension are produced. On the other hand, since the control groups did almost as well as the groups with reduced tensions in obtaining successful outcomes, it does not appear that, in this simulation, tension reduction was a *necessary* precursor to attaining agreement. In relation to Singer's (1962) three approaches to disarmament, these results thus tended to indicate that agreements could be achieved prior to a complete resolution of all outstanding conflicting issues and prior to a complete removal of all tensions—contrary to the predictions of the "tensions-first" and "political-settlements-first" approaches. In short, when tensions are not extreme, it may be possible to reach agreements; on the other hand, an aggravation of existing tensions is likely to detract substantially from the ability of negotiators to reach agreement.

Advantages and Limitations of the Simulation Methodology

There are, of course, some significant limitations in the simulation methodology, which involve some trade-offs in comparison with research in a laboratory experiment of the more traditional variety or with research "in situ." Compared with the strict laboratory experiment, the simulation permits us to create a much broader context for the negotiations. Context is generally ignored in the traditional laboratory experiment, and this makes it very difficult to investigate systematically the effects of the external system on negotiating behavior. In contrast, the scenario of events within a simulation and the roles that negotiators are asked to play provide an opportunity to introduce a rich contextual setting for negotiations. An additional advantage of the simulation is that it is more readily conducive to the use of complex issues, free verbal interactions, and cumulative payoffs than the traditional PD game. In short, the simulation enables us to model the negotiation process in a way that is more directly analogous to the process as it occurs in the referent environment—namely, international politics. It may thus produce findings that can be generalized to the real world with greater validity.

On the other hand, simulations may be less reliable than more traditional experimental methods. The number of interacting variables within a simulation often makes it difficult for the experimenter to maintain adequate control of the conditions being manipulated. Similarly, the lack of structure, which allows for freer verbal interactions, for example, may also reduce the replicability of findings from session to session.

In the simulation described above, we have tried to find some middle ground between two alternative approaches to laboratory research. On the one hand, researchers such as Guetzkow et al. (1963) have developed in the Inter-Nation Simulation a full-scale model of the entire international system in which a large number of variables are allowed to interact simultaneously.

On the other hand, the tradition of more tightly controlled laboratory experiments, which we have already reviewed, has tended to overlook such components as context and verbal interactions. We have chosen instead to emphasize limited models of specific processes where only a few essential variables enter but where context and verbal interactions are central. We hope that further efforts will be made to construct such limited simulation models for investigating such specific phenomena as the impact of tensions on bargaining.

Of course, simulations also have some of the same limitations as laboratory studies. However realistic one may be in constructing a scenario, the fact remains that the laboratory conditions are in some sense artificial. The roles of negotiators are generally played by students and not by real diplomats, and the stakes of the situation are not generally the same for the players as are those that pertain in the real world. For these reasons, we have also found it desirable to test hypotheses derived from the laboratory in the real world of international relations.

RESEARCH "IN SITU"

The Test Ban Case

To date, most research on international negotiations (e.g., Iklé, 1964; Lall, 1966) has been primarily impressionistic in its evaluation of specific propositions. There has been little effort to apply findings that are generated within laboratory experiments and simulations to actual negotiations in international politics. As a first step in this direction, Hopmann and King (1976) have examined the negotiations in the Eighteen-Nation Disarmament Conference in 1962-1963, which led to the agreement on the Partial Nuclear Test Ban Treaty.

The test ban negotiations provided a case study that is interesting for several reasons. First, the negotiations gained some momentum during a period of substantial Soviet-American tension. Throughout most of the period following the U-2 incident and the breakup of the Paris Summit Conference scheduled for May 1960, tensions between the Soviet Union and the United States had been high. The primary focus of these tensions was Berlin, where the Soviet threat to turn over to the East German authorities control of the access routes leading from West Germany into West Berlin had prompted President Kennedy to call up the National Guard in the summer of 1961. This was followed on August 13 of that year by the construction of the Berlin Wall. The crisis, however, culminated in the midst of the test ban negotiations, not in Berlin, as most officials had predicted, but rather in the Cuban missile crisis of late October 1962. At this point, perhaps, the United States and Russia came closer to nuclear war than at any other time, and so these events should enable us to analyze the impact that extreme tensions had on the test ban negotiations.

A second reason for being interested in the test ban negotiations is that these deliberations broke a long stalemate, which had endured for about fifteen years, in disarmament negotiations between the two nuclear powers. Thus, although the agreement reached was limited, it certainly occurred in a climate that otherwise had not been conducive to agreement, and it was followed by a series of agreements on arms control that have contributed significantly to subsequent Soviet-American political détente.

Hypotheses and Research Design

The theoretical framework of this study is based on the "mediated stimulus-response" model of Osgood (1958) as applied to international relations research by North (1968). Specifically, it sought to determine the effects of externally generated tensions on the perceptions negotiators had of one another's actions and on their own bargaining behaviors during negotiations. The general framework is diagrammed in Figure 10.1, and six principal relationships were investigated:

(1) The impact of external conflict and cooperation on the bargaining behavior of each actor within negotiations (the effects of the external stimulus [EXS] on the internal stimulus [INS]); these bargaining behaviors were defined on a "hard"-"soft" strategy dimension.

(2) The perceptions of the second actor of these two stimuli—namely, of actions taken by the first actor toward it both in the external environment and within negotiations (that is, the effects of EXS and INS on perceptions [PER]).

(3) The effect of perceptions upon the second actor's plans for responding (namely, the effects of PER upon PLAN).

(4) The impact of plans on actual overt behaviors in both the internal responses (INR) within negotiations and the external responses (EXR) outside negotiations.

(5) The direct influence on responses in both the external and the internal environment by the stimuli without the mediating variables intervening (that is, INS may be related to INR directly, and EXS may be directly connected with EXR).

(6) The feedback effects of the internal bargaining behaviors on the level of conflict and tension in the external environment (namely, the effects of INR on EXR). Thus the model hypothesized that external tensions would affect the negotiation process directly through its impact on bargaining behaviors and indirectly through its impact on perceptions and plans of individual negotiators.

The hypotheses linking these variables are all based on the following three general principles:

(1) The Symmetry Principle: Overt stimuli (S) and overt responses (R) will tend to be symmetrical both within and outside negotiations; that is, actors will respond to the behavior of others toward them in a symmetrical fashion.

(2) The Consistency Principle: The behaviors of actors within negotiations (IN) will tend to be consistent with their external behaviors (EX).

(3) The Congruence Principle: An actor's perceptions (PER) of overt stimuli will tend to be congruent with the objective stimuli (S); his plans for responding (PLAN) will be congruent with his perceptions (PER) of the behavior of other actors; and an actor's overt responses (R) will tend to be congruent with his planned responses (PLAN).

In short, the framework predicts that external tensions will tend to generate more "hard-line" bargaining behaviors within negotiations and greater perceptions of negative actions. These "hard-line" behaviors will tend to be reciprocal, especially since they will be reinforced by increasingly negative mutual perceptions. In this manner, tensions are likely to detract from the ability to reach agreement. Conversely, reduced tensions should produce more "soft-line" reciprocal bargaining behavior within negotiations and more positive mutual perceptions that are likely to enhance the prospects for agreement.

Three research techniques were used to operationalize the three major sets of variables in this study. First, the external interactions were measured along scales of cooperation and conflict developed by Corson (1970), which were applied to chronologies of the major events taking place among the United States, the Soviet Union, and the United Kingdom—the three participating nuclear powers—across the entire range of their interactions. The chronologies

FIGURE 10.1
Postulated Model Relations

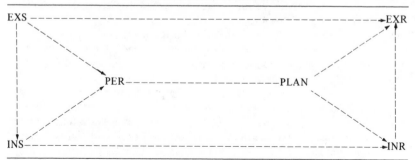

EXS = External Stimulus (external events — other to self)
INS = Internal Stimulus (internal bargaining — other to self)
PER = Perception (internal bargaining evaluation — other to self)
PLAN = Plan (internal bargaining evaluation — self to other)
INR = Internal Response (internal bargaining — self to other)
EXR = External Response (external events — self to other)

used included an American source, the *New York Times Index,* a British source, *Keesings' Contemporary Archives,* and a Soviet source, *New Times.*

Second, the internal bargaining behaviors were measured using a slight variant of the Bargaining Process Analysis system (Walcott and Hopmann, 1975), which was employed in the laboratory simulation discussed earlier. "Soft-line" bargaining behaviors included making new proposals, making concessions, using promises, indicating agreement on specific issues, and acknowledging the contributions of the other party to agreement; "hard-line" bargaining behaviors included retracting previous proposals and concessions, issuing threats, employing commitments, disagreeing on specific issues, and making accusations about the other parties' responsibility for the failure of negotiations.

Third, the perceptions and plans variables were measured along the evaluative dimension of the "semantic differential" (Osgood et al., 1957), that is, from positive to negative, using the Stanford version of the General Inquirer content analysis program (see Holsti, 1969: ch. 7). Perception thus involved each actor's evaluations of the behavior of the other party toward himself, whereas his plans involved his expressed intentions for his own behavior toward the other party.

All variables were aggregated monthly for the period from March 1962, when the Eighteen Nation Disarmament Conference began its meetings, through July 1963, when the Partial Test Ban Treaty was signed in Moscow. Several lag models were used in addition to simultaneous correlations, including a one-month lag and a decaying-memory lag, in which the dependent variable in one month was related to a composite version of the independent variable in the same month and in the two preceding months, weighted to give greatest influence to the most recent time periods.

Major findings

First, we found that usually the external stimulus was significantly related to the internal stimulus. Thus, Soviet behaviors toward the Western nations (the United States and the United Kingdom combined) outside the negotiations correlated with their behavior within the negotiations at .46 (p = .088), whereas Western behaviors toward the USSR outside and inside negotiations were correlated at .69 (p = .005). Thus, external conflict and tensions were clearly projected into the negotiations in the form of harder bargaining strategies.

Second, we looked at the impact of these actions on the perceptions of the negotiators, and we found substantial differences among the three countries. As was predicted, American perceptions of Soviet actions tended to be highly congruent with the actual behaviors of the USSR. The multiple R between Soviet external and internal actions toward the United States and American perceptions of these actions reached .83 (p = .001). In the case of Great Britain, the perceptions of Soviet actions were related only to Soviet behaviors within the external environment (r = .45, p = .096). On the other hand, Soviet perceptions were almost completely unrelated to the actual behaviors of the Western nations toward them. Thus, only for the Western nations did increased external tensions appear to result in increasingly negative perceptions. Since Soviet perceptions were fairly consistently negative throughout most of the negotiations, it is possible that a floor effect prevented significant changes in response to increased international tensions.

Third, the effects of perceptions on plans for responding were examined, although this relationship was generally found to be weak. Indeed, only in the British case were perceptions converted into congruent plans, and in this case the strongest relationship applied with a one-month lag (r = .59, p = .022).

Fourth, plans were projected in behaviors also only in the British case using the decaying lag model (r = .45, p = .097). In this case only, plans seemed to affect subsequent British external behavior. In the Soviet and American cases, the perceptual variables seemed to play relatively little role in mediating between stimuli and responses.

Fifth, we did find strong direct connections between stimuli and responses for all countries, supporting the assumption of the symmetry principle noted above. Looking primarily at the internal environment, we found that there were strong simultaneous correlations between the actions of each nation toward its opponents and its opponents' responses. Thus, within negotiations, Soviet bargaining behaviors toward the United States were correlated with American responses at .68 (p = .006); Western behaviors toward the USSR were correlated with Soviet responses at .77 (p = .001); and Soviet actions toward Great Britain were correlated with British responses at .84 (p < .001). Since in all three cases the stimuli were correlated with external events and since stimuli and responses tended to be symmetrical, we may assume that international tensions generally exerted a hardening effect on mutual interactions within the test ban negotiations. This process of symmetry can cause a spiral of increasing tensions and tough bargaining to become "locked in."

Sixth, the feedback effects from internal responses into responses in the external environment were also significant for all three countries, with the strongest results always appearing in the decaying-lag model. Thus U.S. actions toward the USSR within negotiations were related to subsequent U.S. actions outside negotiations (r = .74, p = .002), while Soviet actions toward the West within negotiations were also related to later external responses (r = .57, p = .027); finally, British behaviors inside the negotiations were correlated with subsequent actions toward the Soviet Union within the external environment as well (r = .68, p = .005).

A summary model of the strongest findings for all three countries is provided in Figures 10.2, 10.3, and 10.4. All three figures give strong evidence of the mutually reinforcing nature of international tensions and tougher bargaining within negotiations. Only in the British case did these relationships appear to be reinforced by the intervening perceptual variables, however. Nevertheless, in the negotiations on the Partial Test Ban Treaty, there is strong evidence that external tensions were related to some increased negative perceptions and especially to tougher bargaining, and this had some reciprocal effect by enhancing tension. Conversely, reduced external tensions seemed to contribute in the Western case to more positive perceptions of the opponent and in all cases to softer bargaining. The latter pattern was particularly evident in the last few months before agreement on the Test Ban Treaty was reached. By June of 1963, one month before the treaty was signed, American behaviors within negotiations toward the USSR had become 100 percent "soft," in contrast to a low of 3 percent "soft" in December

FIGURE 10.2

United States Significant Relationships
(at or below .10 level of significance)

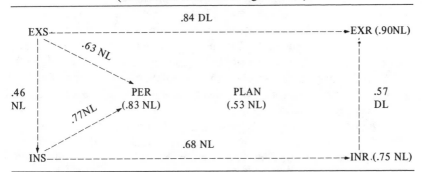

Note: NL = No Lag; L = One-Month Lag; DL = Decaying Lag. Data on lines indicate simple rs, and these are reported only in cases where the relationship was significant at or below the .10 level. Data within parentheses indicate multiple Rs, with all preceding variables entering into the regression equation as independent variables. All multiple Rs are included regardless of significance.

FIGURE 10.3

Soviet Union Significant Relationships
(at or below .10 level of significance)

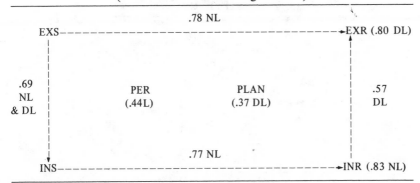

Note: For an explanation of these data, see the note in Figure 10.2.

1962. Similarly, Soviet behaviors toward the West climbed from a low of 5 percent "soft" in December of 1962 to 40 percent "soft," the highest point for the entire negotiations, by June of 1963.

There is considerable debate about the direct effect of the tensions generated by the Cuban missile crisis of October-November 1962 on these negotiations. For example, Hilsman (1967: 228-229) has written the following about the effects of the Cuban missile crisis on the test ban negotiations:

> The irony is that these same problems, which brought the world so near to nuclear war, later brought about the so-called détente—a relaxation of Cold War tensions. For it was the same pressures that led the Soviets to put missiles in Cuba that later led them to take up Kennedy's proposal for a treaty banning nuclear testing.

On the other hand, the data collected by Hopmann and King (1976) tend to suggest that the immediate effect, at least, of the Cuban missile crisis on the test ban negotiations was negative. Perhaps the most significant retractions of earlier proposals occurred in December 1962, especially when a tentative Soviet acceptance of three on-site inspections annually was withdrawn after an alleged private acceptance by the United States of three or four such inspections was renounced. The United States maintained its position in favor of its most recent public offer of seven inspections a year.

Although the Cuban missile crisis appeared to have had a negative immediate effect on negotiations, in the longer run it undoubtedly did have an impact on the perceptions of leaders in the United States, the USSR, and the United Kingdom of the dangers of nuclear war, which prompted a general effort at détente. A major effort to improve the political climate and reduce tensions was made by President Kennedy in his speech at American Univer-

FIGURE 10.4
United Kingdom Significant Relationships
(at or below .10 level of significance)

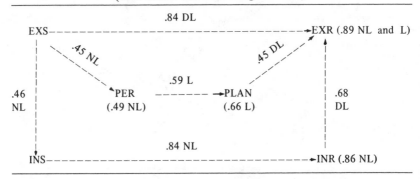

Note: For an explanation of these data, see the note in Figure 10.2.

sity on June 10, 1963. At that time, he announced a unilateral suspension of U.S. nuclear tests and called for a general relaxation of East-West tensions. The Soviet Union responded to this gesture by ceasing their jamming of Voice of America broadcasts and by a general indication of a desire to reduce tensions. The effects of these moves were also reflected within the test ban negotiations, where there was the highest level of "soft" bargaining, as was noted earlier. This paved the way for the secret meeting in Moscow in July 1963, where the final details of the Partial Nuclear Test Ban Treaty were negotiated. The post-missile-crisis détente thus seems to have contributed to this agreement, and the agreement seems in the long run to have contributed to an expanded political détente between the nuclear superpowers.

CONCLUSIONS

There does seem to be some convergence in the evidence derived from laboratory experiments, simulations, and research in situ, all indicating that stresses and tensions generally tend to be dysfunctional for negotiations. They tend to create greater hostility among negotiators; they tend to produce harder bargaining strategies; and they tend to lead to successful outcomes less often than when such tensions are not so strong.

Clearly, this relationship needs further testing. Even though we now have some evidence of its validity in the case of one set of international negotiations, we still need additional real-world research before we can have enough confidence in the generality of these propositions. This will require more case studies. Furthermore, we need to explore more "full-blown" theories of the entire negotiation process at the real-world level. To date, the few studies made have used only isolated hypotheses or limited frameworks, such as the "mediated stimulus-response" model. In real-world negotiations, we need to deal with the impact of external stresses and tensions on bargaining strategies, attitude change, bargaining styles, influence tactics, and the outcomes of negotiations—all contained within one synthesized model. This should provide us with a better opportunity to validate some of the major findings of experimental and simulation research.

The process doesn't necessarily end here, however. Although studies at the real-world level have some obvious advantages over any laboratory studies, they are not without their disadvantages. The absence of systematic controls, for example, makes it most difficult to draw causal inferences. The interaction of many processes at the same time makes it difficult to separate out the independent effects of different variables. While statistical techniques that are now available may help to alleviate some of these problems, they cannot eliminate them altogether. Thus, we may need to take findings from the real world, or even broad insights that have been generated at this level, back into the laboratory, either in tightly controlled experiments or in simulations, in order to isolate independent effects and causal relationships more effectively.

This process of mutual interaction between the laboratory and the real world should be enhanced with techniques such as the Bargaining Process Analysis system (see Walcott and Hopmann, 1975), which may be used for data collection both in the laboratory and in real-world negotiations. By using similar methods with identical operationalizations of the crucial variables in our theories, we should have greater confidence than we do at present in the generalizability of our findings from one environment to another.

It is our general hope that research in both environments, at all three levels, undertaken with specific concern for the theories and methods used at the other levels of research, will enable us to bridge the gap that currently exists between real-world and laboratory studies of negotiations. Our ability to bridge this gap should enhance our prospects for developing a comprehensive theory of the effects of stresses and tensions on the processes and outcomes of negotiations. And a better conceptual understanding of this relationship, if translated into policy, should help us reduce international tensions and achieve more extensive international agreements through the negotiation process.

REFERENCES

CORSON, W. H. (1970) Measuring Conflict and Cooperation Intensity in East-West Relations: A Manual and Codebook. Ann Arbor: University of Michigan Institute of Social Research.

COSER, L. A. (1956) The Functions of Social Conflict. New York: Free Press.

DRUCKMAN, D. (1973) Human Factors in International Negotiations: Social Psychological Aspects of International Conflict. Beverly Hills: Sage Professional Papers in International Studies.

GUETZKOW, H., C. F. ALGER, R. A. BRODY, R. C. NOEL, and R. C. SNYDER (1963) Simulation in International Relations: Developments for Research and Teaching. Englewood Cliffs, N.J.: Prentice-Hall.

HILSMAN, R. (1967) To Move a Nation. New York: Dell.

HOLSTI, O. R. (1969) Content Analysis for the Social Sciences and Humanities. Reading, Mass.: Addison-Wesley.

HOPMANN, P. T. (1972) "Internal and external influences on bargaining in arms control negotiations: The partial test ban," pp. 213-237 in B. M. Russett (ed.) Peace, War, and Numbers. Beverly Hills: Sage Publications.

––– and C. WALCOTT (1976) The Impact of International Conflict and Détente on Bargaining in Arms Control Negotiations: An Experimental Analysis. International Interactions 2: 189-206.

HOPMANN, P. T. and T. KING (1976) "Interactions and perceptions in the test ban negotiations." International Studies Q. 20 (March): 105-142.

IKLE, F. C. (1964) How Nations Negotiate. New York: Praeger.

JENSEN, L. (1962) "Postwar disarmament negotiations: A study in American-Soviet bargaining behavior." Unpublished doctoral dissertation. Ann Arbor: University of Michigan.

KALB, M. and B. KALB (1974) Kissinger. Boston: Little, Brown.

KRAUSS, R. M. (1966) "Structural and attitudinal factors in interpersonal bargaining." J. of Experimental Social Psychology 2: 42-55.

KRETCH, D. and R. S. CRUTCHFIELD (1958) Elements of Psychology. New York: Alfred A. Knopf.

LALL, A. (1966) Modern International Negotiations: Principles and Practice. New York: Columbia Univ. Press.

LANZETTA, J. T. (1955) "Group behavior under stress." Human Relations 8: 29-52.

MILBURN, T. W. (1972) "The management of crisis," pp. 259-277 in C. F. Hermann (ed.) International Crises: Insights from Behavioral Research. New York: Free Press.

NORTH, R. C. (1968) "The behavior of nation-states: Problems of conflict and integration," pp. 303-356 in M. A. Kaplan (ed.) New Approaches to International Relations. New York: St. Martin's.

OSGOOD, C. E. (1958) "Behavior theory and the social sciences," pp. 217-244 in R. Young (ed.) Approaches to the Study of Politics. Evanston, Ill.: Northwestern Univ. Press.

--- (1962) An Alternative to War or Surrender. Urbana: Univ. of Illinois Press.

---, G. J. SUCI, and P. H. TANNENBAUM (1957) The Measurement of Meaning. Urbana: Univ. of Illinois Press.

PALLY, S. (1955) "Cognitive rigidity as a function of threat," J. of Personality 23: 346-355.

POSTMAN, L. and J. BRUNER (1948) "Perception under stress." Psych. Rev. 55: 314-323.

RAPOPORT, A. (1960) Fights, Games, and Debates. Ann Arbor: Univ. of Michigan Press.

RAY, W. S. (1965) "Mild stress and problem-solving." Amer. J. of Psychology 78: 227-234.

SAWYER, J. and H. GUETZKOW (1965) "Bargaining and negotiation in international relations," pp. 466-520 in H. Kelman (ed.) International Behavior: A Social Psychological Analysis. New York: Holt, Rinehart & Winston.

SINGER, J. D. (1962) Deterrence, Arms Control, and Disarmament. Columbus: Ohio State Univ. Press.

SMOCK, C. D. (1955) "The influence of psychological stress on the 'intolerance of ambiguity.' " J. of Abnormal and Social Psychology 50: 177-182.

WALCOTT, C. and P. T. HOPMANN (1975) "Interaction analysis and bargaining behavior." Experimental Study of Politics 4: 1-19.

WALTON, R. E. and R. B. McKERSIE (1965) A Behavioral Theory of Labor Negotiations: An Analysis of a Social Interaction System. New York: McGraw-Hill.

PART IV

COMPLEX SETTINGS AND PROCESSES

EDITOR'S INTRODUCTION

All of the previous contributors relied on data obtained from laboratory experiments as the primary source of information about negotiation process and structure. The choice of this method is based on a preference for rigor in design in order to attain clarity in the interpretation of findings. A cost of this choice is to relinquish consideration of those aspects of a situation that allow one to make a case for the relevance of findings to any particular setting. Extrapolation is forfeited in the interest of interpretability. For many experimentalists, this is not an issue: They are more interested in general knowledge than in relevance to specific cases. For others, specific cases are important: The applicability of the information obtained is just as important as interpretability. The former achieve their goals through tight experimental designs (see, e.g., McClintock, and Hermann and Kogan). The latter strive for representative designs: These are designs that incorporate aspects of particular contexts (see, e.g., Druckman et al.; Hopmann and Walcott). Adequate representative designs are based on an understanding of that context. The chapters in this section attempt to facilitate such understanding.

Two of the chapters emphasize complexity, and each presents a framework for analyzing complex negotiations. Midgaard and Underdal call for an extended conceptualization, while Winham promotes a new one. The Midgaard and Underdal treatment considers the distinctive features of multiparty conferences. These are the structures and processes that differentiate between simple and complex negotiating situations. To understand their operation requires a research strategy that combines several of the analytical approaches that have been used in studying bargaining processes, small groups, and coalition-formation or collective action. Winham's work is a departure from current conceptualizations of negotiation. Like Midgaard and Underdal, he also concentrates on the variables that begin to differentiate between simple and complex negotiations. For him, however, the critical variables are cognitive—relating to factors that affect information-processing. The negotiator's problem is in keeping abreast with developments—"Where are we at?" "Where are they at?" Having identified the problems, Winham then uses his framework to suggest strategies that can help the negotiator to function more effectively in complex, multilateral negotiating situations.

Complexity is also treated in the Stern et al. chapter. However, rather than providing a framework for organizing complex situations, they focus on devices that can be used to restructure *such situations. These are the mediational mechanisms of exchange of persons, superordinate goals, and diplomacy. Each of these has received considerable attention in the literature on interparty conflict resolution. Much of this work has consisted of speculation (especially with regard to diplomacy) or demonstration of effectiveness (note the classic studies on superordinate goals). Stern et al. move this literature forward by making apparent the subtle processes that underlie operation of the mechanisms. An understanding of these processes could lead to a more systematic appraisal of the conditions under which their use is likely to be successful.*

The chapters in this section highlight processes that have implications both for experimental work and for representative design. Each discusses more general cognitive or social-psychological processes that underly certain aspects of negotiating behavior. Information-processing, dependency and power, and coalitions or collective action are some of the general processes concerning which principles can be adduced through laboratory experimentation. Each chapter also discusses more specific negotiating functions or processes that can be observed in situ. Specialized working committees and networks of informal communication, concession-making behavior in multilateral trade conferences, and the "art" of diplomacy are some of the negotiating processes that must be represented in a model of negotiation. The importance of both types of factors for understanding negotiating behavior suggests the plausibility of a methodological strategy that combines experimentation with on-site observations. The former can be used to explore general processes; the latter is necessary for obtaining insights into context-specific processes. This dual emphasis is recognized in the chapters of this section. It is also reflected in many of the contributions of the previous sections.

Chapter 11

MULTIPARTY CONFERENCES

KNUT MIDGAARD

and

ARILD UNDERDAL

Institute of Political Science
University of Oslo

INTRODUCTION

The Meaning of "Multiparty Conferences"

In this chapter, we shall investigate the implications and the consequences of the number of negotiating parties for process and outcome. This may appear to be a well-defined project; the dependent variables—process and outcome— are treated at length in Part II of this volume, and the independent variable— number of parties—may seem unambiguous and easily measureable. In fact, however, it is not always clear what should be considered a party, or what should be considered one and the same conference, or what are the critical distinctions to be made in terms of numbers. So we propose to start this chapter by considering these three questions briefly.

With respect to the first, there are at least three problems to be faced: One is how to designate those that clearly seek to influence the outcome of a negotiation process without being a regular participant (e.g., New Zealand in the negotiations on British membership in the European Economic Community). The second is how to deal with coalitions (e.g., the so-called "group of 77" in UNCTAD sessions). Third is the question of what to do about parties that split into two or more factions fighting out their disputes in the open.

The first problem leaves us with a choice between the criterion of attempted or real influence and that of formal participation (which does not necessarily imply influence). The formal criterion is no doubt the clearest and the most economical being used, while the influence criterion provides us with a distinction that is more significant from a theoretical, as well as from a practical, standpoint. The latter two problems both imply that the number of formal parties may be different from the number of positions or interests that are to be integrated. The forming of coalitions may turn a multiparty conference into an essentially bipolar one, while open internal conflict can give two-party talks a flavor of multilaterality.

The second question (What shall be considered to be one and the same conference?) seems to arise particularly in two kinds of situations: (a) where a conference is part of an integrated series stretched out over some time (such as the UN Conference on the Law of the Sea) and (b) where a formally multilateral conference is divided into a number of (bilateral) subprocesses. (For example, the negotiations on enlargement of the European Economic Community (EEC) were generally conducted bilaterally—i.e., with each applicant separately.) In both cases, concepts like "supra-process" and "subprocess" could be used to give a conference its proper contextual location.

We bring up these questions here to emphasize the fact that there are several forms of multilaterality and that the consequences of the number of parties may to some extent vary from one kind of multilaterality to another. Here we can do little more than identify this complication; a full discussion of the different kinds of multilaterality would go far beyond the scope of this chapter. To make the task manageable, we shall concentrate on the "purer" forms of multilaterality.

The question of the most interesting distinction as to numbers is perhaps even more central to our concern. Clearly the distinction between "bilateral" (n = 2) and "multilateral" negotiations (n > 2) is essential—particularly, it seems, to the analysis of bargaining processes. This is not the only "watershed," but it is much harder to be precise as to the exact location of others. We shall suggest that there are at least two more significant distinctions, one somewhere around five to seven, the other around twenty. Conferences of less than five to seven parties will be referred to as "small," those having more than approximately twenty (e.g., several UN conferences) as "large," and those between as "intermediate." The reasons for making these distinctions will be given throughout the analysis.

"The State of the Art"

There is a rich literature on negotiations and a considerable amount of research on decision-making processes with more than two participants. Unfortunately, however, less has been written directly on the subject of *multilateral negotiations* per se. Most of the theoretical literature on negotiation deals with bilateral bargaining. Although much of this theorizing is relevant to multilateral negotiations as well, theories of bilateral processes can provide at best a starting point for considering our specific problem. Most of the research on multiparty decision-making does not deal specifically with negotiation. There is no evidence that concepts and propositions from other kinds of group processes apply equally well to negotiation. This reservation pertains to inter alia, coalition theories. So some parts of this chapter will attempt to extend (or reformulate) conceptualizations and propositions from other settings to the analysis of multilateral negotiations.

At least three traditions, or "schools," have contributed to an understanding of our specific problem. One is the deductive tradition of game theory, concentrating on the logic of situations or "games," rather than on the empirical study of negotiation processes. The main concern of game theory is a search for "solutions," which in the case of n-person theory, generally refers to coalitions. Second, there is the largely inductive tradition of social psychology, which relies essentially on experiments and is distinguished also by focusing on a number of aspects and variables not germane to game theory (Druckman, 1973). Relevant to our problem are, of course, the studies on coalition formation and maintenance and also much of small group theory— particularly research on the consequences of group size for actor behavior, the character of interaction, and outcome. The third tradition (we might call it the "eclectic" and comparative study of historical cases) shares with social psychology its empirical orientation and its broad focus, but it is less integrated and cumulative. Nonetheless, it is included here, first, because its reservoir of observations and insights can provide a basis for the critical evaluation of models and propositions derived from deductive or experimental studies and, second, because it brings to our specific problem an understanding of conference organization and structure that takes us beyond the achievements of the other traditions.

Among these "schools," there is a considerable amount of overlap in terms of phenomena studied, and there is a continuous exchange of ideas. For this and other reasons, we will not discuss their distinctive features or compare their overall contributions. Together, they make up the sources from which we shall extract our propositions and suggestions. But our concern is the problem, and this is the basis on which the subsequent review and discussion is organized.

More specifically, we shall organize the analysis in the following way: There will below be a broad, general survey of implications and consequences of conference size for (a) actor calculations, (b) manifest negotiating behavior, and (c) outcome. Later we shall discuss more thoroughly one of the distinctive features of multiparty negotiations, the forming of coalitions, and some of the existing theories that attempt to predict or explain coalition formation.

CONSEQUENCES OF CONFERENCE SIZE: A GENERAL SURVEY

Basic Actor Calculations

One of the most fundamental consequences of increasing the number of actors is that the negotiating situation tends to become less lucid, more complex, and therefore, in some respects, more demanding. First, as conference size increases, there will be more values, interests, and perceptions to be integrated or accommodated. This means that an actor will have to consider more interests when deciding upon his moves, as well as that there are more moves and systems of interaction to be coordinated. Second, since there are more interests to consider, there will probably also be more *uncertainty* as to the interests and motives of some of the others and as to their perceptions of one's own utilities. This suggests the general proposition that *conference size tends to make it more difficult to decide on own moves and to find satisfactory solutions to the problems involved.* This may not apply equally well to all actors; thus the most dogmatic and the most indifferent are both probably less sensitive to such complications. But to the average actor, increased conference size generally means, inter alia, increased situational complexity and also increased individual "powerlessness."

The impact of this is felt in all types of negotiation, but perhaps most strongly in bargaining.[1] Let us therefore proceed to consider what size means for actor calculations in bargaining processes.

Bargaining. One way of characterizing pure bargaining, as opposed to what we shall call "cooperative negotiations," is to say that it consists of trying to get the other party or parties to make the largest possible concessions, while making the smallest possible concessions oneself. Thus, one of the core problems in bargaining is that of determining the relative strength of bargaining positions or finding out who will have to make the first concession. In fact, little is known about the way(s) in which actors go about solving this problem. However, several formulas have been suggested as to how bargaining strength should be calculated. Most of these formulas have been developed within the context of bilateral bargaining, and actors will often run into severe problems in trying to undertake the prescribed calculations in multilateral situations. This can be illustrated by considering one of the more interesting models—that of Zeuthen/Harsanyi (Harsanyi, 1956; cf. Luce and Raiffa, 1958: 135-137). Midgaard (1974) has discussed the relevance of this model, and we shall not go into the details of the problem here. The main purpose of the following discussion is to indicate the kinds of problems and possibilities involved in applying this and similar models to multilateral situations.

According to the Zeuthen/Harsanyi model, a party's bargaining strength is determined by the ratio between (1) the utility difference to the party between his own demand and that of his opponent, and (2) the utility difference to the party between his own demand and no agreement. The party for whom this fraction is smaller has to yield or make a concession. This criterion leads to the Nash solution—i.e., the outcome that maximizes the product of each party's gain over no agreement (Nash, 1950; cf. Luce and Raiffa, 1958: 124-128).

Since there may be doubt about the plausibility of the Zeuthen/Harsanyi formula, it should be noted that it is equivalent in its consequences to the criterion obtained by substituting "the demand of his opponent" for "his own demand" in point 2. The present authors find that this version of the criterion, which focuses on what each party can gain, as compared to what he can lose, by insisting on his demand, is more plausible both descriptively and prescriptively.

The Zeuthen/Nash model and the modification suggested require that an actor with at least some confidence can establish the utilities attached by others to his own proposal, the utilities to himself and to others of the position of (each of) his opponent(s), and the utilities attached by each to the possibility of breakdown (deadlock). Clearly these requirements will not always be met even in bilateral bargaining, and as conference size increases, it becomes increasingly difficult to meet them. This is due in part to the fact that, with limited resources, there will be more preferences and alternatives to consider. But, in addition, there may be further complications because of the possibility of incomplete proposals—a distinctive feature of multilateral bargaining; while in bilateral bargaining a demand for a certain share is equivalent to a proposal that stipulates a complete distribution, this will not necessarily be the case when there are more than two parties.

If, however, the actors have the information needed about each other's utilities, and everyone submits complete proposals, the natural method of extending the Zeuthen/Harsanyi model (or the modification suggested) to multilateral negotiations is to deal with each pair of parties the same way two parties are dealt with in the bilateral case.

Under certain favorable conditions, the method of pairwise comparisons can provide a powerful clue. However, it is as likely that an actor trying to run through a set of such calculations will face insurmountable problems. First, the method is clearly feasible for only a small number of parties. Second, and more important, it is not clear how the conclusions produced by this method should be interpreted. Third, pairwise comparisons may lead to intransitivity—i.e., and inconclusive or contradictory outcome. And the probability that this will happen is likely to increase with the number of actors.

Given the fact that a direct extension of the Zeuthen/Harsanyi formula, or the suggested modification, is highly problematic, we would suggest the following reformulation, which retains something of the mode of comparison of the original Zeuthen/Harsanyi formula: For each party we establish the relation between (1) the utility loss involved in the "least possible" concession he can make, or the least concession that would "make sense," and (2) the utility loss involved in breakdown. We then compare these relations: The larger the quotient, the stronger the bargaining position of the party in question.[2]

While the denominator in the fraction that our criterion establishes is the same as in the Zeuthen/Harsanyi criterion, the numerator to be considered is not related to any other party's demand, as is the case in the Zeuthen/Harsanyi formula. Of course, the "least possible" concession a party can make, or the least concession that would "make sense," is in general not a precise entity. It may be, however, that this is a kind of vagueness that one has to live with in multilateral bargaining.

It should also be noted that considering each concession separately may lead to conclusions that are different from those produced by considering all concessions in sum. Parties that have to make concessions at the outset may have to make more concessions in the former case than in the latter.

Our formula should be supplemented with at least one additional criterion: (3) the share of the total gains demanded by the party in question. Other things being equal, it seems that the larger this share is, the weaker is a party's bargaining position. Linking the two criteria, we suggest that a party's bargaining position will be proportional to 1 divided by the product of 2 and 3.

This discussion points to the lack of a criterion of bargaining power in multilateral settings that is precise and feasible as well as compelling. Probably the main conclusion to be inferred is that for multilateral bargaining no such criterion exists. At least we believe that *as the number of parties increases, there will be ample room for the art of creating suggestive clues* (Schelling, 1960), *and a more prominent role for chance as a determinant of bargaining outcomes.*

Cooperative negotiations. To the extent that an increase in the number of parties brings about more heterogeneity in terms of interests and perceptions, and more uncertainty within each party as to the preferences of others, the search for *fair or integrative solutions* (see the Pruitt and Lewis chapter) will become more difficult as size goes up. For one thing, uncertainty as to the exact preferences of others implies uncertainty as to which criteria should be met if a solution is to be satisfactory. And even if the criteria are clear, the wider the range of interests, the harder it is to generate solutions that satisfy them all.

What is said above refers to the calculations of one individual actor. From a *process* perspective, however, these difficulties are more or less offset by the fact that, as conference size increases, there will be more parties and thus more resources working on their solutions. For small groups, and at least for certain kinds of integrative problems, the marginal increase in resources tends to outweigh the added complications. Above that level, however, *further increase in the number of parties will probably, more often than not, be inversely related to conference performance in cooperative negotiations.*

Choice of approach. So far we have examined processes that clearly have the character either of bargaining or of cooperation. However, the choice of approach may also be affected by conference size. Thus, uncertainty about another's motives tends to make open, cooperative behavior more risky, since the probability that someone will turn cooperative moves against you can be expected to increase with the number of actors. On the other hand, the significance of some factors that normally make for bargaining can in fact be reduced in multilateral settings. Asymmetrical interdependence relationships are a case in point. In bilateral negotiations the stronger party will probably be tempted to exploit the asymmetry through bargaining strategies. To do so may be more difficult in multilateral settings, where the presence of additional parties often serves to neutralize, or at least diminish, the power gap, and thereby weaken the stronger party's incentives to bargain. The fact that such contradictory implications may be found precludes generalizations as to the effect of size on the choice of approach.

Negotiation Behavior

Behavioral adaptation to conference size can take place at three different levels: First are what we might call "joint" efforts—i.e., measures established by a conference decision. In principle, these measures are intended to provide for orderly and efficient talks, and deal mainly with process organization. Second are "subgroup" efforts, in which two or more, but not all, of the parties participate. Finally, there is "unilateral" adaptation.

Joint measures. In this section we shall examine three partially interrelated measures for coping with the problems of size: One is the formalization of rules, another is differentiation in terms of roles, and the third is the introduction of special mechanisms for "cutting through" stalemate situations.

Formalization: In any negotiation process, it is vital that there are certain basic interaction rules known and largely observed by all parties. As long as the number of parties is quite small, a tacit agreement may be developed on which rules to adopt. *As conference size increases, however, the need for formalization (i.e., explicit codification) of rules seems to grow stronger.* This is so partly because there will normally be more heterogeneity in terms of premises in a large group than in a small one and partly because tacit coordination itself is possible only among a small number of parties. Berelson and Steiner (1964: 358) suggest that the "watershed" is "around size 5-7," so that formalization—up to a point—tends to increase rapidly as group size grows beyond that number. Moreover, once a rule is adopted, it seems to be harder to change (and perhaps also more risky to violate) the larger the number of parties (Iklé, 1964: 221).

It is difficult to point to clear contrasts between bargaining and cooperative negotiations with regard to the *need* to formalize rules, though the factors that make for stalemate and therefore create a need for good organization are particularly striking in bargaining (see "unilateral measures"). But since procedural rules may have substantial implications, disagreement on substance will often be reflected in conflict over procedure, so we may expect the *ability* to agree on a set of rules to be higher, the more cooperative the atmosphere.

Differentiation: Two roles that are not present in bilateral negotiations are familiar, and sometimes even essential, to multiparty conferences; one is that of chairman or *leader,* the other is that of go-between or *mediator.*

The need for a chairman or leader reflects an inability to conduct orderly and efficient interaction through informal and largely tacit coordination. Again, we suggest, the critical number will be somewhere around five to seven, perhaps slightly lower for bargaining than for cooperative processes. Thus, it seems that the introduction of a chairman contributed decisively to breaking the stalemate in the negotiations among Japan, the Netherlands, Norway, and the United Kingdom on their quotas for pelagic whaling in the Antartica (Midgaard and Overrein, 1970: 98-110; Midgaard, 1974). Small groups may find it useful to appoint a leader, while for larger groups the services of a chairman come close to being necessary for a satisfactory rate of progress. Moreover, the gap in patterns of participation between leader and follower tends to increase with size, so that the larger the group, "the more the active members dominate interaction within the group" (Berelson and Steiner, 1964: 358).

The main purpose of *mediation* is to help conflicting parties converge on a viable agreement. Often the chairman will himself take, and be expected to play, the role of mediator. For analytical purposes, however, the two roles should be distinguished.

Another aspect of role differentiation is the splitting up of processes into a number of subprocesses. This may occur when tasks are delegated *vertically*—i.e., to a subordinate within the delegations—as well as *horizontally*—i.e., to a committee or subgroup at the same hierarchical level. Vertical delegation is primarily a response to complexity and overload of topics (Kaufmann, 1968: 49), while horizontal delegation is a measure designed primarily to overcome the problems created by conference size itself.

Mechanisms of "cutting through": The basic idea of negotiation is to arrive at some kind of agreement—i.e., at a unanimous decision. *Other things being equal, the larger the conference, the harder it is to find a solution that will be readily accepted by everyone.* Large conferences seem to respond to this in at least two ways: First, they tend to develop explicit rules and/or informal norms against certain kinds of "perfectionism." Thus, once an acceptable solution is found, there will be a strong pressure not to delay progress by searching for the "perfect" one. Moreover, even in negotiations that are supposed to be clearly cooperative, certain rules may be introduced to prevent a party from reopening a discussion concerning a point on which he has had second thoughts. In a small forum, such thoroughness would often be considered laudable—or even essential—to integrative negotiations (Walton and McKersie, 1965: 151). In a large conference, however, such behavior is likely to appear misplaced or even actually obstructive.

Such norms will not always be enough to promote progress. Thus, large conferences tend to provide for a special mechanism for "cutting through" stalemate situations, namely, the mechanism of voting. Voting implies some kind of majority decision. In several settings, however, majority "decisions" are not considered binding for and by those who record their opposition. In this case, voting should not be considered primarily a method of making decisions; rather, the point may be to step up pressure on a minority by attaining some kind of "collective legitimization" (Claude, 1967) of a majority position or policy, or even outright stigmatization of uncontrollable opponents.

Whatever the status and purpose of a vote, the introduction of this mechanism is likely to affect the nature of the official proceedings, probably turning them more into a debate or even a battle of propaganda, and leaving most of the search for common ground and acceptable compromises to be pursued informally and within subgroups. Thus, we suggest, *negotiation in a strict sense is a practical method of making plenary decisions primarily for small and intermediate conferences.*

Subgroup measures. The most important measures to be considered here are the forming of self-initiated subgroups and of unofficial channels of communication.

We have previously mentioned that subgroups may be formally appointed by the conference in full session. Of course, subgroups may form also on the initiative and decision of their own members. Usually these two subgroups differ in terms of purpose and composition: Subgroups appointed by the conference generally have the character of committees; i.e., their main purpose is to study a specific problem and come up with suggestions for some broadly acceptable solution (s). To achieve this purpose, a committee should be representative of the whole conference with regard to values, interests, and perceptions. Though exceptions may easily be found, self-initiated subgroups often are referred to as "coalitions," being composed of parties who have largely compatible interests in the topics involved and who are striving to promote these interests against opposition.

It is hard to imagine a large conference that does not have networks of informal channels of communication. At least two reasons can be given why the volume as well as the significance of informal talks tend to increase with conference size. First, the more parties there are, the more time each will need to communicate with others. The practical consequence of size is most often that each gets *less* time to communicate in the official proceedings. Informal talks are one way of compensating for this. Second, as conference size increases, most actors will feel a stronger need to differentiate their messages and to make contacts that are strictly selective in terms of participants and listeners. This can be achieved only to a limited extent through the framework of the formal proceedings.

Taken together, these two points seem to suggest *that the functions of the plenary proceedings vary with conference size.* In general, the larger the conference, the more likely it is (a) that the formal plenary proceedings will turn into a discussion of some simple, clearly defined problem—e.g., a repetitive review of arguments for and against one or a few alternative texts or principles, and (b) that the agreements concluded will confirm what have been achieved through informal (subgroup) talks (Traavik, 1973: 157).

Unilateral measures. In the previous section, on actor calculations, one of the propositions was that conference size tends to make it more difficult for most actors to decide upon their moves. A second was that powerlessness tends to increase with size. Let us now look at some of the unilateral efforts that are designed to cope with these problems, and also at likely emotional reactions.

Aside from trying to simplify the problems (see the next chapter, by Winham), the most conspicuous *attack* on the complications of large numbers is simply to spend more time and/or energy analyzing the situation and making and implementing decisions. In the case of organizational actors, such measures may include efforts to increase the size and/or improve the quality of the delegation, as well as simply to spend more time on preparations.

If more analysis cannot solve the problems, at least two other strategies are available: One may be labelled "nonaction," or, more precisely, "wait-and-see." Although this is a rational response to uncertainty and dilemmas in cooperative negotiations as well as in bargaining, it seems that the incentives to adopt it will often be stronger in bargaining. If we are correct to assume that the criteria of bargaining strength are less clear in multilateral than in bilateral negotiations, effective convergence is less likely in the former for several interrelated reasons. First, the lack of a common, precise criterion of bargaining strength makes it less likely that everybody expects a specific party to move. Second, if somebody nevertheless feels he should try to get the convergence process going by making a concession, he will perhaps find that this is likely to be futile. The reason for this may be partly that no general criterion makes it clear who should make the next move, and partly that his move has no specific addressee; i.e., no specific party is called upon through his move to reciprocate. Moreover, a concession may even be interpreted as a sign of weakness and lead others to expect that the same party should make the next concession also. So a bargaining situation in some cases is probably best interpreted as a (tacit) contest not to be the one who concedes first. Such contests can lead to at least a temporary stalemate even in situations where a generally acceptable compromise or package-deal seems "objectively" possible.

Furthermore, when an actor decides to make a move in a situation that he perceives to be complex, he will often do so either by taking a stand only on some limited aspect of the problem or by making his statements more tentative, vague, or ambiguous. The incentives to do this are probably stronger in bargaining, but the costs of an infelicitous statement can be considerable in cooperative negotiations as well.

In sum, then, these three points support the proposition suggested by Berelson and Steiner (1964: 358) that *as size increases beyond a certain level, conference discussion tends to become "less exploratory and adventurous."*

The strategies referred to above can in part be understood also as a response to individual "powerlessness." But powerlessness may express itself more directly in other ways, notably in efforts to avoid being a single dissident against a united or overwhelming majority. Several studies indicate that "group size is an important factor in determining the amount of yielding to conformity pressures" (Thomas and Fink, 1963: 377). This probably applies to cooperative negotiations as well as to bargaining.

The problems created by size can produce strain and frustration. Along with this, size tends to make interaction more anonymous and thus to weaken the norms of interpersonal discussion (Hamburger et al., 1975). Thomas and Fink (1963: 375) conclude their review with the observation that "tentatively it would appear that smaller groups inhibit expression of disagreements and dissatisfactions more than larger groups." This conclusion is based on studies of interpersonal communication, so caution should be taken in generalizing it to interorganizational processes, where the negotiators act as *agents,* more or less restricted by organizational decisions and norms.

Outcome

What we have said about actor calculations and behavior indicates at least two propositions concerning the implications of conference size for the outcome itself.

First, if we define a "perfect" agreement as one covering all agenda topics and involving the perfect meeting of minds of all parties, it seems clear that the difficulties involved in arriving at such agreements tend to become more serious as conference size increases. Thus, *the larger the conference, the more likely it is that an agreement, if concluded at all, will be "partial" in at least one of three ways:* (a) covering only some of the agenda topics; (b) leaving some disagreement latent in an ambiguous text; and (c) being signed and accepted by only some of the parties.

Second, *the risk of suboptimal outcomes seems to increase with size, at least as far as collective goods are concerned.* This is in line with the main argument of Mancur Olson (1968: 35), although his proposition, "The larger the group, the farther it will fall short of providing an optimal amount of a collective good," seems to refer less to the outcome of negotiations than to the difficulties in getting negotiations started at all. Unfortunately, his hypothesis does not easily lend itself to empirical testing, except in the context of very simple experimental situations. There are a few experimental studies that seem to support it (e.g., Vinacke, 1971; Hamburger et al., 1975), but this is clearly one of the questions where more research will be needed to permit more precise and definite statements.

DISTINCTIVE FEATURES OF MULTIPARTY NEGOTIATIONS

Reference has been made above to a few distinctive features of multiparty negotiations. Among these, *mediation* and the formation of *coalitions* seem to be the ones that attract the greatest interest among students of bargaining. Mediation is analyzed in the chapter by Stern et al. For this reason we shall concentrate here on coalitions.

Coalitions

More than most other topics, the formation of coalitions has served as an integrating focus for deductive, experimental, and historical research. Most of the efforts have been concerned with two questions: (1) Which coalition(s) will form? (2) How is the payoff of the coalition divided among its members?

At least two "groups" of coalition theories could be distinguished: On the one hand, there are the "apolitical" theories of, e.g., Riker (1962) and Gamson (1961); on the other, there are the so-called "policy distance" theories of, e.g., Axelrod (1970) and DeSwaan (1973). Although there are significant differences between these traditions, they both formulate most of their answers within the context of decision-making processes that, in one or more important respects, differ from that of negotiation. So one main point to be made in this section is that the "apolitical" theories are unable to deal adequately with the formation of coalitions in negotiations, and that even "policy distance" theories need some rethinking, or at least translation, to fit this particular kind of process. To substantiate our argument, let us now try to run through the calculations that an intendedly rational actor would have to make in deciding whether or not to join a coalition.

When to opt for coalition membership? For an intendedly rational actor, the general answer is that to seek a coalition if he expects to achieve something that, taking costs into consideration, he could not achieve himself and *perhaps* join a coalition if he thinks he thereby will obtain as much as he would by going it alone. If more than one coalition meets that criterion, he will prefer the coalition that gives him the highest expected net gain.

This leads to another question: When (i.e., in which circumstances) will an actor benefit? At the very general level, three requirements can be indicated: First, the coalition must pursue some purpose that the actor finds attractive and have no side effects that will neutralize that purpose. Second, the coalition must succeed in promoting its purpose. Third, joining must "make some difference"; i.e., by joining he should either (a) increase his share of the net benefits of cooperation, and/or (b) "improve" coalition purpose, and/or (c) contribute to coalition success.

In the "apolitical" theories, the first requirement will be met by any conceivable coalition since in their kind of game there is only one purpose to aim at. Not so in most real-life negotiations. Thus, in this respect, "policy distance" theories are clearly more realistic, in that they consider the extent of agreement on coalition policy to be a crucial variable in explaining coalition formation.

The second requirement—that of coalition success—is vital to every coalition theory that we are aware of. However, the precise meaning of this requirement will depend on the rules of the game. In the simple world of most coalition theories, to "succeed" means to "win" some "winner-take-all" game. To win means to reach a decision point prescribed in the rules (usually 50 percent + 1 of relevant resources). A winning coalition is a "subgroup which, by the rules accepted by all members, can decide for the whole" (Riker, 1962: 12). Each coalition will either win, lose, or block the game. Once a winning coalition is formed, every other coalition becomes a losing one. The "pot" is fixed in the sense that as soon as the decision point is reached, the gain of a coalition will not depend on the total amount of resources commanded. If, for example, the decision point is 50 percent + 1, a coalition commanding just this amount of resources will have the same gain as one commanding 90 percent, other things being equal. Since every actor is assumed to be maximizing his own payoff in that particular game, and since the winner takes all, there is no point whatsoever in forming a losing coalition. Success is an all-or-nothing affair. On the other hand, no coalition would give a party less than he would obtain by going it alone.

Clearly, negotiation is a different kind of game. From our perspective, the most fundamental difference is in terms of decision rules. The basic purpose of negotiation is to arrive at some kind of *agreement*—i.e., a unanimous decision. This has a number of implications; the most immediately relevant one to be noted here is that it implies a need for a different concept of coalition success. To repeat, the traditional criterion of winning is that a coalition must be able to meet a generally accepted rule that confers upon a subgroup the legitimate authority to make decisions for the whole. Obviously this criterion is not very useful when it is applied to processes where no such rule exists. In negotiations, the general purpose of forming a coalition will usually be to make (through information, arguments, or sheer pressure) someone agree to something that he/they would otherwise not have considered or accepted. A coalition succeeds to the extent that it is able to fulfill that purpose. Second, as is indicated by the centrality of concepts like, e.g., "compromise" and "package-deal," most negotiations are not "winner-take-all" games. Thus, in negotiation, success will usually be a matter of degree. Moreover, success will often be "nonexclusive" in the sense that more than one coalition can form and (to some extent) succeed in the same process. In sum, this suggests that when studying negotiations, the dichotomous concept of winning should be replaced by a continuous or incremental concept of success.

As was indicated above, the method of voting will often be used in large conferences. This may imply that the traditional concept of winning will be more relevant to large than to small conferences. But, if so, the explanation is simply that decision-making in large conferences occurs also by methods other than negotiation.

As for the third requirement, two brief points should be made: First, joining a coalition is not always, as is assumed in most theories, a necessary condition for benefitting from its success. In the case of collective goods, an actor may reap the benefits of cooperation without joining at all. Second, the resources of a coalition should not generally be conceived of simply as the sum of member resources. The formation of a coalition may create new resources as well as destroy some of the individual member resources (Stenelo, 1972: 56-57).

Which coalition is the "best"? What, then, if two or more coalitions both (all) fulfill these requirements? Which should an actor prefer? Roughly speaking, the answer of the "apolitical" theories is that he should choose the coalition that maximizes his share of total coalition resources—i.e., the "minimal winning" coalition. The "policy distance" theories recognize that this answer neglects what may be the most important dimension in explaining coalition formation—that is, policy (dis)agreement. However, some of them retain the concept of "minimal winning," which in our context remains a rather unmanageable tool.

To overcome this problem, we would suggest the following reformulation, based upon the preceding discussion: When choosing among coalitions fulfilling the minimal requirements, an individualistically motivated and intendedly rational actor should compare alternatives along the following dimensions: One is the quality or value to him of coalition purposes and policies if he does not join (Q). This depends first and foremost on his "distance" from the "policy center" of the coalition. Second, he should look for possible non-purpose effects of that coalition (N). Third, he should consider the extent to which each coalition would succeed without him (E). This depends on coalition resources. Fourth, he should compare what would be his own proportions of coalition payoffs if he did not join (P). Finally, he should consider to what extent his joining would affect Q, N, E, or P—i.e. (Δq, Δn, Δe, Δp). The value of a given coalition, C, could be conceived of as a function of these dimensions:

$$V_c = f\ [Q_c, E_c, P_c, N_c, \Delta\ q_c, \Delta\ e_c, \Delta\ p_c, \Delta\ n_c]\ .$$

Using the mathematical symbol for multiplication in the rather loose sense of "trading off," we suggest that the form of the function is

$$V_c = (P_c + \Delta\ p_c) \bullet (Q_c + \Delta\ q_c) \bullet (E_c + \Delta\ e_c) \bullet (N_c + \Delta\ n_c).$$

Consequences of coalition formation. The consequences of coalition formation for negotiation process and outcome have so far attracted less interest than has the process of formation itself. This is due in part to the fact that most coalition theories and experiments have focused on kinds of situations where the only consequence to be studied is the distribution of payoffs. In fact, the question of consequences for *process* becomes meaningless if it is asked in relation to situations where the formation of a winning coalition marks the end of the game and where nonwinning coalitions do not form.

What then are the main consequences for a negotiating conference of the formation of a coalition? Perhaps the most conspicuous proposition is that *the formation of a coalition tends to reduce situational complexity* (Stenelo, 1972: 58). The extent to which this will happen, however, depends not only on coalition size, but also on coalition achievement in terms of increasing unity among its members. Thus, a coalition consisting of members whose positions were identical in advance may reduce complexity less than will a somewhat smaller coalition that effectively coordinates positions and strategies that previously diverged.

Kaufmann (1968: 150) suggests that the formation of coalitions (or "groups," as he calls it) "would be a gain in conference efficiency." At first thought, this seems a plausible hypothesis; no doubt, coordination within a coalition can save a considerable amount of conference time. However, as suggested by Kaufmann, coalitions themselves may be rather slow and inflexible actors, and thus the net gain in conference efficiency may be less evident than one might expect. In particular, there seems to be a serious risk that conferences that turn into bipolar bargaining between coalitions will end in breakdown because neither side is able to engage in a sufficiently constructive search for integrative solutions (see the Pruitt and Lewis chapter).

Similar findings are reported by Underdal (1973) in a study of the negotiating behavior of the EEC coalition. Comparing the coalition to state actors, Underdal found that the pluralistic structure affected community decision-making capacity, as well as the substance of the decisions arrived at.

First, since failure to reach agreement among its members most often means failure to produce a decision at all, *the decision-making capacity of a pluralistic actor is, other things being equal, lower than that of more unitary actors.* In general, *low decision-making capacity favors a "passive" approach to negotiation,* at least as far as topics involving internal conflict are concerned. On such topics, coalitions will usually be less able to adopt the searching and flexible approach of cooperative negotiations. Low decision-making capacity may be a liability also in bargaining, but not always: If two actors are to converge on an agreement, the one who will have to move is in fact the one who is able to do so.

Second, in bargaining, the requirement of agreement tends to favor the coalition member(s) who are most opposed to further concessions. Furthermore, once a coalition has succeeded in hammering out a "difficult" decision, that decision is likely to be hard to modify or change. Often it may be easier to split a conflict-ridden coalition than to make it retreat from an established position. In sum, *coalitions tend to be slow and inflexible actors.*

These propositions are, however, based on the study of a particular kind of coalition in one particular process. In fact, Underdal himself reserves his conclusions for coalitions that (a) adhere to the principle of agreement, (b) are faced with some internal conflict, and (c) have a broad scope and a high value to their members. Obviously there are other kinds of coalitions, so caution should be used in generalizing his observations.

Finally, we have attempted, in this chapter, to review the current knowledge on the consequences of the number of parties for negotiation processes and outcomes. As was indicated by the preceding discussion, however, there are several areas yet to be explored and a number of propositions that should be subjected to further empirical investigation. Some of these topics include calculations of bargaining strength, rules and norms in large conferences, and the problem of collective action through negotiation. Other topics are suggested in the concluding section of this volume.

NOTES

1. As used in this chapter, the term "bargaining" corresponds to Walton and McKersie's (1965: 13) "distributive bargaining"—i.e., the process by which each party attempts to maximize his own payoff in relation to that of his opponent(s). The term "cooperative negotiations" includes what Walton and McKersie (and also the Pruitt and Lewis chapter) refer to as "integrative bargaining" and also negotiations that concern the distribution of fixed-sum payoffs, but still take on the character of a largely cooperative effort at achieving a solution that is "fair."

2. Some implications of adopting this criterion should be spelled out. First, we may note that if concessions can be measured in objective terms, like amounts of money, utility may decrease in different ways as the concessions increase. There may be a uniform utility loss for each unit of concession, or the utility loss curve may be particularly steep in the beginning or toward the end.

The probability that a party will have to make a concession at the outset will be higher if its initial utility loss per unit of concession is relatively low than if it is relatively high. This means that, if the total amount of concessions required is rather modest, the probability that a party will have to make *some* concession will be higher in the former case than in the latter.

REFERENCES

AXELROD, R. (1970) Conflict of Interest. Chicago: Markham.

BERELSON, B. and G. A. STEINER (1964) Human Behavior. New York: Harcourt, Brace & World.

CLAUDE, I. (1967) The Changing United Nations. New York: Random House.

DE SWAAN, A. (1973) Coalition Theories and Cabinet Formations. Amsterdam: Elsevier.

DRUCKMAN, D. (1973) "Human factors in international negotiations: Social-psychological aspects of international conflict." Sage Professional Paper in International Studies, 02-020, Beverly Hills: Sage Publications.

GAMSON, W. A. (1961) "A theory of coalition formation." Amer. Soc. Rev. 26: 373-382.

HAMBURGER, H., M. GUYER, and J. FOX (1975) "Group size and cooperation." J. of Conflict Resolution 19: 503-531.

HARSANYI, J. (1956) "Approaches to the bargaining problem before and after the theory of games: A critical discussion of Zeuthen's, Hick's, and Nash's theories." Econometrica 24: 144-157.

IKLÉ, F. C. (1964) How Nations Negotiate. New York: Harper & Row.

KAUFMANN, J. (1968) Conference Diplomacy. Leyden: Sijthoff.

LUCE, R. D. and H. RAIFFA (1958) Games and Decisions: Introduction and Critical Survey. New York: John Wiley.

MIDGAARD, K. (1974) "Cooperative negotiations, and bargaining: Some notes on power and powerlessness." Unpublished manuscript, Oslo.

MIDGAARD, K. and P. OVERREIN (1970) "Spillet om hvalen i Antarktis." Unpublished manuscript, Oslo Institute of Political Science.

NASH, J. (1950) "The bargaining problem." Econometrica 18: 155-162.

OLSON, M., Jr. (1968) The Logic of Collective Action. New York: Schocken.

RIKER, W. H. (1962) The Theory of Political Coalitions. New Haven: Yale Univ. Press.

SCHELLING, T. C. (1960) The Strategy of Conflict. Cambridge, Mass.: Harvard Univ. Press.

STENELO, L. G. (1972) Mediation in International Negotiations. Lund: Studentlitteratur.

THOMAS, E. J. and C. F. FINK (1963) "Effects of group size." Psych. Bull. 60: 371-384.

TRAAVIK, K. (1973) "Et nytt territorium apnes." Unpublished cand. polit.-thesis, Oslo Institute of Political Science.

UNDERDAL, A. (1973) "Multinational negotiation parties: The case of the European Community." Cooperation and Conflict 8: 173-182.

VINACKE, W. E. (1971) "Negotiations and decisions in a political game," in B. Lieberman (ed.) Social Choice. New York: Gordon & Breach.

WALTON, R. E. and R. B. McKERSIE (1965) A Behavioral Theory of Labor Negotiations. New York: McGraw-Hill.

Chapter 12

COMPLEXITY IN INTERNATIONAL NEGOTIATION

GILBERT R. WINHAM

Centre for Foreign Policy Studies
Dalhousie University

Sometime between the great world wars, a Whitehall civil servant took to admonishing visitors with a few words framed on the wall behind his desk; they said: "If you know what you think, you don't understand the problem." The name and exact vintage of this professional skeptic are not reliably recorded, but one doubts that he and his contemporaries grappled with problems as labyrinthine, or as treacherous, or as rich in paradox, contradiction, and abstraction as those covered by SALT, the Strategic Arms Limitation Talks. If the term itself is by now among the world's best-known acronyms, its substance is available only to initiates—to the assorted bureaucrats and scientists who are professionally involved. And many of them are confused; their thinking shifts and oscillates, because the analysis flowing from SALT mocks, if it doesn't overwhelm, tidy, clear-cut points of view [Newhouse, 1973: 1].

Modern international negotiation is an exercise in complexity. It is theoretically possible that the issues being negotiated can be narrowed to clear-cut alternatives, but this is usually not the case. The frequency of multilateral international negotiations is rising, which in turn increases the size of the issues and the number of viewpoints that must be accommodated in the negotiating process. The issues brought to negotiations are complex in themselves, and important aspects of them may be little understood because information is inadequate and the cost of improving it is high. Some issues are complex because they are unknowable—for example, the relationship between numbers of nuclear missiles and national security. The content of international negotiations reflects the content of international transactions,

AUTHOR'S NOTE: The author is grateful for research support from the Canada Council, and for the time spent and the insights provided by the persons interviewed in connection with this project. The author also thanks Mr. S. Bruce Wilson, office of the Special Representative for Trade Negotiations, who read and commented on this paper.

and these transactions are becoming increasingly complex. Recent negotiations have handled such problems as conventional and nuclear weapons, multilateral trade and payments, human population, environment, and food. In each of these issue areas, complexity is created by the interrelatedness of major variables, by technologies associated with the issue area, and by inherent uncertainties of the issue area. Negotiators in these issue areas must contend with complexity, and this affects the style and content of their negotiating behavior.

Modern negotiations relate increasingly to a man-made technological infrastructure. This infrastructure is characterized by a growth of international relations and by a corresponding growth in demands for further interaction (Scott, 1974). In this context, negotiations are an attempt to manage and to maintain control over an increasingly complex system. Similar problems of management and control have been examined by students of organizational decision-making (March and Simon, 1958; Cyert and March, 1963). Their findings indicate that decision-making processes in complex situations differ from those in situations where alternatives are clear-cut and priorities are easily ordered. These decision-making studies underscore the importance of studying complexity in international negotiation, and they provide useful analogies for addressing the problem.

The research methodology used in this study has been to compare findings from field research in an actual negotiation with findings obtained through simulations of that same negotiation. This procedure has some advantages for the study of complexity and avoids the difficulties that arise when either methodology is used alone. One problem with field research is that it is difficult to reconstruct enough detail about the negotiation process to appreciate the impact of complexity on a negotiator's decision. This problem can be alleviated through simulation, which permits direct observation of a representative process. However, simulating a large negotiation is a ponderous task. Complexity must be retained in the model, but the time and effort involved in running the simulation make frequent repetitions of the experiment difficult. As a result, the findings from simulation research are not amenable to the usual statistical testing, but rather have been confirmed through comparisons with the actual negotiation.[1]

The negotiation selected for this study was the Kennedy Round of trade negotiations (Winham, 1973). Conducted among eighty-two nations over the period 1963-1967, these negotiations resulted in a multilateral agreement to make the most significant and widespread tariff reductions since the formation of the GATT. The subject of the negotiation was objectively complex, for it involved multilateral trade in thousands of products (many of which defy standardized description), as well as trade restrictions of many varieties. The objective complexity of the material can be seen in the five-volume report by the GATT Secretariat on the outcome of the negotiation. The negotiation was also subjectively complex; that is, it was felt to be complex by the major participants. In unstructured interviews, participants (negotiators and GATT officials) freely admitted that the material was beyond mastery and indicated that major efforts were made to gather, maintain, and process the information needed to make intelligent strategic decisions.

The simulation, which replicated the Kennedy Round, consisted of four fictitious nations—each having an economy, an international trade position, and a tariff schedule (Winham et al., 1973). Two negotiators and one minister (internal decision maker, IDM) represented each nation. Each negotiating team operated on the basis of public information about its nation's position and on private instructions provided by the IDM. The simulation was scheduled to run for one week, with five four-hour negotiating sessions. The simulation was run twice for pretesting and twice for data collection, with graduate students as subjects in each run. More recently, an abbreviated three-session version of the simulation has been used for training government officers. The abbreviated session has been run twice in training courses on negotiation of the Department of External Affairs, Ottawa, and three times at the Department of State, Washington, D.C.

The complexity of the real situation was replicated in the simulation in two ways. First, the scenario replicated the data mass of the Kennedy Round by providing a large amount of data relative to the time available for negotiation. Specifically, the scenario provided for 215 products which were traded among the four nations. Assuming that nations table demands and offers on each product, and assuming that tariff reductions range in integers from nil to 50 percent, the theoretical number of decisions that each nation must handle at any one point during the negotiation can be calculated as follows: demands, 215 x 51 x 3 nations = 32,895; offers, 215 x 51 = 10,965; total, 43,860. Of course, in practice the problem is simpler. Products are grouped and negotiated by sectors (save for exceptions), and negotiators by agreement concentrate on one area at a time to the exclusion of others. However, the simulation clearly provided scope for studying complexity. By a perverse Peter's Law, if things *can* get complicated, they *will* get complicated; and subjects in the simulation uniformly commented on the problems of keeping track of their own and the other nations' positions.

Second, the scenario replicated the economic uncertainties of the Kennedy Round. Economists are generally in agreement that there is no satisfactory way to measure the effects on trade of tariff reductions (Curzon, 1965). Several means have been devised for assessing the value of tariff agreements, but these often produce inconsistent results in the real world, and in any case their relationship to trade effects is unclear (Preeg, 1970). The simulation incorporated two measures that are commonly used in trade negotiations, and, as was expected, these measures produced inconsistent results when used on simulation data. This introduced the problem of not having any firm guidelines with which to evaluate agreements and left subjects in the difficult position of having to negotiate over the measures to be used as well as over the tariff reductions themselves. Furthermore, the problem was compounded by the fact that the simulation provided for two large nations and two small nations. As in the real world, the simulation subjects faced the argument that equality pertains only among equals, and thus they were forced to consider the problem of distributing benefits among units of different size, regardless of the methods used for calculating those benefits.

THE NATURE OF THE PROBLEM

Complexity is a common problem in human affairs and warrants at the outset a definition. Essentially, "complexity" means "complication"; it presents a challenge to comprehension because, in Simon's words, it consists of "a large number of parts that interact in a nonsimple way" (Simon, 1969: 86). This definition will become more elaborate for use in analyzing international negotiation, but the essence remains the problem of complication. In international negotiation, as in life generally, complication inhibits the prospects for rational choice and value maximization. As Newhouse observed about the Strategic Arms Limitation Talks, "SALT mocks, if it doesn't overwhelm, tidy, clear-cut points of view."

Complexity in international negotiation can result from various factors. The most obvious is the size of the negotiation or the variety in the decision-making environment that is faced by the negotiators. International negotiations become complex when there are a lot of "things" to be kept in mind, either issues being debated or positions taken by different parties, or implications that the negotiation might have for the external environment. Complexity is created also under conditions of uncertainty, when information needed for decision-making is difficult or costly to obtain or is simply unavailable. Both these factors challenge the negotiator's comprehension, but the mechanism is different in each case. Size or variety creates problems of processing and is best understood in the sense of information overload. Uncertainty creates problems of the discovery or generation of information and is best understood in terms of learning behavior. These two factors can be incorporated into a working definition of complexity: For example, a negotiation approaches complexity when

(a) the size of the negotiation situation (i.e., environmental variety) is such that the relevant information cannot easily be memorized, and

(b) there is uncertainty in the information available to the negotiators.

This definition is intended to be suggestive and not necessarily precise simply because it is difficult and probably pointless to establish binary categories of "simple" and "complex" negotiations. Complexity is a matter of degree, and the definition adequately isolates those variables that begin to differentiate simple from complex situations in international negotiation.

Many writers suggest that complexity is a factor in negotiation. Observers of contemporary negotiations regularly note the presence of complexity and allude to its effect on the negotiation process. Newhouse, quoted above, finds that the subject matter of SALT produces "confusion"; Bellany (1973: 658) notes that assessments in conventional force-reduction negotiations are necessarily tentative, given "the recognized difficulty of understanding the nature of conventional (especially) military power, particularly as it relates to the numbers and kinds of troops and equipment making up standing forces." In economic matters, complexity has been noted in the Kennedy Round of tariff negotiations (Preeg, 1970: 66). Similarly, Zartman (1971: 56) commented on the complexity of issues in the economic negotiations between African nations and the EEC and observed that: "The complexity of issues . . . delayed agreement until late in the game as members held out on one point in the hope of gaining a final agreement on another." The author notes in this case that complexity was manipulated as a bargaining advantage by one party over the other.

Theoreticians of negotiation have also commented on complexity, and the main theme running through these comments is that complexity affects a negotiator's perception of the situation and thus presumably affects expectations and negotiating behavior as well. Druckman (1973: 53) has noted that complexity affects the capacity of a negotiator to learn an opponent's strategy in a laboratory setting, and that this problem may be further enhanced in international negotiations, where issues are more complex yet. Iklé and Leites (1962: 22) observe that complexity reduces the tendency of negotiators to estimate a bargaining range, which probably has the effect of producing less continuity between the positions of the negotiating partners. Research on labor negotiations suggests that complexity of the decision situation increases the ambiguity of information available to negotiators and makes the information subject to more varying interpretations (Walton and McKersie, 1965: 295-296). A reasonable conclusion from the practical and theoretical literature is that complexity is widely regarded as an important factor in understanding negotiating behavior, and that its importance is increased as one moves from theoretical or experimental conceptions of the negotiating process to practical negotiating situations in international politics. Yet little work has been devoted to this phenomenon in studies of negotiation, even though complexity has been a major focus in studies of the decision-making process.

At this point, the student of negotiation can profit from theories about the decision-making process in government and other large organizations. In essence, decision-making and negotiation are analogous activities, for they both involve choice behavior in the pursuit of certain goals or values.[2] Normally, one assumes that the choice behavior in both instances is rational, that is, that it is preceded by some attempt to order the values that are sought and to assess which choices will maximize the most important values. Current decision theory has sharply challenged the assumption of rational choice behavior (e.g., Braybrooke and Lindblom, 1963) and has substituted various other models to explain how political decisions actually are made. Interestingly, these alternative models are most plausible when decisions are being analyzed under complexity.

A recent contribution to decision theory (Steinbruner, 1974) suggests that the main preoccupation of decision-making in complexity is uncertainty control. The decision unit achieves uncertainty control by adjusting to the environment, either by decomposing a complex environment into simpler sub-systems (Simon, 1969) or by creating hierarchy in the decision process, which matches variety in the environment with variety in the decision unit (Ashby, 1956). The evolution of assembly lines and bureaucracies is a common manifestation of the process of uncertainty control. In complex environments, decision makers usually focus on processes and not on end-states, and they break down decision-making into a sequence of well-understood operations. Decision-making consists of monitoring a few crucial feedback variables to keep them within tolerable ranges, but beyond this, the decision maker generally ignores the complexity in the environment. The perspective of the decision unit is thus "bounded" (March and Simon, 1958); it learns instrumentally and proceeds incrementally (Lindblom, 1965), and it adapts to the environment by gradually adjusting the operations that are included in the decision process.

The theory of decision behavior in complexity provides a new approach for analyzing multinational negotiations, such as the Kennedy Round. Superficially, the activity of large negotiations is similar to decision-making in large organizations, particularly since it is a bureaucratized activity (e.g., negotiation by "working groups") and deals with a subject matter that has been decomposed into compatible subgroups (e.g., "product sectors" in trade negotiations). On further analysis, the rationale of large negotiations can be seen as similar to the rationale behind large-scale organizations. Modern negotiations, especially multilateral negotiations, usually do not develop for the purpose of resolving specific points of dispute between the parties. Rather, they occur out of an attempt by parties to manage some aspect of their environment. The impetus for international negotiations like the Kennedy Round is the same as the impetus behind the growth of bureaucracy within nation-states; and the reason why this impetus does not take the same form at the international level is that there is usually insufficient cooperation among nations to permit an administrative/bureaucratic solution to problems. An essential purpose of the Kennedy Round and other GATT tariff negotiations was uncertainty control; that is, to secure a regulated level of tariff support that would preclude the destabilizing forces of competitive protectionism. Once tariffs are regulated by international agreement, the nations participating in these agreements are locked into a pattern of mutual obligation. Observance of these obligations effectively reduces unilateral action and, hence, reduces the uncertainty in tariff levels with which exporting nations must contend.

The principal behavior in large-scale negotiation is a process of adapting to the complex environment created by the demands and offers of other nations. Large-scale negotiations like the Kennedy Round evolve over considerable time. Negotiators proceed toward agreement by first tabling a position that is exploratory at best. At this stage, negotiating teams rarely have much of an idea what a final acceptable agreement might look like, for two reasons. The first is lack of attention by governments; often there is serious thought about what is acceptable only after earnest negotiation has begun. The second reason is that what is acceptable is a function of what is available, and this is demonstrated only in the act of negotiating. The result is that negotiators proceed with more understanding of and attention to the process of negotiation than where this process will lead. The process is a programmed set of operations that has evolved out of considerable experience. It consists of tabling a position, decomposing and aggregating the relevant information wherever possible, and then setting about, point by point, to reconcile the different positions of the parties. Negotiators explore incrementally the interface between the bargaining positions of nations much as army ants explore the interface of their colony and the environment.

Over time, the negotiation accumulates a settlement from the bottom up—a process the participants refer to as "building a package." In this process, negotiators monitor certain feedback variables, such as domestic support for the negotiation, which indicate the willingness of their government and others to cooperate in a negotiated settlement. Inherent in the programmed nature of the negotiation is the risk that negotiating procedures will not be sufficiently flexible to take advantage of unusual or unorthodox opportunities. This occurred in the Kennedy Round when agricultural products were not included in the general agreement. Agricultural restrictions are generally not amenable to the same negotiating procedures as industrial tariffs; and, in the opinion of several interviewees, opportunities to liberalize agricultural trade were missed because this area was outside the "ground rules" of the negotiation.

HYPOTHESES AND FINDINGS

Complexity influences the negotiation process in a number of ways, but no attempt will be made here to analyze exhaustively the effects of this variable. Rather, the effects of complexity on three important areas of bargaining behavior will be explored. First, it is hypothesized that complexity encourages negotiators to develop simplified and sometimes unrealistic cognitive structures that facilitate bargaining and decision-making. Second, complexity affects the importance of concessions and concession strategy in negotiation. Third, complexity can affect the outcome of negotiation—specifically, the probability that the negotiation will end in a settlement or agreement.

Structuring

Complexity, by definition, entails a limited comprehension of one's environment. One might therefore expect complexity to create paralysis in decision-making, but this is usually not the case in international negotiation. Negotiators generally manage to cope with complexity; and if they fail to reach a settlement, incapacity to take action in a complex situation is usually not the reason for the failure. One reason why negotiators retain a capacity for action is that the human mind acts as a mechanism for resolving complexity by imposing structure on otherwise ambiguous information (Steinbruner, 1974). Much of this structuring is done without conscious thought and is independent of the information-processing or choice behavior we associate with decision-making. This structuring is supported by mechanisms that maintain simplicity and consistency in the information perceived by decision makers (Deutsch and Merritt, 1966). The implication of this argument is that the mind is not necessarily a rational information processor, but rather operates to impose structure on information that is beyond the rational capabilities of decision makers.

An interesting example of cognitive structuring is that which occurs in trade negotiations. At the most basic level, the Kennedy Round, like other trade negotiations, was set up on the basis of a bargained exchange of benefits. Economists have noted that this may not be the most rational way to handle tariff reductions since "concessions" (i.e., tariff reductions) are often more beneficial to the nation making the reduction than to the other parties. However, the concept of bargained exchange is the basic structure of trade talks, and thus these talks are consistent with concepts of exchange in liberal economic theory as well as historical practices related to diplomatic bargaining. The notion of exchange suggests a quid pro quo, leading in turn to a concern for *reciprocity*. Reciprocity is a central structuring concept in trade negotiation in that no negotiator will accept an agreement unless he can defend it as "reciprocal." There is no common definition of reciprocity beyond some simple idea of "fair exchange"; nor are there exact procedures available for measuring reciprocity. Essentially, the meaning of reciprocity is left to each negotiator to determine, applying his own system for assessing the results of the bargaining.

Despite its flexibility and obvious imprecision, reciprocity serves to channel behavior and communication in trade negotiations. By invoking reciprocity, negotiators implicitly conceptualize the interaction in terms of a single value, and they ignore other values that might confound the bargaining process.[3] Negotiators focus on a concept that provides a simple and consistent rationale for what they are doing, and they subjectively manipulate the information at the negotiation into their assessments of reciprocity. This procedure, which was developed in trade negotiations, has analogies in other kinds of negotiations. For example, in the naval arms-control negotiations of the 1920s and 1930s, negotiators defined the problem as one of achieving "parity" between naval powers. Like reciprocity, parity defined the process without providing precise criteria for evaluating its results. Likewise, negotiation based on the principle of parity may not have been the most rational way to approach strategic arms control between the parties. As Bull (1973: 42) has noted, "It seems doubtful whether 'parity,' expressed as equal numbers or tonnages of ships, bore any relationship to the actual strategic needs of either Britain or the United States."

The concept of reciprocity helps establish communication between the parties. Negotiators know roughly how others will evaluate their proposals, which establishes a common language and is a crucial preliminary step in bringing about convergence on issues of substance. This point has been emphasized by Evans (1971: 23), who states: "When a negotiator invokes his right to reciprocity, he is speaking a language that both he and his fellow bargainers understand." In tariff negotiation, the notion of a bargaining language can actually be carried considerably beyond the simple invoking of ideas of reciprocity. Tariff reductions are a quantitative problem, and thus reciprocity can be a more useful notion if there is some procedure for deriving a quantitative assessment of tariff reductions. Tariff reductions cannot be measured precisely, as is well known, but this has not prevented the development of simple indices for quantitatively assessing prospective concessions. One such measure is an average depth of cut (weighted by import values), which has been described as "a practical approximation of reciprocity" (Preeg, 1970: 132). Another index, defined as a "50 percent equivalent" (Preeg, 1970: 132), relates import values and tariff cuts on single products and is applicable in areas where nations follow a piecemeal rather than an across-the-board approach. Use of these indices established a peculiar sort of bargaining language between negotiators. In economic terms, however, they were little more than fiction; as one interviewee put it, "People used calculations of reciprocity even though they understood it made no sense." Nevertheless, these indices were used because they provided a structure for communication and decision-making. They were a mechanism for simplifying information—even to the point of inaccuracy—by which negotiators ignored the variety inherent in the problem of comparing tariff reductions.

The findings from the simulation experiments confirmed the observation that negotiators tend to make simple measurements in order to negotiate over complex data. Both the weighted average depth of cut and the 50-percent equivalent measures were available to simulation participants. Both measures are conceptually simple and use the same variables—(i.e., percentage tariff cut and volume of imports), but they differ somewhat in application. The former is inherently an aggregative measure that is used after a number of tariff reductions have been made; the latter can be applied to each tariff reduction, but then the results of separate transactions can be added to compile an aggregate assessment. In practice, the latter method was used extensively by simulation participants, whereas the former measurement was used much less often, even in some cases after the relevant calculations had been made by the mediator (thus saving participants the time and effort involved in calculation). The concentration on 50-percent equivalents did not represent rational bargaining behavior in many cases. All participants were aware the two measures did not produce consistent results, and, hence, one would have expected them to make use of whichever calculations gave them a bargaining advantage. However, the 50 percent equivalent measure was easier to calculate in practice, and it produced units (i.e., "equivalents") that were readily understandable and that could be summed up in terms of debits and credits as the negotiation proceeded. Thus, concentration on this measure created a simple structure for the bargaining process, even at the cost of realism judged in terms of the information available in the simulation. Behavior in the simulation, as in the Kennedy Round, supported the contention that negotiators restrict the information they deal with in order to permit action in complex situations.

Concessions

Concession strategy is an area of negotiation that is affected by complexity. Concession-making is regarded as important in the literature because concessions presumably move a negotiation toward agreement, and yet there is usually a cost associated with making a concession. This creates a tradeoff situation in which a choice is required, which clearly involves ideas of rational or analytic decision-making behavior. The opportunity to make concessions arises often in any negotiation. Hence, the problem of what strategy to apply in concession-making is one that arises for negotiators and researchers alike.

Researchers are divided as to which concession strategy produces the most satisfactory payoff for the concession giver. Siegel and Fouraker (1960) have argued that concessions raise an adversary's level of aspiration, making it more difficult to reach an agreement that is advantageous to the concession maker. The conclusion from this research is that a "tough" policy is desirable and that concessions should be given only when the opponent is unyielding. Osgood (1959) has taken the opposite position, suggesting that concessions dispel distrust in negotiation and thus remove the main obstacle to concessions by one's opponent. This research supports a "soft" policy and suggests that it is advantageous for parties to initiate unilateral concessions. Both positions have found support in subsequent research (Hamner, 1974; see also the Hamner and Yukl chapter in this volume).

Because of its seeming importance—indeed, one can almost define negotiation as a process of exchanging concessions—concession behavior in the Kennedy Round was examined. Interviews with negotiators did not shed much light on the hypotheses advanced by Osgood or Siegel and Fouraker. Interviewees frequently volunteered some variation on the theme that it is necessary to give a concession in order to get a concession (i.e., to reciprocate concessions), but beyond this, few had a reasoned argument for supporting either a "tough" or a "soft" strategy. Indeed, it appeared that the negotiators had given relatively little thought to concessions, certainly in comparison to other problems, such as organizational phenomena or the manner of presenting their position. This raised the question whether concession-making was one of the "key problems" (Hamner, 1974) in a negotiation situation. Some of the apparent differences between the findings in previous literature and the Kennedy Round findings may be due to research methodology. Most of the literature on concession behavior is experimental. This method allows the researcher and subject alike to concentrate on concession-making behavior apart from other phenomena that clutter a negotiation, and it permits a number of concessionary moves between subjects to be observed rather than basing conclusions on one or two concession attempts. In the Kennedy Round, however, concessions occurred less frequently, and they often were buried in a mass of other details. Nevertheless, it is still possible they were of crucial importance, even though they may have appeared to be less than a key problem to the negotiators.

A second research strategy was used in examining concession-making in the Kennedy Round. The action in a negotiation is usually discontinuous, and convergence of the parties' positions often occurs in spasms, or "breakthroughs." It is reasonable to expect that these breakthroughs are occasioned by concessions made by one or more of the parties. It seemed possible that by interviewing various negotiators about a specific breakthrough, one might gain insight into the concession strategies used when different negotiators interacted in the same situation.

The situation chosen was a decision to continue negotiating which broke a deadlock in the crucial chemical sector that had developed between the United States and the EEC on Monday, May 8, 1967 (Preeg, 1970: 192). The interviews produced varying results. On the one hand, nothing gleaned from interviews suggested that negotiators consciously pursued a concession strategy in connection with the incident. Of course, this finding may be due to the negotiators' unwillingness to reveal or inability to remember the details related to any such strategy. Hence, these results were considered inconclusive, even though they were consistent with simulation results.[4] On the other hand, the negotiators seemed uncertain about details of the breakthrough that one would have expected some agreement on. For instance, there seemed to be substantial differences among interviewees about the timing of the breakthrough, about whether positions had indeed changed in substance, and about whether there had been any effective mediational efforts by GATT officials or third parties. In short, it was difficult to reconstruct the situation with any confidence. Each participant or observer seemed to have an idiosyncratic and subjective perception of the incident after the fact. This finding seems significant for concession strategy, for if individual perceptions were equally subjective at the time of the incident, it places in doubt the notion of clear alternatives and analytical choice behavior that is implied in concession strategy.

The problem of concession-making was explored more systematically in the simulations. Negotiation in the simulations took place in a series of meetings—multilateral and bilateral—that occurred on the initiative of the participants. There were twelve multilateral and nineteen bilateral meetings in the first data run, and thirteen multilateral and twenty-eight bilateral meetings in the second run. Questionnaires were administered to the participants of each meeting when it ended. Included were the following questions designed to assess the importance of concession behavior for reaching agreement:

> [In terms of this meeting only] "What was the most important concession you gave—either demands dropped or offers increased—and to which nation was it given?"
> "What was the most important concession given to you . . . and from which nation?"

These questions provide a test for congruence of perception in concession-making. The test assumes that if Participant A indicates that he has made a concession to Participant B, one can check and find out whether B felt he had received a concession and, if so, whether it was roughly the same concession indicated by A. The questions were coded for *agreement* (i.e., respondent agrees with at least one representative of named nation as to the nature of the concession) or *no agreement*. The results (see Table 12.1) showed that more than half the time participants either failed to agree on the nature of concessions or failed to perceive when concessions were made to them. Certainly there did not seem to be much convergence on the matter of

TABLE 12.1
Agreement With One Representative of Named
Nation on Concessions Given/Received[a]

	Data Run 1		
	Agree	*Not Agree*	
Concession given	45%	55%	= 100% (N = 83)
Concession received	57%	43%	= 100% (N = 88)
	Data Run 2		
	Agree	*Not Agree*	
Concession given	47%	53%	= 100% (N = 122)
Concession received	43%	57%	= 100% (N = 123)

[a]Difference in frequency between runs due to fewer concessionary moves in Run 1.

evaluating concessions or even recognizing them when given. In order to provide a more rigorous test, a separation was made between bilateral and multilateral meetings. Presumably, with three or four nations there might be some difficulty in keeping track of concessions given and received in a busy meeting. This should not be the case with bilateral meetings, however, which often were brief and designed to resolve one or two points which arose during the course of a multilateral session. Results indicated that congruence was higher in the bilateral meetings (see Table 12.2), but not much higher. Bilateral meetings produced congruent perceptions in participants slightly more than half the time on the average, and this occurred using a minimal definition of congruence (i.e., agreement with only one person from named nation).

The conclusion seems to be that, in a complex negotiation, concessions lose much of the meaning usually attributed to them. If parties cannot agree on concessions or are sometimes unaware that they have received them, then theories other than those based on a concept of bargained exchange may be needed in order to understand the role of concessions in complex negotiations.

Here the notion of cybernetics (Steinbruner, 1974) is attractive. Cybernetic theory suggests that in complex situations decision makers will monitor a few key variables, will attempt to control uncertainty, and will screen out much of the information flow around them. In comparison with other issues, concessions may be of small concern to negotiators and may be screened out much of the time. In fact, individual concessions are a fairly structured phenomenon: Either you win or you lose the point. There was less structural uncertainty associated with concessions than with other areas of concern to Kennedy Round negotiators, such as the constant risk that a delicate domestic consensus might come unhinged, or the organizational

TABLE 12.2
Meeting Type and Agreement on Concessions Given/Received

			DATA RUN 1		
Concession Given			**Concession Received**		
Meeting Type	*Agree*	*Not Agree*	*Meeting Type*	*Agree*	*Not Agree*
Multilateral	49%	61%	Multilateral	60%	53%
Bilateral	51%	39%	Bilateral	40%	47%
	100%	100%		100%	100%
	(N=37)	(N=46)		(N=50)	(N=38)
			DATA RUN 2		
Concession Given			**Concession Received**		
Meeting Type	*Agree*	*Not Agree*	*Meeting Type*	*Agree*	*Not Agree*
Multilateral	40%	60%	Multilateral	38%	61%
Bilateral	60%	40%	Bilateral	62%	39%
	100%	100%		100%	100%
	(N=57)	(N=65)		(N=53)	(N=70)

problem of keeping on top of a complex negotiating position (the phrase "figure out where we are" was frequently repeated by participants in simulations). Thus, negotiators in complex negotiations pay relatively little heed to individual concessions, but rather monitor them as a trend, noting in that trend a key variable of the "will to negotiate" as reflected in the behavior of other parties.

Concessions are unimportant individually, but they become important when one nation perceives in another's behavior, including its concession behavior, a backing away from the agreed principles of the negotiation. In this case, deadlocks develop, usually around some specific point at issue, but the argument covers a broader area than just the point in question. Deadlocks thus have different meanings for different parties, and in cases where they are resolved, it is through a process whereby parties convince each other of their continued will to negotiate. There may or may not have been concessions involved, as the term "concession" is usually understood.

Outcome

Complexity not only affects the way in which a negotiation is framed, and the way in which compromises are reached and concessions are exchanged, it also affects the process of concluding a negotiation. All negotiations end in decision-making, whether the decision is to conclude with a settlement or to break off without agreement. There is some evidence that complexity places special burdens on this kind of decision-making, although ironically there are some ways in which the negotiator's task is made easier as well.

The situation when complex negotiations like the Kennedy Round conclude is that many outstanding issues must be woven together into a package deal. This is necessarily the task of senior negotiators who work within guidelines set by their instructions and the advice of their delegation. Decision-making in the final stages is concerned with achieving a settlement that is acceptable to all parties; and technical notions of balance (such as 50-percent equivalents) that delegations may have previously relied on are less relevant. This creates a shifting situation and new uncertainties beyond those inherent in the data. Decision-making at this point is more a matter of educated political guesswork than a precise calculation of advantage. The cost of not reaching agreement is likely to be substantial, especially if considerable time and effort have been expended on the negotiation. The decision strategy that is most likely to emerge under such conditions is for negotiators to adopt a bias in favor of settlement because of the momentum built into the negotiation and the costs of not reaching agreement. At this point, complexity works in favor of reaching agreement because the inherent lack of precision in the material makes it difficult to argue effectively against an agreement.

The conclusion of a negotiation can be demonstrated from simulation data, even though the real situation cannot be observed. The following excerpt from a Department of External Affairs exercise illustrates the pressure that is exerted on negotiators to conclude a settlement, and it points out (perhaps in overstated terms) the uncertainty participants feel about the value of alternative proposals. The excerpt covers the conclusion of a bilateral settlement between the two large nations in the exercise; both negotiating teams at this point are operating in accordance with their instructions, although they are aware that their instructions and the amount they have conceded will be public knowledge at the end of the simulation.

Conclusion of Alba-Tristat bilateral meeting, approaching deadline.

Tristat (1):[5]   Wait, we just need one more minute.

Alba (1):   All right, you said 25 on steamboilers in return for accepting the 22, and all the other offers in the package stand.

Tristat (2):   Uh ... uh ... yes ... I just asked you that one question for now.

Alba (1):   Well, it's related, if you want to tie those two. . . .

Tristat (1):   Uh yes, everything else, uh . . . that's the only variable, that's the only change I'm making at the present time.

Alba (1):   If that's the only thing you ask for, other than the basic package we offer, if that's the only adjustment, without having had a chance to make our own calculation, we're risking losing our shirts and we'll take it.

Tristat (2):   O.K., Well one. . . .

Alba (1):   No!

Tristat (2):   One small annex to that. . . .

Alba (1):   No! You better be very careful . . . very careful.

Tristat (2):   One other small point, one small annex to the. . . .

Alba (2):   It better be very minor.

Tristat (2):   No, no, no! Wait just a minute! It won't cost you anything simply to help us out with Medatia on one small tariff item.

Alba (1):   What's that?

Tristat (2):   Change your . . . hanging paper . . . which is a minor item for you and which you were willing to change before anyways, and take on shoeboard.

Alba (1):   Um . . . you'll have to drop your 25 on the steamboilers for that, because that's going to complicate the negotiation. We've got 25 minutes! Umm . . . we will help you to get agreement with the others, in general . . . we won't change our exceptions!

Tristat (2):   Well is that 25 important to you?

Alba (1):	Yes.
Tristat (2):	This is worth 100 points.
Alba (2):	Listen, that 25. . . .
Tristat (2):	That 25 . . . that 25. . . .
Alba (3):	We had to go . . . we had to sacrifice some of our . . . our instructions, as a matter of fact.
Alba (1):	We will try. . . .
Tristat (3):	You're talking about 7 percent on trade of 460 (million)!
Alba (1):	We will try to get cooperation.
Tristat (1):	We need one more minute before we say yes or no.
Alba (1):	You can't . . . oh, hurry, O.K.?
Tristat (1):	O.K.
Alba (1):	We're going to go in [bilateral with Medatia] to start talking. Just come and say yes or no—if it's no, I think it's no agreement on the whole show.
Tristat (1):	O.K., yes.

[Alba delegation leaves room]

Tristat (1):	John, we've got to have a yes or no from you. You got the figures, gut feeling, anything you want.
Tristat (3):	I've got . . . uh . . . O.K., what was that last change?
Tristat (1):	They're going to give us 25 percent on steamboilers.
Tristat (3):	O.K. [pause] . Well, if you want a gut feeling . . . 25 percent on steamboilers . . . and they've demanded 15 on furnaces and turbines . . . we'll give them 10!
Tristat (1):	So you want to go back and negotiate on those other two?
Tristat (3):	Yup.
Tristat (1):	Well, we'll have to call them back in and negotiate again—they've gone into another meeting.
Tristat (3):	Well just drop. . . .
Tristat (1):	So you can't accept that?
Tristat (3):	Drop an offer on them . . . ahh, I don't have the faintest idea what I could accept . . . but I. . . .
Tristat (2):	No, no, we don't have time now.
Tristat (1):	Well, could we, now how important is it? How important is the 5 percent?
Tristat (3):	Umm [pause] . . . quite frankly, at this point I haven't got the vaguest idea. . . .
Tristat (1):	O.K., we accept the offer!
Tristat (3):	You want to accept it?

Tristat (1):   [Nods affirmatively]
Tristat (2):   It's more important I think at this point to reach
                 an agreement.

The simulation excerpt suggests that, under deadline pressure, complexity and especially uncertainty can improve the prospects for reaching agreement. The mechanism is as follows. As momentum builds in the search for an agreement, negotiators become increasingly preoccupied with the puzzle of fitting contending positions into a multilateral settlement. Reaching such a settlement is a challenge in itself. Negotiators tend to concentrate on those aspects that are relatively certain, such as the positions of nations, and to pay less attention to the aspects that are less understandable, such as the value of alternative proposals. The final choices in a large negotiation like the Kennedy Round are political, and this was made clear by Kennedy Round interviewees. If some aspects of the final settlement are "vague," which was a point admitted by interviewees and confirmed in the simulation, then it simply leaves negotiators a wider scope in defining for themselves the limits of an acceptable political settlement.

Can this reasonably be extended to the proposition that complexity generally facilitates agreement in negotiation? To carry the argument to this point requires the analysis to go beyond the immediate interaction between negotiating teams. Complexity is a variable that not only affects how negotiators interact, but also affects both the relationship of negotiators with the society they represent and the way those societies frame the issues that get negotiated. Analysis of these latter factors is admittedly speculative, but some progress must be made here to understand the general impact of complexity on negotiation.

It is generally agreed that complexity can strengthen the hand of a negotiator vis-à-vis the organization he represents. For example, Walton and McKersie (1965: 334) note: "The complexity of issues gives the union leadership tremendous control and flexibility." This point was confirmed by Kennedy Round interviewees, who indicated that the complexity of the trade agreements provided the flexibility needed to convince constituents that they had concluded a good deal. This was the case especially with U.S. negotiators, who were subject to close political surveillance by members of Congress and various concerned businessmen. To the extent that negotiators become personally committed to the success of a negotiation (interviewees generally admitted this) and are in a position to be caught up in the momentum of the process, one would expect that any factor that increased negotiators' competence would also increase the probability of reaching agreement. Hence, complexity increases the probability of agreement because it increases the authority of those who are likely to be disposed toward agreement.

The argument can be carried further, however. Complexity, and especially uncertainty, promote ideology in political decision-making (Downs, 1957). As complexity reduces the possibility that governments will comprehend the issues before a negotiation, it increases the probability that ideological positions will influence the attitude of governments toward the negotiation. Furthermore, complexity increases the probability that governments will become committed to simplified, overriding goals (Tee, 1975), which may sharply constrain negotiating flexibility. Hindsight would suggest that in the Kennedy Round ideology was a crucial variable in determining the outcome of negotiation. The Kennedy Round was conducted within the ideology of trade liberalism, and many negotiators and GATT officials were open advocates of this ideology. Certainly none was a committed protectionist. In the face of complexity, these negotiators generally made decisions in favor of negotiated agreement because agreement was a highly valued norm for most of the major governments participating in the Kennedy Round. Decision-making in uncertainty entailed some risks, but they were risks taken in the direction of the predominant ideology of the negotiation. Had that ideology changed substantially, the effect of complexity on outcome might have been different. Without a strong commitment to trade liberalism, it is possible that complexity might have fostered doubt and hesitancy, and led to a much less substantial settlement.

This argument puts negotiation in perspective within the international political process. The capacity for variables within the negotiation process to affect the course of agreements between nations is indeed limited. Broad concerns dictate what issues nations will negotiate and when they will reach agreements. The scope for negotiation to affect this process is small. However, in an age of increasing international transactions, the probability is that large-scale negotiation will be used with increasing frequency in international politics, and its purpose will be in part to manage the complexity of the international system. Such negotiations would probably be conducted in a favorable environment, which is normally a sine qua non for major multilateral negotiations. It seems likely then that complexity will facilitate and certainly not impede agreements in other negotiations in the future, just as it appears to have facilitated agreement in the Kennedy Round.

NOTES

1. Most laboratory models of the negotiation process are not useful for studying complexity because they are too simple and because it is assumed that the attention of both players is focused on the bargaining situation. However, in real-world negotiations, the situation is usually complex, and mutually focused attention itself seems to be in greatest doubt.

2. Negotiations necessitate choice behavior, and, hence, it is assumed they can be analyzed along lines similar to those used in analyzing decision-making. In pure form,

decision-making involves choices against the environment, while negotiation involves choices against an opponent and is accompanied by persuasion and haggling. In practical terms, negotiators make social decisions (or they force social decision-making on governments), and they are similar in their consequences to any other acts of government.

3. One example is the failure of EEC representatives to make much headway with the notion of "tariff harmonization"—a concept that the EEC has successfully applied to its internal tariff reductions. Tariff harmonization was not consistent with the practice of reciprocal exchange as the latter has developed in GATT negotiations, and would have required greater restructuring of the negotiating process than was acceptable to other nations.

4. A similar specific example of deadlock and breakthrough was analyzed during one simulation. In this case, the author had the advantage of direct observation of the behavior. Subsequent interviews with the principals indicated that they had framed the confrontation in very different terms, which were not sufficiently overlapping or continuous for them to have applied a concession strategy. In fact, the interview accounts did not seem to describe the same situation, and it would have been impossible to reconstruct the essentials of the original confrontation (which was tape recorded) from the interviews. It did not appear the principals had thought much about a concession strategy, beyond believing they had given "too much" and that it was about time they "got something."

5. Numbers denote the seniority of the negotiator—three negotiators for each nation. Participants in this simulation were junior-to-middle-rank FSOs and had had between one and three field postings. Several had had prior negotiating experience.

REFERENCES

ASHBY, W. R. (1956) An Introduction to Cybernetics. London: Chapman & Hall.

BRAYBROOKE, D. and C. E. LINDBLOM (1963) A Strategy of Decision: Policy Evaluation as a Social Process. New York: Free Press.

BELLANY, I. (1973) "The problems of balancing reduction in conventional forces." J. of Conflict Resolution 17: 657-671.

BULL, H. (1973) "Strategic arms limitation: The precedent of the Washington and London Naval Treaties," in M. A. Kaplan (ed.) SALT: Problems and Prospects. Morristown, N.J.: General Learning Process.

CURZON, G. (1965) Multilateral Commercial Diplomacy. London: Michael Joseph.

CYERT, R. M. and J. G. MARCH (1963) A Behavioral Theory of the Firm. Englewood Cliffs, N.J.: Prentice-Hall.

DEUTSCH, K. W. and R. L. MERRITT (1966) "Effects of events on national and international images," in H. C. Kelman (ed.) International Behavior: A Social-Psychological Approach. New York: Holt, Rinehart & Winston.

DOWNS, A. (1957) An Economic Theory of Democracy. New York: Harper & Row.

DRUCKMAN, D. (1973) Human Factors in International Negotiations: Social-Psychological Aspects of International Conflict. Beverly Hills, Calif.: Sage Publications.

EVANS, J. W. (1971) The Kennedy Round in American Trade Policy: The Twilight of the GATT? Cambridge, Mass.: Harvard Univ. Press.

HAMNER, W. C. (1974) "Effects of bargaining strategy and pressure to reach agreement in a stalemated negotiation." J. of Personality and Social Psychology 30: 458-467.

IKLÉ, F. C. and N. LEITES (1962) "Political negotiation as a process of modifying utilities." J. of Conflict Resolution 6: 19-28.

LINDBLOM, C. E. (1965) The Intelligence of Democracy: Decision Making through Mutual Adjustment. New York: Free Press.

MARCH, J. G. and H. A. SIMON (1958) Organizations. New York: John Wiley.

NEWHOUSE, J. (1973) Cold Dawn: The Story of SALT. New York: Holt, Rinehart & Winston.

OSGOOD, C. E. (1959) "Suggestions for winning the real war with Communism." J. of Conflict Resolution 3: 295-325.

PREEG, E. H. (1970) Traders and Diplomats: An Analysis of the Kennedy Round of Negotiations under the General Agreement on Tariffs and Trade. Washington: Brookings Institution.

SCOTT, A. M. (1974) "The Global System and the Implications of Interactions." International Interactions 1: 229-36.

SIEGEL, S. and L. E. FOURAKER (1960) Bargaining and Group Decision Making: Experiments in Bilateral Monopoly. New York: McGraw-Hill.

SIMON, H. A. (1969) "The architecture of complexity," in H. A. Simon The Sciences of the Artificial. Cambridge, Mass.: MIT Press.

STEINBRUNER, J. D. (1974) The Cybernetic Theory of Decision: New Dimensions of Political Analysis. Princeton: Princeton Univ. Press.

TEE, J. (1975) "Yalta: A perspective on negotiations." Unpublished manuscript, McMaster University.

WALTON, R. E. and R. B. McKERSIE (1965) A Behavioral Theory of Labor Negotiation: An Analysis of a Social Interaction System. New York: McGraw-Hill.

WINHAM, G. R. (1973) "International trade negotiation." International Studies Newsletter A: 30-32.

———, G. R. BERRY, and D. MAGEE (1973) "Trade negotiation simulation." Unpublished manuscript, McMaster University.

ZARTMAN, I. W. (1971) The Politics of Trade Negotiations between Africa and the European Economic Community: The Weak Confront the Strong. Princeton: Princeton Univ. Press.

Chapter 13

MEDIATIONAL MECHANISMS IN INTERORGANIZATIONAL CONFLICT

LOUIS W. STERN

Northwestern University

RICHARD P. BAGOZZI

University of California at Berkeley
and
RUBY ROY DHOLAKIA

Indian Institute of Management (Calcutta)

This chapter examines the social-psychological processes (as well as the potential problems) associated with implementation of three distinct mediational mechanisms that have been suggested for use in managing, reducing, or resolving conflict in *inter*organizational relations. While numerous mechanisms have been suggested elsewhere as appropriate for application to interorganizational relations (Stern, 1971a), concentration here is on (1) exchange of persons, (2) superordinate goals, and (3) diplomacy.

Because the focus of this chapter is on mediational devices or strategies for managing *conflict* between organizations, attention is devoted first to developing a perspective of conflict in such a context. The discussion then turns briefly to an investigation of the structural preconditions that seem likely to foster the most effective use of the mechanisms. Next, each of the three mechanisms listed above is examined in turn, with attention being given to the probable consequences of its use, as well as to some important caveats with regard to meaningful implementation.

INTERORGANIZATIONAL CONFLICT

Conflict among commercial, social-welfare, or government organizations may be viewed as a form of opposition that is opponent-centered; based on incompatibility of the goals, aims, or values of opposing organizations; direct; and personal; and in which the opponent or opposing organization controls the goal or object desired by both parties (Stern, 1971b). Such conflict—behavior that frustrates, thwarts, injures, or destroys an opponent—is present in all socioeconomic systems.

Typically, conflict arises as a natural consequence of an organization's activities. As a social system, the organization moves toward greater differentiation and complexity in the division of its functions and task responsibilities (Durkheim, 1933). This internal diversity stimulates organizational innovation, which in turn increases the need for resources (Aiken and Hage, 1968). To obtain needed resources, the organization has to engage in exchange with other organizations, and the resulting web of interdependencies sets the stage for incompatibility of goals and for other causes of conflict.

For any given organization, conflict with other organizations may have ambivalent consequences. On the one hand, some degree of conflict may be highly functional for the long-term viability of the organization (Coser, 1956). Thus *inter*organizational conflict often serves as a motivational force stimulating *intra*organizational creativity and change. It may even lead to increased solidarity and cohesion within the organization and may also function as a mechanism for eliciting or altering norms relative to its interactions with other organizations.

On the other hand, at some point interorganizational conflict becomes dysfunctional and has a disequilibrating effect on the organization. When interdependent organizations perceive their relationships with others as thwarting expectations, they are pressured to reduce the discrepancy between role prescriptions and role behavior by modifying the conflict. Mediational mechanisms of all types are concerned primarily with limiting disequilibrating effects and with managing conflict so that the conflict process produces positive benefits within interorganizational systems.

The use of mediational mechanisms for managing conflict is constrained by three major variables that structure interorganizational relationships and affect the likelihood that such relationships will persist under conditions of strain and conflict. These variables are (1) dependency, (2) power, and (3) intensity.

Dependency

In a very general sense, "dependence" means that "two or more organizations must take each other into account if they are to accomplish their goals" (Litwak and Hylton, 1962: 401). According to Emerson (1962: 32), "The dependence of actor A upon actor B is (1) directly proportional to A's motivational investment in goals mediated by B, and (2) inversely proportional to the availability of the goals to A outside of the A-B relation." A positive relationship exists between dependence and conflict; it has been observed that the greater the level of dependence, the greater will be the opportunity for interfering with goal attainment (Schmidt and Kochan, 1972: 361-363), and, hence, the greater the potential for conflict between interdependent organizations. However, a relatively high level of mutually recognized interdependence is also necessary if the organizations are to seek to further the relationship and thus to invest in mediational mechanisms for the containment or management of conflict.

Power

Following Thibaut and Kelley (1959), power is the capability one organization has for affecting the outcome of another in a relationship. It is not a characteristic or attribute of an organization or person in the relationship. Rather, power is a property of the relation itself (Emerson, 1962). In particular, the power of A over B is the range of outcomes that A determines or influences for B.

As a characteristic of the relation between two organizations, power may occur in two generic states. A *symmetric power relation* occurs when each party controls a range of outcomes for the other of relatively equal strength.[1] In a practical sense, this occurs when both parties have essentially the same capability for affecting the outcomes of the other. A symmetric power relationship facilitates mediational mechanisms that involve bilateral involvement in their design and implementation. An *asymmetric power relationship* occurs when one of the parties can control a range of outcomes greater than that controlled by the other. Asymmetrical power relationships usually lead to unilateral attempts at changing conflictual relationships.

Intensity

The intensity of a relationship between two organizations represents the degree of involvement demanded of the parties (Marrett, 1971). Intensity expresses the energy level of a relationship and may be measured by (1) the size of the resource investment and (2) the frequency of interaction. Where the resource investment and/or the frequency of interaction is high, the intensity of a relationship has a positive effect on its persistence. Organizations in an intense relationship realize the ongoing contingencies that their actions will create for each other and, as a result, will strive to arrive at mutual solutions.

The levels of dependency, power, and intensity define the basic structure of an interorganizational relationship and determine the use of mediational mechanisms. For bilateral mechanisms, such as exchange-of-persons and superordinate goals, a strong level of mutual dependence, symmetric power, and a relatively intense relationship are required for their implementation. Under such conditions, the organizations are capable of making rewards, punishments, threats, offers, and counteroffers at comfortable levels. These factors motivate the parties to avoid unilateral attempts to influence one another in favor of cooperative activities that are aimed at achieving mutual outcomes. Typically, the orientation of organizations in such situations is one of collaboration (Thomas, 1976), negotiation, bargaining, or problem-solving (Walton and McKersie, 1965).

On the other hand, it is likely that the presence of each of these variables is relatively less significant when the use of diplomacy as a mediational mechanism is being considered. Diplomacy can even be used when the level of dependency is relatively low and unequal and when power is asymmetrical. By its very nature, diplomacy may be the product of a unilateral move. However, an intense relationship between the interacting parties is necessary; otherwise, the diplomats will lack the level of interaction necessary for developing an informational base. It is important to note, though, that in asymmetrical power relations, diplomacy may simply be the means by which influence messages are conveyed. In fact, in order for diplomacy to avoid being viewed as a short-run means of deception, it would probably function best in situations where there are mutual dependence and symmetric power relationships.

The mediational mechanisms discussed in this chapter set the stage for meaningful negotiations by fostering an atmosphere of trust and attraction between conflicting parties. As a result of adopting any of these mechanisms, organizations are likely to enter the negotiation process with greater understanding and empathy. For example, "diplomats" not only implement policies at the negotiating table, but also influence the perception of the other party and structure the conflict relationship by providing and interpreting information and by recommending policy alternatives before the actual negotiations ensue. Similarly, the acceptance of a superordinate goal tends to enhance the attractiveness of the relationship and facilitates negotiations on means-conflict. Exchange of persons requires that preliminary bargains be struck with regard to implementation. Thus, these mechanisms lay the groundwork for agreement on broader goals and specific means—the outcomes of successful negotiation processes.

EXCHANGE OF PERSONS

As a mediational mechanism for resolving conflict, an exchange-of-persons strategy entails a bilateral trade of personnel for a specified time period. In interorganizational relations, exchange of persons could take place on several different levels of an organization or on all levels. The technique involved in such programs is, in one sense, similar in logic to role reversal, a procedure where one (or each) of the participants in a discussion presents the viewpoint of the other (Muney and Deutsch, 1968).

The idea that conflict will dissipate merely as a function of the occurrence (or frequency) of interactions is an intuitively appealing one. Indeed, many have proposed such an approach as a means for reducing conflict in racial and ethnic relations (Allport, 1954), as well as in interorganizational and inter-group disputes (Nielsen, 1972). The assumption underlying this "contact" hypothesis is twofold. First, it is thought that intergroup contact will lead to the formation of positive intergroup attitudes, which, in turn, will produce a reduction in conflict and improved relations. Second, it is felt that the improved communication associated with an exchange of persons will result in more cooperation and greater joint outcomes for all parties involved. In general, research from the experimental game and bargaining literatures tends to support both conjectures (e.g., findings consistent with the first include Swingle, 1966; Morgan and Sawyer, 1967; and McClintock and McNeel, 1967, while those supporting the second include Deutsch, 1958; Cole, 1972; Druckman, 1968; Swingle and Santi, 1972; Voissem and Sistrunk, 1971; and Wichman, 1970, to name a few).

Despite the logic of the approach, however, there is evidence indicating that contact between warring groups may just as often lead to increased tension and negative attitudes and even produce an escalation in the conflict under certain conditions (e.g., Deutsch and Krauss, 1962; Hornstein, 1965). The important research question to address is what are the social-psychological processes underlying the contact between conflicting groups which may lead to a reduction or an increase in hostilities.

In his review of the literature dealing with intergroup conflict and the contact hypothesis, Amir (1969) concludes that the circumstances surround-ing the relations are crucial for determining the outcome of the contact. On the one hand, he found that contact leads to a reduction in negative attitudes when

(1) the contact occurs between group members of equal status,
(2) the members of a majority group interact with higher-status members of a minority group,
(3) an authority and/or the social climate are in favor of and promote the contact,
(4) the contact is of an intimate rather than a casual nature,
(5) the contact is pleasant and rewarding, or
(6) "the members of *both* groups in the particular contact situation interact in functionally important activities or develop common goals or superordinate goals that are higher ranking in importance than the individual goals of *each* of the groups" (Amir, 1969: 338).

On the other hand, he found that negative attitudes are reinforced when

(1) the contact situation produces competition between the groups,
(2) the contact is unpleasant, involuntary, or tension-laden,
(3) the prestige or status of one group is lowered as a result of the contact,
(4) members of a group or the group as a whole are in a state of frustration,
(5) the groups in contact have moral, ethnic, or other normative standards which are objectionable to each other, or
(6) in the case of contact between a majority and a minority group, the members of the minority group are of a lower status or are lower in relevant characteristics than are the members of the majority group (Amir, 1969).

As a mechanism for reducing conflict, the exchange-of-persons approach is conceptually similar to programs intended to improve contact between combative groups (Stern et al., 1975). By exchanging members, it is hoped that each will become familiar with the problems, procedures, and personnel of the opposite organization and that this will promote mutual understanding and favorable attitudes. Upon their return to their home organizations, it is anticipated that the members will better implement, or at least influence, policies and procedures that accord with—rather than conflict with—the opposing organization.

It is important to realize that the exchange-of-persons mechanism operates at two levels. First, at the interpersonal level, the exchange of persons affects the feelings of like or dislike, trust or distrust, or other personal aspects of the relationship. In this sense, it is the person-to-person orientations, understandings, and affect that come into play when contact and exchange occur. Second, the exchange of persons also influences the normative and role structures within and between the organizations. The social actors experiencing an exchange carry with them a set of official prescriptions of how they ought to behave and what is expected of them by both organizations. The exchange crystallizes any discrepancy or opposition between norms by forcing the actors to function within the conflicting normative environments. It is hoped that any confrontation in norms and expectations will induce discussion, debate, and adjustment both in personal orientations and in the norms themselves. Thus, the exchange-of-persons approach can be designed to influence the interorganizational relations associated with the boundary positions sanctioned by organizations, as well as with the interpersonal dimensions that are relatively independent of those "official" positions.

The underlying philosophy of the exchange-of-persons mechanism is to facilitate ·the interchange and adjustment of rights and responsibilities between two interdependent organizations by changing the character of the dyadic interactions between social actors, both across the organizations and within them. In particular, the goal is to transform an interaction from one that is characterized predominantly by unilateral influence to a fully integrated bilateral interaction, where both parties negotiate mutually beneficial outcomes. Using the scheme of Thomas (1976), the objective is to move from the competitive or accommodative orientations to one of collaboration. Or, in Walton and McKersie's (1965) terminology, the purpose is to shift from competitive or distributive orientations to mutual problem-solving. Overall, the aim is to facilitate the exchange of needs, preferences, and intentions and to stimulate cooperative actions on the part of both organizations.

Summary

The exchange-of-persons strategy for interorganizational conflict management is a mediational mechanism designed to facilitate the mutual communication of needs, preferences, and intentions by increasing the amount of meaningful contact between organizations through a bilateral trade of personnel for a specified time period. If successfully employed, the mechanism should stimulate cooperative actions on the part of organizations participating in such programs. Operating at the interpersonal level, exchanges can influence the normative and role structures within and between organizations. However, it is important to note that increased contact leads to improved relations only when the conditions for the contact are supportive. These include a number of interpersonal conditions, as well as the structural conditions of mutual dependence, equal power, and intense relations.

SUPERORDINATE GOALS

Superordinate goals are "those ends greatly desired by all those caught in dispute or conflict which cannot be attained by the resources and energies of each of the parties separately but which require the concerted efforts of all parties involved" (Sherif, 1967: 467). The Sherifs and their associates (1961) have compiled impressive research data to indicate that the introduction of superordinate goals into a conflict situation is a sound mediational mechanism. Establishment of, agreement on, and pursuit of superordinate goals permit conflicts to be suspended in the interest of values that transcend immediate, parochial concerns. The success of superordinate goals in conflict situations is dependent upon the creation of a cooperative context, in which the conflicting parties interact on problems of joint interest and attempt to achieve solutions that are mutually satisfactory.

The Sherifs (1969: 256) reason that if conflict develops from mutually incompatible goals, then common goals should promote cooperation. However, these goals must be of such importance that conflicting groups or organizations are motivated to forget their differences and to work together to achieve a common goal. Successful introduction of a superordinate goal appears to be constrained by the following parameters: (1) it must be introduced by a third party; (2) it must be seen as a natural event in no way identified with the third party; and (3) it must not be perceived by the adversaries to be aimed at resolving the conflict (Johnson and Lewicki, 1969).

In spite of the wealth of data reported by the Sherifs on the effectiveness of superordinate goals, this mediational mechanism seems to have been rarely used, in a purposive fashion, in interorganizational settings. However, in the television receiver industry and in the liquor industry, the desire for stabilized prices has served as an ad hoc superordinate goal for certain manufacturers, distributors, and retailers (see Biederman and Tabak, 1967; and Mingst and Soriano, 1967).

A type of superordinate goal that is sometimes referred to as a separate technique is the "common enemy." The common-enemy approach involves two groups or organizations uniting against an external threat and has been referred to as a superordinate threat (Blake et al., 1964) and as a "defensive" superordinate goal (Stern, 1971a). The Sherifs (1969) and Blake et al. (1964) criticize the use of the common-enemy approach because it is said to be (1) a temporary method of resolving conflict and (2) a widening of the scope of the original conflict. On the other hand, as Stern et al. (1973) observe, the unified reaction on the part of conflicting parties to an external threat can be viewed as a behavior change; and, as behavior changes, attitudes may be modified to become more consistent with the new behavior. These new attitudes may remain after the threat is removed. In addition, during the process of countering the threat, information will be exchanged, some of which may have a bearing on sources of conflict beyond that posed by the threat. Because of the information exchanged and because of the monetary and psychological costs borne jointly by the parties during the time when they were combating the threat, future relationships between the parties may be significantly different from those during previous interactions. Parties may gain empathy by seeing other parties' points of view, perhaps for the first time. Finally, the original conflict issues—prior to the occurrence of threat— may decay over time as energies are directed toward the outside threat. Until further research is performed, it is often impossible to distinguish between the common-enemy approach and other superordinate goal techniques. Therefore, it is best for present purposes to consider such mediational mechanisms in one broad category.

While contact between conflicting parties involving interdependent action toward superordinate goals is conducive to cooperation, a single episode is usually not sufficient to reduce established interorganizational hostility and negative stereotypes (Hunger and Stern, 1976; Stern et al., 1975). Only if a series of superordinate goals is implemented is the cumulative effect of cooperative activities likely to be successful in developing procedures specifically to foster such orientations and behavior and in transferring them to new situations (Sherif, 1966). Thus, it appears that the frequency of superordinate goals may be a more important determinant of successful reduction of interorganizational conflict than the specific conceptualization of the superordinate goal itself.

A second factor influencing the effect of superordinate goals on conflict reduction is the success or failure in achieving the desired end through the cooperative efforts of the conflicting parties. Most of the empirical evidence in support of superordinate goals has confounded the relationship between the effects of cooperation on conflict reduction and the effects derived from goal achievement. For example, in the Sherif et al. studies (1961), the conflicting groups successfully solved the several problems confronting them. The common predicaments that led to cooperative and problem-solving behaviors were reinforced by positive results of the behavior. Therefore, the effectiveness of superordinate goals in reducing intergroup conflict was a joint product of a cooperative process *and* successful achievement of the goals.

However, the individual contributions of these two variables are still unassessed. The question remains whether cooperation initiated by a superordinate goal is a sufficient condition for conflict reduction or whether conflict reduction is contingent upon the specific outcome obtained in achieving the superordinate goal. Hunger and Stern (1976) indicate that the effectiveness of the superordinate goal as a conflict-reducing mechanism *is* contingent upon the achievement of the goal itself; however, the findings are not conclusive.

It should be pointed out that the empirical investigations of superordinate goals have been studies conducted under conditions of symmetric power relations supporting the effectiveness of a goal initiated by third parties. When Johnson and Lewicki (1969) attempted to initiate a superordinate goal by one of the parties involved in the conflict—but where the relationship was symmetric—it led to greater conflict than when the goal was initiated by a third party.

The effect of a superordinate goal in producing cooperation facilitates intergroup and interorganizational communication. Maximum exchange of information was conceived as an initial step in integrative tactics by Walton and McKersie (1965). Deutsch (1973: 363) found that cooperation led to

> open and honest communication of relevant information between the participants. The freedom to share information enables the parties to go beneath the manifest to the underlying issues involved in the conflict and, thereby to facilitate the meaningful and accurate definition of the problems they are confronting together. It also enables each party to benefit from the knowledge possessed by the other and thus to face the joint problem with greater intellectual resources.

The initiation of a superordinate goal also affects intergroup attraction. The necessary property of a superordinate goal that it "be greatly desired by all those caught in dispute or conflict" influences the parties' perceptions of similarity of their judgments. Byrne (1971) has found judgment similarity to be positively related to attraction. When attraction is high, two parties are more likely to engage in cooperative interaction than when it is low.

Moreover, since a superordinate goal cannot be achieved without the joint effort of all the parties in conflict, the perceived usefulness of other parties in achieving the goal must be high if cooperation is to take place. The importance of a superordinate goal, together with the perceived instrumentality of the other party, leads to the development of favorable intergroup and interorganizational attitudes. This facilitates the growth of mutual trust, which increases sensitivity to similarities and common interests while minimizing the salience of differences. It stimulates a convergence of beliefs and values (Deutsch, 1973). Information is given freely, and there is minimal distortion of the other party's values, beliefs, or intentions.

The success of superordinate goals as a mediational mechanism for conflict reduction presupposes frequent interaction between the two parties so that opportunities for implementing such goals exist and transfer of the cooperative process to other situations in which the parties may interact is possible. The development of communication, attraction, and trust are facilitated when both parties expect the interaction to be relatively enduring and frequent.

Summary

The seminal research of the Sherifs has led to the realization that superordinate goals may be very powerful mediational mechanisms in intergroup conflict situations. Additional research by Hunger and Stern (1976) and Stern et al. (1973, 1975) indicates that the mechanism may be transferred to interorganizational settings with a moderate degree of success. However, in the latter research, single episodes were used; that is, an individual goal of high appeal value was introduced by a third party into a conflict situation. It is likely that a series of such goals would have to be introduced in order to achieve maximal impact in such settings. Benefits are likely to accrue from their use, irrespective of whether they are the result of a threat from an external source or the result of positive, nonthreatening desires imposed into the conflict situation by a third party. The implementation of superordinate goals is likely to lead to enhanced communication and information exchange, greater attraction among the parties to the conflict, and the growth of mutual trust. All of these factors are critical to the establishment of an integrative, problem-solving atmosphere and, thus, should lead to more functional negotiations between conflicting organizations.

DIPLOMACY

The use of diplomacy is most commonly associated with relations between two or more nation-states. In such a relationship, the role of diplomacy is "to raise and clarify social issues and problems, to modify conflicting interests, and to transmit information of mutual concern to parties" (Werne, 1974: 95). The concept of diplomacy can also be extended to use in interorganizational settings where "ambassadors," "envoys," or other boundary-spanning persons rely on diplomatic procedures to conduct, adjust, and manage the relations between interdependent organizations (Stern, 1971a).

Diplomacy has been viewed as "a process of representation and negotiation" (Padelford and Lincoln, 1967: 314), based on information, communication, and interpersonal relationships. Morgenthau (1967) believes that diplomacy consists of four broad tasks:

(1) Diplomacy must determine its objectives in light of the power actually and potentially available for the pursuit of these objectives.
(2) Diplomacy must assess the objectives of other parties and the power actually and potentially available for the pursuit of their objectives.
(3) Diplomacy must determine to what extent these different objectives are compatible with each other.
(4) Diplomacy must employ the means suited to the pursuit of its objectives.

The functions of an interorganizational "diplomat" would be, again in the widest interpretation, to help shape the policies he is to follow, to conduct negotiations with organization-set members to which he is assigned, to observe and report on everything that may be of interest to the organization employing him, and to provide information concerning his organization to the operatives in counterpart organizations (Van Dyke, 1966). As Schleicher (1962: 139) observes, "Implicitly, if not explicitly, these reports contain recommendations which may influence a (collectivity's) policy. In any case, a diplomat is likely to shape policy more at this stage than in the actual negotiating process, where he may be allowed little discretion." In situations where diplomacy is employed, communication—or the transmission of messages, impressions, and interpretations from one human source to another—is crucial. The interorganizational diplomat is, or can become, a key link in this human network.

Very little empirical research is available on the use of diplomacy or diplomatic procedures in the management of conflict. Much of the information that does exist on the subject is anecdotal in nature. For example, Webster (1961: 3) observes that the performance of diplomacy is related to *how:*

(1) a climate of opinion is produced, in which the desired ends can be most easily obtained;
(2) forms of agreement are devised, in which the ends can be translated into practical accomplishment; and
(3) the timing of the effort for achieving the objectives is perceived and created.

Beyond these and similar generalities, there are very few studies that specify the effects of diplomatic procedures on the relationships between collectivities, such as organizations or nations.

On the other hand, it has been found that background characteristics of diplomats influence their patterns of interaction. For example, their relative statuses are apparently important for the development of positive interpersonal attitudes from interactions (Amir, 1969). Modelski (1970) operationalized status as solely a function of the diplomat's demographic, educational, and attitudinal orientations; he found considerable similarity in the backgrounds of foreign ministers. However, such a definition of status was not enough to predict the pattern of interactions among the foreign ministers studied because it ignored the underlying structural relationship in which the ministers operated.

Like the two mechanisms discussed earlier in this chapter, diplomacy works at the interpersonal level through feelings of liking, trust, attraction, and other personal aspects of the relationship. However, diplomats are often subject to important strains that tend to impede their ability to help resolve conflict. In a study of personnel who must rely on diplomacy as they operate on the boundaries of their various organizations, Kahn et al. (1964: 123-124) concluded:

> Lacking formal power over role senders outside his work unit, a person at the boundary has a reduced ability to guarantee that the performance of these outsiders will be as he needs and wishes. In compensation for this lack of formal authority, a boundary person relies heavily on the affective bonds of trust, respect, and liking which he can generate among the outsiders. But these bonds are unusually difficult to create and maintain at the boundary. For the outsiders, the failings of a person's unit are all too easily identified as failures of the person, thus weakening their affective bonds with him.
>
> [A consequence of the role senders' inadequate understanding of boundary positions] is the failure of role senders, especially in other departments, to appreciate the urgency or necessity of a boundary person's requests to them. They are likely to present him with self-interested demands and to be intolerant if these demands are not met.
>
> A person in a boundary position is faced, therefore, with a sizable body of role senders whose demands are hard to predict and hard to control. . . . Most difficult of all, the boundary person faced with such demands has at his disposal only limited power resources with which he may attempt to induce their modification.

This extended quotation shows clearly the problems that are likely to face the interorganizational diplomat. As a result of these problems, it is possible that diplomats can become "marginal men."

A "marginal man" is defined as a person who belongs to neither one group nor another, but who stands "between" the groups (Stouffer et al., 1949).

Thus, the marginal man faces the psychological difficulties of uncertainty and instability. Boundary roles serve the function of maintaining the boundary of the focal organization against pressures exerted on it by other organizations, but the performance of this function often produces *role conflict*. In some respects, a diplomat faces problems similar to those encountered by salesmen in industrial settings. A "good" salesman, for example, is supposed to be client-oriented. In this role, the individual must learn to understand the needs and wants of the client and then must transmit the client's desires to his own firm. At the same time, a "good" salesman is also supposed to have a strong allegiance to his employer's norms and goals. However, the latter are often poorly defined for the salesman, and because most of his time is spent "in the field," he has little opportunity to seek clarification. In fact, it can be hypothesized that his identification with the client and the client's problems (e.g., delivery dates, discounts, etc.) will increase as his interpersonal contact with his own organization decreases. And if he must frequently "do battle" with his own organization in seeking to satisfy his client's needs, he will probably begin to feel alienated. This feeling will be accentuated if his organization shows little interest in developing means whereby he can participate in decision-making processes. On the other hand, despite his increased identification with the client, the salesman may continue to be perceived by the client as the supplier's "man." He may not be fully accepted as a member of the client's organization. Thus, uncertainty and instability may be significant attributes of his position.

It is essential that the status of the diplomat be high enough so that the power which the diplomat holds is at least relatively obvious to the parties with whom he interacts. The suggestion of Kahn et al. (1964: 393) appears appropriate to the concept of creating diplomatic positions:

> With respect to the liaison of the organization with the outside world, create specialized positions for which liaison is the major and continuing function. Provide strong support for such positions, in terms of power, ancillary services, and organizational recognition.

The authors further suggest that the organization should create multiple rather than single liaison arrangements whenever the workload justifies it; as they point out, "All truth is seldom contained in one channel." Finally, they urge that formal procedures be built into the organization for maintaining agreement and understanding between the boundary personnel and those personnel within the organization who are "inwardly oriented" (Kahn et al., 1964).

Summary

The lack of empirical research on the functions and processes of diplomacy limits the ability to provide many useful insights into the diplomat's potentially significant role in managing conflict among organizations. Nevertheless, some broad generalizations can be made, which should be subjected to rigorous testing either in the laboratory or in field settings. First, the diplomat can be an extremely important actor in the communication network among organizations. As such, he/she can assume a critical role in shaping policy and in conducting negotiations. Second, the diplomat's status and background characteristics must facilitate the building or maintenance of liking, trust, and attraction if he is to perform his role adequately. In fact, diplomats, especially in industrial settings, must frequently rely on affective bonds because they often lack the power or the status to command the attention of others both within and outside their own organizations. Thus, diplomats may be subject to a considerable amount of role strain. Finally, it may be postulated that diplomats must be provided with support in terms of power, ancillary services, and organizational recognition if they are to live up to their potential for adjusting, conducting, and managing interorganizational relations.

SUMMARY AND CONCLUSIONS

This chapter has analyzed three mediational mechanisms—exchange of persons, superordinate goals, and diplomacy—for managing, resolving, or reducing conflict between two or more organizations. Exchange of persons entails a bilateral trade of personnel for a specified period of time. The technique involved in such programs is essentially the same as role reversal, a procedure where one or both participants in a discussion present(s) the viewpoint of the other. Superordinate goals, in contrast, are "those ends greatly desired by all those caught in dispute or conflict which cannot be attained by the resources and energies of each of the parties separately but which require the concerted efforts of all parties involved" (Sherif, 1967: 457). Establishment of, agreement on, and pursuit of superordinate goals permit conflicts to be suspended in the interest of values that transcend immediate parochial concerns. Finally, using the analogy from international relations, diplomacy is the method by which interorganizational relations are conducted, adjusted, and managed by "ambassadors," "envoys," or other persons operating at the boundaries of organizations. In general, organizations may find it useful to engage in, cultivate, and rely on diplomatic procedures in managing the conflict that is inevitable between and among them.

Each mechanism can be used most successfully when the structural relations among the organizations are typified by mutual dependence, symmetric power, and relative intensity. In the case of superordinate goals, for example, the parties to the conflict will not share the motivational investment required to activate the process involved in adhering to the goals if these structural preconditions do not hold. For exchange of persons, the costs incurred in implementing the exchange will tend to be borne too heavily by the weaker party if power is asymmetric. And for diplomacy, the mediational process may be used in a deceptive fashion when power is unequal. In other words, the use of diplomacy may simply mask the threats and other manipulative efforts that the more powerful party will eventually employ. For all three mechanisms, the energy level in the interorganizational relations must be high enough to promote appropriate attention to the negotiations which, implicitly in the case of superordinate goals and explicitly in the cases of exchange of persons and diplomacy, underlie them.

There are a number of plausible social-psychological processes that operate when these mediational mechanisms are used. From the previous discussion, four kinds of processes appear to be highly relevant: (1) interpersonal attraction/similarity; (2) humanizing processes; (3) comparison processes; and (4) communication/reactivity relations.

Interpersonal Attraction/Similarity

Perhaps the most influential process leading to a reduction in conflict is interpersonal attraction. Because the parties in a dependent relation mediate rewards to each other, the basis exists for developing a liking relationship since people tend to like those who reward them (Berscheid and Walster, 1969; Huston, 1974). Although there are conflicting findings with regard to the relation between attraction and reward mediation, there is some support for the notion that attraction may be a function of the perceived similarity between two parties.

Interpersonal attraction may be facilitated by similarity in attitudes, personality characteristics, physical characteristics, or social attributes (Berscheid and Walster, 1969). Apfelbaum and Moscovici, for example, studied the effect of perceived similarity or dissimilarity of a partner on subsequent interpersonal conflict (Apfelbaum, 1974). In their experiment, it was found that

> over time, the subjects became significantly less and less cooperative . . . toward a partner whom they perceived as different. . . . In the case of a similar partner . . . however, the level of positive choices was high from the start and remained stable throughout the interactions [Apfelbaum, 1974: 113].

One of the hypotheses that Apfelbaum proposes as explaining the nature of the similarity and conflict relation is the role that similarity plays in regard to uncertainty.

> Cooperation depends on the ability to reduce uncertainty. Thus, similarity enables the individual to perceive a situation from the point of view of the other. The more he perceives other people as similar to himself, the more will his behavior be determined by his perception of their behavior [Apfelbaum, 1974: 117-118].

Thus, the exchange-of-persons approach and diplomacy may reduce conflict in highly dependent relations if the contact is between similar actors. Agreement on superordinate goals may also be facilitated under such conditions.

Attraction may have other consequences. Tedeschi et al. (1973) present research that supports the position that interpersonal attraction between a target and source of communications will authenticate promises or warnings. The various mediational mechanisms examined in this chapter should lead to increased interpersonal attraction; therefore, a basis should exist for enhanced compliance and cooperation when they are implemented. Three studies support the hypothesis that the greater the perceived similarity between pairs of subjects, the greater the cooperation (Krauss, 1966; Kaufmann, 1967; and Tornatzky and Geiwitz, 1968). Finally, in a bilateral monopoly game, Druckman and Bonoma (1976) found that bargainers were softer against similar opponents (to whom they were attracted). But, interestingly, when the similar opponent disappointed the bargainer's expectations of softness, the bargainer retaliated by being tougher than he was against a "tough" dissimilar opponent.

Humanizing Processes

The three mediational mechanisms can be viewed as humanizing processes, where people who normally have only superficial relations with role partners in another organization come to view these others in a more personal sense. Many experimental studies show that when an opponent is viewed as human, similar to oneself, or likeable, there is a greater probability of cooperative interchanges. Abric and Kahan (1972), for instance, found that subjects interacting with "real live" partners (i.e., "a student like yourself") were more cooperative (54 percent versus 35 percent) than were subjects paired with a nonhuman partner (i.e., "a programmed strategy devised by a machine"). Similar results were obtained by Sermat (1964) in his test of behavior in mixed-motive games. Subjects who interacted with a program tended to maximize their payoffs and did not emit cooperative responses regardless of the actions of the other, while those who knowingly interacted with a real party tended to cooperate to a greater extent.

Comparison Processes

Various comparison processes may also play a role when one is exchanging persons, arriving at superordinate goals, or instituting diplomacy. Two main types of comparison processes are *interpersonal comparisons* between those within a relationship[2] and *external comparisons* and pressures between one actor in a conflict relation and third parties or normative standards. For example, an exchange of persons between two organizations might require that the social actors participating in the exchange be chosen from comparable levels within each organization so as not to produce disparities in status. To do otherwise would be to create a situation of imbalance, marked by loss of esteem, or to induce other emotional reactions that could interfere with the establishment of a cooperative relation (Adams, 1965). Similarly, the outcome of an exchange of persons may be affected by the nature of the role relations and normative pressures exerted on the exchangee by his home organization. In a study of contract negotiations between the United Auto Workers Union and International Harvester, McKersie et al. (1965) found that negotiators on both sides experienced strong pressures from their constituents, which affected both their behaviors and felt tension and thus, presumably, the outcome of their encounters. Gruder (1971) manipulated the accountability that a subject experienced in a two-person bargaining game by telling him that he would (would not) meet his constituent partner after the game. Those subjects who thought they were to meet their constituent were more demanding and made small initial concessions. More research is needed, however, to test the nature and effects of comparison processes in the contexts of the three mediational mechanisms discussed here.

Communication/Reactivity Relations

Exchange of persons, superordinate goals, and diplomacy may serve as the vehicles for enhancing the nature of communication or "reactivity" between boundary personnel and others in two conflicting organizations. Apfelbaum (1974) defines the process whereby each individual takes into account the anticipated response of another before acting as "interpersonal reactivity." Briefly, interpersonal reactivity allows two parties to engage in reciprocal processes of communication, whereby the relationship can evolve into a state of mutual satisfaction. Each party is encouraged to respond with cooperative actions. The effect of interpersonal reactivity may be summarized as follows:

> An increase in the partner's responsiveness increases (a) the understandability of the partner's behavior, which becomes more predictable; (b) the impact of the subject's own behavior on the future of the relationship, in particular through the influence he can exert on his partner's choices; and (c) the willingness of the subject to initiate a cooperative process because he expects his initiatives to be reciprocated; but it simultaneously limits his competitive attempts for fear of possible retaliation [Apfelbaum, 1974: 133].

A number of experiments support these conclusions. For example, in a Prisoner's Dilemma game, Apfelbaum (1967) found that there was "markedly more cooperation toward a partner who was perceived as reactive than toward a partner whose behavior was assumed to be independent of the subject's responses." Reactivity was manipulated by informing the partner as to the other's attitude as reactive, unconditionally cooperative, or unconditionally competitive. The reactive conditions resulted in 66 percent positive (cooperative) choices, while the other conditions yielded 47 percent positive choices taken together. Rapoport and Chammah (1965) found similar results in that more cooperative exchanges, on the average, were found in tit-for-tat than in noncontingent cooperative encounters. Finally, a number of studies report more cooperative choices (or other measures of effective bargaining) when communication is available than when no opportunity for communication exists, thus lending support to Apfelbaum's notion of reactivity (Deutsch, 1958; Cole, 1972; Voissem and Sistrunk, 1971; and Wichman, 1970).

In sum, each of the mediational mechanisms examined in this chapter can be used to set the stage for meaningful negotiations by fostering an atmosphere of trust, attraction, and liking between conflicting parties. Given their hypothesized underlying social-psychological processes, implementation of the mechanisms should lead to greater understanding and empathy, thereby permitting organizations to enter into negotiations with an increased probability of achieving successful accommodation and compromise.

NOTES

1. By "range of outcomes," we mean the standardized interval of possible outcomes for a party in a power relation.

2. Interpersonal comparisons have been exemplified in equity theory (Adams, 1965), distributive justice (Homans, 1974), stereotyped utility functions (Harsanyi, 1962), and self-esteem maintenance (Goffman, 1959).

REFERENCES

ABRIC, J. C. and J. KAHAN (1972) "The effects of representations and behavior in experimental games." European J. of Social Psychology 2: 129-144.

ADAMS, J. S. (1965) "Inequity in social exchange," pp. 267-299 in L. Berkowitz (ed.) Advances in Experimental Social Psychology. New York: Academic Press.

AIKEN, M. and J. HAGE (1968) "Organizational interdependence and intraorganizational structure." Amer. Soc. Rev. 33: 912-929.

ALLPORT, G. W. (1954) The Nature of Prejudice. Reading, Mass.: Addison-Wesley.

AMIR, Y. (1969) "Contact hypothesis in ethnic relations." Psych. Bull. 71: 319-342.

APFELBAUM, E. (1974) "On conflicts and bargaining," pp. 103-156 in L. Berkowitz (ed.) Advances in Experimental Social Psychology. New York: Academic Press.

——— (1967) "Representations du partenaire et interactions à propos d un dilemme du prisonnier." Psychologie Francaise 12: 287-295.

BERSCHEID, E. and E. H. WALSTER (1969) Interpersonal Attraction. Reading, Mass.: Addison-Wesley.

BIEDERMAN, R. G. and R. L. TABAK (1967) "The television receiver industry," pp. 247-298 in H. Assael (ed.) The Politics of Distributive Trade Associations: A Study in Conflict Resolution. Hempstead, N.Y.: Hofstra University.

BLAKE, R. R., H. A. SHEPARD, and J. S. MOUTON (1964) Managing Intergroup Conflict in Industry. Houston, Texas: Gulf Publishing Co.

BYRNE, D. (1971) The Attraction Paradigm. New York: Academic Press, 1971.

COLE, S. G. (1972) "Conflict and cooperation in potentially intense conflict situations." J. of Personality and Social Psychology 22: 31-50.

COSER, L. (1956) The Functions of Social Conflict. Glencoe, Ill.: Free Press.

DEUTSCH, M. (1973) The Resolution of Conflict. New Haven, Conn.: Yale Univ. Press.

——— (1958) "Trust and suspicion." J. of Conflict Resolution 2: 265-279.

——— and R. M. KRAUSS (1962) "Studies of interpersonal bargaining." J. of Conflict Resolution 6: 52-76.

DRUCKMAN, D. (1968) "Prenegotiation experience and dyadic conflict resolution in a bargaining situation." J. of Experimental Social Psychology 4: 367-383.

——— and T. V. BONOMA (1976) "Determinants of bargaining behavior in a bilateral monopoly situation II: Opponent's concession rate and similarity." Behavioral Sci. 21: 252-262.

DURKHEIM, E. (1933) The Division of Labor in Society (trans. by G. Simpson). Glencoe, Ill.: Free Press.

EMERSON, R. E. (1962) "Power-dependence relations." Amer. Soc. Rev. 27: 31-41.

GOFFMAN, E. (1959) The Presentation of Self in Everyday Life. Garden City, N.Y.: Doubleday Anchor.

GRUDER, C. L. (1971) "Relationships with opponent and partner in mixed-motive bargaining." J. of Conflict Resolution 15: 403-416.

——— (1970) "Social power in interpersonal negotiation," pp. 111-154 in P. Swingle (ed.) The Structure of Conflict. New York: Academic Press.

GUETZKOW, H. (1966) "Relations among organizations," pp. 13-44 in R. V. Bowers (ed.) Studies on Behavior in Organizations. Athens: Univ. of Georgia Press.

HARSANYI, J. C. (1962) "Bargaining in ignorance of the opponent's utility function." J. of Conflict Resolution 6: 29-38.

HOMANS, G. C. (1974) Social Behavior: Its Elementary Forms. New York: Harcourt Brace Jovanivich.

HORNSTEIN, H. A. (1965) "The effects of different magnitudes of threat upon interpersonal bargaining." J. of Experimental Social Psychology 1: 282-293.

HUNGER, D. J. and L. W. STERN (1976) "An assessment of the functionality of the superordinate goal in reducing conflict." Academy of Management J. 19: 591-605.

HUSTON, T. L. [ed.] (1974) Foundations of Interpersonal Attraction. New York: Academic Press.

JOHNSON, D. W. and R. J. LEWICKI (1969) "The initiation of superordinate goals." J. of Applied Behavioral Sci. 5: 9-24.

KAHN, R. L., D. M. WOLFE, R. P. QUINN, and J. D. SNOEK (1964) Organizational Stress: Studies in Role Conflict and Ambiguity. New York: John Wiley.

KAUFMANN, H. (1967) "Similarity and cooperation received as determinants of cooperation rendered." Psychonomic Sci. 9: 73-74.

KRAUSS, R. M. (1966) "Structural and attitudinal factors in interpersonal bargaining." J. of Experimental Social Psychology 2: 42-55.

LITWAK, E. and L. F. HYLTON (1962) "Inter-organizational analysis: a hypothesis on coordinating agencies." Administrative Sci. Q. 6: 395-426.

McCLINTOCK, C. G. and S. P. McNEEL (1967) "Prior dyadic experience and monetary reward as determinants of cooperative and competitive game behavior." J. of Personality and Social Psychology 5: 282-294.

McKERSIE, R. B., C. R. PERRY, and R. E. WALTON (1965) "Intraorganizational bargaining behavior in labor negotiations." J. of Conflict Resolution 9: 463-481.

MARRETT, C. B. (1971) "On the specification of interorganizational dimensions." Sociology and Social Research 56: 83-99.

MINGST, J. and R. A. SORIANO (1967) "The liquor industry," pp. 351-386 in H. Assael (ed.) The Politics of Distributive Trade Associations: A Study in Conflict Resolution. Hempstead, N.Y.: Hofstra University.

MODELSKI, G. (1970) "The world's foreign ministers: A political elite." J. of Conflict Resolution 14: 135-175.

MORGAN, W. R. and J. SAWYER (1967) "Bargaining, expectations, and the preference for equality over equity." J. of Personality and Social Psychology 6: 139-149.

MORGENTHAU, H. J. (1967) Politics Among Nations. New York: Alfred A. Knopf.

MUNEY, B. F. and M. DEUTSCH (1968) "The effects of role-reversal during the discussion of opposing viewpoints." J. of Conflict Resolution 12: 345-356.

NIELSEN, E. H. (1972) "Understanding and managing intergroup conflict," pp. 329-343 in J. W. Lorsch and P. R. Lawrence (eds.) Managing Group and Intergroup Relations. Homewood, Ill.: Richard D. Irwin.

PADELFORD, N. J. and G. A. LINCOLN (1967) The Dynamics of International Politics. New York: Macmillan.

RAPOPORT, A. and A. CHAMMAH (1965) Prisoner's Dilemma: A Study in Conflict and Cooperation. Ann Arbor: Univ. of Michigan Press.

SCHLEICHER, C. P. (1962) International Relations: Cooperation and Conflict. Englewood Cliffs, N.J.: Prentice-Hall.

SCHMIDT, S. M. and T. A. KOCHAN (1972) "Conflict: Toward conceptual clarity." Administrative Sci. Q. 17: 359-370.

SERMAT, V. (1964) "Cooperative behavior in a mixed motive game." J. of Social Psychology 62: 217-239.

SHERIF, M. (1966) In Common Predicament: Social Psychology of Intergroup Conflict and Cooperation. Boston: Houghton Mifflin.

––– (1967) Social Interaction. Chicago: Aldine.

––– and C. W. SHERIF (1969) Social Psychology. New York: Harper & Row.

SHERIF, M., O. J. HARVEY, B. J. WHITE, W. R. HOOD, and C. W. SHERIF (1961) Intergroup Conflict and Cooperation: The Robbers Cave Experiment. Norman: Univ. of Oklahoma Press.

STERN, L. W. (1971a) "Potential conflict management mechanisms in distribution channels: An interorganizational analysis." pp. 111-145 in D. N. Thompson (ed.) Contractual Marketing Systems. Lexington, Mass.: Heath Lexington Books.

––– (1971b) "Antitrust implications of a sociological interpretation of competition, conflict, and cooperation in the marketplace." Antitrust Bull. 16: 509-530.

–––, B. STERNTHAL, and C. S. CRAIG (1973) "Managing conflict of distribution channels: A laboratory study." J. of Marketing Research 10: 169-179.

––– (1975) "Strategies for managing interorganizational conflict: A laboratory paradigm." J. of Applied Psychology 60: 472-482.

STOUFFER, S. A. et al. (1949) Studies in Social Psychology During World War II: The American Soldier, I and II. Princeton, N.J.: Princeton Univ. Press.

SWINGLE, P. G. (1966) "Effects of the emotional relationship between protagonists in a two-person game." J. of Personality and Social Psychology 4: 270-279.

––– and A. SANTI (1972) "Communication in non-zero sum games." J. of Personality and Social Psychology 23: 54-63.

TEDESCHI, J. T., B. R. SCHLENKER, and T. V. BONOMA (1973) Conflict, Power, and Games. Chicago: Aldine.

THIBAUT, J. W. and H. H. KELLEY (1959) The Social Psychology of Groups. New York: John Wiley.

THOMAS, K. W. (1976) "Conflict and conflict management," in M. D. Dunnette (ed.) Handbook of Industrial and Organizational Psychology. Chicago: Rand McNally.

TORNATZKY, L. and P. J. GEIWITZ (1968) "The effects of threat and attraction on interpersonal bargaining." Psychonomic Sci. 13: 125-126.

VAN DYKE, V. (1966) International Politics. New York: Appleton-Century-Crofts.

VITZ, P. C. and W. R. KITE (1970) "Factors affecting conflict and negotiation within an alliance." J. of Experimental Social Psychology 6: 322-247.

VOISSEM, N. H. and F. SISTRUNK (1971) "Communication schedule and cooperative game behavior." J. of Personality and Social Psychology 19: 160-167.
WALTON, R. E. and R. B. McKERSIE (1965) A Behavioral Theory of Labor Negotiations: An Analysis of a Social Interaction System. New York: McGraw-Hill.
WEBSTER, C. (1961) The Art and Practice of Diplomacy. London: Chatto & Windus.
WERNE, L. (1974) International Politics: Foundations of the System. Minneapolis: Univ. of Minnesota Press.
WICHMAN, H. (1970) "Effects of isolation and communication on cooperation in a two-person game." J. of Personality and Social Psychology 16: 114-120.

EDITOR'S CONCLUSIONS:
WHERE DO WE GO FROM HERE?

This volume is presented as a social-psychological treatment of negotiation. Each of the contributions reflects this theme. Taken together, the wide range of perspectives and emphases represented can all be considered within the purview of a social-psychological analysis of negotiation. This purview is defined by certain concepts and methods. The concepts are those that refer to processes of and influences on behavior in negotiating situations. The methods are *primarily* those of experimentation and simulation. We believe that these are the ideas and tools that will further our understanding of the *human factors* in negotiations. The chapters are demonstrations of what *has* been done and therefore of what *can* be done. But this is just a beginning. In this concluding section, the critical areas for future development are outlined. In particular, eight areas are identified as those that are most likely to lead to important breakthroughs in understanding. These are as follows (*not* listed in order of importance).

(1) Can negotiation settings be distinguished in terms of the relative importance of cognitive and motivational factors? Can this distinction also be made for stages of a negotiation? In order to make these distinctions, it is necessary to separate behaviors that are primarily driven by preferences from those that are directed by a plan. Such a separation would form the basis for analyses designed to explore the interplay between the two sources for negotiating behavior as it occurs in situ.

(2) Are there acceptable strategic solutions to the bargaining problem? Is there an acceptable outcome? What is (are) the bargaining process(es) that is (are) likely to lead to such an outcome? A solution that often occurs in experimental situations is one that gives each side exactly one-half the maximum payoff it can rationally expect to get. (This is the Nash solution.) Most bargainers might agree that this is the "fair" solution. Agreeing that it is an acceptable outcome, however, does not suggest a bargaining strategy for achieving it, which depends on the ability of bargainers to coordinate their moves—offers and demands—by making acceptable opening bids, by calibrating the size of their sequential concessions, by developing criteria for evaluating progress toward the expected outcome, and so on. The problem of converging incrementally toward an acceptable outcome is an empirical issue

that would benefit considerably from both systematic laboratory research and observations made in field settings.

(3) Can the persuasive and problem-solving functions of debate be distinguished? Are negotiators' intentions revealed in their rhetoric? Progress toward understanding the rhetorical aspects of negotiation depends on the development of reliable indicators of intentions, which can help an analyst "see through the rhetoric" of the dialogue. This has advantages for the researcher and for the tactician. The former could use the indicators as variables in exploring process-outcome relationships; the latter could use them as aids for distinguishing between cultural or idiosyncratic style and strategy. By so doing, the researcher might be able to demonstrate stronger relationships, and the tactician might be able to assess more realistically the other's intentions. Achievements to date are encouraging. However, more stringent tests of the indicators already developed would seem appropriate.

(4) Can the relative importance of negotiators' personalities, their role obligations, and the negotiating situation be determined? How does this vary from one type of negotiation to another? At different times and under certain conditions or in certain settings, the negotiator may be relatively impervious to the situation, his role, or the unique qualities of his personality. It has been suggested that these effects can be observed more clearly in the negotiating process. If this is so, then it should be possible to develop indicators by linking aspects of the process to selected influences as these occur during different stages of a negotiation. Such indicators should enable investigators to extend their base of observation from the laboratory to the field.

(5) What tactical recommendations are likely to be effective in helping a negotiator manage the impressions conveyed to his opponents and constituents? How can he resolve Stevens' negotiation paradox: being firm without appearing too rigid and at the same time being willing to yield without appearing too conciliatory? The negotiator's challenge is to influence his opponents' actions and to structure his constituents' expectations in directions that promote a favorable agreement. Among the tactics that can be used to affect the opponents' actions are casuistry (commitment devices) and magnifying the size of concessions already made. The constituents' expectations can be influenced by efforts to manipulate their perception of his performance and outcome and by tacit bargaining. The negotiator/tactician could benefit considerably from the results of experiments designed to evaluate the impact of alternative postures intended to convey the desired impressions.

(6) To what extent is negotiating behavior shaped by the context within which it occurs? What is the relative importance of external (contextual) and internal (conference) variables as determinants of negotiating behavior? A systematic evaluation of the importance of external versus internal variables requires the development of a broad perspective on negotiating as well as

indicators of variables that operate at the two levels. The perspective is one that should clarify linkages among the external-system and internal-conference level variables. The indicators should permit investigators to explore simultaneously the effects of variations in both context and immediate conditions on negotiating behavior.

(7) What are the more effective strategies for managing complexity in negotiation? Are analytic or synthetic approaches likely to be more useful? The analytic versus synthetic distinction is the difference between reducing a problem to its "essentials" and confronting the problem by organizing its various components into a conceptual framework. The distinction turns on attempts to develop calculation aids for determining bargaining strength or mutually acceptable concessions as opposed to developing broad conceptual schemes for organizing complexity. The effects on the course of a negotiation of using either (or both) of these types of strategies is a research problem worth investigating.

(8) What forms of mediation are likely to be most effective at different junctures of a negotiation? Does the way in which they are used make a difference? These questions turn on matters of appropriateness, timing, and style. Certain procedures are likely to be helpful for establishing a climate for negotiating; others are more appropriate for helping to assuage a crisis during the negotiation. Some problems require a restructuring of the situation while others merely depend on an outside decision for their solution. The mediator can be helped by research that addresses the following issues: Which procedures should be used? When should the intervention take place? How should the intervention be framed?

These are the topics that are deemed appropriate for further study. The achievements to date, reported in this volume, provide a foundation on which to build. As we move forward with the work suggested above, we should come closer to the time when the process of *accumulating* knowledge gives way to the task of *consolidating* knowledge. These tasks consist of: (a) inventorying our findings, noting consistencies and divergencies in effects obtained by parallel experiments conducted in several negotiation settings; (b) formulating propositions that depict critical relationships between subsets of variables contained in the inventory; and (c) forging linkages among the variables in the set treated in the propositions. From these efforts, a structure that is capable of organizing the diverse processes and influences of negotiation will emerge. This is our goal. We are prepared to meet the challenge. So, let us move forward!

AUTHOR INDEX

SUBJECT INDEX

Affective behavior, 205, 206: of diplomats, 380; positive affect as proportion of total, 207; positive affect score, 207; role of affect, 312-313; vs. task, 312

Agreement (See also Agreements, integrative; Disagreements): chance of finding, 100, 128, 151, 156; cognitive aid for reaching, 92; effect of negotiator's toughness on, 145, 146, 150; effect of prenegotiation issue formation on, 198, 199; effects of tension and stress on, 312-313; means of reaching, 115, 158; pressure to reach, 148, 150, 151; probability of reaching, 143, 151, 178, 182, 312, 316; progression toward, 34, 138; ratio of to disagreement, 205, 312; satisfaction with, 138, 142; type, level, nature of, 33, 90, 93, 138, 139-140, 167-169, 171-172, 195, 332; utility of own demand vs. no agreement, 332-333

Agreements, integrative (See also Agreement; Integrative bargaining): 163, 167, 170-171, 174, 175, 177, 180-181, 185, 187, 188; and conflicts, 184; and debate, 194; and flexible rigidity, 182; and norm following, 185, 187; and time pressures, 182

Aggression, 233, 276, 282, 302: in bargaining, 233, 234; and coercion, 215, 234; counter-aggressive responses, 237; preemptive, 216

Alternating schemes: vs. compromise, 164

Ambiguity: tolerance of, 306; of information, 354

Anxiety: effect of on bargaining, 249, 253; and conciliation, 262; and cooperative vs. exploitative orientation, 262, 269; and forgiveness, 264, 269; as personality measure, 258, 260, 269, 270; and repentance, 264

Arms control negotiations, 235, 307, 308, 309, 315, 355

Arms races, 22, 24, 25, 108, 308: concession-making model, 140, 154; East-West, 222

Aspiration, level of: effect of concessions on, 356; and conflicts, 184; high and inflexible, 177-181; maintaining, 172; reducing, 172; rise of, 182, 183; and time pressure, 182

Aspirations in bargaining, 180-184

Attitudes: changes in, 199, 203, 204, 236, 321; and effectiveness of bargaining, 305; and interaction, 199; interpersonal attitudes of negotiators, 305; positive and negative, 305, 371, 372, 376; similar and dissimilar, 224, 381; similarity of, effect of on interpersonal attraction, 381; effect of stress on, 303

Authoritarianism, 253, 258-259, 260, 263: effect of on bargaining, 249, 253, 254; and self-esteem, 263

Authority, legitimate, 371: distribution of, 220; and response to influence attempts, 220

"Balancing" process, 109, 110, 112-123, 126

Bales' interaction process analysis system, 203, 204, 206, 209

Bargainer (See also Negotiators; Opponents; Strategies): aspirations of, 141-142, 181; behavior of, 141-142, 150-151, 153, 156, 170, 177, 223, 249, 253-254, 382; effects of authoritarianism on, 249-254; number of bargainers, 334, 383; and payoffs, 145-146; relationship to other (see also Opponents), 141, 142, 156, 163, 171, 173, 175-177, 180-183, 222-223, 332-333; strategies used by (see also Bargaining tactics and strategies)

ABOUT THE EDITOR AND CONTRIBUTORS

The Editor
DANIEL DRUCKMAN is Senior Research Analyst at Mathematica Inc., in Betheseda, Maryland. He received his Ph.D. in social psychology at Northwestern University. His primary interests are in the areas of interparty conflict resolution, policy decision-making, negotiations, and simulation. He is the author of a number of articles and monographs on such topics as the interplay between conflict of interest and value dissensus, factors affecting agreement in negotiations, coalition formation, and simulation methodology. Among his current concerns is the interface between behavioral science and political (including intergovernmental) decision-making.

The Contributors
RICHARD P. BAGOZZI is presently affiliated with the College of Business Administration at the University of California, Berkeley. He holds a Ph.D. in Marketing from Northwestern University. His research interests are in the areas of theoretical foundations of marketing, the behavior of salesmen, marketing and social change, and mathematical models of social and psychological behavior in marketing.

THOMAS V. BONOMA is Associate Professor of Business Administration at the University of Pittsburgh. He was awarded his Ph.D. by the State University of New York at Albany in 1972, with his major concentration in social psychology. His areas of research interest include power, conflict, and social influence; individual and group decision-making; sex roles and influence; field studies of power; and simulation and gaming.

BERNDT BREHMER is Chairman of the Department of Psychology at the University of Umea, Sweden, where he received his Ph.D. in 1971. He has authored many articles in the methodology of learning and in the general area of conflict research. He was 1976-1977 President of the Scandinavian Association for Psychological Research.

BERT R. BROWN is Associate Professor and Chairman of the Psychology Department, University College, Rutgers University. He received his Ph.D. from Columbia University in 1967. His recent book (with Jeffrey Rubin),

The Social Psychology of Bargaining and Negotiation (1975) reviews and integrates previous research on the bargaining process as an instrument of conflict resolution.

RUBY ROY DHOLAKIA is Assistant Professor of Marketing at the Indian Institute of Management in Calcutta. She recently received her Ph.D. in Marketing at Northwestern University.

KENNETH R. HAMMOND is presently affiliated with the Institute of Behavioral Science at the University of Colorado at Boulder. He received his Ph.D. in 1948 from the University of California. His major concentration has been on inductive inference, to which he has applied Brunswik's "lens model" of behavior. His recent research includes studies of interpersonal conflict which arises from differing cognitive systems.

W. CLAY HAMNER is a Professor of Organizational Behavior in the Graduate School of Management at Boston University. He received his Ph.D. from Indiana University. He has contributed articles to many professional journals, and is coeditor of *Contemporary Problems in Personnel,* and *Organizational Behavior and Management: A Contingency Approach* (both published in 1974 by St. Clair Press).

MARGARET G. HERMANN is a Research Associate at the Mershon Center, Ohio State University. She received her Ph.D. in psychology from Northwestern University. Her current research is on ways in which the personal characteristics of political leaders affect what they do politically. Her general areas of interest include political leadership, political psychology, and decision-making.

P. TERRENCE HOPMANN is Associate Professor of Political Science and Associate Director of the Center of International Studies at the University of Minnesota. He received his Ph.D. in political science from Stanford University in 1969. His major research and teaching interests are in international politics, with an emphasis on bargaining and negotiations, and on coalition theory applied to international alliances.

TIMOTHY D. KING is a Ph.D. candidate in the Department of Political Science at the University of Minnesota, where he has also served as Coordinator of the World Order Studies Program in the Quigley Center of International Studies. His principal interests are in the application of social-psychological concepts to international negotiations, and he has done research on the use of techniques of role reversal.

NATHAN KOGAN is a Professor of Psychology at the New School for Social Research in New York City. He received his Ph.D. in Psychology from Harvard University. His major research interests focus on risk-taking behavior and on cognitive development and he is the author of a number of articles on these topics.

STEVEN A. LEWIS is Assistant Professor of Psychology at Wayne State University. He received his Ph.D. in 1973 from the State University of New York at Buffalo. His major research interest is the study of conflict resolution—specifically the study of variables important to, and the processes involved in, successful integrative bargaining.

CHARLES G. McCLINTOCK is Professor of Psychology at the University of California, Santa Barbara. He received his Ph.D. in 1956 from the University of Michigan, majoring in social psychology. His primary areas of interest are in experimental social psychology, social motivation, decision-making, game behavior, conflict behavior, and international relations. He is the editor of *Experimental Social Psychology.* (1972, Holt, Rinehart & Winston).

KNUT MIDGAARD is Associate Professor at the Institute of Political Science of the University of Oslo. He received the Norwegian Mag. art. degree from that university in 1959. His areas of concentration are in the applications of game theory in political science; debates, negotiations, voting; and normative political theory.

DEAN G. PRUITT is Professor of Psychology and Director of the Social Psychology Program at the State University of New York at Buffalo. He received his Ph.D. degree in 1957 from Yale University. His current major areas of research interest are social conflict and bargaining, and he has published extensively in these fields.

RICHARD M. ROZELLE is Professor of Psychology at the University of Houston. He received his Ph.D. from Northwestern University. His research interests are in the fields of conflict resolution; experimental and quasi-experimental methodology; attitude-behavior change and persuasion; and nonverbal behavior and impression formation.

LOUIS W. STERN is Professor of Marketing in the Graduate School of Management at Northwestern University. He received his Ph.D. from Northwestern in 1962. Among his many publications are *Distribution Channels: Behavioral Dimensions* 1969, Houghton Mifflin), and *Competition in the Marketplace* (with John R. Grabner, Jr., 1970) and *Perspectives in Marketing Management* (with others, 1971), both published by Scott, Foresman.

JAMES T. TEDESCHI is Professor and Director of the Social Psychology Program at the State University of New York at Albany. He received his Ph.D. in Experimental Psychology from the University of Michigan (1960). He has published extensively in professional journals, and is the editor of *Perspectives on Social Power* (1974) and *The Social Influence Processes* (1972) (both published by Aldine).

ARILD UNDERDAL is Research Fellow at the Institute of Political Science of the University of Oslo. He received his Mag.art. degree from the same university in 1972. His areas of concentration are in international decision-making, with particular focus on international negotiations; and in foreign policy decision-making.

CHARLES WALCOTT is Assistant Professor of Political Science at the University of Minnesota. He received his Ph.D. from the University of California at Santa Barbara in 1971. His major research and teaching interests are in bargaining and decision-making in organizations and other political groups; and applications of experimental methodology to political analysis.

GILBERT R. WINHAM is Associate Professor of Political Science and Director of the Centre for Foreign Policy Studies at Dalhousie University, Halifax, Nova Scotia. He was awarded his Ph.D. in 1968 by the University of North Carolina at Chapel Hill. His current research is on international trade negotiations. He is interested in teaching in the areas of international relations and foreign policy-making.

GARY A. YUKL is Associate Professor of Organizational Behavior at Baruch College of the City University of New York. He received his Ph.D. in Industrial Psychology from the University of California, Berkeley, in 1967. His general area of interest is industrial psychology and organizational behavior, and his areas of specialization are in organizations, leadership, job attitudes and motivation, bargaining and conflict resolution.

KATHLEEN ZECHMEISTER was a Research Associate at the Institute for Juvenile Research and a Research Consultant at Children's Memorial Hospital in Chicago. She is currently self-employed. She received her Ph.D. in psychology from Northwestern University. Her major interests are in the areas of conflict resolution and interparty decision-making, and she has published a number of articles on these topics.